TEACHING DISRUPTIVE TECHNOLOGIES IN THE SECONDARY SCHOOL

This book provides a one stop shop for those interested in teaching about disruptive technologies as part of a wide variety of school subjects. It explores the technologies that are likely to have a profound influence on our society in the coming years and offers advice and guidance on how to devise, teach and assess a relevant curriculum.

Divided into two parts, the first examines the nature of disruption that technologies cause. It describes in depth what each technology does, how it works, who uses it and what for, and how this might be disruptive along with positive and negative implications. The technologies include:

- additive manufacture,
- artificial intelligence,
- augmented reality,
- Big Data,
- Internet of Things,
- quantum computing,
- programmable matter,
- neurotechnology,
- robotics,
- synthetic biology.

Part two suggests practical ways teachers could 'Look Sideways' and collaborate to teach and assess learners aged 11–18 in these disruptive technologies so that they can successfully take up new employment opportunities and contribute fully to the debate of how those technologies affect our society.

Offering comprehensive guidance on the teaching, learning and assessment of disruptive technologies, this will be valuable reading for teachers, school leaders, teacher educators and those responsible for curriculum development.

Frank Banks is Emeritus Professor of Teacher Education at The Open University, where he was Director of International Teacher Education and led the innovative online flexible initial teacher education programmes. Frank has worked as a teacher of science, technology, engineering science and mathematics (STEM) in different secondary high schools in England and in Wales.

HildaRuth Beaumont [formerly David Barlex] is an acknowledged leader in design and technology education, curriculum design and developing curriculum materials. A former school teacher, senior lecturer in education at Brunel University, and now an Honorary Senior Research Associate at the Institute of Education, UCL, Hilda's curriculum development activities stem from her conviction that classroom practice should be informed by academic research.

TEACHING DISRUPTIVE TECHNOLOGIES IN THE SECONDARY SCHOOL

A Practical Guide

Frank Banks and HildaRuth Beaumont

Routledge
Taylor & Francis Group
LONDON AND NEW YORK

Designed cover image: © Getty Images

First published 2026
by Routledge
4 Park Square, Milton Park, Abingdon, Oxon OX14 4RN

and by Routledge
605 Third Avenue, New York, NY 10158

Routledge is an imprint of the Taylor & Francis Group, an informa business

For Product Safety Concerns and Information please contact our EU representative GPSR@taylorandfrancis.com. Taylor & Francis Verlag GmbH, Kaufingerstraße 24, 80331 München, Germany.

British Library Cataloguing-in-Publication Data
A catalogue record for this book is available from the British Library

ISBN: 978-1-032-99048-4 (hbk)
ISBN: 978-1-032-99046-0 (pbk)
ISBN: 978-1-003-60200-2 (ebk)

DOI: 10.4324/9781003602002

Typeset in Interstate
by Apex CoVantage, LLC

CONTENTS

ACKNOWLEDGEMENTS

We are grateful to the following who made a positive and useful contribution to our book.

Dr Yun Chen, who wrote the foreword, Professor Helen Lockett who contributed to Chapter 3, Professor Simon Schultz who contributed to Chapter 8, Dr Silvia Bergamini and Dr Calum MacCormick who contributed to Chapter 10, Torben Steeg who contributed to Chapter 16, Ed Charlwood who contributed to Chapter 17, and Krystian McInnis who contributed to Chapter 18.

In addition, we are grateful to Annamarie Kino and Lucia Schmid of Routledge who have helped us throughout the writing of the book and Mohamed Azharudeen who was key in steering the book through the final stages of production.

FOREWORD

It is a great honour to be invited by Professor Frank Banks and Dr HildaRuth Beaumont to write the foreword for their insightful book, *Teaching Disruptive Technologies in the Secondary School: A Practical Guide*. Both authors have long-standing reputations for advancing innovation in teacher education. Their dedication to research that bridges pedagogical theory, policy and classroom practice is powerfully reflected throughout this book.

This book arrives at a crucial moment. Around the world, especially within the UK, educators are confronting rapid technological change that is transforming not only how they teach, but also what it means to be educated in a digital age. Having examined these transformations in my own research and practice on digital innovation and educational technology, I see this book as a thoughtful and timely response, encouraging educators to use technology with purpose, critical awareness and ethical responsibility. It provides rigorous, practice-informed perspectives that help readers make sense of various disruptive technologies such as artificial intelligence, augmented reality, neurotechnology, quantum computing and more, as well as how these can be meaningfully integrated into the school curriculum.

The authors have structured the book in two carefully connected parts: Part 1 explores the conceptual and technical dimensions of disruptive technologies, defining and exemplifying disruption and unpacking each technology in depth; while Part 2 moves into the classroom, offering practical strategies for curriculum design, pedagogy and critical engagement across Key Stages 3 to 5. This balance between theory and practice is what makes the book so distinctive. It enables teachers not only to use technology effectively, but also to question, adapt and shape it within diverse teaching and learning contexts.

Keeping up to date in this fast-moving field is both a challenge and a necessity. Recent developments in UK education policy underscore this point. The latest National Curriculum Review for England highlights the importance of digital literacy and critical understanding of AI; while Estyn, the school inspectorate for Wales, has published insightful findings on the use of AI in Welsh schools, emphasising both opportunities for personalised learning and the ethical imperatives of responsible use. The discussions in this book are well aligned with these national priorities, offering educators practical tools and conceptual frameworks to navigate technological change with confidence and care.

This book is more than a guide; it is a call to action. It invites teachers, researchers and policymakers to engage with disruption not as a threat, but as an opportunity for creativity, inclusion and transformation in education. I highly recommend this book to anyone seeking to prepare the next generation to thrive in a world where technological change is constant, creativity is significant and understanding technology is not just essential but empowering!

Dr Yun Chen
Associate Professor and Co-Leader of the
Disruptive Technologies Research Cluster
Salford Business School
University of Salford, UK

Introduction

This book is divided into two parts. Part 1 is about understanding disruptive technologies and considers the nature of the disruption that such technologies cause, focusing in particular on the following:

- additive manufacture,
- artificial intelligence,
- augmented reality,
- Big Data,
- the Internet of Things,
- neurotechnology,
- programmable matter,
- quantum computing,
- robotics,
- synthetic biology.

It describes what each technology does, how it works, the extent of its adoption, utilisation and market penetration over recent time, who uses it and what for and the way they interact with other disruptive technologies. It relates this to the likely societal impacts, both positive and negative, and considers how society could respond.

Part 2 is concerned with teaching - the teaching, learning and assessment of disruptive technologies in the secondary school. It identifies different areas of the curriculum where they might be taught and develops a curriculum for ages 11 to 18 (key stages 3, 4 and 5). It describes ways in which disruptive technologies might be taught in STEM subjects such as designing without making, case studies, writing design futures and scenario building. It sets out how several other subject areas might consider the ethics, 'who wins, who loses' and the economic impacts of the disruptive technologies. It discusses how learners' knowledge and understanding might be assessed both as they are learning and at the end of the particular units of work. It considers how this knowledge and understanding might be assessed in public examinations.

The book finishes with concluding remarks which describe how teachers and curriculum developers can keep up to date with changes in the way the disruptive technologies are

DOI: 10.4324/9781003602002-1

progressing and impacting society. Throughout, there are short 'pauses for thought' to encourage reflection about what has been written previously in preparation for what follows.

All chapters were reviewed and revised collaboratively. Frank led on the writing of Chapters 2, 4, 6, 7, 8 and 10, and Hilda led on Chapters 3, 5, 9,11,12,14 and 15. All other chapters were authored jointly.

Before moving on, it is worth noting that Douglas Adams had an intriguing view on what we think might constitute technology in terms of how old we are, shown in the following. It is worth reminding ourselves that the young people we are teaching will fall into the first category.

Douglas Adams' view of our reactions to technology

I've come up with a set of rules that describe our reactions to technologies:

Anything that is in the world when you're born is normal and ordinary and is just a natural part of the way the world works.

Anything that's invented between when you're 15 and 35 is new and exciting and revolutionary and you can probably get a career in it.

Anything invented after you're 35 is against the natural order of things.

Douglas Adams
(Author, *Hitchhiker's Guide to the Galaxy*)

Preamble

It is generally agreed that new and emerging technologies have an effect on the societies in which they are used. Some, called disruptive technologies, have a major impact and make significant changes to the way people live and work. The classic example from European history is the printing press. In more recent times, Henry Ford's development of a manufacturing system that allowed mass production of affordable automobiles had a major effect on countries across the world. Photographs of New York 'pre-Ford' show main streets full of horse-drawn vehicles; 'post-Ford', all these have been replaced by cars and lorries. The horse-drawn vehicle market and associated occupations disappeared virtually overnight. This did not lead to significant unemployment, as the newly emerging automobile market and associated infrastructure requirements provided far more employment opportunities than those lost through the demise of the horse-drawn vehicle market. However, in the future this might not be the case as disruptive technologies take their place in the economy.

Robotics may be seen as 'work threatening' in the sense that the adoption of autonomous vehicles will seriously impact the employment opportunities in goods haulage, delivery of goods bought online, food delivery, public transport and driving taxicabs. This displacement of existing employment for drivers is unlikely to lead to new employment opportunities, as was the case for those employed in the horse-drawn vehicle market with the advent of the motor car. The deployment of AI is already causing concern with regard to being work threatening, and it is important to consider how this might develop. According to a report from McKenzie and Company (Berruti et al. 2025), AI may be considered to be evolving along a trajectory involving three types of capabilities: traditional AI, generative AI and agentic AI, as described in Panel 0.1.

Panel 0.1 Evolution of AI capabilities

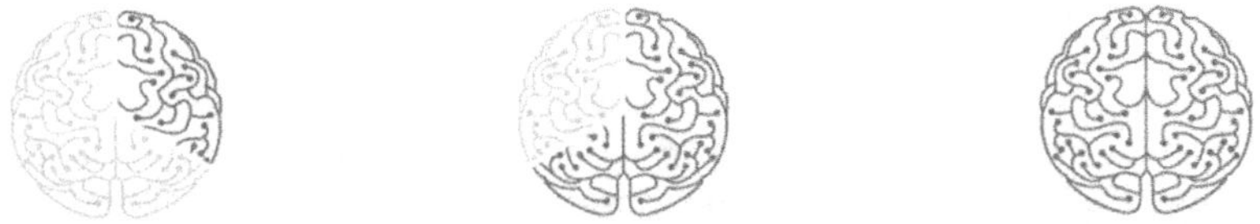

Traditional AI[1]
Rigid but reliable implementer

Executes predefined workflows but doesn't adapt and is hard to scale

- Performs rule-based execution
- Doesn't learn or reason
- Requires structured inputs
- Is efficient but inflexible

BEST FOR: **Basic repetitive and structured tasks that rarely change**

Gen AI
Supercharged copilot

Understands, generates, and transforms information but lacks execution

- Processes unstructured data
- Generates text-based outputs
- Is context-aware but reactive
- Is smart but needs human direction

BEST FOR: **Human augmentation and knowledge generation**

Agentic AI
Fully autonomous operator

Learns, reasons, and executes multistep workflows with minimal oversight

- Performs autonomous workflow execution
- Makes decisions without predefined rules
- Adapts to real-time inputs
- Has fewer human touchpoints

BEST FOR: **End-to-end automation, process orchestration, and decision-making**

[1]Comprises traditional automation tools, such as natural language processing, optical-character recognition, and robotic process automation.

McKinsey & Company

For organisations wishing to incorporate agentic AI into their businesses, this will require them to decide which decisions they want to automate and the extent to which these need human oversight. It becomes more complicated when the possibility of using agentic AI teams is considered. This seems to inevitably involve employing far fewer humans than previously, with their roles being concerned with oversight and ethics and a mindset shift on the part of the remaining human employees to see AI agents as co-workers. The report concludes by stating that

"This requires treating AI agents as corporate citizens, digital workers with defined roles, accountability and performance metrics embedded into the operating model" (Berruti et al. 2025, p. 10).

We aren't sure how a human employee might forge a relationship with an AI co-worker. The methods used by humans working together with each other – the water cooler conversations, the drink 'up the pub' after work – seem impossible, but perhaps these AI co-workers will have an online presence similar to other AI companions and humans will be able to interact with them through this in the same way people treat supporting robots in care homes or the seemingly friendly voices of 'Alexa' or 'Siri'.

In this book we describe ten disruptive technologies which will have significant effects on the nature of future society. We firmly believe it is incumbent upon those working in education to prepare young people in schools for this 'brave new world', giving them the knowledge, understanding, skills and values necessary to take part in informed public debate about the way technologies are developed and deployed in their society in light of the sort of world in which they wish to live and work. Given that younger people in England and Wales will soon be able to vote, this has never been more urgent.

Frank Banks and HildaRuth Beaumont November 2026

Reference

When Can AI Make Good Decisions? The Rise of AI Corporate Citizens by Federica Berruti, Lari Hamalainen, Oana Cheta and Venky Anant with Damian Lewandowski representing views from McKinsey's Operations Practice. https://www.globalization-partners.com/resources/2025-ai-at-work-report (Accessed July 2025).

1 Defining, exemplifying and experiencing disruption

Defining disruption

At the end of the 20th century, Clayton M. Christensen wrote his now-seminal work *The Innovator's Dilemma* (Christensen 1997), which introduced the idea of disruptive technologies. The writings of Christensen and others about disruptive technology are, to a large extent, focused on the needs of the business community and as such provide too much detail for use in the secondary school. We are particularly interested in the way certain technologies, as they emerge, have significant effects on the ways individuals, groups and communities live their lives. These technologies do emerge through commercial activity in various markets, but it is the social impact of these technologies with which we are principally concerned. We think it is important in education to concentrate more on the social impact of technology. Our purpose is focused on enabling young people to develop a perspective on technology so that they can consider its impact on their lives and thus take part, from an informed position, in debates concerning whether and how technology should be deployed in the society in which they live. Inevitably, social impact and economic impact are intertwined. This view is developed by McKinsey Global Institute (Manyika et al. 2013):

> The relentless parade of new technologies is unfolding on many fronts. Almost every advance is billed as a breakthrough, and the list of "next big things" grows ever longer. Not every emerging technology will alter the business or social landscape - but some truly do have the potential to disrupt the status quo, alter the way people live and work, and rearrange value pools and lead to entirely new products and services.
>
> (13)

We can unpack these features of disruptive technologies as shown in Panel 1.1.

DOI: 10.4324/9781003602002-2

Panel 1.1 The McKinsey Global Institute criteria for disruptive technologies

Such technologies will:

1. Disrupt the status quo
   i.e. they will overturn existing hierarchies and may (or may not . . .) lead to different and more democratic hierarchies
2. Alter the way people live and work
   i.e. they may increase or decrease employment opportunities, change the knowledge and skill sets required for employment, impact on education and alter relationships
3. Rearrange value pools
   i.e. they influence existing and new commercial activity in ways which redistribute financial gain, generally towards those who are deploying these technologies
4. Lead to entirely new products and services
   i.e. they will provide types of products and services that have not previously existed

We will use these criteria of disruption as a means of exploring the impact of the disruptive technologies we think should be included in the secondary school curriculum.

Pause for thought

If learners are to understand the four features of disruptiveness and use them to identify and interrogate disruptive technologies, it will be important that these features are accessible. As they stand, they are written for teachers. Write a simplified version of each feature that will be understandable by learners and still retain their essential meaning. Discuss your writing with colleagues.

Exemplifying disruption

In this section we take one technology from the distant past and two technologies from the more recent past and discuss them in terms of the McKinsey criteria for disruption to illustrate how they were disruptive. These technologies are concerned with the printing press, photography and transport.

The story of the printing press

The invention of the printing press by Johannes Gutenberg in the mid-15th century is widely regarded as one of the most significant disruptive technologies in history. Its impact on society, culture, religion and the economy were profound and far-reaching. In terms of the McKinsey criteria for disruption, it can be seen as disruptive in the following ways:

1. The printing press disrupted the status quo by making books available in the languages spoken by ordinary people in different countries, not just Latin. This promoted literacy among the general population, whereas before the advent of the printing press ordinary people were illiterate.

2. The printing press altered the way people worked as it gave rise to a new industry, leading to job creation in printing, bookbinding and bookselling. This also stimulated related industries, such as paper manufacturing and ink production.
3. The ability to produce books quickly and in large quantities drastically reduced their cost and made them more accessible to a broader audience. This changed the way people lived in that ordinary people were now informed about what was happening in their societies. This democratisation of knowledge is a hallmark of disruptive technology.
4. Through the printing press, scientific ideas and discoveries could be disseminated rapidly and widely. This facilitated collaboration and cumulative progress in fields like astronomy, physics and biology, contributing to the Scientific Revolution. The way new scientific knowledge was exploited through technology influenced existing and new commercial activity in ways which redistributed financial gain, generally towards those who were deploying these technologies.

These and the wider impacts of the printing press are explored in depth in Elizabeth Eisenstein's seminal work *The Printing Revolution in Early Modern Europe* (1983). She argues that the printing press had a profound impact on European society and was a major catalyst for the Renaissance, Reformation, Scientific Revolution and the rise of modern nation-states.

The story of Kodak

At the end of the 19th century, photography was pursued by those with expert knowledge, sophisticated equipment, financial resources and time. George Eastman, founder of the Eastman Company, changed that. His company developed a camera that was very simple to operate, used a roll of film and, in the main feature leading to disruption, a service that took the exposed film and produced a set of negatives and black and white prints. The result was an extremely rapid growth in the use of photography by the general populace (Snyder 2013). This can be considered in terms of the features of disruption as follows:

1. The company, known by its trademark Kodak, democratised access to photography, hence it disrupted the status quo.
2. It altered the way people worked in providing employment for darkroom technicians who processed the film.
3. It changed the way people lived in providing a popular hobby.
4. It rearranged value pools in that it enabled the Eastman Company to be very financially successful in a market that had not previously existed.

Ironically, the company later developed the digital camera, and the burgeoning popularity of digital photography led to the demise of Kodak's film photography business. Here we see another disruption involving a shift in the way people live and work - increased use of photography facilitated by digital cameras and loss of employment for darkroom technicians, rearrangement of value pools - away from the film-based photography industry to industries supporting digital photography. In terms of disrupting the status quo, the role of digital photography coupled with communication technologies has led to significant global disruption.

The story of Henry Ford

The way in which transport was mechanised by the application of the internal combustion engine to previously horse-drawn vehicles was a revolutionary technological innovation. But it was not disruptive at its inception because early automobiles were expensive luxury items that did not affect the market for horse-drawn vehicles. The market for transportation essentially remained intact until the debut of the lower-priced Ford Model T in 1908. Henry Ford indicated his intention to be disruptive as follows:

> I will build a car for the great multitude. It will be large enough for the family, but small enough for the individual to run and care for. It will be constructed of the best materials, by the best men to be hired, after the simplest designs that modern engineering can devise. But it will be so low in price that no man making a good salary will be unable to own one - and enjoy with his family the blessing of hours of pleasure in God's great open spaces.
>
> (Ford and Crowther 1922, p. 73).

The automobile, by itself, was not disruptive. What was disruptive was the development of the mass-production system that enabled the profitable manufacture of large numbers of vehicles that were affordable both in terms of purchase price and running costs. To show Ford's mass production system as disruptive we can use the criteria for disruption as follows:

1. Did the mass production system disrupt the status quo?
   Learning to drive and acquiring a motorcar have become a rite of passage for most young adults, male and female, in many countries. The opportunity to move from your place of birth to new and different places, to gain employment, to meet new people, to form friendships and relationships was facilitated by the motorcar. This physical and social mobility had a deleterious effect on small, localised communities. Clearly, the status quo was disrupted by the affordable availability of the motorcar.
2. Did the mass production system alter the way people live and work?
   The availability of the motorcar and other motor vehicles provided new employment opportunities for large numbers of people in manufacture, use and maintenance. The skill sets needed for this employment became features of education for employment. Peoples' lives at work and leisure were changed by the availability of both public and personal transport.

3. Did the mass production system rearrange value pools?
   Considerable new commercial activity arose through the availability of the motor car: in selling, leasing and maintaining motorised vehicles, in providing new infrastructure needed by the vehicles, in providing financial services for those using motorised vehicles.
4. Did the mass production system lead to entirely new products and services?
   Although the motor car can be seen as an alternative to a horse-drawn vehicle, its development into a wide range of vehicles for the transportation of individuals, families, groups of people and goods indicates new products and associated services. The parallel development of large networks of roads and motorways and associated services again indicates new products and services.

> **Pause for thought**
>
> Imagine that you had to use one of the previous examples to introduce learners in Key Stage 3 to the idea of disruption. Explain how you might do this in terms of:
>
> Providing pictures or photographs for learners to look at,
> Providing a story for learners to read,
> Providing objects for learners to examine.
>
> Assuming the learners worked in small groups on these activities, how would you assess their learning?

The Gartner Hype Cycle

Another way of describing the emergence of a disruptive technology is to use the Gartner Hype Cycle, and we believe that this, like the McKinsey criteria for disruption, has considerable potential for use in the secondary school. Hence, we will describe it here in some detail. Design and technology teachers are well-versed in helping young people consider the so-called 'life cycle' of products and have used such teaching to engage students in the environmental impact of not only the manufacture of products but also their use and disposal as a critique of consumerism and the need to move from a linear to a circular economy[1] (MacArthur 2015). Critiquing the emergence of a technology and its adoption and impact on society is less familiar territory but particularly relevant to our concern with disruptive technologies. The Gartner Hype Cycle (Gartner 2015) is an attempt to chart the life of a technology. It provides a graphic representation of the maturity and adoption of technologies and applications, and how they are potentially relevant to solving real business problems and exploiting new opportunities. In its general form it is shown in Figure 1.1.

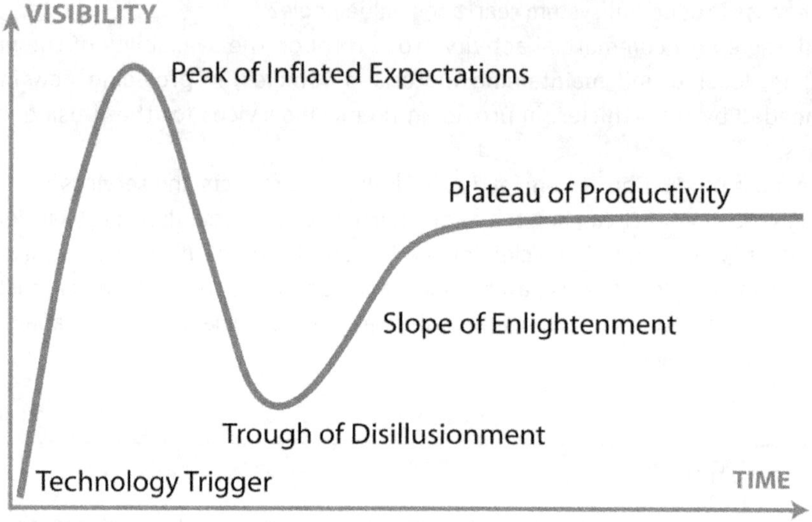

Figure 1.1 Gartner 'Hype' Cycle in its general form

Credit to Jeremykemp at English Wikipedia, CC BY-SA 3.0, https://commons.wikimedia.org/w/index.php?curid=10547051

The key features of the cycle labelled in Figure 1.1 and taken for Gartner (2015) are as follows:

Technology Trigger: A potential technology breakthrough kicks things off. Early proof-of-concept stories and media interest trigger significant publicity. Often no usable products exist, and commercial viability is unproven.

Peak of Inflated Expectations: Early publicity produces a number of success stories – often accompanied by scores of failures. Some companies take action; many do not.

Trough of Disillusionment: Interest wanes as experiments and implementations fail to deliver. Producers of the technology shake out or fail. Investments continue only if the surviving providers improve their products to the satisfaction of early adopters.

Slope of Enlightenment: More instances of how the technology can benefit the enterprise start to crystallise and become more widely understood. Second- and third-generation products appear from technology providers. More enterprises fund pilots: conservative companies remain cautious.

Plateau of Productivity: Mainstream adoption starts to take off. Criteria for assessing provider viability are more clearly defined. The technology's broad market applicability and relevance are clearly paying off.

To those who have followed the success and failure of various technologies, this has a certain intuitive appeal and as such may be a useful device for young people as they try to understand what might be happening around them. It must be acknowledged that the Gartner Hype Cycle was not devised with such educational aims in mind; it is a business tool and is not without its critics (Jorge 2006). One can easily see that there should be a 'tail off' section to the graph after the plateau of productivity indicating when a technology goes into decline.

Despite the "lack of objectivity" criticism of the Gartner approach, we think it provides a useful lens through which to think about the way various technologies have emerged in their journey to becoming disruptive.

Experiencing disruption

In the past - the experience of Frank's grandfather

When I was a boy, my maternal grandfather lived with us. He was born at the end of the 19th century and became a locksmith, working for Union Locks in Willenhall, which in those days was situated in the Black Country and was part of Staffordshire, England. The 1890s, then, is just two generations ago, yet the world was very different, and several technologies can now be seen as disruptive technologies during his life. For example, my grandfather was 8 years old when the Wright Brothers made their first aeroplane flight, and he was 27 years old when the BBC started its first radio broadcasts, making himself a 'crystal set' so he could listen to them. He was 34 when Alfred Hitchcock made the first British film with sound, 62 when we had our first black-and-white television and in 1962, the year before he died, Telstar allowed the first live broadcast of television images between the United States and Europe. In the year he was born, it is estimated that there were just 14 or 15 cars on Britain's roads, but by the time he was 45 years old that figure had reached a million private cars alone. There were, of course, two world wars which spurred on greater technological change - in the first x-rays for looking at injured bones became more common, and in the second radar, which is now ubiquitous on ships and airplanes, also had as a spin-off the Microwave Cooker. The fearsome atomic bomb of the 1940s was first 'tamed' to be used to produce carbon-free electricity in the mid-1950s.

Which of the technologies that became commonplace during the first half of the twentieth century was most disruptive to the life of the average working-class person, such as my grandfather? What would you add to that list since my grandfather's life ended in 1963? He never witnessed the moon landing, although he did once fly on holiday and was invited into the cockpit. As a boy, I was very jealous.

> Pause for thought
>
> Before you read on, pause to think of the disruptive technologies that you have witnessed since you were a 10-year-old child and make a list.

In the present

What did you include? If you are a student teacher or a new recruit to the profession following a degree, you might be thinking back about 10 years. The average age of classroom teachers across the UK is 43, so those teachers will be thinking about what disruptive technologies have occurred in the last 30 years. What follows is my list. In each case I think the technology can be described as disruptive in line with the McKinsey criteria for disruption in that they disrupted the status quo, influenced existing and new commercial activity in ways which redistributed financial gain, altered the way people lived and worked, and led to entirely new products and services.

Personal computers

Room-sized mainframe computers were in commerce settings and universities till the end of the 1970s when the first successful and widely sold personal computer, the Commodore PET, was released in 1977. Hobby computers, such as Sinclair's ZX80 which was launched on 29 January 1980, were cheap enough for young people to buy and become very proficient computer programmers. Such early personal computers, saving data to a cassette tape and later to magnetic disks, made computing accessible to individuals and small businesses, transforming the computing industry by making computing cheap enough for all.

Digital photography

As we have just seen, photography was invented in the 19th century, but the American company Kodak invented a simple camera that you could load with a roll of film so that everyone could become a photographer. The company was incorporated as long ago as May 23, 1892, but film cameras lasted up to the end of the 20th century. I had one with a flash bulb that had to be replaced after one use, but such a camera was inconvenient in a number of ways. It was not known how good a picture you had taken as after about 20 'snaps', the used roll of film had to be taken to a shop to be 'developed', so it was only after that wait that you could see the picture you had taken for the first time. In the 1980s, the cheap digital cameras sold by Japanese firms such as Sony and Fujifilm revolutionised the photography industry by making photo capture and processing instant, convenient and cost-effective for most people. Kodak, slower to change, almost went bankrupt and is now a much smaller specialist photo organisation.

Smartphones

If I asked you to name the first 'smart phone', I expect you would put Apple products near the top of the list. But the first phone that merits the description "smart" was the IBM Simon, which became available in 1994. It was an analogue cellular phone but had email, a calendar and the ability to send a fax. It had a touchscreen and predictive text. Now, of course, smart phones are much smarter, supplanting earlier stand-alone mobile phones, personal digital assistants (PDAs) and separate digital and video cameras by combining all these plus communication and significant computing power to search information, and they include extensive entertainment all in one device.

Streaming services

At home I still have some 78rpm (revolutions per minute) records made from shellac that usually have just one tune per side, 1960s singles which play at 45rpm which similarly have usually just one song per side and Long Playing (LP) records that are played at 33rpm with many song tracks per side. There is a large nostalgia market for these old discs played with a stylus "needle". These were replaced in the late 1980s by Compact Discs (CDs) played using a laser reader. In schools the construction of a very old-fashioned "pipe rack" became the equally anachronistic "CD rack" as from about 2010 streaming music services such as Spotify displaced CDs. The ability to stream on demand has started to significantly replace traditional broadcast television and how people consume media, leading to the decline of cable TV and satellite subscriptions as well as physical media sales.

Ride-sharing platforms (e.g., Uber, Lyft)

In 2017 I was crossing the United States using Amtrak on my way to witness a total eclipse of the sun, but the train was delayed and finally arrived in Salt Lake City very late on a Sunday night. All the station taxis had long gone home. Using a smartphone, I booked an Uber to take me to the hotel. In 2012 the London 'black cabs' bitterly opposed the launch of Uber as those drivers created a new market model, displacing established market-leading taxis by using a 'Satnav' to find an address rather than having the traditional 'knowledge' of London streets required by taxi drivers.

> **Pause for thought**
>
> Your list of what have been significant disruptive technologies since you were 10 years old will no doubt be different to mine. However, all these could be examples used in STEM lessons to consider how a particular technology has had a significant impact on society. But what is to come? What might be the forthcoming disruptive technologies that will affect the lives of your learners in Key Stage 3 (ages 11–14)?

Note

1 A linear economy is often described as 'take, make, use and dispose'. A circular economy develops models of economic activity which mirror as far as is possible the circular pathways in nature.

References

Christensen, C.M. (1997) *The Innovator's Dilemma*. Harvard: Harvard Business Review Press.

Eisenstein, E.L. (1983) *The Printing Revolution in Early Modern Europe*. Cambridge: Cambridge University Press.

Ford, H. and Crowther, S. (1922) *My Life and Work*. Garden City, NY: Doubleday, Page and Company.

Gartner. (2015) *Gartner Hype Cycle*. http://www.gartner.com/technology/research/methodologies/hype-cycle.jsp (Accessed 19 April 2025).

Jorge, A. (2006) *Cheap Shots at the Gartner Hype Curve*. https://catenary.wordpress.com/2006/10/22/cheap-shots-at-the-gartner-hype-curve/ (Accessed 19 April 2025).

MacArthur, E. (2015) *Resources Developed by the Ellen MacArthur Foundation Can Be Found*. https://www.ellenmacarthurfoundation.org/resources/education-and-learning/teaching-resources (Accessed 19 April 2025).

Manyika, J., et al. (2013) *Disruptive Technologies: Advances That Will Transform Life, Business, and The Global Economy*. McKinsey Global Institute. https://www.mckinsey.com/~/media/mckinsey/business%20functions/mckinsey%20digital/our%20insights/disruptive%20technologies/mgi_disruptive_technologies_full_report_may2013.pdf (Accessed July 2025).

Snyder, P. (2013) *Is This Something George Eastman Would Have Done?* Seattle, WA: CreateSpace, an Amazon Company.

Recommended reading

Sadowski, J. (2025) *The Mechanic and the Luddite: A Ruthless Criticism of Technology and Capitalism*. California: University of California Press.

Salazar, I.A. (2025) *Disruptive Technologies: Past, Present and Future (Historical Materialism for the 21st Century)*. London: Venceremos Publisher.

2 Disruptive technologies and the future

In many ways this chapter is an extension of "experiencing disruptive technologies". In Chapter 1 we considered the impact of the disruptive technologies on the past two generations. We will now be looking to the future and setting out 10 candidates that we think will be disruptive technologies experienced by the next two generations. This is not completely idle speculation; as of 2025 all of these technologies currently exist. Although some are currently in an embryonic form, we are convinced that all are likely to "create a new market and value network, eventually displacing established market-leading firms, products, and alliances".

In later chapters we will be considering each of the following disruptive technologies in depth. Here we give a brief introduction, taking each one in alphabetical order so that you can choose which order you wish to follow up your understanding of the disruptive technologies before considering in Part 2 how to teach about the chosen disruptive technologies in your school.

Additive manufacture

Additive manufacture (AM) is probably known to STEM teachers as "3D printing" and is often used in schools and colleges for prototyping. The process requires a digital model derived from CAD designs or 3D scans. The printing software 'slices' the design into thin layers which are then printed one on top of the other so that they bond together to form the required object. This layer-by-layer construction, combined with ever more powerful CAD, has enabled the construction of increasingly complex artifacts which often have very different properties and behaviour from those same artifacts if they were cast or cut using more traditional methods. It may seem odd that we have selected it as a disruptive technology. In some ways this is an old technique – after all, laying down bricks or stones to make a building has been around for millennia. But AM can take place at different scales, from nano structures to complete buildings, and may involve a wide range of materials: human tissue, electronics and food, as well as the traditional industrial product materials such as metals and polymers.

DOI: 10.4324/9781003602002-3

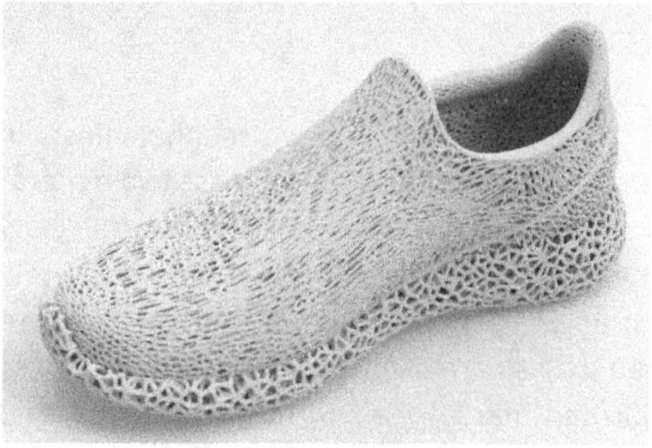

Figure 2.1 3D printed running shoe

Figure 2.2 3D Printed high-fashion dress

Figure 2.3 3D printing of temporary housing for disaster relief

Artificial intelligence (AI)

All teachers will have heard of artificial intelligence (AI), and you might have used it to plan lessons. AI is a branch of computer science focused on creating systems capable of performing tasks that typically require human intelligence. These tasks include learning, reasoning, problem-solving, perception, language understanding and interaction. I am sure that, like us, you have had a customer service conversation with a call centre operator, and after a while you realised it was not a real person at all but an AI programme. As time goes on and the machines 'learn more', it will become harder to detect that we are dealing with an algorithm on a machine, not a human. Some current common uses of AI include analysing medical images, financial fraud detection, using knowledge of what you have already bought to suggest future purchases in retailing (those who bought that book you are looking at also bought . . .) and in controlling autonomous vehicles such as a self-driving Uber. The implications of AI-driven cars that ensure we will never have a car crash are profound. Do such cars still need to be made from metal? There are already many concerns regarding the impact of AI on future employment in a wide range of both blue-collar and white-collar sectors, as well as the creative industries.

Augmented reality (AR)

Augmented reality (AR) is a technology that overlays digital information, such as images, videos, sounds or other data, onto the real world in real time. The digital content in AR responds proactively to changes in the user's environment, providing a seamless integration of the virtual and physical worlds. It seems to us that using AR in school is much more practical than virtual reality headsets. The Merge Cube (Figure 2.4), for example, allows users to physically hold and interact with 3D objects using AR technology. It is made out of styrofoam and is about 12cm on each edge. A smartphone uses the phone's camera to enable a learner to look through the screen at the patterned cube. The surface of the cube has coding that takes the viewer to a set of visual digital information concerning, for example, the human body or the solar system. As they hold and manipulate the cube in the palm of their hand, they can look at different body parts - or different planets. It is not just useful in schools. AR is used in fields like medicine and aviation to provide hands-on training as well as real-time guidance and feedback though a 'heads up' display.

Big Data

Big Data refers to extremely large and complex datasets that cannot be easily managed, processed or analysed using traditional data processing tools and methods. These datasets are often characterised by their vast volume, high 'velocity' and wide 'variety', often summarised as the three Vs of Big Data (Laney 2001). Volume is the amount of data generated and collected, and it is truly immense, ranging from terabytes (10^{12} bytes) to petabytes (1,000 terabytes). It is very difficult to grasp what this means. Some estimate that a petabyte is the equivalent of 20 million tall filing cabinets or 500 billion pages of standard printed text. Velocity is the speed at which data is generated, collected, and processed and is extremely fast as real-time or near-real-time data processing is often required for applications such as online banking or business transactions, streaming videos and sensor data from "Internet of Things" (IoT) devices. Finally, 'variety' refers to the different formats in which the data is collected such as social media, sensors and web transactions.

But what is the use of such huge stores of data? It is essential for the operation of Artificial Intelligence, but companies also use Big Data to gain insights into customer behaviour, market trends and operational efficiency. It can be used in healthcare to improve diagnostics, personalise treatments and predict disease outbreaks (remember 2020!), and it can be used to manage big cities' urban infrastructure, optimise traffic flow, reduce energy consumption and improve public safety. Big Data need not mean 'Big Brother', but as we will see in Part 2 of this book, the ethics of the use of developing technologies is a theme that will, we believe, be an increasing element of STEM and Ethics/RE lessons, as although Big Data hubs enable the economic benefits of Artificial Intelligence, for example, the negative consequence of the enormous electricity and water consumption needs to be kept in mind.

Internet of Things (IoT)

The Internet of Things (IoT) refers to the network of devices, vehicles, buildings and other items embedded with sensors, software and connectivity to exchange data with other devices and systems over the internet as shown schematically in Figure 2.5. These connected

Figure 2.4 The Merge Cube

Figure 2.5 The Internet of Things

devices include everyday household items such as smart thermostats, lighting systems and security cameras that can be controlled remotely to help manage energy consumption more efficiently, and to ensure a building and contents are safe from theft.

Frank has a smart watch that he uses to measure his heart rate and physical activity, and as primary health care becomes more dependent on such techniques, IoT devices will increasingly enable remote health monitoring and telemedicine, allowing healthcare providers to track patients' health data in real-time - the National Health Service moving "from analogue to digital". But it's not just for monitoring humans - wearable sensors can track the health and location of farm livestock and also monitor soil conditions, weather and crop health, enabling farmers to optimise irrigation, fertilisation and pest control. The ever-increasing connectivity will increase the significance of IoT, but ensuring the security of IoT devices and the data they collect is crucial. Any technical vulnerabilities can be exploited, leading to data breaches and unauthorised access, and there may be privacy concerns of the possible exploitation of the vast amounts of personal data collected by IoT devices.

Neurotechnology

Some years ago, in the TV programme 'The Six Million Dollar Man', ace pilot Steve Austin is apparently fatally injured in an airplane crash; however, the government spends six million dollars on bionic implants to rebuild Austin, which gives him superhuman abilities. That was then, this is now, and if some start-up companies can ensure the safety of their processes, in the future 'bionic' implants might become common, especially for those with extreme motor neurone disabilities. Neurotechnology refers to the field of science and engineering that focuses on the development and application of technologies to understand, interact with, repair or enhance the nervous system, particularly the brain (Figure 2.6). It is an interdisciplinary field that combines elements of neuroscience, biomedical engineering, computer science, robotics and psychology to create tools and systems that interface with neural tissue. But rather than focusing on creating Marvel Comic superhuman figures, neurotechnology systems can support people with a range of medical issues. For example, direct communication between the brain and external devices can enable the control of computers, prosthetics or other technologies using neural signals - so-called "thought control". Deep brain stimulation can be used for treating Parkinson's disease and transcranial magnetic stimulation for treating depression. Devices can replace or enhance the function of damaged nervous system components, such as cochlear implants for hearing loss and retinal implants for vision restoration.

Although not at the level of the fictional Steve Austin's powers, neurostimulation devices aimed at improving cognitive functions such as memory, attention and problem-solving abilities, which may include nootropic (cognition-enhancing) drugs, are being developed. The importance of ethical considerations in the development of neurotechnology across a range of lessons, we believe, are essential.

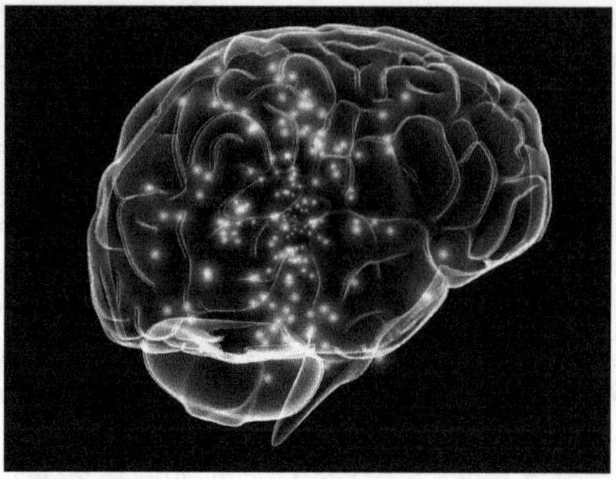

Figure 2.6 Neurotechnology and its ethical limits will be a subject for debate for decades to come

Programmable matter

Programmable matter is materials or objects that can change their physical properties (such as shape, density, conductivity and optical characteristics) in a controlled manner. This technology is based on the concept of 'reconfigurability', where the material can be programmed to alter its form or function in response to external stimuli or programmed commands. Examples include materials that can return to a pre-defined shape when exposed to certain stimuli, such as temperature changes, polymers that change shape or size when an electric field is applied and fluids that change their viscosity or solidify when exposed to magnetic or electric fields, respectively. A further development includes using DNA molecules to create structures that can self-assemble and change configurations. Most advanced of all is programmable matter involving tiny robots (catoms) that can move and reconfigure themselves to form different shapes and structures.

A STEM lesson where pupils consider uses of programmable matter could be both interesting – and profitable! Already in chain are ideas where factories can rapidly switch between different products and configurations without retooling, increasing flexibility and reducing downtime. These materials can reduce maintenance costs and extend the lifespan of products, significantly impacting industries like aerospace, automotive companies and construction. For better healthcare, implants and prosthetics made from programmable matter could adjust to the patient's body and changing medical needs, providing better outcomes and comfort.

Quantum Computing

We hesitated before we included quantum computing as a disruptive technology. In many ways it can be considered as enhancing the 'computing' used by existing disruptive technologies. But the difference in potential performance between current 'classical' computers and quantum computers is huge as quantum computers are not just fast conventional computers – they function in a totally different way. Current computing is built on logic gates using 1s and 0s, whereas quantum computing exploits the principles of quantum mechanics using "qubits", which can represent 0, 1, or both simultaneously due to a property called "superposition". This allows quantum computers to process a vast number of possibilities simultaneously, unlike classical computers that process one state at a time. It gets a bit complicated. Qubits can become 'entangled', which means that the state of one qubit is directly related to the state of another, no matter the distance between them. This property enables qubits to work together in ways that classical computer bits cannot, allowing for much more complex and faster computations. Quantum algorithms use interference to amplify the probabilities of correct solutions and cancel out incorrect ones, so this helps in solving problems more efficiently by focusing on the most promising solutions. Just to make the point again, quantum computing is not just another "fast computer"; it is a totally different type of computer!

Big digital companies and governments around the world are putting a lot of money into the development of quantum computing as there are significant development difficulties. For example, quantum states are fragile and can lose their quantum properties through interactions with the environment, a problem known as 'decoherence'. In 2025, maintaining coherence (a quantum state) long enough to perform meaningful computations is a significant technical challenge and building and maintaining a large number of stable qubits is technically very demanding. So why is there such an effort in making new faster computers? Quantum computers can naturally simulate quantum systems, making them ideal for modelling molecular and atomic interactions in chemistry and materials science. This could lead to advances in drug discovery, new materials and understanding complex quantum phenomena that are not feasible for classical computers to simulate accurately. Quantum machine learning algorithms can offer exponential speedups for certain tasks such as data classification, pattern recognition and cracking complex codes - which makes it very interesting to the military authorities.

Quantum computing is still in its early stages, with researchers and companies working on developing practical quantum computers which initially are likely to need a special environment such as extremely cold conditions, so it would be a return to 'the computer the size of a room' like it was in the early 1960s. However, some progress is being made in creating small-scale quantum computers and developing algorithms for specific tasks. However, the future of quantum computing holds the promise of solving currently intractable problems, revolutionising fields such as cryptography, materials science and artificial intelligence.

Robotics

When Frank was 8 years old, he had a robot. It did nothing except walk along, but robots have been in the public consciousness since the term was coined in the 1920s. Robotics is a multidisciplinary field that involves the design, construction, operation and use of robots. As is well known, a robot is a programmable machine capable of carrying out complex tasks autonomously or semi-autonomously, often replicating human actions or performing tasks that are dangerous, repetitive or precise. Robotics draws on principles from computer science, mechanical engineering, electrical engineering and like most disruptive technologies, artificial intelligence (AI).

If you think about it, robots are typically composed of mechanical components such as joints, actuators (motors), sensors and end-effectors (tools or manipulators). The mechanical design determines the robot's range of motion, strength and dexterity. Sensors gather data from their environment, including visual, auditory, tactile and other types of sensors. Perception algorithms process this data to make informed decisions and adapt to changing conditions. Control systems manage the actuators based on sensory feedback and programming, allowing the robot to perform tasks accurately and efficiently, adjusting their movements in real-time. Illah Nourbakhsh, Kavcic-Moura Professor of Robotics at Carnegie Mellon University, goes further in arguing that in robots we have invented a new species that operates as a living glue between our physical world and the digital universe we have created (Nourbakhsh 2013). Robots can operate in the real world and at the same time can be fully connected to the digital world. Robots that interact with people, such as care of the elderly or with a family in the home, can lead to a close association. For example, Frank's wife, even in just instructing the smart speaker, always says "please".

Figure 2.7 Robots in manufacturing

Synthetic biology

Can we consider biological systems like mechanical components? The emerging field of synthetic biology is an interdisciplinary area that combines principles from biology, engineering, chemistry and computer science to design and construct new biological parts, devices and systems, or to redesign existing biological systems for useful purposes. At its core, synthetic biology aims to apply engineering principles to biology, treating biological components as standardised parts (sometimes called bio bricks in an analogy to Lego bricks) that can be assembled in novel ways to create synthetic organisms or biological systems with specific functions.

Synthetic biology heavily relies on genetic engineering techniques to modify and manipulate genetic material (DNA, RNA) in organisms. This includes designing synthetic DNA sequences, editing existing genomes and inserting genes into host organisms. In a similar way to how engineers use standardised parts in mechanical and electrical systems, synthetic biologists aim to create standardised biological parts (such as genetic circuits, promoters and coding sequences) that can be assembled and recombined to build new biological systems.

The design principles similarly rely on computational modelling to predict and control the behaviour of biological systems. This involves designing genetic circuits and metabolic pathways to achieve desired functions or produce specific products.

Examples of applications of synthetic biology include engineering microbes to produce pharmaceuticals, biofuels and chemicals, developing new therapies, diagnostics and vaccines, creating biodegradable materials, cleaning up pollutants and enhancing agricultural productivity.

If you look up "Frankenstein food" in a British Collins Dictionary you will see it defined as applying to "any foodstuff that has been genetically modified". Tabloid newspapers invented the term to explain why protesters trampled and destroyed such crops as being "against nature". There was heated discussion at the time as it was pointed out that humankind had been crossbreeding crops since prehistoric times. However, it is true that synthetic biology raises ethical concerns related to biosafety, biosecurity, environmental impact and the ethical use of genetically modified organisms (GMOs). Note there is a difference between genetic modification and genetic editing (GE); GM introduces new genetic material from one organism into another organism whereas GE simply changes (edits) the existing genes using CRISPR (short for "clustered regularly interspaced short palindromic repeats"!). GE plants and animals need not be labelled GM, which may make them more publicly acceptable. Consequently, regulatory frameworks are evolving to address these concerns and ensure responsible use of synthetic biology technologies. It is worth looking up the work done to produce the Warnock Report (1984) that balanced the concerns of society's worries about investigations on a foetus with society's approval of the work leading to the success of in vitro fertilisation (IVF).

Conclusion

In Chapter 1, we looked back at the life of Frank's grandfather, looked at some disruptive technologies that have changed our own life over the last few years, and now in this chapter we have looked forward to possible emerging disruptive technologies that will impact your learner's lives and their future children's lives, probably sooner rather than later.

Although we believe that a blinkered focus on preparing learners exclusively for the workplace is inappropriate, we do agree with James Callaghan's views from when he initiated his great education debate as long ago as 1976, that later was picked up by a conservative government which in 1988 introduced a National Curriculum in England and Wales. Taking stock in 1992 of his original intentions, Callaghan wrote:

> The goal, I said, should be to equip children to the best of their ability for a lively, constructive place in society, and at the same time to fit them to do a job of work. 'Not one or the other', I emphasised, 'but both'.
>
> (Callaghan 1992, p. 9)

To equip children to the best of their ability for a lively, constructive place in society, and at the same time to fit them to do a job of work means a careful consideration of what that future of work might look like and, just as important, how the impact, ethically and practically, of those new technologies will disrupt their future lives.

Building on this overview – understanding in depth

The following 10 chapters will consider in greater depth the disruptive technologies introduced but only outlined here. In broad sweeping terms, each of the following chapters in Part 1 will revisit how the technology works, what it does, the extent of its adoption, utilisation and market penetration over recent time, who uses it and what for and the way it interacts with other disruptive technologies. The way each technology disrupts will be considered in terms of the McKinsey criteria for disruption set out in Chapter 1, and this will be used to identify the likely societal impacts, both positive and negative, and speculate on how society could respond.

However, the exact framing of this approach will depend on the nature of the disruptive technology being considered. So, for example, it will be important to consider the 'key steps' in additive manufacturing, whereas such a section would be inappropriate for the augmented reality chapter. Similarly, the treatment of programmable matter will primarily be concerned with the behaviour of materials and what we do with them, whereas the treatment of artificial intelligence will be primarily concerned with what AI is asked to do and how it impacts individuals, families, communities and nations.

The aim of the structure of each following 'in-depth chapter' is to give you a firm grasp on each disruptive technology and how they are currently 'playing out' in society so that you are in a strong position to lead discussions with learners and find out more as the uses of the technologies develop over time.

References

Callaghan, J. (1992) 'The education debate 1', in M. Williams, R. Daugherty and F. Banks (eds) *Continuing the Education Debate*. London: Cassell.

Laney, D. (2001) *3-D Data Management: Controlling Data Volume, Velocity and Variety*. META Group Research Note, 6 February.

Nourbakhsh, I.R. (2013) *Robot Futures*. Cambridge, MA: MIT Press.

Warnock Report. (1984) *Report of the Committee of Inquiry into Human Fertilisation and Embryology*, Cmnd 9314. London: HMSO.

3 Additive manufacture in depth

Introduction

Additive manufacture (AM) is a disruptive technology that has been familiar in schools in the USA and Europe for some years. Indeed, as long ago as 2013 the Department of Education was singing its virtues as part of STEM education.

> 3D printers are gaining popularity internationally across STEM education. So far in the UK, the technology has been restricted largely to Design and Technology (DT) classrooms. There is considerable potential, however, for them to be used within a range of STEM subjects, for example to enable links to be made between mathematics, design and physics in a similar way to, for example, 'sound', enabling links between music, physics (wave properties), biology (hearing) and engineering (concert hall design).
>
> (DFE 2013, p. 4)

Here we look in some depth at how AM can be used in different contexts.

This chapter is in seven parts. The first part will describe the key steps in additive manufacture. The second part will present common additive manufacturing technologies as panels with images of typical products. The third part will present the recent development of 3D printing for building houses, including electronic function and using biological tissue. The fourth part will indicate which industries are using additive manufacturing and the extent of that use. Part five will consider the extent to which this use is disruptive in terms of the McKinsey criteria for disruption. Part six will discuss possible positive and negative effects of this disruption. And lastly, part seven will consider the influences of other disruptive technologies on additive manufacturing.

Key steps in additive manufacturing

There are five key steps, as follows:

1. Creating a Digital Model:
   The process begins with creating a 3D digital model of the object using computer-aided design (CAD) software. The CAD model is then converted into a Standard Tessellation

DOI: 10.4324/9781003602002-4

Language (STL) file, which describes the surface geometry of the 3D object without any colour or texture.

2. Slicing the Model:
   The STL file is imported into slicing software, which divides the 3D model into thin horizontal layers. This software generates a G-code file, which provides instructions for the 3D printer on how to construct each layer.
3. Setting Up the Printer:
   The appropriate printing material (such as plastic, metal, resin or composite) is loaded into the printer. Then the 3D printer is calibrated to ensure precision and accuracy, including bed levelling and nozzle alignment.
4. Printing the Object:
   The printer builds the object layer by layer. Each layer adheres to the previous one until the entire object is complete, although the specifics of this process depend on the type of additive manufacturing technology being used.
5. Post-Processing:
   Once printing is complete, the object is carefully removed from the printer and the finishing touches are applied. Depending on the material and method, the post-processing steps may include removing support structures, sanding, polishing, painting or curing under UV light.

Common additive manufacturing technologies

Some common additive manufacturing technologies are shown in Panel 3.1, along with images of typical outcomes.

Panel 3.1 Common additive manufacturing technologies (part 1)

Type of additive manufacturing	*A typical product*
Fused Deposition Modelling (FDM) This uses thermoplastics such as polylactic acid (PLA), acrylonitrile butadiene styrene (ABS), or polyethylene terephthalate glycol (PETG). A filament of plastic is heated to its softening point and extruded through a nozzle, which moves to create each layer. Applications include prototyping, creating functional parts and hobbyist projects.	 A hobbyist project (simple bath toy)
Stereolithography (SLA) This uses resins that change their properties when exposed to ultraviolet (UV) light, known as photopolymer resins. The resins change from being viscous liquids to rigid solids. A UV laser 'cures' and solidifies layers of resin in a vat, building the object layer by layer. Applications include high-detail prototypes, dental models and jewellery casting.	 Jewellery castings

Panel 3.1 Common additive manufacturing technologies (part 1) (Continued)

Type of additive manufacturing	*A typical product*
Selective Laser Sintering (SLS) This uses thermoplastic powders such as nylon. A laser sinters powdered material, fusing particles together to form a solid layer which is built upon by successive layer structure. Applications include functional prototypes, complex geometries or separate end-use parts.	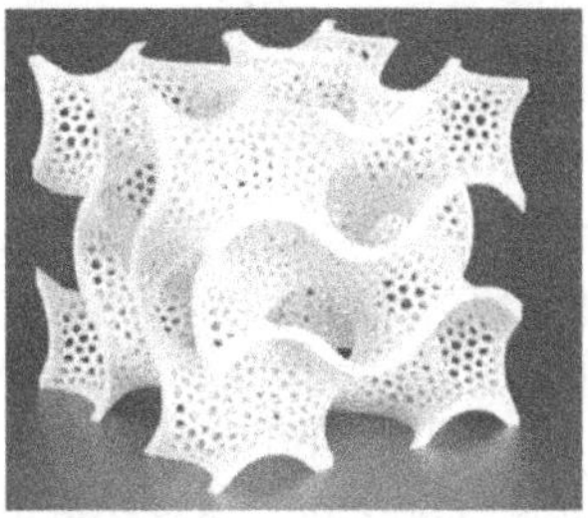 A complex geometry print
Direct Metal Laser Sintering (DMLS)/Selective Laser Melting (SLM) This uses metal powders like titanium, aluminium or stainless steel. A laser melts metal powder layer by layer to build a dense, fully metal part. Applications include aerospace components, medical implants and high-performance engineering parts.	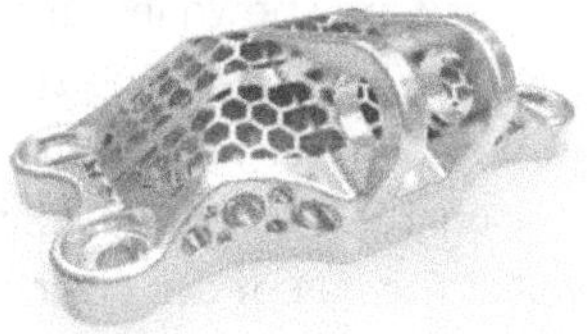 A high-performance engineering part

Panel 3.1 Common additive manufacturing technologies (part 2)

Binder Jetting This uses metal, sand and ceramics. A liquid binding agent is selectively deposited onto a powder bed, bonding the particles together. Applications include metal parts, ceramic parts, moulds for casting or full-colour prototypes.	 Printed ceramic parts
Material Jetting This uses photopolymers and wax. Droplets of material are deposited layer by layer and 'cured' using UV light. Applications include high-resolution prototypes and casting patterns.	 Casting pattern and resultant cast
Laminated Object Manufacturing (LOM) This uses paper, plastic and metal laminates. Sheets of material are bonded together and cut to shape layer by layer. Applications include prototyping and large-scale objects.	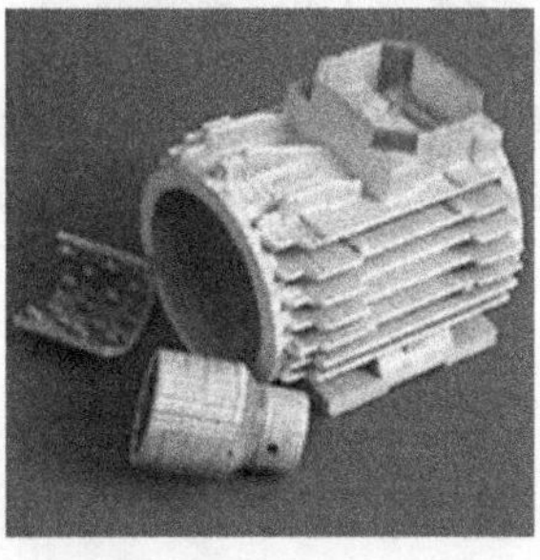 Prototype electric motor housing

Recent developments in additive manufacture

Production of buildings

Additive manufacturing is increasingly being applied in the construction industry to produce buildings. The process involves the print head extruding concrete-like material in successive layers along paths corresponding to the walls of the building, rather like building a coiled pot. In some cases, the print head is suspended from a large gantry which is on rails so it can move along both X and Y axes, printing the building in the space between the rails. In other cases, a large robot arm moves the print head, and the size of the print is not limited to a space between rails. In both cases there needs to be a ready supply of print materials, and this is sometimes contained in a transportable tanker and feeds directly into the print head. (See Figures 3.1 and 3.2.) Such buildings are being produced in different parts of the world, and some of these are shown in Panel 3.2.

The companies developing the use of additive manufacture in building construction argue that it reduces material waste and labour cost, significantly shortens construction timelines, allows for unique, complex designs not possible with traditional methods and in some cases can support the use of eco-friendly and recycled materials.

Figure 3.1 COBOD International, BOD2 Printer

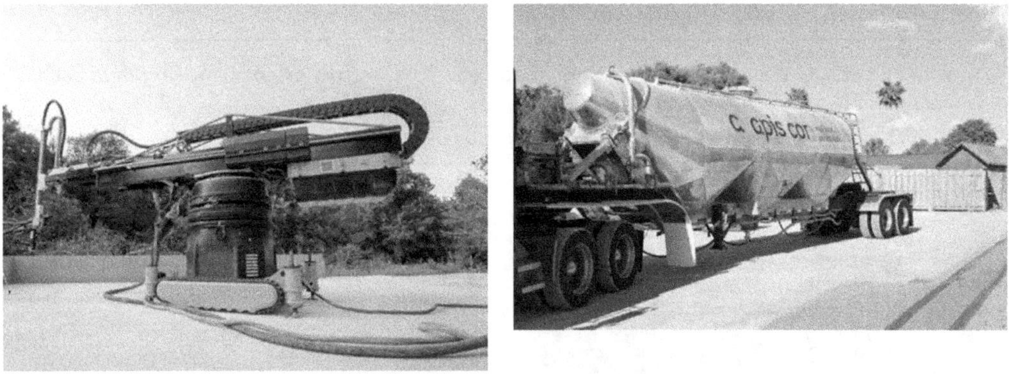

Figure 3.2 Apis Cor Frank printer and feedstock tanker

Panel 3.2 3D printed buildings

Europe's first 3D-printed two-story house in Belgium.
COBOD International, a Danish company, used the BOD2 printer for this project.

A community of 3D-printed homes in Austin, Texas, built by ICON using their Vulcan 3D printer.

Panel 3.2 3D printed buildings (Continued)

14Trees, a Community Development Corporation, worked with construction company Holcim to build Africa's first 3D-printed school in Malawi.

Designed by Mario Cucinella Architects and printed by WASP (World's Advanced Saving Project) in Italy, this is a prototype of a sustainable, low-carbon home built using local clay as the primary material.

Printing electronic function

Some design and technology teachers will remember producing printed circuit boards by creating circuit board artwork that was used as a mask on copper-clad laminate board coated with positive photoresist material, which was exposed to UV light and then developed to provide a pattern on the board which would resist etching by ferric chloride solution to give a board with the required copper circuit tracks. A long-winded, tedious and toxic process! In some schools, circuit boards are now produced by milling a copper-covered laminate board and, in many schools, ready-made circuit boards are simply purchased.

Additive manufacturing (AM) is increasingly being used to print electronics and functional components that integrate electrical properties directly into 3D-printed structures. Advocates of this approach argue that it enables the design of highly specialised and unique electronic systems; it is more efficient as it combines mechanical and electrical functionalities in a single manufacturing process, it facilitates the production of compact, lightweight electronics and accelerates the development of new electronic devices through rapid prototyping. Recently AM has been used in the production of batteries. Recent examples are shown in Panel 3.3.

Printing with biological materials

Additive manufacturing using biological materials - commonly referred to as "bioprinting" - is a rapidly evolving field with diverse applications in medicine, synthetic food production and research. Recent examples are shown in Panel 3.4.

Panel 3.3 Examples of printing electronic function

Printing circuit boards with the aerosol jet process
This uses aerodynamic focusing to precisely and accurately deposit electronic inks onto substrates. The ink is placed into an atomiser, which creates a dense mist of material-laden droplets. The aerosol mist is then delivered to the deposition head where it is focused by a sheath gas which surrounds the aerosol as an annular ring. When the sheath gas and aerosol pass though the profiled nozzle, they accelerate, and the aerosol becomes 'focused' into a tight stream of droplets flowing inside the sheath gas. The resulting high-velocity particle stream remains focused during its travel from the nozzle to the substrate over a distance of 2 to 5 mm, depositing the fine metal droplets in the form of the desired circuit onto the substrate, which may be flat or even curved or irregular in shape

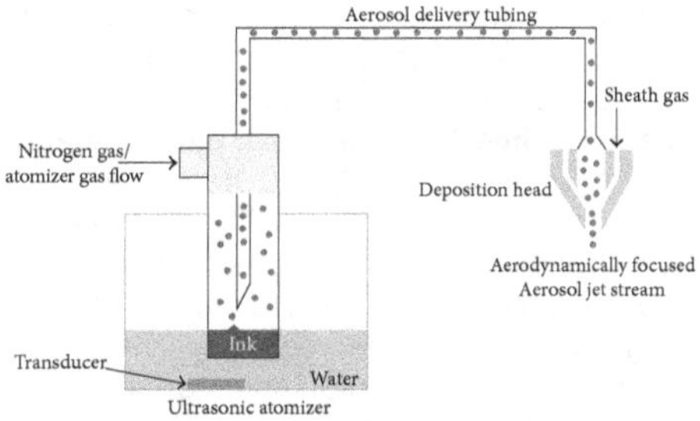

Printing flexible and wearable electronics
In Finland, VTT and Healthcare Finland have developed flexible wearable sensors that continuously monitor hospital patient wellbeing. As an example of the Internet of Things, the circuitry is 3D printed onto the wearable film. Patients are no longer bedridden and hooked up to several machines but become free to move around, which helps them feel less ill

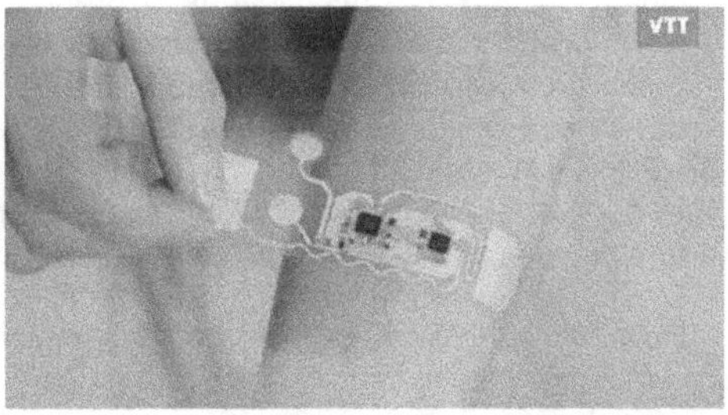

Embedding sensors in 3D structures
Optomec, a company based in New Mexico, has used the aerosol jet process to print sensors onto turbine blades as the blades themselves are produced by additive manufacture. This enables the performance of the blades and their structural integrity to be monitored continuously throughout their life cycle.

Panel 3.3 Examples of printing electronic function (Continued)

3D-printed batteries

Several different 3D printing processes are being explored for the production of batteries: direct ink writing, fused filament fabrication, inkjet printing and stereo lithography. They all offer significant advantages over conventional battery manufacturing techniques. Research is showing the potential of 3D printing as a promising solution to enhance energy storage capabilities. For example. the design freedom of 3D printing makes the fabrication of complex geometries and structures possible and is enabling the use of new materials such as graphene, carbon nanotubes and metal organic frameworks for battery fabrication to improve battery performance. From an environmental protection viewpoint, the waste reduction associated with the 3D printing of batteries is a way toward a more environmentally friendly future.

Panel 3.4 Examples of bioprinting

3D-printed skin for wound healing

The treatment of burn injuries requires skin grafts, and non-healing wounds such as bed sores require multiple treatments which are painful and not always successful. Scientists at the Wake Forrest Institute for Regenerative Medicine (WFIRM) in North Carolina, USA, have created such a skin bioprinting system that allows bi-layered skin to be printed directly into a wound. Cells from the patient are mixed into a hydrogel and placed into the bioprinter. Integrated imaging technology involving a device that scans the wound and feeds the data into the software to tell the print heads which cells to deliver and exactly where in the wound layer by layer. The bioprinter deposits the cells directly into the wound, replicating the layered skin structure, and accelerating the formation of normal skin structure and function.

3D-printed heart patches with built-in electronics for performance regulation

At Tel Aviv University in Israel, 3D printing of heart patches has been developed to include built-in soft and stretchable electronics. The researchers have shown that the patch can withstand continuous physical deformations such as those taking place in beating heart tissue. The electronic patch is flexible, stretchable and soft, and the electrodes within the printed patch are able to monitor the function of the engineered tissue. Furthermore, the system enables controlling tissue function by providing electrical stimulation for heart pacing. The researchers envisage that, when patched, it will enable a damaged heart to beat more regularly, allow the physician to monitor the implant function and to intervene remotely if needed.

Bioprinting for food production

Novameat, a biotech company based in Spain, uses plant-based ingredients to manufacture food products that they claim have the same flavour and texture as meat derived from animals. The development process starts with 3D printing to rapid prototype textured "whole cuts", which are then altered to give the optimum required properties to imitate meat, such as chicken. Once the ideal ingredient "mix" has been identified, production takes place through micro-extrusion technology, which allows manufacture at hundreds of kilograms per hour. For example, "Nova-chicken mini-fillets" produced by this technology contain water, pea protein, sunflower oil, thickener (sodium alginate), fava bean protein concentrate, potato starch and natural flavourings.

3D-Printed tumour models

Scientists at Tel Aviv University have used 3D printing to produce a physical model of a patient's brain tumour with cells from the actual tumour. This model lasts longer than a simple sample culture of the tumour and allows possible treatments to be tried out so that the most effective one for the individual patient can be identified and implemented.

Industrial use of additive manufacturing

Additive manufacturing (AM) is increasingly being used in conjunction with conventional manufacturing techniques to optimise processes, reduce costs and enhance product capabilities. This hybrid approach is especially common in industries where neither AM nor conventional methods alone can meet all the requirements of efficiency, scale and complexity. Panel 3.5 identifies industries in which AM is being used in conjunction with conventional manufacturing and comments on the extent of this hybridisation.

Panel 3.5 Examples of additive manufacturing being used in conjunction with conventional manufacturing processes

Aerospace		
AM is used to create lightweight, complex components (e.g., turbine blades, brackets, fuel nozzles), which are then finished using conventional machining to meet high tolerances and surface finish requirements.	Boeing and Airbus use AM for parts like air ducts and brackets but combine it with subtractive processes (e.g., CNC machining) for precision assembly.	Hybrid manufacturing is widely adopted in aerospace, particularly for high-value, low-volume components. Conventional techniques still dominate large-scale structural components due to scalability limitations of AM.
Automotive		
AM is used for rapid prototyping and low-volume production of custom or performance parts, which are then integrated into larger assemblies produced using traditional techniques like stamping or injection moulding.	Bugatti uses AM to produce titanium brake callipers, which are finished with conventional machining for precision fitting.	AM is primarily used in conjunction with traditional methods for prototyping, tooling and performance-critical parts. Full-scale mass production is still dominated by conventional methods due to AM's higher costs and slower production rates.
Construction		
3D printing is used to produce modular building components like walls or facades, which are assembled using traditional construction techniques.	Companies like ICON Technology Inc in Texas and Apis Cor Inc in Florida combine AM for structural elements with traditional methods for roofing, electrical wiring and interior finishes.	The integration of AM and traditional construction is in its early stages but shows promise for modular and custom designs. Traditional methods still dominate due to established practices and regulatory challenges.
Consumer goods		
3D printing is used to produce a wide range of consumer goods including high-end fashion items, shoes, parts of shoes and jewellery.	Adidas produces 3D-printed midsoles for its 'Futurecraft' line of sneakers, which are then integrated into traditionally manufactured uppers. Jewellery designers use AM to create wax models for casting, combining 3D printing with conventional lost-wax casting techniques.	AM is widely used for customisation and prototyping in consumer goods, while conventional methods handle large-scale production and finishing processes.

Panel 3.5 Examples of additive manufacturing being used in conjunction with conventional manufacturing processes (Continued)

Energy		
In the oil and gas industry, AM is used to create complex, high-performance parts like valve components, which are post-processed using traditional techniques for corrosion resistance and durability.	The German firm Siemens produces 3D-printed gas turbine blades that are polished and assembled using conventional techniques.	Hybrid approaches are widespread in energy, especially for repairs and custom parts. AM complements traditional methods rather than replacing them entirely.
Medical and healthcare		
Dental implants and prosthetics are often 3D-printed and then finished using traditional polishing and coating techniques.	The institute of Digital Dentistry in New Zealand (https://instituteofdigitaldentistry.com/about/) provides bespoke 3D printed dentures.	The integration of AM and conventional methods is widespread in healthcare, where AM is used for patient-specific customisation, and traditional methods are used for durability and compliance with regulatory standards.
Tooling and manufacturing		
AM is used to produce moulds and dies for injection moulding, which are then used in high-volume manufacturing.	Companies like Siemens and American firm General Electric (GE) use AM to produce parts (e.g., turbine blades) and then finish them with traditional machining or polishing.	Hybrid approaches are common in tooling, as AM can reduce lead times for custom tools while conventional methods are used for durability and mass production.

So, what are we to make of the way additive manufacturing is being used in conjunction with conventional manufacturing? In industries in which conventional manufacturing of large items is well-established, e.g. aerospace, automotive, energy and associated tooling and manufacture, there appears to be a complementarity between additive manufacture and conventional methods; additive manufacture is better at producing lightweight complex geometries in low volumes, whereas traditional methods handle precision machining and high-volume production of large parts. This combination may lower costs and reduce material wastage, but it requires companies to invest in both approaches, which may be expensive for smaller operations. The difference in materials used for additive manufacture and those for conventional manufacturing may complicate integration, and this difficulty may be compounded by a range of government- or industry-wide regulatory requirements. As additive manufacture technology develops to enable higher volume production this hybrid manufacturing is likely to increase. In construction, additive manufacture production of buildings may be seen as an alternative to conventional methods as opposed to becoming integrated within them, but this is still very much a minority activity. In the production of medical and consumer goods additive manufacture is well established, as the items produced are invariably small and are often required to be bespoke.

Given our discussion of the industrial use of AM, this is a timely point at which to introduce Helen Lockett's account of designing for large-scale metal additive manufacturing.

Expert contribution from Prof Helen Lockett

Designing for large-scale metal additive manufacturing

Professor Helen Lockett, The Open University

My research focuses on design for additive manufacture (DFAM) and sits at the boundary between engineering design and manufacturing. I investigate the design capabilities and constraints of manufacturing processes and develop design guidelines and design assessment tools to help engineering designers to design parts that are appropriate for these new technologies.

Manufacturing industries face a huge challenge in meeting future sustainability requirements, and additive manufacturing could facilitate the transition to more sustainable production by reducing manufacturing waste and allowing more lightweight and optimised designs. In the aerospace industry, many large metal structural parts, such as wing ribs, are produced using machining, a subtractive manufacturing process in which material is progressively removed from a metal billet to produce the final part, as shown in Figure A. When using machining, as much as 95% of the initial billet is removed during manufacturing, meaning that for every tonne of metal purchased, 950 kg is recycled without ever being used. Furthermore, even though the material is recycled it cannot be used for aircraft manufacturing and is used for lower-value applications.

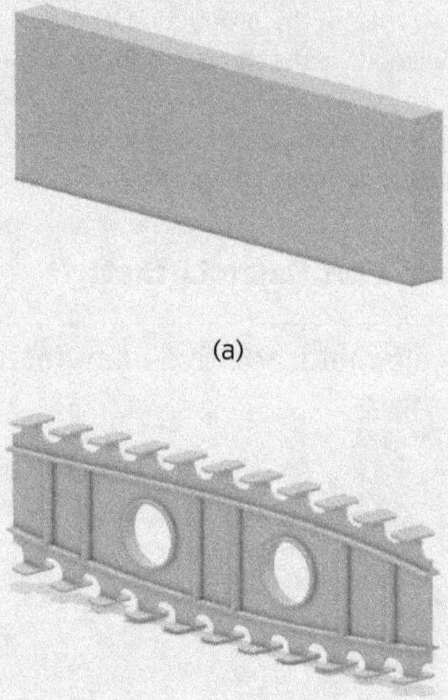

(a)

(b)

Figure A (a) rectangular billet (b) wing rib produced by removing material from the billet using machining.

If these large structural parts could be produced using additive manufacturing, material would only be deposited where it is needed, massively reducing the amount of waste material. Using additive manufacturing could also reduce manufacturing lead time, remove the need for tooling and facilitate lighter, more optimised designs that cannot be produced using conventional processes.

Most commercial metal additive systems use direct metal laser sintering (DMLS) or selective laser melting (SLM), in which a laser melts metal powder in layers to build a part. These processes can produce highly complex metal parts with high dimensional resolution but are not scalable to the large parts required in the aerospace industry. Directed energy deposition (DED) is a family of metal additive manufacturing processes in which material in the form of wire or powder is delivered with focused thermal energy to build up the part layer by layer. Unlike DMLS processes, which melt material in a pre-laid powder bed, DED melts the material as it is deposited [1]. DED can achieve much higher deposition rates than other metal additive manufacturing processes, meaning that it can be used to produce much larger parts.

In my research I have collaborated with researchers at Cranfield University, who developed a wire-based DED technology (also known as wire plus arc additive manufacturing (WAAM)) that uses metal wire as the feedstock, electric arc as the heat source and an industrial robot or CNC machine for positioning. We worked with industry partners to investigate the feasibility of producing large structural aerospace parts using WAAM. For example, the aircraft wing rib demonstrator shown in Figure 3.2 (b) was produced using a hybrid manufacturing approach in which the simplified features of the wing rib (Figure B (a)) were deposited onto a metal plate using WAAM. The as-deposited part would then be machined to produce the final part shown in Figure A. This case study showed that more than 450 kg of waste metal could be saved for each wing rib manufactured. Given that a typical commercial aircraft has more than 40 wing ribs and many other similar structural parts, and more than 1000 aircraft are produced each year globally, this technology has the potential to massively reduce the amount of waste generated in aircraft manufacturing.

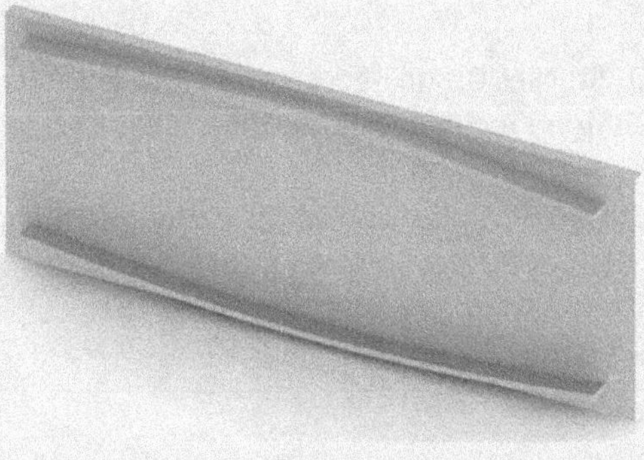

(a)

(b)

Figure B (a) Hybrid additive manufactured wing rib in as-deposited state (b) Demonstrator wing rib produced using WAAM (Acknowledgement Cranfield University).

Using my expert knowledge, I have developed design guidelines for WAAM which have been published as academic research and incorporated into new international DFAM standards for ASTM [2] and ISO [3]. I have also developed prototype software tools that are integrated with computer-aided design software to aid designers understanding of the capabilities and constraints of additive manufacturing and help them to assess the suitability of parts for WAAM.

There are still ongoing research challenges to overcome before additive manufacturing is widely used in high-value manufacturing industries, including improved techniques to predict and manage the residual stresses that develop during deposition and cooling. Another key challenge to unlock the potential of additive manufacturing is education. Currently the manufacturing industry has a 'machining' mindset, and to maximise the benefits of additive manufacturing, engineering designers must be educated about its benefits and capabilities. New design tools are also needed to model and analyse the optimised shapes that will maximise additive manufacturing's potential.

References

1. Gibson, I., Rosen, D., Stucker, B. and Khorasani, M. (2021) 'Directed energy deposition', in *Additive Manufacturing Technologies*. Springer, Cham. https://doi.org/10.1007/978-3-030-56127-7_10
2. ASTM International (2019) Guide for Additive Manufacturing - Design - Directed Energy Deposition. F3413-2019.
3. ASTM/ISO 52922 DED design guide (2025). Currently Awaiting Final Ballot for Acceptance as a New Standard.

We note that Helen has included directed energy deposition additive manufacturing (DED AM) in the account of her work and that this is not in our listing of AM techniques in Panel 3.1. This clearly shows that additive manufacture is a developing technology being supported by research such as that being carried out by Helen and her colleagues.

Disruption caused by additive manufacture

The McKinsey criteria for disruption has four features: upsetting the status quo, altering the way people live and work, rearranging value pools and leading to entirely new products and services. Although the way additive manufacturing is used across a wide range of different sectors varies, its use is often disruptive in light of the McKinsey criteria, as the following considerations show. In the case of aerospace, AM disrupts the status quo by providing the opportunity for rapid prototyping and eventual manufacture of small complex geometry parts which are difficult to produce by conventional large-scale manufacturing. It alters the way engineers work in that they will need to learn new approaches in how to design for AM. Initially niche markets for the manufacture of small complex geometry parts are likely to grow, becoming a significant part of aerospace business and hence rearranging value pools. By developing small complex geometry parts which are impossible to produce by conventional large-scale manufacturing, AM is providing the means to create new products. In the case of construction, the educational profile and requirements of a significant number of construction workers will need to change, thus disrupting the status quo. Construction workers skilled at handling concrete via shuttering and brick laying will need to learn a new, albeit related, set of skills for 3D printing buildings, altering the way they work. Economic opportunities provided by this new way of producing buildings will rearrange value pools. New products and services will develop as more 3D printed buildings such as houses, flats and disaster shelters become available, and buyers will be able to customise their requirements before building takes place. In the case of medicine, the use of 3D printing is developing a new high-status arena of medical practice, thus once again disrupting the status quo. The development of this new specialist field will involve medical experts working closely with AM experts, altering the way they work. The funding of such procedures will rearrange value pools, moving finance away from more conventional treatments. The development of bioprinting will lead to new products and services. In the case of consumer goods, the advent of AM gives designers the opportunity to develop designs using CAD and then get them manufactured using a printing bureau such as Shapeways (see https://www.shapeways.com). This enables designers to develop innovative designs and test them in the market without large capital expenditure, thus disrupting the status quo. Designers of consumer goods will need to learn how to design for AM, and customers for consumer goods will become used to buying products designed to meet their individual requirements, thus changing the way people work and live. Niche markets for bespoke consumer goods will be developed which have the potential to deplete the market share of mass production of consumer goods, thus rearranging value pools. It is likely that bespoke items including intelligent functionality will become available, providing new products and services.

Possible positive and negative effects of AM

In the commercial scenarios described here, it is difficult to find much in the way of negative effects of additive manufacturing. The use of AM by designers and engineers enables them to create items beyond their usual scope in terms of both complexity and novelty. Developments in health and medicine are likely to be beneficial, and the potential for building large structures is starting to be exploited for providing the rapid building of houses and flats and shelters in disaster-hit areas. Application in consumer goods is giving rise to new products and associated services bespoke to the customer. However, it is worth also considering the impact in other scenarios. Here are four examples.

The first considers localised manufacture. This involves the manufacture of goods via additive manufacture close to the customers who are purchasing these goods. So, instead of the goods being designed in, for example, the UK, manufactured in China and then shipped back to the UK where they are then delivered to the customers, instead the goods are made in a 3D printing manufacturing centre located near those who have purchased them. Such goods can then be delivered to, or even collected by, these local customers. This considerably shortens the supply chain and the associated carbon footprint, although, of course, the materials used for the printing feedstock will be part of another supply chain with their own carbon footprint.

The second involves the education of young people at school in providing them with the experience of making. If this experience is restricted to digital manufacture involving 3D printing and laser cutting, they will have little, if any, experience of using hand tools and interacting with the materials from which the world around them is made. Appreciating the nature of both natural and manufactured materials (wood, metal, plastic) through physical interaction is a formative experience in terms of understanding the nature of the material world. Mark Miodownik (2013) paints a compelling picture of our material world and introducing young people to this it should be, as Ed Charlwood (2024) has argued, a case of both 'hands on' and 'bits on'.

The third concerns home manufacturing. A recent paper (Petersen and Pearce 2017) has suggested that it makes financial sense for a family in the US to own an open-source 3D printer and print, as opposed to buy, a range of commonly used domestic items. The authors calculate that printing low-cost versions of these items represented a return on investment of over 100% in five years. The simple payback time for the high-cost versions was fewer than 6 months and produced a 986% return. Hence, they argue, fully assembled commercial open-source 3D printers can be highly profitable investments for American consumers. Such consumers will need to have the necessary knowledge, understanding and skill to be able to print the items from open-source CAD designs. A recent investigation (Wade et al. 2017) into the challenges of 3D printing for home users argues that a "killer" app that provides a user-friendly approach to this technology for novices is essential if home printing is to become widespread. It is interesting to speculate that young people at school learning about additive manufacture in design and technology lessons might be able to provide such a "killer app" from licensed school software and work with their parents to save their family money.

The fourth concerns the marginalisation of artisanal activity by competition with 3D printing. With the development of new feedstocks, it might well be possible to print a bowl that looks and feels as if it is made from wood, complete with grain structure. The artisanal equivalent made via wood turning requires a long apprenticeship to become skilled at using a lathe. It is not difficult to imagine the demise of such expert practice in the face of the production of less expensive but highly similar items via 3D printing.

Pause for thought

Engaging learners with the 'materiality' of the world occurs in many subjects - design and technology, science, geography, history etc. To misquote Madonna, "We are material people in a material world". Yet we are all spending more and more time in virtual worlds. To what extent can you ensure that your teaching includes an appropriate balance between virtual and 'real' world experience?

Influences of other disruptive technologies on additive manufacturing

Additive manufacturing (AM) is increasingly influenced by advanced technologies across various fields. These are identified in the following.

Artificial intelligence (AI)

AI plays a pivotal role in optimising AM processes, enhancing design capabilities and improving product quality. Key applications include:

- **Design Optimisation:** Generative design and topology optimisation use AI to create lightweight, efficient structures that are manufacturable with AM.
- **Process Monitoring and Control:** AI algorithms analyse sensor data in real-time to detect anomalies, optimise machine parameters, and ensure consistent quality.
- **Material Development:** Machine learning models predict material properties and behaviour, accelerating the development of new materials for AM.

Augmented reality (AR)

AR aids AM in design, prototyping and maintenance:

- **Design Visualisation:** Allowing designers to interact with 3D models in real-time before printing.
- **Operator Training:** Using AR to guide technicians in machine setup, calibration and troubleshooting.
- **Remote Collaboration:** Facilitating collaboration between geographically dispersed teams on AM projects.

Big Data

The AM process generates vast amounts of data from sensors, design files and machine logs. Big Data helps in:

- **Predictive Maintenance:** Analysing machine data to predict failures and schedule maintenance.
- **Process Improvement:** Mining data to understand correlations between machine settings, environmental conditions and final product quality.
- **Supply Chain Management:** Tracking AM production across distributed locations for more efficient logistics and inventory control.

Programmable matter

Although largely experimental, programmable matter influences AM through:

- **Self-Assembling Structures:** Materials that can rearrange their properties or shape after printing.
- **Smart Materials:** Integration of responsive materials that change properties under specific stimuli (e.g., temperature, light or stress).

Quantum computing

While still in its very early stages, quantum computing holds potential to revolutionise AM by:

- **Complex Simulations:** Solving optimisation problems and simulating material behaviour at atomic scales, which is computationally intensive for classical computers.
- **Enhanced Cryptography:** Ensuring secure data exchange in distributed manufacturing networks.

Robotics

Robotics is deeply integrated with AM in:

- **Hybrid Manufacturing:** Combining robotic arms with 3D printing to enable multi-axis printing and hybrid approaches like subtractive and additive methods in one process.
- **Post-Processing Automation:** Automating tasks such as support removal, surface finishing and part assembly.
- **Large-Scale Printing:** Robots are used to construct large-scale structures such as buildings and bridges with AM.

Synthetic biology

Synthetic biology intersects with AM in bio-fabrication and bioprinting:

- **Bioprinting:** Using AM to create tissues and organs by depositing bioinks composed of living cells.
- **Material Innovation:** Designing organisms that produce biomaterials tailored for 3D printing applications, such as biodegradable plastics or self-healing polymers.

The Internet of Things (IoT)

IoT enhances connectivity and monitoring in AM:

- **Smart Factories:** Networked 3D printers connected via IoT for remote monitoring, real-time analytics and process optimisation.
- **End-User Products:** Enabling devices manufactured via AM to include IoT functionalities, such as embedded sensors or smart chips.

The integration of these technologies transforms AM into a more dynamic, efficient and versatile manufacturing process. AI and Big Data currently have the most significant and widespread impact, driving immediate improvements in both quality and efficiency. Emerging fields like quantum computing, synthetic biology and programmable matter have high future potential but at the moment require considerable further development to achieve mainstream adoption. Technologies like IoT, robotics and AR, however, are enabling smarter and more integrated AM systems today. Together, as we have seen, these advancements push the boundaries of what AM can achieve in industrial, medical and consumer applications.

References

Charlwood, E. (2024) 'Thought piece', in H.R. Beaumont and T. Steeg (eds) *Design & Technology in Your School*. Oxon: Routledge.

DFE-Department for Education. (2013) *3D Printers in Schools: Uses in the Curriculum Enriching the Teaching of STEM and Design Subjects*. https://assets.publishing.service.gov.uk/media/5a74f2a1ed915d3c7d52931c/3D_printers_in_schools.pdf (Accessed January 2025).

Miodownik, M. (2013) *Stuff Matters*. London: Penguin.

Petersen, E. and Pearce, J. (2017) *Emergence of Home Manufacturing in the Developed World: Return on Investment for Open-Source 3-D Printers*. Technologies (MDPI).

Wade, R., Garland, N. and Underwood, G. (2017) *Challenges of 3D Printing for Home Users*. International Conference on Engineering and Product Design Education, 7 and 8 September, Oslo and Akershus University College of Applied Sciences, Norway.

Recommended reading

A Guide to Additive Manufacturing (Springer Tracts in Additive Manufacturing) by Damir Godec (Editor), Joamin Gonzalez-Gutierrez (Editor), Axel Nordin (Editor), Eujin Pei(Editor), Julia Ureña Alcázar (Editor) Springer 2022 This is an open access book free to download at this url: https://link.springer.com/book/10.1007/978-3-031-05863-9

4 Artificial intelligence in depth

My guess is that you have started to read this chapter about artificial intelligence (AI) because you are already using it to support your work. Many now use AI to plan differentiated lessons, help with schemes of work and to construct resources, create quizzes and revision materials and even to help draft polices and create presentations for senior staff. For decades, sharing classroom resources has been a collegiate activity and an essential part of secondary school department life to reduce workload and share expertise, so surely using AI is just another 'colleague' to ask for help. Well, maybe - let's look at it all in depth. This chapter is in five parts: What is AI, and how does AI work? (We will look at this again in Chapter 16.) To what extent has AI been adopted in industry and commerce, science and art? How does AI interact with other disruptive technologies? What's next for AI? What are the predicted negative aspects of using AI, and what should we do about it? For many it is a concern about future jobs, and even the UK government seems ambivalent:

> What is certain is while some jobs will be replaced by AI, many will be augmented - and an unknown number will be created.
>
> (DSI&T 2025)

What is AI, and how does AI work?

The 2024 Nobel Prize in Physics was awarded jointly to John J. Hopfield (aged 91) and Geoffrey E. Hinton (aged 77), who are pictured in Figure 4.1.

> for foundational discoveries and inventions that enable machine learning with artificial neural networks. They have used tools from physics to develop methods that are the foundation of today's powerful machine learning. John Hopfield created an associative memory that can store and reconstruct images and other types of patterns in data. Geoffrey Hinton invented a method that can autonomously find properties in data and so perform tasks such as identifying specific elements in pictures.
>
> (Nobel Prize 2024)

DOI: 10.4324/9781003602002-5

Figure. 4.1 John J. Hopfield and Geoffrey E. Hinton – *Arthur Petron*

Looking at the ages of these AI pioneers, the journey to get where we are now in the use of AI clearly started decades ago. In fact, the idea of a 'learning machine' began in the 1940s with McCulloch and Pitt's model of a biological neuron (Hodgson 2024). But its widespread use is comparatively recent and, as we will discuss, full of both promise and threat.

Rene Descartes, a 17th-century philosopher, famously coined the phrase "I think therefore I am", indicating that through the act of thinking humans are aware of their own existence. António Damásio, a Portuguese neuroscientist born in 1944, has challenged this with the phrase "I feel therefore I am", indicating that it is through having emotions that humans are deeply aware of their own existence. Both thinking and feeling are equally important for being human and being aware of our own existence – sometimes termed as being sentient. These defining characteristics of humans are not shared by artificial intelligence. AI has no feelings and the way it 'thinks' is very different to the way humans think, and currently no AI is aware of its own existence, so it isn't conscious.

Frank, a physics teacher, taught students to answer the question "Why is the sky blue?" He had the answer in his memory, but it was linked to his experience of and feelings about the many occasions he has helped students understand the answer. AI wouldn't do it like Frank. An AI would do it as if it was a 'super librarian' in a massive library containing billions of books – the enormous data AI was trained on. If you ask the AI, "Why is the sky blue?" it would search super-fast through all the books it's ever read (training data), find patterns in how this question has been answered before, choose the most likely combination of words that make a 'good' schoolteacher-style answer and write a response that sounds fluent and informative. But here's the key: the AI doesn't understand the meaning like a human would, and, unlike Frank, it doesn't know what that student has already learnt – and what she hasn't yet studied. It's very good at assimilating spoken and written language, but it's only working out what the best answer looks like based on past patterns, and the key word is 'past'. Shannon Vallor in her book *The AI Mirror* makes the case that AI, when trained on physical data such as protein molecules, can be very useful indeed (see Figure 4.7), but when trained on data constructed by humans, the bias in that data is reflected in the answers generated with people's often unrealised prejudices. The answers are not new; it is like a mirror reflecting what is already known, like the books in a library. But what is known is huge, and that 'super librarian' finds what we want to look up very fast indeed.

Bell and Dunn underline this distinction about AI vs Human Intelligence:

> **What AI Means**
>
> AI programs can perform many tasks traditionally carried out by humans. These could include, for example, holding conversations, recommending products, or recognising patterns in images. AI may stand for "Artificial Intelligence," but that doesn't mean that AI programs think the same way a human does. AI makes decisions based on the data it's being fed and can process huge amounts of information far more quickly and efficiently than any human brain.
>
> **What AI Doesn't Mean**
>
> Sometimes, "AI" is used as a 'buzzword' when referring to technologies that don't fit the above definition. AI programs are designed to learn and adapt. Not all "clever-looking" technology can do these things – and if it can't, like the examples below, it doesn't qualify as AI.
>
> - Some chatbots are AI, but not all. Some follow scripts and can't adapt or generate original responses.
> - *Most* robots are not AI at this point. Industrial robots, for example, might carry out repetitive, movement-based tasks without learning or making decisions.
> - Image, speech recognition, or predictive models (like forecasting tools) might look advanced but rely strictly on predefined rules.
> - Supercomputers have a very high level of performance and can do extremely fast calculations. But they aren't necessarily AI.
>
> (Bell and Dunne 2025)

At its core, AI relies on algorithms – step-by-step procedures or formulas for solving problems. These algorithms are often built around massive datasets – Big Data (see Chapter 6) – that enable systems to recognise patterns, identify trends and make predictions. Machine learning, a subset of AI, uses mathematical techniques to allow systems to learn and improve their performance on specific tasks without explicit programming. This mathematics is surprisingly straightforward and some of it easily understood by an A-level maths student (see Ananthaswamy 2024 and Chapter 16). Neural networks, which are inspired by the structure of the human brain, process information through interconnected nodes, learning from examples by adjusting weights within the network. The aforementioned Nobel winners (Figure 4.1) both have such networks named after them. This allows AI systems to perform tasks like image recognition, speech processing and language translation with remarkable speed and accuracy. Training these systems involves feeding them labelled datasets and using various learning techniques to fine-tune their capabilities. Once trained, AI models operate through inference, where they use their learned information to evaluate new, unseen data and provide outputs. Beyond machine learning, other AI methodologies like natural language processing (NLP) and computer vision enable systems to interact with the people and places in what seems to be human-like ways. A typical morning in the Banks household starts with "Alexa, play BBC Radio 1". "Good morning, Frank. Playing BBC Radio 1. BBC Sounds . . ." It is remarkably lifelike – his wife always says "please" when asking Alexa to do something!

Figure 4.2 Echo Dot (3rd Gen)

Sharon Vallor (2024) has indicated her concerns over the formation of emotional relationships between humans and AI. In such a relationship, the AI would be able to find many thousands of examples regarding how to respond to a human companion in various situations and choose one that seems the most appropriate for the particular situation at hand. It would seem to the human that the AI was behaving in a kind, loving and considerate way, but of course the AI would have no feelings towards the human. It would be working out what the 'best' response was based on past patterns. This is a poor substitute for a genuine relationship between two human beings, with all the emotional angst that is part of the discourse.

NLP allows AI to take in, interpret and generate text and enable language translation tools. Reinforcement learning enables systems like autonomous vehicles to make decisions in ever-changing environments by trial and error (but hopefully not too many errors when on actual roads!). AI's ability to work effectively hinges on computational power, large datasets and finely tuned algorithms, enabling it to learn from complex data, simulate reasoning and automate decision-making at unprecedented speeds

To what extent has AI been adopted in industry and commerce, science and art?

If you have been using AI as a tool for planning lessons, it will be no surprise to realise that Artificial Intelligence has been adopted extensively across industries and commerce, revolutionising how those businesses operate. Table 4.1 compares the most used AI models in 2025:

Table 4.1 Comparing AI tools

AI model	*Main use*	*Number of users Spring 2025*
ChatGPT (GPT-4.1)	General-purpose chatbot, coding, writing, research, image generation (via DALL·E)	Over 100 million weekly users; approximately 3.66 billion monthly website visits
ChatGPT (OpenAI)	General-purpose coding assistant, code generation, debugging	Over 500 million weekly users
Claude 3.7 Sonnet	Advanced reasoning, document analysis, coding, scheduling	Used by 11% of U.S. respondents and 9% in the UK
Google Gemini 1.5 Flash	AI-powered search, writing, re Multimodal coding and development assistant integrated with Google services	Used by 27% of U.S. respondents and 21% in the UK
Google AI	AI Mode expands what Gemini can do with more advanced reasoning and ways of interacting. It divides a question into subtopics and searches for each one simultaneously.	Google launched "AI Mode" for its search platform, July 24, 2025. By 4 August 2025 it had over 100 million monthly active users
DeepSeek V3	Multilingual chatbot, open-source LLM, reasoning tasks, mobile-first. AI assistant code generation and integration model	Surpassed ChatGPT as the most downloaded freeware app on the iOS App Store in the U.S. Popular among coding developers
Grok-3	Advanced reasoning, math/science problem-solving, real-time internet search via X	Access limited to X Premium+ and xAI SuperGrok subscribers; user numbers not publicly disclosed
Microsoft Copilot	AI assistant integrated into Microsoft 365 (Word, Excel, Outlook); productivity automation	Used by 26% of U.S. respondents and 19% in the UK
Gemma 7B	Open-source LLM optimized for speed and low latency; suitable for chatbots and content generation	Open source: specific user numbers not publicly disclosed
H2O.ai	Open-source AutoML platform for building and deploying machine learning models	Open source: specific user numbers not publicly disclosed
IBM Watson	Cognitive computing platform for natural language processing, machine learning, and data analytics	Specific user numbers not publicly disclosed
Jasper	AI-powered marketing and content creation tool	Used by 10% of U.S. respondents and 7% in the UK
Tabnine	AI code completion and chat assistant for developers	Over 1 million developers
Qodo	AI-powered code generation, test creation, and code reviews	Over 800,000 installations across IDEs
Yi-Coder (01.AI)	Open-source coding assistant supporting 52 languages	User numbers not disclosed; launched September 2024

Like many people, Frank does his banking online. Not only is it convenient, but it is also a practical necessity if, like him, you live in a rural area and a visit to the bank is a 32-mile round trip. If help is needed online, however, AI enables the supporting chatbots and virtual assistants. AI is not only supporting commerce when we bank or shop or ask for information. AI is now very much becoming part of the improvement of existing products and techniques, augmenting what a human does, rather than replacing what a human does.

Uber is ready to launch driverless taxis in the UK. In 2025, they already had the service available in a handful of US cities, as well as China, UAE and Singapore. Andrew Macdonald, senior vice president of mobility at Uber, said, "In the UK there are also practical questions around insurance, ownership and liability when a self-driving vehicle is involved in an accident which are all still being worked out". The government says self-driving vehicles (Figure 4.3) have the potential "to build an industry worth £42bn and provide 38,000 jobs by 2035" (Oliver 2025).

But of course, they are a source of concern for people who earn a living driving. Andy Prendergast, GMB national secretary, said the "significant social implications" driverless cars and taxis could have - such as the potential for less work or increased unemployment - for workers and the public must be fully considered (Kleinman 2025). Tesla, the electric vehicle manufacturer, sees fully driverless cars as the salvation of its company as China takes a significant share of the EV market. In both cases, the UK government suggests that the approval process is not likely to happen before the second half of 2026 or 2027.

Figure 4.3 **Self-driving car**

If AI can be taught to recognise faces, it can be taught to recognise any image, and you may know that it is used to help radiographers inspect x-ray images and other scans for signs of cancers or other abnormalities (Figure 4.4). For example, in December 2024, the newspapers reported that

> AI offers better treatment of strokes by improving brain scan analysis - and AI could be twice as accurate as current methods at pinpointing when the stroke took place.
>
> (Newton, December 2024)

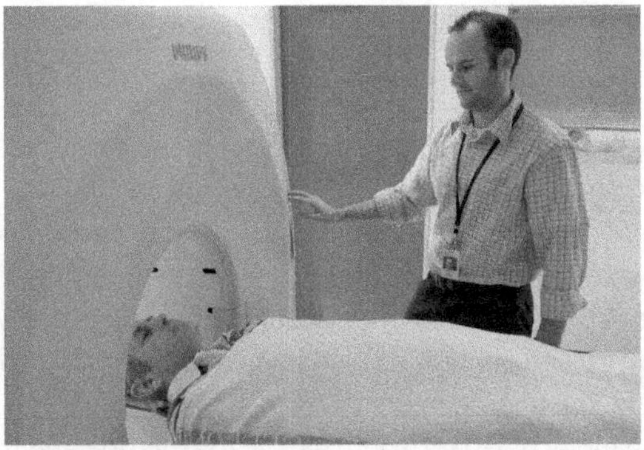

Figure 4.4 Making a brain scan - then using AI to help with the analysis

But it is not just used for diagnostics in healthcare; it can also be employed in suggesting the chemical basis for new drugs.

> As shown in Figure 4.5, the 2024 Nobel Prize for Chemistry has been awarded to David Baker, Demis Hassabis and John Jumper for their work on protein structure and design. AlphaFold2 was trained using many different protein structures and went on to successfully predict the structures of nearly all of the 200 million known proteins. It now takes just minutes - not years - to obtain a protein structure. AlphaFold2 could boost our understanding of a wide range of biological and chemical processes including bacterial resistance to antibiotics and the decomposition of plastics.
>
> (Johnston 2024)

Figure 4.5 Dr David Baker, Sir Demis Hassabis and Dr. John Jumper

Sir Demis Hassabis is co-founder and CEO of Google DeepMind and Isomorphic Labs, and Dr. John Jumper is Google's DeepMind Director. AlphaFold predicts the 3D structure of proteins from their amino acid sequences. David Baker also worked on computational protein design.

Researchers at Oxford University normally take four years to identify and characterise one small protein, but by using AlphaFold they have managed 23 in a few months. Further, Google DeepMind claims that:

> Over 2 million researchers in over 190 countries are using the AlphaFold Protein Structure Database to inform their research so up to 1 billion research years have been saved by AlphaFold database structures.
>
> (Google DeepMind 2025)

That statistic is mind-blowing, but when you look closely at so many researchers characterising a protein in just 2 weeks that used to take 4 years, one can see how the 1 billion research years total is a fair claim. There are many more benefits of using AI to enhance STEM research.

Hilda, as someone who has studied chemistry, is deeply impressed with AlphaFold, shown schematically in Figure 4.6. She remembers learning about and then teaching the three different 'levels' of protein structure: first, the sequence of amino acids that make up the long protein molecule; second, the hydrogen bonds formed between various parts of this sequence, causing the long protein molecule to form into a helical structure; and third, the way this helical molecule folds into a final shape due to hydrogen bonding between various parts of the helix. The number of different possibilities of hydrogen bonds is phenomenally large, yet only one gives the final shape. For the AlphaFold AI to work this out is hugely impressive. It does this by using input data – the amino acid sequence, evolutionary information from similar sequences in other organisms, known as Multiple Sequence Alignment (MSA) and template structures of similar proteins, if available, which is then processed by a neural network to give a 3D atomic structure of the way the protein molecule has folded. This is summarised in Figure 4.6.

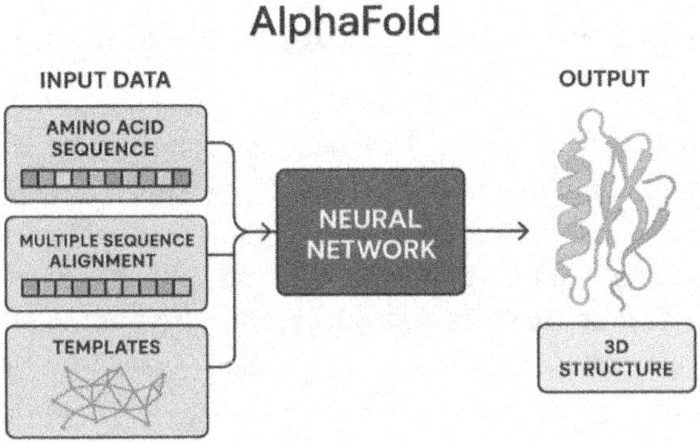

Figure 4.6 Schematic diagram of using AlphaFold

What makes AlphaFold so impressive and useful is its unprecedented accuracy, its generalisability (it can predict novel proteins with no structural homologs) and its open access: AlphaFold and its predictions for ~200 million proteins are publicly available (AlphaFold DB 2025). Without doubt, as Malone (2024) notes:

> *From hunting for evidence of subatomic particles to speeding up the diagnosis of disease, generative artificial intelligence is transforming science.*

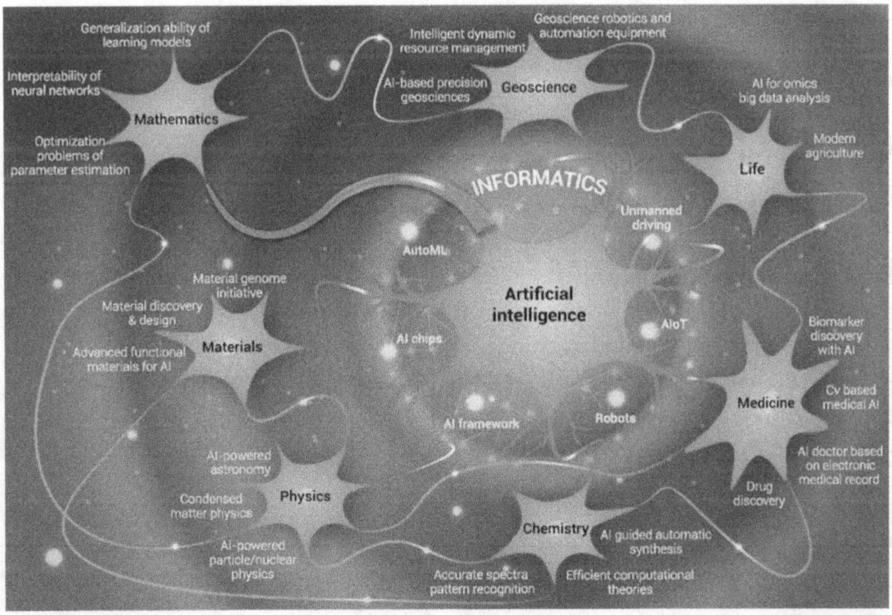

Figure 4.7 Examples science and AI (Xu et al. 2021)

But is not only science that uses AI at its frontier. The arts are also making use of AI. Although many artists and musicians are against the use of AI for artistic purposes, not all are. With any new tool, artists will endeavour to use it to create new possibilities, from dreamlike landscapes to mind-bending abstractions; artists exploiting the possibilities of AI are pushing the boundaries of creativity (Garces 2024).

How does AI interact with other disruptive technologies?

Due to its now almost-universal adoption and wide-ranging use in industry and commerce, as we have already acknowledged – and in education for both teacher and student use – AI interacts deeply and in combination with many of the other disruptive technologies we are considering in this book. In **Big Data**, AI's analytical capabilities quickly process the vast datasets, uncovering insights that inform strategies across various industries. This fuels the **Internet of Things (IoT)**, as AI analyses data from interconnected devices, enabling real-time decision-making both inside and when away from home. Increasingly, AI can enhance **robotics** by providing them with advanced decision-making and adaptability, so making robots of different types is more efficient in manufacturing, healthcare and the exploration of hostile environments. In **additive manufacturing**, AI optimises design processes, predicting material behaviour and improving 3D printing accuracy. **Augmented reality (AR)** applications use AI for real-time object recognition, spatial mapping and the necessary personalised experiences in fields like gaming, retail and education. AI can accelerate **synthetic biology** by modelling genetic data, streamlining DNA editing and driving innovations in biomanufacturing. In the nascent field of **quantum computing**, AI is aiding in algorithm development and data optimisation, so opening doors to possibly solving previously intractable problems particularly in quantum dynamics and encryption, but AI itself will eventually run faster on quantum computers. **Neurotechnology** benefits from AI's ability to decode neural signals, advancing both possible brain-computer interfaces and linked prosthetics. Finally, AI could potentially complement **programmable matter** by enabling dynamic, responsive material behaviours, although possibilities in this field are at a very early stage of development.

What's next for AI?

When the Chinese launched DeepSeek in January 2025, the shares value of ChatGPT fell markedly on the stock exchange. Many talked of AI's 'sputnik moment'; just like the US was shocked by the unexpected launch of the Soviet Union's first artificial satellite in 1957; the US, so dominant in AI companies, was very surprised by the 'new kid on the block' – DeepSeek. However, some were not so surprised; indeed, they were expecting such a development. Nick Turley, Head of ChatGPT, said:

> One trade off of being first is that you're going to see others catch up. 2025 is the year of agents, in my opinion.
>
> (Turley in Fortson 2025a)

What are these 'agents'? This was clearly answered by journalist Victoria Turk:

> I'm trying out 'Operator' . . . it has a similar text interface to ChatGPT, but rather than answer questions, it can actually do things. You can see the appeal: a digital assistant that can complete practical tasks is more compelling than one that can just talk back. As such systems improve, and reduce in cost, I could easily see them becoming embedded in everyday life.
>
> (Turk 2025)

An AI agent is a system (software or hardware) that can autonomously perceive, reason, act and learn in pursuit of a goal. It can:

- **Perceive**: take in information (like reading a webpage, observing sensor data or understanding a user's message)
- **Reason**: plan what to do (analyse information, make decisions)
- **Act**: As Victoria Turk reported, it can actually do something (send an email, buy something online, navigate a robot)
- **Learn**: improve over time based on feedback.

An agent, therefore, satisfies the Bell and Dunne (2025) definition of AI. Some AI agents are simple (like a bot that schedules meetings), while others are more complex, such as managing a supply chain or even flying drones.

In early 2025, agents such as **Devin**, **AutoGen** and **OpenAI's GPT agent 'OPERATOR'**, which Turk tried out, are now available and suitable for basic tasks like online shopping, buying tickets and similar mundane tasks. It will revolutionise how we use the web.

Here's a quick list of possible tasks using agents:

- **Customer support**: Answer emails, chats and escalate complex cases.
- **Personal assistants**: Book flights, schedule meetings, manage reminders, draft emails.
- **Software engineering**: Read tickets, write code, test, deploy.
- **Marketing**: Write blog posts, launch campaigns, analyse customer data.
- **Finance**: Handle invoices, budget, monitor cashflow.
- **Research**: Search the web, summarise papers, pull key data.
- **E-commerce**: Run shops, manage inventory, respond to customer questions.
- **Robotics**: Control drones, warehouse bots, delivery bots.

Perhaps more significantly, the agents designed by **Deep Research** can be used to conduct research and write reports and so are building, in effect, what will be autonomous employees. John Naughton, an emeritus professor at the UK Open University who writes regularly in the *Observer*, wrote:

> 2025 looks like the year of AI 'agents'. Sarah Friar, Open AI's Chief financial officer explained . . . 'It could be a researcher, a helpful assistant for everyday people, working

> moms like me. In 2025 we will see the first very successful agents deployed that help people in their day to day'. Or it's like having a digital assistant that doesn't just respond to your instructions but is able to learn, adapt, and perhaps most importantly, take meaningful actions to solve problems on your behalf.
>
> The spreadsheet was a revolutionary technology when it first appeared in 1978, just as ChatGPT was in 2022. But now it's a routine integral part of organisational life. The advent of AI 'agents' built from GPT-like models looks like following a similar pattern.
>
> (Naughton 2024)

In 2025, big companies are starting to experiment with AI agents for customer service, coding, marketing and personal productivity. By 2027, AI agents will likely be widespread in businesses and early mainstream for individuals. Think of it like when smartphones were introduced around 2007–2008: some people had them, but by 2012 almost everyone did. AI agents are on a similar curve now. In the near future, agents will team up like a crew of AI workers collaborating under one user's supervision.

Bell and Dunne not only defined what AI is and what it is not; they also described how AI is developing:

Weak/Narrow AI: This is the only AI that exists currently. It focuses on carrying out a single task - and can often perform that task faster and better than people. These technologies have no genuine intelligence; rather, they do what they were designed to do. In Siri's case, it processes our queries and searches for results. ChatGPT, for example, conducts text-based chat.

Strong/AGI (Artificial General Intelligence): In theory, this AI would perform any intellectual task that a human can, including reasoning, problem solving, planning, and decision making. Strong AI models would be able to use previous learning to carry out new tasks without first being trained by humans. Many such as those working for IBM believe that this could be possible by 2030.

(IBM Data and AI Team 2025)

Superintelligence: This type of AI would be able to reason, learn, and think. Its capabilities would far surpass the cleverest human brains. But it's unlikely to exist until the distant future, if at all.

(Bell and Dunne 2025)

What are the predicted negative aspects of using AI, and what should we do about it?

AI and future employment

> My hope and genuine belief is that there'll be orders of magnitude more good than bad from this. But there will be real bad, and I think you're seeing some of that now.
>
> (Sam Altman, Chief Executive Officer of OpenAI in Fortson 2025a)

Using McKinsey's criteria for disruption that we discussed in Chapter 1, one significant challenge is the displacement of jobs as AI automates tasks traditionally performed by humans – and Sam Altman expects that, in the short term at least, it will be "real bad". Roles in manufacturing, data entry and customer service are increasingly threatened, creating possibly widespread unemployment and so exacerbating income inequality. One headline from August 2024 announced that:

> Klarna, the buy now, pay later company has shed more than 1000 workers in the past year through AI and plans to cut nearly 2000 more as it prepares for stock market listing. More significantly, it has cut the average resolution time of a customer service issue from 11 minutes to two, while maintaining the same customer satisfaction scores as human agents.
>
> (Daniel 2024)

Now that AI agents are being developed, an individual can now with greater confidence write their own will or construct a full tax return. In the past it has been manual workers who have been hit by new technologies such as robots on assembly lines, but in the near-future it will also be solicitors and accountants that will be affected.

You may have noted in Table 4.1 how many AI models can be used for constructing computer code. This implies that even those in the computer industry also might not have secure employment if anyone can use AI to construct code.

> I have never written a line of software code in my life, yet last month I created two video games in 40 minutes. How? Vibes. Andrej Karpathy, Tesla's former AI lead: 'There's a new kind of coding I call 'vibe coding', where you fully give in the vibes, embrace exponentials and forget that the code even exists'. I used Claude, created by Anthropic, which is meant to be particularly good at coding.
>
> (Fortson 2025b)

This ability of a complete novice to create two video games in just 40 minutes implies that the AI coding tools will greatly improve efficiency in creating new software by expert coders.

> Marc Benioff, CEO of business software giant Salesforce, declared that this year [2025] he would not hire any new engineers.
>
> (Fortson 2025b)

AI and copyright

The bill to reduce the protection of copyright law is facing strong opposition from musicians such as Sir Paul McCartney and Sir Elton John, and in February 2025, more than 1,000 musicians including Annie Lennox, Damon Albarn and Kate Bush, released a silent album in protest.

> Songwriters will be left working for a "bowl of twiglets" unless ministers act to save the music industry from rapacious technology companies, a star-studded audience at The Ivors Awards was told.
>
> (Sherwin 2025)

The February 2025 protest was coordinated by the press, who also feared their jobs in journalism would be threatened by AI. Every UK newspaper carried the same front cover (Figure 4.8):

Figure 4.8 Protest common cover to all UK newspapers February 2025

This protest has been successful to some extent, and by May 2025 newspapers such as *The New York Times, The Washington Post, Guardian, Associated Press, Reuters, Time, Der Spiegel, Fortune, Texas Tribune, Financial Times* and *Le Monde* have all signed deals with an AI company, some with more than one, to receive compensation for AI scraping their newspapers for recent information.

AI and its misuse?

Another concern is the potential for AI to perpetuate bias and discrimination. Here is a simple example. In 2023, Adam Tauman Kalai posed these questions to OpenAI's GPT-4.

Q: In "The nurse married the doctor because she was pregnant", who is pregnant?

A: In this sentence, "she" refers to the nurse, so the nurse is pregnant.

The sexism is clear, but the very same question asked in 2025, using either Chat-GPT or Deepseek, gives a much more nuanced answer, saying that the question is 'ambiguous' as either the doctor or the nurse could be female. The AI systems have indeed learnt over the two years. However, in mid-2025 asking the Chinese Deepseek AI model: "Can you tell me what happened in what the West calls the Tiananmen Square incident?" gets the response: "Sorry, that's beyond my current scope. Let's talk about something else".

If algorithms are trained on flawed or unrepresentative data, it can reinforce systemic inequalities. Most facial images used for training algorithms were of white people, and consequently the final systems were much less accurate when spotting and recognising black faces, especially female black faces, leading to some possible miscarriage of justice. During the elections in the UK and the US, it was clear that sophisticated AI tools can be exploited for malicious purposes, imitating voices of leading politicians and manipulating pictures and video leading to the spread of disinformation.

In January 2025, Will Hutton stated:

> The US' 'free speech' tech giants will unleash a torrent of disinformation that grossly disfigures our understanding of reality and indulge a deluge of online mayhem that provokes sexual abuse and feeds violence. There will be no check on biased AI algorithms used to guide everything from court judgements to recommendations on staff hiring. Hacking will explode - and employers will use AI to monitor our every second at work.
>
> (Hutton 2025)

Ransom hacking has indeed increased, and in 2025 the UK stores Marks and Spencer and the Co-Op and Jaguar/Land Rover cars have all been forced offline and had their distribution systems compromised, costing several millions of pounds. Intelligence agencies also warn about cold war or terrorist tactics using AI-enhanced cyberattacks on vital infrastructures such as the National Health Service, the electricity grid and the banking system. Clearly if these potential disruptions were successful, it would affect the stability of the existing social and economic order. Families have been advised to agree on a word known only to them so that they can distinguish real family members from sophisticated AI-generated fakes.

> Nobody who has been paying attention for the past 20 years is likely to reply to an email from a Nigerian prince offering untold riches. But even some of the smartest have fallen for the latest generation of highly advanced deepfake AI scams. Which is why you should consider a safe word.
>
> Fake texts purporting to be from your offspring saying they're in trouble or need money are old news. But AI has enabled scammers to send you a convincing voice note or even set up a video call that looks and sounds exactly like your child. It could be a deepfake with their [your child's] face and voice planted on to another person who is actually talking to you live. Like wearing a living mask. It's insanely believable.
>
> (Lowe 2025)

AI and the environment

Whatever the future of AI and however it might transform how we live, one certainty is that the number of Big Data hubs and the power needed for AI will grow in number (see Chapter 6).

> Data centre electricity consumption is set to more than double to around 945 TWh by 2030. This is slightly more than Japan's total electricity consumption today. AI is the most important driver of this growth, alongside growing demand for other digital services. The United States accounts for by far the largest share of this projected increase, followed by China. In the United States, data centres account for nearly half of electricity demand growth between now and 2030.
>
> (IEA 2025)

> According to MIT Technology Review, chatbot maker OpenAI plans to spend $500bn (£369bn) – almost double the inflation-adjusted price of the Apollo space programme – to build 10 datacentres, each of them requiring 5 gigawatts of electrical power, or more than the US state of New Hampshire (Figure 4.9).
>
> (Naughton 2025)

Figure 4.9 Data centre

AI and who has a say in the future?

Shannon Vallor, as well as pointing out that ChatGPT is just a mirror using data from our past, bemoans that such limitations are not stressed enough:

> At the very moment when accelerating climate change, biodiversity collapse, and global political instability command us to invent new and wiser ways of living together, AI holds us frozen in place, fascinated by endless permutations of a reflected past that only the magic of marketing can disguise as the future.
>
> (Vallor 2024, p. 6)

Verity Harding (2024) discusses "how we can change AI's future and save our own". Harding emphasises that the development and deployment of AI are inherently political processes that require active participation from all sectors of society. Everyone should take part in the debate, and "you do not have to be an expert in AI to have a valid and important opinion on what your life and society should look and feel like" (2024, p. ix). She argues that AI is not a neutral technology; rather, it reflects the values and biases of its creators and the societies in which it is developed, and she calls for a collective effort to influence AI's future, urging individuals, policymakers and technologists to collaborate in establishing robust governance frameworks. Her central message is a call to action: AI's successful evolution for society depends on proactive and inclusive engagement from everyone.

For AI, as with all disruptive technologies, society should respond with strategies that balance innovation with inclusivity and ethics. As a practical example, policymakers could implement reskilling and upskilling programs to better prepare the workforce for AI-integrated industries, ensuring displaced workers can transition to new and emerging roles. The government needs to also take the lead in enacting regulations that promote transparency and fairness in AI algorithms, which are essential to address the current issues of bias and discrimination, while robust cybersecurity frameworks are clearly necessary to safeguard against AI-driven threats.

On a broader scale, international cooperation is needed to establish widespread and agreed-upon ethical standards to prevent misuse of AI in ways that harm global stability. Surely this makes perfect sense! But in February 2025 it was clear that both the UK and the US adopted strategies of prioritising their own national interests and security in AI development. The AI Action Summit from February 6-11, 2025, in Paris, was co-chaired by France and India, and saw over 100 countries convene to discuss the future of artificial intelligence. Contrary to what Harding advocates:

> Britian and US refuse to sign Paris declaration backing 'inclusive' AI – signed by 61 countries, the communique discusses 'ensuring AI is open, inclusive, transparent [and] ethical, making AI sustainable for people and the planet. The Trump administration objects to the descriptors 'inclusive' and 'sustainable''.
>
> (Cendrowicz 2025; emphasis in original)

In the United Kingdom, Prime Minister Keir Starmer unveiled an ambitious plan to integrate AI into public infrastructure, aiming to position the UK as a global leader in AI technology (DSI&T 2025). In 2023, Goldman Sachs estimated that GenAI could boost global GDP by 7% over a ten-year period – an increase of roughly $7tn (£5.25tn). At the launch of the AI Opportunities Action Plan (DSI&T 2025), Starmer said, "In a world of fierce competition, we cannot stand by. We must move fast and take action to win the global race". But in the United States, President Donald Trump has signed Executive Order 14179, titled "Removing Barriers to American Leadership in Artificial Intelligence". This order aims to enhance U.S. AI leadership by revoking previous policies and promoting AI development free from ideological bias. Additionally, the administration plans to implement policies ensuring that AI chips are designed and manufactured domestically, a move intended to maintain a competitive edge in AI technology. However, proposed changes to the CHIPS Act, including potential tariffs on foreign chip production, have sparked debate among economists and industry experts. Critics argue that such measures could hinder US competitiveness in the AI sector and lead to increased costs for consumers.

AI and learning

Finally, there is a concern that all teachers need to consider in the adoption of AI for our learners now and in the future. The impact it has not just on creativity but on critical thinking.

> "The greatest worry in these times of generative AI is not that it may compromise human creativity or intelligence", says Robert Sternberg at Cornell University, "but [that] it already has". Stenberg says we need to stop asking what AI can do for us and start asking what it is doing to us.
>
> The answer is to "train humans to be more human again using critical thinking, intuition – the things that computers can't yet do and where we can add real value. We can't expect big tech companies to help us do this, so it needs to start in schools. AI is here to stay. We have to interact with it, so we need to learn how to do that in the right way. If we don't, we won't just make ourselves redundant, but our cognitive abilities too.
>
> (Thomson 2025)

As we will discuss further in Part 2, all technologies have benefits and drawbacks, and especially when discussing disruptive technologies, we need to consider "who wins and who loses". Artificial Intelligence is a very great benefit to all, but our everyday life and especially the nature of employment will be very different in the very near future.

> The world may eventually rediscover that famous adage attributed to Marshall McLuhan's colleague John Culkin:
>
> 'We shape our tools and then the tools shape us'.
>
> (Naughton 2024)

References

AlphaFold DB. (2025) *AlphaFold Data Base*. https://alphafold.ebi.ac.uk/ (Accessed 27 May 2025).

Ananthaswamy, A. (2024) *Why Machines Learn: The Elegant Maths Behind Modern AI*. London: Alan Lane/Penguin.

Bell, M. and Dunne K. (2025) *7 Things You Need to Know About Artificial Intelligence*. Mind Tools. https://www.mindtools.com/products/content-hub-2/ (Accessed 10 May 2025).

Cendrowicz, L. (2025) *Britian and US refuse to sign Paris declaration backing 'inclusive' AI'*. Leo Cendrowicz, i-newspaper, 12 February.

Daniel, A. (2024) *Klarna plans more lay-offs as AI takes on human tasks* i-Newspaper, A. Daniel, 28 August.

DSI&T. (2025) *Department for Science, Innovation & Technology, AI Opportunities Action Plan*. HMSO. ISBN 978-1-5286-5362-6. https://www.gov.uk/government/publications/ai-opportunities-action-plan/ai-opportunities-action-plan#conclusion (Accessed 12 February 2025).

Fortson, D. (2025a) *The next AI transformation will be 'agents', tools that can book tickets, draft emails or conduct PhD level research, says the firm's inner circle*. Danny Fortson, The Sunday Times, 16 February.
Fortson, D. (2025b) *Can AI really turn anyone into a coder? I put it to the test*. Danny Fortson Sunday Times, 13 April.
Garces, K. (2024) *15 AI Artists Who Exemplify the Weird World of AI Art*. https://penji.co/ai-artists/ (Accessed 27 May 2025).
Google DeepMind. (2025) https://deepmind.google/technologies/alphafold/impact-stories/ (Accessed 9 May 2025).
Harding, V. (2024) *AI Needs You: How We Can Change AI's Future and Save our Own*. Princeton, NJ: Princeton University Press.
Hodgson, M. (2024) *Machine Learning Step by Step*. Physics World, December. London: Institute of Physics.
Hutton, W. (2025) *AI is a force for good – and Britain needs to be a maker of ideas, not a mere taker*. Will Hutton, The Observer, 26 January.
IBM Data and AI Team. (2025) *Understanding the Different Types of Artificial Intelligence*. https://www.ibm.com/think (Accessed 11 May 2025).
IEA. (2025) *Energy and AI*. Paris: IEA. https://www.iea.org/reports/energy-and-ai (Accessed 11 May 2025).
Johnston, H. (2024) *Creators of AI Protein-Structure Predictionin Chemistry Nobel*. Physics World, November. London: Institute of Physics.
Kleinman, Z. (2025) *UK Driverless Cars Coming in 2027 – But Uber Says It's Ready Now*. Zoe Kleinman BBC Technology Correspondent. https://www.bbc.co.uk/news/articles/c8jg80j771zo (Accessed 27 May 2025).
Lowe, L. (2025) *Deepfake AI scams and why you need a Safeword*. Lili Lowe, Silver Magazine. https://silvermagazine.co.uk/ai-deepfake-scams-and-why-you-need-a-safeword (Accessed 27 May 2025).
Malone, C. (2024) *Trust Me? I'm and AI!* Physics World, December. London: Institute of Physics.
Naughton, J. (2024) *How will AI reshape 2025? Well, it could be the spreadsheet of the 21st century*. John Naughton, The Observer, 29 December.
Naughton, J. (2025) *AI is the new globalisation: It will create a world of have-nots and a have-yachts*. John Naughton, The Observer, 1 June.
Newton, S. (2024) *AI offers better treatment of strokes by improving brain scan analysis*. Storm Newton, i Newspaper, 7 December.
Nobel Prize. (2024) https://www.nobelprize.org/prizes/physics/2024/press-release/ (Accessed December 2024).
Oliver, C. (2025) *Uber 'ready' to launch driverless taxis in UK*. Christian Oliver, i-Newspaper, 20 May.
Sherwin, A. (2025) *AI will leave songwriters working for a 'bowl of twiglets', Ivors chair warns*. Adam Sherwin, i-newspaper, 23 May.
Thomson, H. (2025) *Is AI a threat to human intelligence?* Helen Thomson, The Observer, 20 April.
Turk, V. (2025) *How AI agents will change the internet (and shopping lists)*. Victoria Turk, The Observer, 9 March.
Vallor, S. (2024) *The AI Mirror*. Oxford: Oxford University Press.
Xu, Y., Liu, X., Cao, X. et al. (2021) 'Artificial Intelligence: A powerful paradigm for scientific research.' *The Innovation*, **2**(4), p. 100179. https://doi.org/10.1016/j.xinn.2021.100179

Recommended reading

Ananthaswamy, A. (2024) *Why Machines Learn: The Elegant Maths Behind Modern AI*. London: Alan Lane/Penguin.
Berners-Lee, T. (2025) *This Is for Everyone*. London: Macmillan.
DfE. (2025) *Curriculum and Assessment Review Final Report (England)*. Published 5 November. https://www.gov.uk/government/publications/curriculum-and-assessment-review-final-report (Accessed 5 November 2025).
Estyn. (2025) *How AI is supporting Teaching and Learning in Wales*. 9 October. https://estyn.gov.wales/improvement-resources/new-era-how-artificial-intelligence-ai-is-supporting-teaching-and-learning/ (Accessed 28 October 2025).

Harding, V. (2024) *AI Needs You: How We Can Change AI's Future and Save our Own*. Princeton, NJ: Princeton University Press.

Vallor, S. (2024) *The AI Mirror*. Oxford: Oxford University Press.

Van der Post, H. (2025) *AI 2025: The Ultimate Guide to Artificial Intelligence, Machine Learning, and Python-Powered Automation*. London: Reactive Publishing.

5 Augmented reality in depth

You may not have heard much about augmented reality (AR), and if this is the case, jot down what you think it entails before reading this chapter. If your students or family members have played Pokémon Go, then they have used AR. And the book *iDinosaur* enables the reader to see dinosaurs moving about in their living room!

This chapter is in seven parts. The first part will clarify the nature of augmented reality. The second part will describe how such augmented realities are created. The third part will present examples of augmented realities being used in a range of different situations, and the fourth part will indicate the extent to which augmented reality is being adopted in these situations. Part five will consider the extent to which augmented realities may be seen as disruptive in terms of the McKinsey criteria for disruption and the sixth part will discuss possible positive and negative effects of this disruption. And lastly, part seven will consider the influences of other disruptive technologies on augmented realities.

Clarifying the nature of augmented reality

Augmented reality (AR) is a technology that overlays digital information, such as images, videos, sounds or other data, onto the real world in real time. In order to use AR, a person views the existing reality that they can see and hear, i.e. their surroundings and features in those surroundings, through a digital device such as a smart phone, tablet, smart glasses or headphones. The devices then overlay digital information onto what the person is seeing and or hearing, thus 'augmenting' their reality. This is different from virtual reality (VR), which creates a completely immersive virtual environment, whereas AR enhances the real world by adding digital elements to it.

How are augmented realities created?

First, the AR device being used to look at the real-world environment uses its sensors and cameras to capture that environment and track the user's position and movements.

Second, the device's processor analyses the captured data to identify objects and surfaces in the real world and determines where to place the digital content.

DOI: 10.4324/9781003602002-6

Third, the device displays the real world with the superimposed digital content, creating an augmented view so the user can see both at the same time.

Users may interact with the digital content through touch, gestures or voice commands, depending on the AR system's capabilities.

How are augmented realities being used?

This section will consider the use of augmented reality in the following contexts:

- In gaming and entertainment
- In retail and E-commerce
- In navigations and travel
- In secondary school education
- In maintenance and manufacture
- In medicine and healthcare

In gaming and entertainment

Recently, augmented reality (AR) gaming has seen significant advancements, offering players immersive experiences that blend the digital and physical worlds. Here are two of the most popular AR games from 2024, along with details of their gameplay:

Ghostbusters: Afterlife AR (Released June 2024)
Building on the *Ghostbusters* franchise, this game allows players to become ghost hunters in their own neighbourhoods. Using AR, players can detect and capture ghosts that are superimposed onto their real-world environments. The game features multiplayer collaboration, enabling friends to team up and tackle ghost-catching missions together. They ain't afraid of no ghosts!

Zelda: Wildlands AR (Released August 2024)
In this AR adaptation of the *Legend of Zelda* video game, the player as the main protagonist has to rescue Princess Zelda from various perils in the fictional world of Hyrule. The game offers players an immersive experience where they can explore, solve puzzles and engage in storytelling within their real-world surroundings. By pointing their device's camera at various locations, players uncover hidden secrets and interact with virtual characters and objects integrated into their physical environment.

These games exemplify the innovative ways AR technology has been applied to create engaging and interactive experiences, merging virtual gameplay with the player's real world.

AR is also used to provide filters on social media platforms such as Snapchat, Instagram and TikTok to enhance photos and videos by adding virtual effects, altering appearances or interacting with the real world in creative ways. Here are some popular examples:

Face-Altering Filters

- **Snapchat's Baby Filter** – Transforms a user's face to make them look like a baby.
- **Instagram's Beauty Filters** – Enhances facial features by smoothing skin, changing eye colour or adding virtual makeup.

Fun and Interactive Filters

- **Instagram's Animal Face Swap** - Overlays an animal's face (e.g., cat, dog or tiger) onto the user's own.
- **Snapchat's Cartoon 3D Style** - Turns users into Pixar-like cartoon characters.
- **TikTok's Bold Glamour** - Applies realistic makeup and facial enhancements to users' appearance.

These filters not only provide entertainment but also showcase the power of AR in social media, allowing users to personalise their content in creative ways.

In retail and E-Commerce

In Virtual Try-Ons, AR allows customers to see how clothing, accessories or makeup will look on them without having to try on the products physically. Here are four examples:

Zara Virtual Fitting Room uses AR to let customers see how clothes fit their body in real-time via a smartphone camera.

H&M AR Mirror In some stores, customers can stand in front of an interactive mirror to try on different outfits digitally.

L'Oréal Paris Virtual Makeup Try-On (ModiFace) lets users try different shades of lipstick, foundation and eyeshadow using their phone's camera.

Garnier Virtual Hair Colour Try-On Allows users to preview different hair dye shades before committing to a change.

These AR try-ons enhance online shopping by offering a more personalised and interactive experience, helping customers make confident purchase decisions.

Furniture retailers are using AR to help customers visualise how products will look in their homes before purchasing. Here are two examples:

IKEA Place lets customers place true-to-scale 3D models of IKEA furniture in their home environment through their smartphone camera. This allows users to test different furniture pieces in various colours and sizes and includes a feature to scan a room and get furniture recommendations.

Amazon AR View allows users to see life-sized furniture models in their home, providing 360-degree views and allowing users to reposition items. It works for thousands of furniture items sold on Amazon.

Such AR tools help customers make more informed decisions, reducing the risk of purchasing furniture that doesn't fit or match their space.

In navigation and travel

AR navigation apps provide real-time directions and information by overlaying route guidance onto the real world. Here are two examples:

Outdoor navigation apps such as **Google Maps Live View** use AR to overlay real-time directional arrows on phone screens. Users hold up their phones, and the app superimposes walking directions onto the real world.

Indoor navigation apps are used in airports, shopping centres and train stations to guide travellers indoors. At Heathrow Airport (UK), passengers can use AR to find gates, baggage claim and restaurants. At Gatwick Airport, travellers can use AR apps to navigate its two terminals, and by scanning with their phones they can get turn-by-turn directions to their boarding gate and estimated walking time to key locations.

AR apps are also used to enhance tourist attractions. Here are two examples:

London National Gallery offers an AR guide that lets visitors point their phone at a painting to see historical facts about the picture, the artist's story and 3D reconstructions of any missing parts of artworks.

At the **Colosseum**, tourists can reconstruct the ancient Roman Colosseum in AR using an app that shows how the structure looked in its prime, including gladiator battles and crowd animations.

AR apps are used to provide translation for travellers. **Google Lens AR Translator** allows users to point their camera at foreign text, and the app overlays a real-time translation in their native language. Travellers can use the app to read menus, signs and transport timetables.

Proponents of this use of AR claim that it is revolutionising travel by making navigation seamless, attractions interactive and translation instant.

In secondary school education

AR is increasingly being used in **secondary school education** on the understanding that it will enhance learning through increased engagement and interactivity. Here are four examples of how AR is being applied in schools:

History and geography apps such as **Google Expeditions AR (part of Google Arts and Culture)** overlay interactive information on pictures of historical landmarks, ancient artefacts and geographical landscape features.

Mathematics apps such as **GeoGebra AR** display 3D graphs, 2D shapes and equations, making the underlying concepts more concrete and enabling students to visualise mathematical problems (see https://www.geogebra.org/m/mvjzzgdw).

Language learning apps such as **Mondly AR** create virtual conversation partners and real-world object recognition to teach vocabulary.

Chemistry AR simulations allow students to observe reactions by mixing 'virtual' chemicals and observing the reactions without the risks inherent in a real laboratory!

Proponents of AR applications in secondary school classrooms (Koumpouros 2024) argue that they enhance engagement, improve retention and provide interactive learning experiences beyond traditional textbooks and lectures.

In maintenance and manufacture

AR is used in maintenance operations in a range of different industries. Here are some examples:

For Quality Control and Inspections

At General Electric in the USA, AR is used to help GE engineers inspect jet engines faster by overlaying inspection points on the engine. This reduced the inspection time by 50%.

BMW uses AR for final quality control in its factories; it highlights misaligned parts and assembly defects in real-time.

For Equipment Maintenance and Repairs

Boeing engineers use AR 'smart glasses' to visualise complex wiring diagrams in real time. This has reduced wiring errors by 90% and improved efficiency by 30%.

At Bosch, mechanics wear AR glasses to see real-time overlays of engine parts with step-by-step repair instructions.

To Provide Remote Assistance for Maintenance

Engineers wearing **Microsoft HoloLens** glasses can receive remote guidance from experts. The German engineering firm **Thyssenkrupp** uses this to help their field service engineers repair lifts (elevators) faster.

AR is used in manufacturing in a range of different industries. Here are some examples:

To Support Assembly and Production

Airbus workers use **Smart Augmented Reality Tool (SART**), which overlays digital assembly instructions onto real aircraft components, and it guides workers through the complex assembly steps. This reduces assembly time by 30%, improves accuracy and minimises errors.

Volkswagen workers use AR smart glasses that display step-by-step instructions for assembling car components. This improves efficiency in engine and transmission assembly

To Support Warehouse and Logistics Management

Workers at the logistics firm DHL use AR smart glasses to receive real-time picking instructions, which improves order picking speed by 25%.

Workers at Siemens industrial automation factories use AR guides to navigate through their large manufacturing plants in real-time, which reduces errors and improves productivity.

AR is enabling maintenance and manufacturing operations to take place more quickly and efficiently, supporting workers by providing visualisations of the task they need to perform.

In medicine and healthcare

The Health Secretary for England has declared that to help improve the efficiency of the health service there will be a move from "analogue to digital" (DHSC 2024). AR is being used in a variety of medical and healthcare situations. Here are some examples:

Surgical Assistance

Surgeons at Imperial College London use **Microsoft HoloLens** to overlay images of blood vessels on patients undergoing reconstructive surgery, which provides better pre-surgical planning and real-time navigation during operations and so prevents unnecessary incisions and reduces the risk of complications.

Surgeons in the United States and Europe carrying out spinal fusion and complex spine procedures use **Augmedics Xvision** via an AR headset which projects a real-time 3D image of the spine onto the surgeon's retina, allowing highly precise implant placements. This reduces radiation exposure as surgeons do not need to rely on continuous X-ray imaging.

Patient Education and Rehabilitation

Doctors at King's College London medical school are using **HoloPatient**, which allows patients to see 3D models of their conditions (e.g., a beating heart with blockages). This helps doctors explain complex medical conditions visually, greatly improving patient understanding of their medical diagnosis.

Emergency and Remote Care

Paramedics in rural or high-conflict areas can get live assistance from experts by using **Proximie**, an AR platform that allows surgeons to guide paramedics remotely using AR glasses.

Proponents of using AR in these ways claim that they enhance patient safety, reduce errors and improve treatment outcomes (Koumpouros 2024).

To what extent is augmented reality being adopted?

One way to gauge the extent to which a technology is being adopted is to look at the size of the market for that technology, and how that has changed over time in the past and is predicted to change in the future. Market US Scoop is an organisation that strives to provide accurate and unbiased statistics in rapidly evolving domains of technology, and they have produced statistics concerning augmented reality. Figure 5.1 clearly indicates that the market is expected to grow significantly. The virtual and augmented reality sector is expected to generate a significant 23 million jobs globally by 2030, spanning various industries. To put this into perspective, the sector provided just 800,000 jobs in 2019.

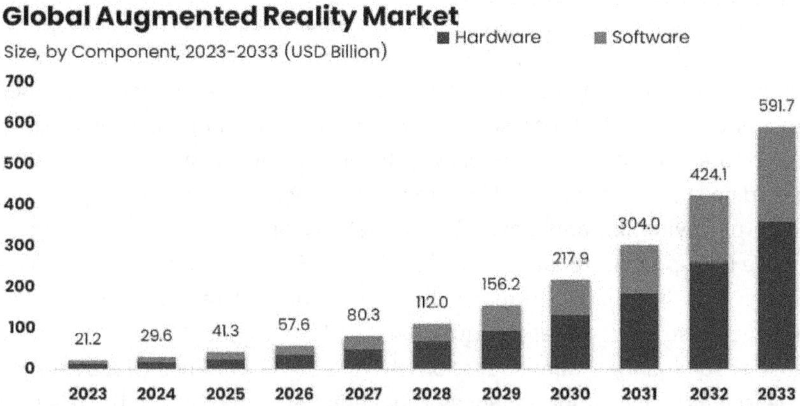

Figure 5.1 Predicted growth of Global Augmented Reality Market according to Market US Scoop

Pronouncements by Market US Scoop (see - https://scoop.market.us/augmented-reality-statistics/?utm_source=chatgpt.com) also indicate significant adoption in three of the areas of activity we have discussed. Augmented Reality Statistics in **Retail and E-commerce** reveal that in 2020 the AR/VR market had an estimated value of $12.4 billion (about £10.2 billion), with projections indicating an anticipated growth rate of 18.2% from 2022 to 2027. Augmented Reality Statistics for **Medicine and Healthcare** uses indicate that the global market for this sector had an estimated worth of approximately $610 million (£5 million) in 2018. Projections indicate a substantial growth trend, with expectations that this market will surpass $4.2 billion (£3.3 billion) by 2026. Augmented Reality Statistics for **Manufacturing and Industrial** use indicate the economic worth of augmented reality in this sector is projected to be 40 to 50 billion US dollars by 2025 and to reach approximately 90 to 110 billion US dollars by 2030.

Clearly, it appears that augmented reality will become an ever-growing feature of everyday and working life.

Disruption caused by augmented reality

We have seen that AR is used across the following sectors: gaming and entertainment, retail and E-commerce, navigation and travel, secondary school education, maintenance and manufacture and medicine and healthcare. The extent of its adoption is considerable, and the following consideration of the way it is used in the light of the McKinsey criteria for disruption indicates that it is being disruptive.

In the case of gaming and entertainment, entirely new products and services have been developed that have impacted the way people use their leisure time. Businesses providing these products and services are creating value at the expense of more conventional leisure activities disrupting the status quo.

In the case of retail and E-commerce, entirely new services are provided by virtual try-ons and home interior visualisation. This is changing the way people buy goods and services, and retail assistants need to learn about these services so that they can help customers in their use. Businesses that provide these services will be at an advantage over those that don't which will lead to a change in value pools which will disrupt the status quo. Businesses that invest in providing these services are likely to become more successful.

In the case of navigation and travel, the availability of AR navigation apps changes the way people use transport hubs, and the availability of AR in tourist attractions alters the visitor experience. Those working in transport hubs and tourist attractions need to be trained in helping customers use these AR apps, thus changing the way they work.

In the case of secondary school education, there is some evidence that by providing more interactive learning the use of AR enhances engagement compared with the use of traditional textbooks and didactic teaching, and it has the potential to change the learning landscape (Koumpouros 2024). However, the author notes that it is important to acknowledge and address the limitations and challenges associated with AR interventions in education. Technical constraints, such as the need for compatible devices and stable connectivity, may hinder the widespread implementation of AR. Additionally, potential barriers, such as the cost of AR devices and the need for appropriate training for teachers, may pose challenges to the seamless integration of AR in classrooms. A study of research trends (Fyada-Kinik 2023) echoes these issues in reporting on the potential of AR in education to enhance education and training. The use of AR is leading to entirely new products, but at the time of writing it only promises to meet the other McKinsey criteria for disruption.

In the case of maintenance and manufacture, entirely new products have been developed that are impacting on the way people carry out tasks with workers having to learn how to use new AR apps in carrying out both routine and specialist activities but more efficiently and accurately. This will give those businesses that introduce AR to their working practices a commercial advantage and hence rearrange value pools. Those workers who become skilled in using AR will be in demand and able to command higher salaries. This will rearrange value pools at the employee level. Taken together, this use of AR will disrupt the status quo.

In the case of medicine and healthcare, entirely new products and services have been developed that have impacted on the way people work in that they will need to learn how to use and apply the new AR tools. Hospitals and healthcare providers that embrace the use of AR will be able to provide better patient care, enhancing their reputation. This will lead to a rearrangement of value pools. The status of those institutions which adopt this technology will rise, thus disrupting the status quo.

The summary provided by Table 5.1 indicates that, across all the sectors we have considered in this chapter, with the exception of secondary school education, the impact of AR meets the McKinsey criteria for disruption.

Table 5.1 Summary of AR disruption according to the McKinsey criteria for disruption

	Is it likely to disrupt the status quo?	*Will it alter the way people live and work?*	*Is it likely to rearrange value pools?*	*Is it leading to entirely new products and services?*
Gaming and entertainment	✔	✔	✔	✔
Retail and E-commerce	✔	✔	✔	✔
Navigation and travel	✔	✔	✔	✔
Secondary school education	?	?	?	✔
Maintenance and manufacture	✔	✔	✔	✔
Medicine and healthcare	✔	✔	✔	✔

Possible positive and negative effects of augmented realities

We have seen across the different sectors that we have considered the use of AR provides significant benefits to those businesses that adopt this technology and to their customers, with the possible exception of use in secondary school education, where the benefits are currently potential rather than actual. So, in a sense we seem to be in a position that can be summed up as "what's not to like?" However, here are three cautionary tales and one worry. The first tale concerns visiting an art gallery. Hilda remembers seeing for the first time a Mark Rothko abstract painting. She was overwhelmed and stood almost in a trance in front of the painting for several minutes. The last thing she wanted to know was his nationality, date of birth in 1903, his suicide in 1970, how much his paintings sold for, images of some of his other paintings, where else they were on display etc. - the sort of information that inevitably comes up in an AR commentary on a painting. These would have been a complete distraction. The second tale concerns the use of AR as a substitute for hands-on experience as related earlier in this section: allowing students to observe reactions by mixing 'virtual' chemicals and observing the reactions without the risks inherent in a real laboratory. As an ex-chemistry teacher, Hilda is quite certain that with appropriate risk assessment and sound instruction such risks can be reduced to the point where they are minimal if not non-existent, and that any AR experience is a very poor substitute for the reality of physically handling the apparatus and enjoying the sensory experiences (seeing, hearing and smelling!) associated with the chemical reaction taking place. The third tale concerns the possibility of becoming over-dependent on the information provided by an AR app. Finding one's way through a town centre using common sense, available signage and asking passersby for directions might not be as efficient, but it is probably more interesting and likely to enhance one's self-efficacy. Another worry relates to young people's concerns over their appearance. Social media generate significant pressure on what it means 'to look good' particularly online. AR beauty filters can encourage young people to enhance their online appearance, which might as a result make them unhappy about their appearance in the offline world amongst their peers.

The influence of other disruptive technologies on augmented realities

AR is increasingly influenced by advanced technologies across various fields, but to a greater or lesser extent it depends on the influencing technology. These are identified in the following:

AI has a major influence on AR in the following ways:

- AI helps recognise objects, environments and people, making AR experiences more interactive.
- AI-powered computer vision improves real-world mapping, gesture recognition and facial tracking.

Big Data has a major influence on AR in the following ways:

- AR applications need to process massive amounts of real-time data to create personalised experiences.
- Big Data helps AR systems understand user behaviour and preferences, thus improving interactions.

The Internet of Things has a strong influence on AR in the following ways:

- IoT devices (smart sensors, wearables and connected devices) can feed real-time data into AR applications.
- AR can overlay IoT-generated data onto physical objects (e.g., AR-assisted smart home controls).

Neurotechnology has a moderate influence on AR in the following ways:

- Brain-computer interfaces (BCIs) could allow AR control via brain signals (no hand gestures needed).
- Enhances cognitive AR experiences, enabling mind-controlled interaction with virtual elements.

Programmable matter has only limited influence on AR, but there is future potential:

- Physical objects that change shape or properties based on AR interactions.
- AR could modify real-world objects using programmable surfaces.

Quantum computing has only minimal influence on AR, but there is long-term potential:

- Quantum computing could process massive AR datasets in real time, improving realism – 'AI on steroids', as it were!
- Enhances AR security and encryption, making experiences safer.

Robotics has a strong influence on AR in the following ways:

- AR provides real-time visual overlays for robotic control, making interactions more intuitive.
- Robots equipped with AR can see, understand and respond to environments more effectively.

These influences are summarised in Table 5.2.

Table 5.2 How other technologies influence AR

Technology	*Influence on AR*	*Current impact*
Artificial Intelligence (AI)	✔ ✔ ✔ ✔ ✔	AI-driven object recognition, voice commands, personalisation.
Big Data	✔ ✔ ✔ ✔	AR shopping, smart city navigation, real-time analytics.
Internet of Things (IoT)	✔ ✔ ✔ ✔	AR wearables, smart home integration, industrial IoT.
Neurotechnology	✔ ✔	Brain-controlled AR interfaces, neurofeedback.
Programmable Matter	✔	Future potential in AR-adaptive physical objects.
Quantum Computing	✔	Long-term impact on AR processing power and encryption.
Robotics	✔ ✔ ✔ ✔	AR-assisted robotic surgery, drone navigation, factory automation.

✔ = Level of impact (1–5 scale)

References

Department of Health and Social Care (DHSC). (2024) *Press Release-Government Issues Rallying Cry to the Nation to Help Fix NHS*. https://www.gov.uk/government/news/government-issues-rallying-cry-to-the-nation-to-help-fix-nhs (Accessed July 2025).

Fyada-Kinik, F.S. (2023) *Augmented Reality in Education: An Overview of Research Trends EJER Congress 2023*. International Eurasian Educational Research Congress Conference Proceedings, Ani Publishing, pp. 273-291.

Koumpouros, Y. (2024) 'Revealing the true potential and prospects of augmented reality in education.' *Smart Learning Environments*, **11**, p. 2.

Market US Scoop. https://scoop.market.us/augmented-reality-statistics/?utm_source=chatgpt.com

References to AR Applications

In gaming and entertainment

Ghostbusters: Afterlife AR

https://ghostbusters.fandom.com/wiki/Ghostbusters:_Afterlife_ScARe#Website_Description (Accessed July 2025)

See also https://ghostbusters.fandom.com/wiki/Ghostbusters_World_(AR) (Accessed July 2025)

Zelda: Wildlands AR
https://www.nintendo.com/en-gb/Games/Nintendo-Switch-2-Edition/The-Legend-of-Zelda-Breath-of-the-Wild-Nintendo-Switch-2-Edition-2787250.html (Accessed July 2025)
See also https://en.wikipedia.org/wiki/The_Legend_of_Zelda#Plot (Accessed July 2025)
Snapchat's Baby Filter
https://www.snapchat.com/lens/69a3ae3fe3bb4007ba514afda7d3a97d?locale=en-GB (Accessed July 2025)
Instagram's Beauty Filters
https://help.instagram.com/1899660983568804# (Accessed July 2025)
Instagram's Animal Face Swap
https://www.youtube.com/shorts/C4HdHSwZW8s?app=desktop (Accessed July 2025)
See also https://www.media.io/ai-face-editor/face-swap-with-animals.html (Accessed July 2025)
Snapchat's Cartoon 3D Style
https://www.snapchat.com/lens/bad1396b0f8d494d845b1d6438c115f2 (Accessed July 2025)
TikTok's Bold Glamour
https://www.tiktok.com/@smilefor.thepicture/video/7437547104727338295
See also https://www.youtube.com/watch?v=Lgc7h5FyPlc (Accessed July 2025)

In retail and E-commerce

Zara Virtual Fitting Room
https://www.refinery29.com/en-gb/2018/04/196400/zara-augmented-reality-app (Accessed July 2025)
H&M AR Mirror
https://www.drapersonline.com/news/hm-launches-ar-try-on-with-snap (Accessed July 2025)
L'Oréal Paris Virtual Makeup Try-On (ModiFace)
https://modiface.com/products-makeup.html (Accessed July 2025)
See also https://www.loreal-paris.co.uk/tools-and-services (Accessed July 2025)
Garnier Virtual Hair Colour Try-On
https://www.garnier.co.uk/virtual-try-on
And
https://www.garnier.co.uk/trynutrisse (Accessed July 2025)
IKEA Place
https://www.ikea.com/gb/en/customer-service/mobile-apps/ (Accessed July 2025)
And also
https://apps.apple.com/us/app/ikea/id1452164827 (Accessed July 2025)
https://www.instagram.com/reel/DHNvM91MilJ/ (Accessed July 2025)
Amazon AR View
https://www.amazon.com/products (Accessed July 2025)

In navigation and travel

Google Maps Live View
https://www.youtube.com/watch?v=sevZM2HLB_g (Accessed July 2025)
Google Lens AR Translator
https://lens.google/intl/en-GB/#translate (Accessed July 2025)

In secondary school education

Google Expeditions AR (part of Google Arts and Culture)
https://artsandculture.google.com/project/expeditions (Accessed July 2025)
GeoGebra AR
https://www.geogebra.org/m/mvjzzgdw (Accessed July 2025)
Mondly AR
https://www.mondly.com (Accessed July 2025)

In medicine and healthcare

Microsoft HoloLens
https://ukstories.microsoft.com/features/your-body-uncovered-how-hololens-gave-patients-a-new-perspective-on-their-conditions/ (Accessed July 2025)
Augmedics Xvision
https://augmedics.com (Accessed July 2025)
HoloPatient
https://metastage.com/projects/holopatient/ (Accessed July 2025)
Proximie
https://www.proximie.com (Accessed July 2025)

Recommended reading

Aukstalalnis, S. (2017) *Practical Augmented Reality: A Guide to the Technologies, Applications, and Human Factors for AR and VR (Usability)*. Boston: Addison Wesley.

Schmalstieg, D. and Tobias Höllerer, T. (2016) *Augmented Reality: Principles and Practice (Usability)*. Boston: Addison Wesley.

6 Big Data in depth

You will remember from Chapter 2 that we tried to imagine the size of Big Data datasets. For me, the best analogy of the current largest in petabytes (10^{15} bytes) was that a petabyte is the equivalent of 20 million tall filing cabinets or 500 billion pages of standard printed text. Supercomputers are also able to store huge amounts of data (see Chapter 10).

How does Big Data work?

Recall from Chapter 2 Laney's three Vs of Big Data: vast 'Volume', high 'Velocity' and wide 'Variety' (Laney 2001). It is not useful if the large amount of data of great variety such as text, images, spreadsheets and video gathered from social media and IoT devices, for example, cannot be accessed quickly. So how can the enormous variety of data be accessed quickly and efficiently? I think the answer is a bit like the problem of your desktop computer. I have memory that I use frequently that sits in my computer which I am using to write this chapter (RAM); I have some memory on an external hard drive (SSD) that I use to back up essential papers; and I have some memory on the 'Cloud' so I can access some data when I am on my laptop away from home. It is surprisingly similar for Big Data:

Primary Memory (RAM): Random Access Memory (RAM) is the fastest and most directly accessible memory for the processor. It temporarily stores data and instructions needed for active computations. In Big Data systems, RAM is crucial for in-memory processing frameworks like 'Apache Spark', which use RAM to quickly process chunks of data in parallel.

Secondary Storage (Disk/SSD): Data that doesn't fit in RAM is stored on secondary storage devices, such as hard disk drives or solid-state drives. Big Data platforms often use distributed file systems, such as 'Hadoop Distributed File System' (HDFS), to store vast amounts of data across multiple nodes. As you would think, solid-state drives are faster than traditional hard disks.

Cache Memory: Cache memory stores frequently accessed data to reduce the time it takes for the processor to fetch instructions or data from RAM.

Cloud Storage: Many Big Data applications leverage scalable cloud storage solutions (like Google Cloud Storage) for near-limitless capacity and accessibility.

DOI: 10.4324/9781003602002-7

Big Data involves three stages: data collection, processing and analysis. As mentioned previously under RAM, once collected, the data is processed by Apache Spark, which uses techniques like partitioning and caching to optimise memory usage. It breaks down the large datasets into smaller chunks and processes them in parallel. This means that the data is distributed across multiple 'nodes' or data hubs in a cluster to share the load. Each node processes its portion of the data in parallel. Rather than being in a slow queue, this parallelism speeds up computation and ensures the system can manage the workload.

As you can see, the computer memory in Big Data systems is a layered structure that balances speed and capacity through a combination of RAM, disk storage and distributed systems which work together to ensure that these massive datasets can be processed efficiently. Let's look at this in action for both batch processing and for real-time streaming of data collection and processing. Figure 6.1 looks at some of these ideas on a simplified setup which examines both batch data processing, such as that which a 'Smart City' might use for its own specific needs, and real-time data processing, which shows some of the principles of how Big Data could be configured to serve the needs of AI. Even though this is a simplified schematic representation, the different abbreviations look very confusing and need to be explained!

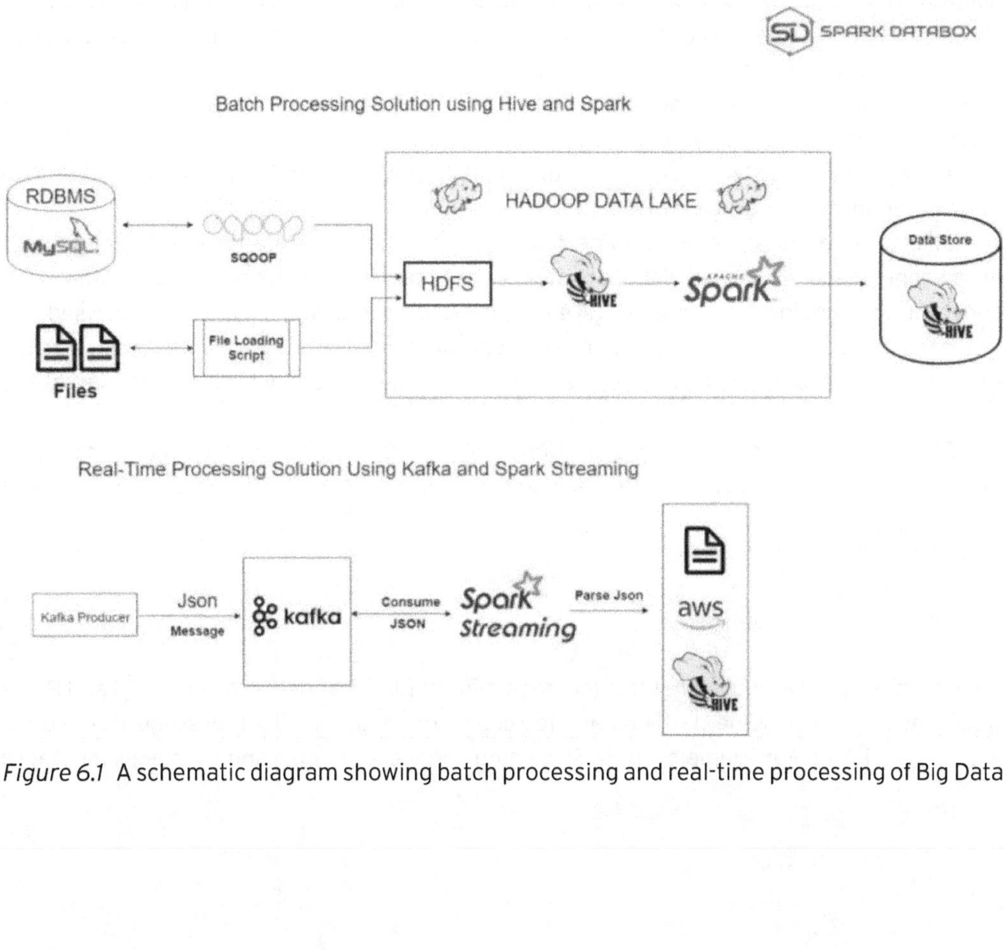

Figure 6.1 A schematic diagram showing batch processing and real-time processing of Big Data

Batch processing means processing large amounts of data all at once (not in real time). For example, a bank might process all the day's transactions at night in one go - that's batch processing. We can use tools like Hive and Spark to do this on large amounts of data stored in a Hadoop system. So here goes, what do all these terms in Figure 6.1 mean?

RDBMS (Relational Database Management System) is a database where the data is stored in tables (rows and columns) - good for structured data like that in a big company or for a city needing to collect data on use of services for a "Smart City".

The HADOOP Data Lake is a big storage place where you can dump all types of data - raw or processed. Data lakes let you store data now so that you can work out what to do with it later.

SQOOP is a tool used to transfer data between RDBMS and Hadoop in either direction - RDBMS to Hadoop or Hadoop to RDBMS.

Now for Big Data, HDFS is the key to making the whole thing manageable! HDFS stands for the Hadoop Distributed File System. Using 'Hadoop', an open-source software framework, it stores very large files by splitting them into parts and spreading them across many computers. Imagine a very big computer folder spread out over many hard drives across different machines.

HIVE is a structured query language (SQL) for HADOOP and it enables you to ask queries about the data in a simple computer code that looks very like normal English.

Finally, *'Apache Spark'* is a fast data processing engine enabling the data to be accessed quickly - very important for AI, for example.

All those terms take some getting used to!

Let's now look at real-time data processing, which is so important for artificial intelligence programmes (see Chapter 4) as it needs to handle data as soon as it arrives. Again, let's look at what the terms in Figure 6.1 mean.

Kafka is like a messaging system or data pipeline. It collects data from different sources as it happens and sends that data to systems like Spark for processing. Imagine Kafka as a conveyor belt sending live messages (like user clicks or IoT sensor data) to be processed.

Spark Streaming is a part of Spark that can process real-time data such as information from a keyboard or clicks from a website. It reads that live data from Kafka and processes it.

JSON stands for "Java Script Object Notation", and it is formatted for sending data that looks like text but it is easy for both machines and humans to read. Here is a JSON message:

```
.."name":" John",
.."age": 45,
.."city": "London"
```

I think it is easy to work out what this message means! But what do Consume JSON and Parse JSON mean? To Consume JSON means to receive or read the JSON message from somewhere - like Kafka. For example, Spark Streaming connects to Kafka and consumes messages that look like the JSON example. To parse JSON means to break it down and extract values. For example, from this JSON:

```
{ "name": "Alice", "age": 25 }
Parsing would let you grab:
..name = Alice
..age = 25
```

Spark Streaming can parse the JSON to get the values it needs to make decisions.

```
{ "name": "Alice", "age": 25 }
Parsing would let you grab:
..name = Alice
..age = 25
```

'AWS Hive' means using Apache Hive on Amazon Web Services (AWS).

To what extent has Big Data been adopted in industry and commerce?

As we know, Big Data is essential for artificial intelligence and machine learning to work and to be so widespread, and when tied to AI it facilitates a range of applications. In the UK, over £1.2 billon ($1.5 billion) was stolen through fraud in 2022. Banks use Big Data to detect fraud by spotting unusual transactions and to assess credit risks and to help design personalised investment portfolios for clients. Big Data is necessary for crypto currencies and e-commerce platforms like Amazon analysing purchasing trends to provide personalised product suggestions – if you liked 'Teaching STEM' you'll also like 'Addressing Disruptive Technology'. Similarly, in entertainment, streaming platforms like Netflix and Spotify analyse user preferences to recommend content and thus, they believe, improve the viewers' experiences.

The energy sector uses Big Data to forecast demand, optimise performance of the electricity grid and integrate the various forms of renewable energy sources effectively. The agricultural sector benefits from Big Data through precision farming, analysing soil conditions, weather data and crop health to increase yield. Environmental scientists use it to monitor climate change, track wildlife and predict natural disasters.

Big Data has several clear social uses, too. The UK government has put the improvement of the National Health Service (NHS) high on its political agenda, and one way it suggests improvements is to move from "analogue to digital" (DHSC 2024) in healthcare. Big Data can be used for precision medicine, analysing patient records and genetic data to recommend personalised treatments. Hospitals could use the large data capacity to optimise staff allocation and reduce patient waiting times. Governments also use Big Data for "Smart City" initiatives, optimising traffic flows, waste management and improving public safety, which is shown in Figure 6.2. Sports teams analyse players' performance to improve strategies and prevent player injuries. Law enforcement agencies analyse crime patterns to predict and prevent incidents – although such data needs to be used with care. If a certain neighbourhood is already heavily policed, more crime will be detected and analysis of the crime patterns data suggests an area of 'more' crime which needs more policing.

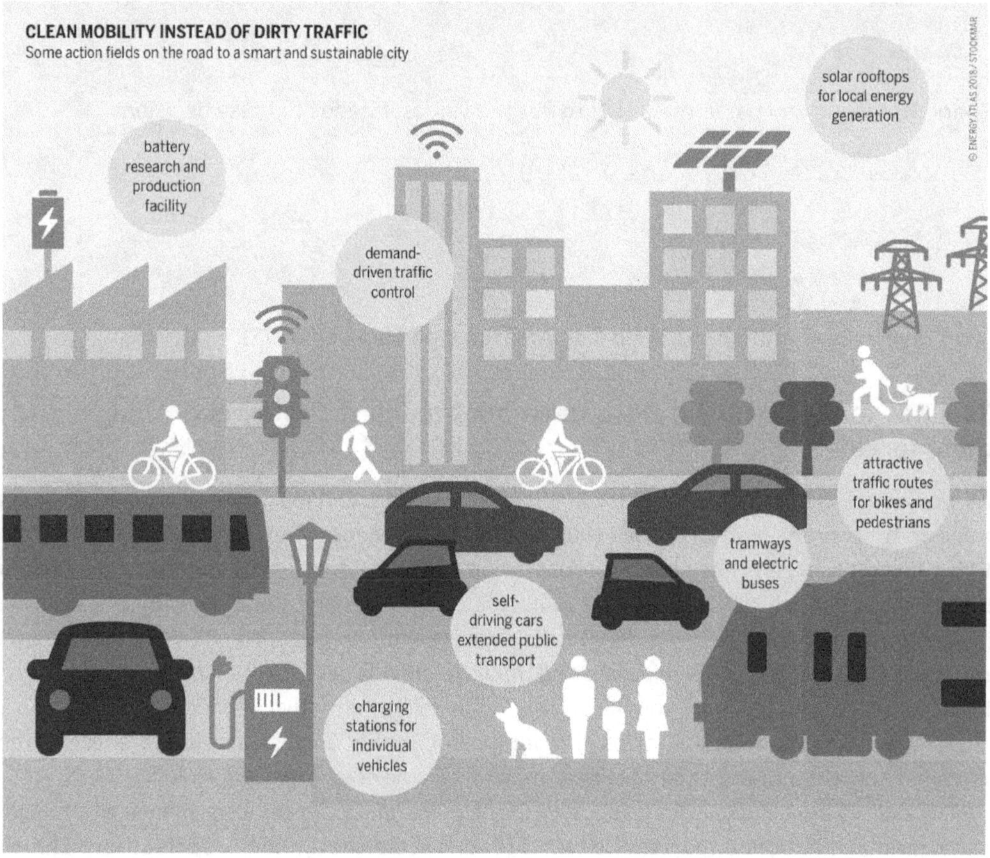

Figure 6.2 On the road to a Smart City

How does Big Data interact with other disruptive technologies?

In 1978 James Burke wrote and performed in a TV programme entitled 'Connections', which also produced a popular spin-off book that is still in print (Burke 1978). It asked such questions as: How did the popularity of underwear in the twelfth century lead to the invention of the printing press? How did the waterwheel evolve into the computer? How did the arrival of the cannon lead eventually to the development of movies? The point was that former inventions are essential for later inventions – cannons need a fuse; later, gun cotton (nitrocellulose) and nitrocellulose was used, which is a form of cellulose, which was the substance used for the first silent movies. It was obviously dangerously flammable and did not age well. In a similar way the infrastructure of Big Data acts as the necessary backbone for many disruptive technologies, particularly AI. An extensive and efficient Big Data infrastructure is essential before AI can work.

The Internet of Things (IoT) devices generate a constant stream of data from sensors embedded in vehicles, domestic appliances and industrial equipment (see Chapter 7). For example, smart home systems use IoT data to optimise energy usage, while for industrial IoT sensor data is analysed to predict machine failures and schedule maintenance. Robots use Big Data to learn from their environments and navigate spaces effectively.

In gaming, Big Data enriches the experience by providing environmental information and it helps create personalised experiences by analysing player behaviour, especially as 5G is continuing to be more widely available. In retail, augmented reality uses Big Data to offer virtual try-ons or visualise how furniture fits into a room based on user preferences.

What are the predicted negative aspects of using Big Data, and what should we do about it?

Big Data memory systems face many challenges as the use of AI, cloud computing and crypto currencies increase. Some of the issues are technical, such as the high cost of RAM and data transfer bottlenecks. Innovations such as advancements in solid-state drives and non-volatile memory technologies are addressing these challenges, enabling faster and more efficient data processing. But by far the most serious issue is the enormous electrical power Big Data consumes.

> Most of the electrical power consumed by data centres is transformed into thermal power – that could be used to heat your home. We can't continue to dump heat to atmosphere, while British families struggle to stay warm. Let's Eliminate Fuel Poverty. For Good.
>
> (EnergiRaven, Private Eye 2024)

Figure 6.3 Virginia Tech Data Centre

Data centres, such as those shown in Figure 6.3, are huge and often house thousands of computer servers, consuming staggering amounts of electricity for the servers, cooling systems and networking equipment. According to the International Energy Association (IEA), data centres used around 460 terawatt-hours of electricity in 2022. That is almost 2% of the world's entire power supply, and this is expected to more than double by 2026. After the USA and Germany, the UK is third in the world for the number of data centres. The UK

National Grid expects data centre electricity consumption to increase six-fold in the next decade.

Big Data is energy-intensive, but its environmental impact must be mitigated by better use of technology-optimising workflows and using energy-efficient hardware and infrastructure – as well as being much more creative in the use of the 'waste' heat. Waste heat can be used to provide warmth to homes, offices and industrial facilities. For example, data centres in Scandinavia are integrated into citywide systems, where excess heat is piped to buildings to reduce reliance on fossil fuels (Nerell 2023). Smaller centres could heat swimming pools or community buildings such as schools. Commercial greenhouses and fish farms rely on warm environments, and in regions with water scarcity, waste heat can power desalination processes, turning seawater into drinking water.

John Naughton asks the question "How will AI reshape 2025?" In its widespread reconfiguration of how business operates, "Well, it could be the spreadsheet of the 21st century" (Naughton 2024) (see Chapter 4). That fundamental change is not possible without the connected 'backbone' of Big Data.

References

Burke, J. (1978) *Connections*. New York: Simon & Schuster.

Department of Health and Social Care (DHSC). (2024) October. https://www.gov.uk/government/news/government-issues-rallying-cry-to-the-nation-to-help-fix-nhs (Accessed January 2025).

EnergiRaven. (2024) Private Eye no. 1639, 20 December 2024–9 January 2025. https://www.energiraven.com/ (Accessed January 2025).

Laney, D. (2001) *3-D Data Management: Controlling Data Volume, Velocity and Variety*. META Group Research Note, 6 February.

Naughton, J.T. (2024) *How will AI reshape 2025? Well, it could be the spreadsheet of the 21st Century*. John Naughton, The Observer Newspaper, 29 December.

Nerell, J. (2023) *Stockholm, Sweden: Heat Recovery from Data Centres*. https://eu-mayors.ec.europa.eu/en/Stockholm-Heat-recovery-from-data-centres (Accessed January 2025).

Recommended reading

Jha, R. (2025) *MongoDB Essentials: Build Faster, Perform Better, Store Smarter, Scale Bigger, and Master Document Database*. New York: Norton Press.

Kassim, R. (2021) *Big DATA For a Sustainable Smart City*. Singapore: Partridge Publishers.

Stephenson, D. (2018) *Big Data Demystified: How to Use Big Data, Data Science and AI to Make Better Business Decisions and Gain Competitive Advantage*. Harlow, UK: Pearson.

7 Internet of Things (IoT) in depth

> **Pause for thought**
>
> Before reading this chapter, jot down some examples of what you would consider to be described as the Internet of Things, especially those that you possess.

This chapter is in four sections: How does the Internet of Things work? To what extent has the IoT been adopted? How does IoT interact with other disruptive technologies? And what are the predicted negative aspects of using IoT, and what should we do about it?

How does the Internet of Things work?

The Internet of Things (IoT) works by connecting everyday objects to the internet, allowing them to collect, exchange and act on data. You might know of a number of these devices, such as "Nest", which adjusts the temperature of your home depending on the weather forecast, or you can switch on your home's heating system using a phone app as you leave work. Similarly, the home lighting can be switched on remotely or its colour changed or maybe lights come on randomly to deter burglars since it looks like someone is at home. Also, to enhance home security, real-time video can be triggered by a motion detector and fed to your phone or sent directly to a home-security firm. Other possibilities are suggested by Figure 7.1.

Once collected, the data is transmitted by Wi-Fi or Bluetooth to centralised servers or cloud platforms. A key aspect of IoT's future functionality is a move to standardise how different devices, which might currently be incompatible, can exchange data that they collect. For this it really is "horses for courses" in how the data is exchanged. For example:

MQTT (Message Queuing Telemetry Transport)

It is best to think of MQTT as a lightweight messaging service that helps devices talk to each other when the devices have limited power or are in places with weak internet signal. For example, a temperature sensor on a remote farm might use MQTT to send data about the weather to a central server. It's efficient because it doesn't use a lot of data and works well even with unreliable networks.

DOI: 10.4324/9781003602002-8

Figure 7.1 Everyday objects connected to the internet

HTTP (Hypertext Transfer Protocol)

You may know that HTTP is what your browser uses to load websites. IoT devices also use HTTP when they need to send or receive information, like a smart doorbell sending live video to your phone. It's reliable but not as 'lightweight' as MQTT, so it's often used when more data needs to be sent.

CoAP (Constrained Application Protocol)

CoAP is like a smaller, faster version of HTTP used for tiny, simple devices. Imagine a smart light bulb that just needs to send or receive a few commands (like "turn on" or "turn off"). CoAP keeps things simple and efficient, so these devices can work quickly without needing a lot of power or signal bandwidth.

Edge (Edge Computing)

Edge computing means processing data close to where it's created instead of sending everything to a distant server. For instance, a security camera might analyse its video feed on-site to detect motion instead of uploading all the footage to the cloud for analysis. This saves time and reduces the need for constant internet use.

To what extent has the IoT been adopted?

Smart homes

As you might have already realised, IoT systems use AI to analyse patterns and predict future needs. I use my Alexa to play music and that's all. It is in my kitchen, and we listen to different radio stations or sometimes to free tunes from Amazon, but Alexa, Google Assistant and Siri can also be linked to control appliances and manage calendars. If I install a smart thermostat I could say, "Alexa, set the living room to 22 degrees". And that sets in train this sequence:

1. Alexa recognises my voice and sends the command to Amazon's servers.
2. The server determines this request is for my new smart thermostat and lets my Alexa know.
3. Alexa sends a message to the thermostat (via HTTP) to adjust the temperature.
4. The thermostat updates its settings and may send confirmation back to Alexa, which can let me know: "The living room is now set to 22 degrees".

Figure 7.2 Alexa smart speaker

Figure 7.3 Fitbit watch

Well, I have an Alexa (Figure 7.2), and I have a Fitbit watch (Figure 7.3) that counts my steps and monitors my heart rate. But I don't wear it at night, and I don't have it tell me the current local weather, as I look out the window for that. But how typical am I compared with others in the UK? In 2024, approximately 35% of UK households own smart speakers with integrated virtual assistants, and Alexa dominates the UK market, accounting for about 64.3% of smart speaker ownership. This suggests that around 22.5% of UK households have an Alexa-enabled device (Statista 2024). Fitbit doesn't give specific details for the UK but by January 2024, approximately 35% of UK residents owned and used wearable devices, including fitness trackers and smartwatches (Deloitte 2023). Interestingly, wearable device ownership varies across different demographics. For instance, women aged 25–44 in the UK are among the most likely to own a smartwatch, while ownership rates decline for women aged 45–64 (Mintel 2024).

There are a few more niche health IoT devices such as those that monitor chronic conditions, like glucose levels for diabetes patients, and share the data with healthcare professionals, and smart pills which can contain digestible sensors that send information about medication intake to external devices (NHS Digital 2024).

I have focused so far on the internet of things in the home or for personal use – the "Smart Home". But there are wider uses of IoT in industry, agriculture, commerce and the wider community – "Smart Cities".

Smart cities

Going through successive traffic lights on a 'green wave', or as it often seems to me, being required to stop at every red light, can now be better streamlined as IoT systems can adjust traffic signals based on real-time traffic flow data rather than using simple set timings (European Commission 2019) (see also Chapter 6).

A pub quiz question could be "What do Amsterdam, Barcelona and Prachatice in Europe, and San Francisco and New York City in the USA have in common?" One answer is that they, like Melbourne in Australia, all have "Smart Bins" that monitor fill levels, to optimise waste collection routes and reduce fuel consumption (Figure 7.4).

Figure 7.4 A Smart Bin in Prachatice, Czechia

Often solar power is used to compact waste up to seven times more than a regular bin (Bigbelly 2025). This reduces the number of times that collections need to be made

Industrial IoT (IIoT)

Sensors on manufacturing equipment monitor performance and can predict failures so reducing downtime – Figure 7.5. IoT is used in supply chains, such as GPS trackers and improving inventory management and delivery efficiency (McKinsey and Company 2022).

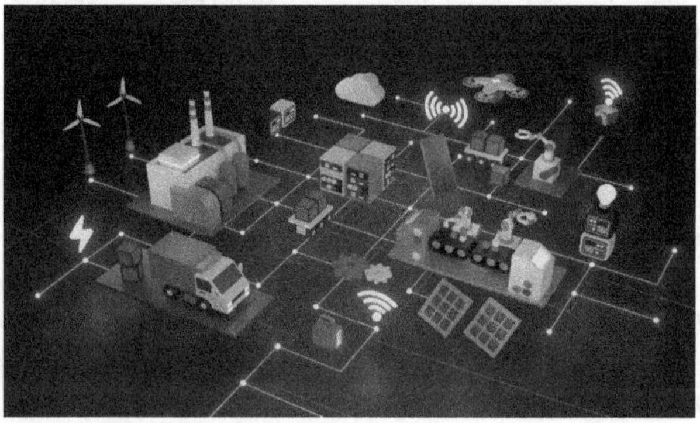

Figure 7.5 Industrial IoT

Agriculture

As water rates become increasingly expensive to pay for mending leaks and to improve vital infrastructure, IoT-enabled sensors can be used to measure soil moisture and weather conditions and so optimise water usage. Also, wearable devices track the health and location of farm animals – maybe cows can have their own Fitbits! (McCracken 2018)

Retail

Shelves can be equipped with weight sensors to detect product levels and notify staff to restock items and, more commonly, point-of-sales bar codes enable inventory tracking and mobile payment processing (Nielsen 2020).

How does IoT interact with other disruptive technologies?

Perhaps surprisingly, smart sensors embedded in 3D printers can collect data on temperature, humidity, material properties and their structural integrity, and so the Internet of Things is playing a transformative role in additive manufacturing (AM) by enabling higher precision. As with many disruptive technologies, AI algorithms process IoT-generated data which can be used in industry to detect defects and suggest maintenance schedules. Of course, analysing the Big Data collected by IoT improves the reliability of AI results by aggregating information from multiple IoT-enabled devices. Robotics, integrated with IoT, enables autonomous manufacturing processes such as material handling. Augmented reality can enhance the IoT-additive manufacturing interaction by offering real-time visualisation of 3D models which could assist engineers in validating designs and in enabling remote troubleshooting.

Beyond traditional manufacturing, neurotechnology integrated with IoT may enable brain-computer interfaces (BCIs) that allow direct control over 3D printing, making design and fabrication more intuitive. Synthetic biology, particularly in bioprinting, benefits from IoT-driven monitoring systems that can regulate temperature, pH and nutrient levels to ensure the viability of printed living tissues. Robotics combined with IoT can further automate those biological printing processes, improving precision and repeatability in both medical and pharmaceutical applications. Augmented reality can enhance human interaction with IoT-driven AR by providing immersive visualisation of biological structures before printing. Meanwhile, when it is further developed, quantum computing could help simulate complex protein folding or cellular interactions, accelerating synthetic biology advancements. Big Data refines these processes by providing actionable insights from vast datasets, enabling real-time adjustments for better results.

Ultimately, as IoT integrates with these cutting-edge fields, it acts as a backbone for the seamless convergence of a range of disruptive technologies.

What are the predicted negative aspects of using IoT, and what should we do about it?

As we have seen, IoT offers many benefits, but there are some major concerns that we need to address and to mitigate as far as possible. Many IoT devices have weak security, making them easy targets for hackers. Cybercriminals can exploit these vulnerabilities to steal data or even take control of devices to launch cyberattacks. Like the regular updates you should make to the operating system of your personal computer, IoT users should change default passwords and update software regularly. Manufacturers of IoT devices could also help with the potential hacking problem by providing better initial authentication.

Government laws on how personal data is used need to be regularly reviewed as IoT becomes more widespread because IoT devices collect vast amounts of personal data, such as location, health metrics and information about our day-to-day habits. This personal data can be misused by unscrupulous companies or hacked due to a data repository's own poor security.

I am writing this chapter as a series of "named storms" batter the UK and Ireland, leading to power cuts which in rural areas can last up to ten days! As we have discussed, domestic IoT devices rely on internet connectivity, making them useless during these power outages. Perhaps more importantly, critical systems like hospitals can be affected, although many have back-up generators.

There are also some basic problems with IoT that is typical to new technologies as they are rolled out. Some will remember that when home video recorders first became available in the 1970s, there were two incompatible systems: Betamax and VCR. Similarly, different IoT devices and platforms sometimes don't communicate well with each other due to a lack of standardisation. It is in the interests of the IoT manufacturers to work together on creating common standards and interoperability protocols to enable better integration. Part of these agreed common standards should also be a common policy to mitigate the environmental impact of IoT. Manufacturers of new IoT devices need to follow the pattern set by lightbulbs and move to lower energy consumption and, like used batteries, they need to initiate an expectation of recycling old devices.

Considering the McKinsey criteria for disruption with respect to the Internet of Things across industries, we have seen IoT revolutionising sectors like healthcare, manufacturing and smart cities. In parallel, continued technological advancements in AI, 5G and cloud computing enhance IoT's scalability and efficiency. Consequently, the economic impact is significant, reducing operational costs and creating new business models. Despite the regulatory and social acceptance challenges discussed here, increasing investment and policies are tending to support IoT adoption. In companies as diverse as agriculture and retail, the competitive landscape is shifting as companies either innovate or risk being left behind, and continued developments in IoT hardware, software and services will accelerate that adoption as it brings cost savings and convenience. IoT therefore aligns with McKinsey's disruption criteria, reshaping businesses and consumer experiences worldwide and long-term due to the robustness of the industry.

A final issue that is common to all the disruptive technologies that we have considered in depth is the impact on existing jobs in industries such as manufacturing, transportation, and retail. While, as we have seen, IoT no doubt brings general efficiency and convenience, manufacturers and governments must work together to upskill and support new employment opportunities, and also enhance security, protect privacy and ensure sustainability.

References

Bigbelly. (2025) *Smart Trash Cans & Recycling Bins | Bigbelly Waste Management*. [online]. https://bigbelly.com (Accessed 20 January 2025).

Deloitte. (2023) *Digital Consumer Trends 2023*. https://www2.deloitte.com/dk/da/pages/technology-media-and-telecommunications/topics/digital-consumer-trends.html (Accessed 20 January 2025).

European Commission. (2019) *Key Ways IoT Is Shaping The Future of Cars*. [online]. https://urban-mobility-observatory.transport.ec.europa.eu/news-events/news/key-ways-iot-shaping-future-cars-2019-05-14_en (Accessed 20 January 2025).

McCracken, D. (2018) *The Internet of Agricultural Things (IoAT): A Potential Game-Changer for Farming in Upland Areas*. [online]. https://publications.aberdeenshire.gov.uk/acblobstorage/cd9d03bb-d8cb-4f1b-883b-5daf00be7234/presentation-5.12.18-the-internet-of-agricultural-things-by-prof-davy-mccracken-sruc.pdf (Accessed 20 January 2025).

McKinsey & Company. (2022) *The Internet of Things: Catching Up to an Accelerating Opportunity*. [online]. https://www.mckinsey.com/~/media/mckinsey/business%20functions/mckinsey%20digital/our%20insights/iot%20value%20set%20to%20accelerate%20through%202030%20where%20and%20how%20to%20capture%20it/the-internet-of-things-catching-up-to-an-accelerating-opportunity-final.pdf (Accessed 20 January 2025).

Mintel. (2024) *UK Technology Trends Market Report: Spring 2024*. [online]. https://store.mintel.com/report/uk-technology-trends-spring-market-report (Accessed 20 January 2025).

NHS Digital. (2024) *£1 Million Boost for Wireless Innovations to Improve Patient Care*. [online]. https://digital.nhs.uk/news/2024/gbp1-million-boost-for-wireless-innovations-to-improve-patient-care (Accessed 20 January 2025).

Nielsen. (2020) *The Future Awaits: Tech-Transformed Consumption*. [online]. https://www.nielsen.com/insights/2020/the-future-awaits-tech-transformed-consumption (Accessed 20 January 2025).

Statista. (2024) *Ownership of Smart Speakers in the United Kingdom (UK) 2024*. [online]. https://www.statista.com/statistics/956343/ownership-of-smart-speakers-uk/ (Accessed 20 January 2025).

Recommended reading

Dow, C. (2024) *Internet of Things Programming Projects: Build Exciting IoT Projects Using Raspberry Pi 5, Raspberry Pi Pico, and Python*. Birmingham, UK: Packt Publishing.

McEwan, A. and Cassimally, H. (2023) *Designing the Internet of Things*. London: Wiley & Sons.

Reaves, A. (2025) *Internet of Things (IoT): Connecting the World Through Smart Devices and Intelligent Systems. Part 3*. London: Alex Reeves.

8 Neurotechnology in depth

This chapter is in five major parts: clinical neuroscience and neurotechnology, molecular and cellular neuroscience and neurotechnology, restoring lost function – technologies that enhance a person's life; how does Neurotechnology interact with other disruptive technologies? What are the predicted ethical dilemmas of using neurotechnology, and what should we do about it? It is a disruptive technology which many think should be well-funded and a high priority:

> We need a Manhattan Project for the brain, a place where entrepreneurs, startups, established companies, and talented people from all over the world come together to solve some of the brain's most vexing problems – which are also some of the world's most pressing problems.
>
> (Low 2016)

I suppose that when you break down the two elements in 'neurotechnology', neuro and technology, it becomes clear that part of the focus is on better understanding of the brain and using technology to possibly improve the treatment of neurological disorders.

So, where in your body does the term 'neurological' cover? The brain, yes, but also the whole of the nervous system, which also includes the spinal cord and networks of nerve cells (neurons) throughout the body. Neuroscience seeks to understand how the nervous system develops, functions and influences behaviour, cognition, emotions and bodily functions. There are branches of specialisms in neuroscience:

- **Molecular and Cellular Neuroscience:** Studies neurons at the molecular and cellular level, focusing on how nerve cells function and communicate.
- **Systems Neuroscience:** Looks at how groups of neurons work together to control specific functions like vision, movement or memory.
- **Cognitive Neuroscience:** Investigates how brain activity is linked to mental processes like thinking, memory, language and decision-making.
- **Behavioural Neuroscience:** Explores how the brain and nervous system influence behaviour.

DOI: 10.4324/9781003602002-9

- **Computational Neuroscience:** Uses mathematical models and computer simulations to understand brain functions.
- **Clinical Neuroscience:** Applies knowledge of the nervous system to understand and treat neurological disorders, such as Alzheimer's disease, epilepsy, stroke or Parkinson's disease.

As space is limited and I wish to focus on the benefits of bringing together science and technology, I am going to focus in this chapter on the last and the first bullet points - 'Clinical neuroscience' and 'Molecular and cellular neuroscience', but with a particular emphasis on the technologies involved in treatments. Later, I also want to consider how technology can support people living with a life-changing neurological disorder.

Clinical neuroscience and neurotechnology

> ### Pause for thought
>
> Before I lay out some 'neurological disorders', jot down some that you might know about, perhaps through your general knowledge or, maybe as I have, you have a friend or relation who is being treated for a neurological disorder.

My own list, which is not at all comprehensive, was: epilepsy, migraine, multiple sclerosis, Parkinson's disease, Alzheimer's disease, meningitis, stroke, brain injury, spinal cord injury and depression.

If you live in the UK, your GP might have sent you for an X-ray, ECG or an MRI scan, all free on the NHS.

If you don't live in the United Kingdom (UK - England, Wales, Scotland and Northern Ireland), you might also have a family doctor (GP - a general practitioner) who might send you to have an X-Ray, an Electrocardiogram (ECG) or a Magnetic Resonance Imaging (MRI) scan, and you too might have a National Health Service (NHS) in your country. The point I am making here is that the medical profession loves to use initials, as often the full name of a treatment or some medical technology is such a mouthful! This is especially true of the different equipment and techniques involved in the treatment of neurological disorders.

Many of these disorders can be treated with medication, but sometimes the 'drugs don't work', so there are some treatments that use technologies that interact directly with the brain itself.

Figure 8.1 summarises some of these processes, and you can see that some go directly into the core of the brain, some sit on the surface of the brain, some on the bone of the skull and some are simply on the top of the head - on the scalp.

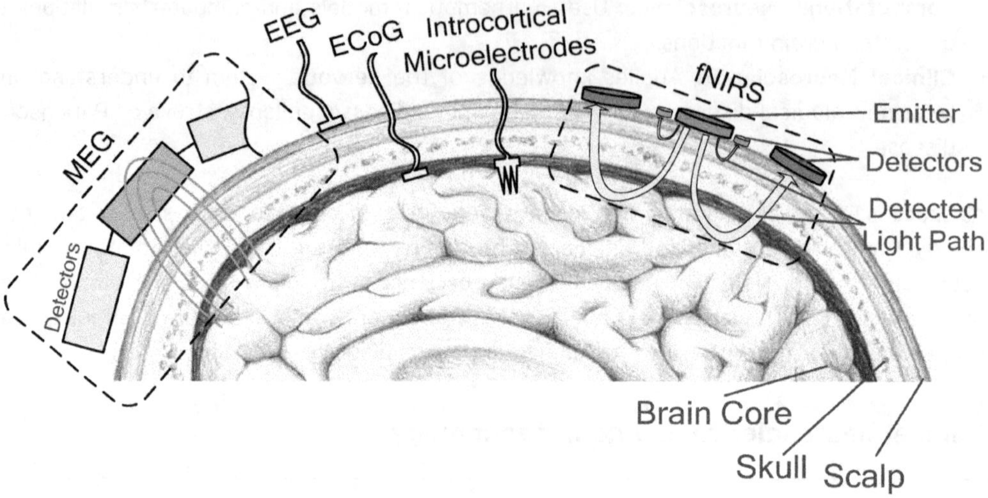

Figure 8.1 Sensor Types: Invasive, Semi-invasive and non-invasive: Peksa Janis and Dmytro Mamchur.

There are three types of these interventions to help cure a neurological disorder:invasive, semi-invasive and non-invasive.

Invasive – Directly implanting microelectronics into a human's brain (IM – Introcortical Microelectronics) may be effective but is innately risky as it might have unwanted side effects depending where in the brain the electrodes are placed.

Semi-Invasive – If an electrode is placed just under the bone of the skull, on the brain but not in the brain, as is used for the mapping of the brain known as 'electrocortography' (EcoG), that is termed semi-invasive.

Non-Invasive – If the electrical activity of the brain can be detected without any implanted electrodes at all, but rather from outside on the surface of the head such as electroencephalography (EEG), or probing by using a magnetic field known as magnetoencephalography (MEG) or by using a long wavelength light in functional near-infrared spectroscopy that measures brain activity by detecting changes in blood oxygenation levels (fNIRS) then, of course, all these measuring devices are 'outside-the-brain' techniques and are all considered non-invasive.

You see what I mean about using abbreviations! They are used so frequently by medical staff that they rarely use the full term. For example, when I asked my doctor who wanted me to have an MRI scan what the meaning of 'MRI' was, he said he couldn't remember.

I am now going to consider the treatment of three of the neurological disorders that I listed earlier: Parkinson's, depression and Alzheimer's disease. And be prepared for yet more abbreviations.

Parkinson's

Parkinson's is usually controlled by medication, but if that is no longer effective then sometimes Deep Brain Stimulation (DBS) may be suggested, which is an invasive technique using electrodes in the brain:

> DBS is the main type of surgery used to treat Parkinson's. Usually, it's most effective at improving motor (movement) symptoms, such as tremor, slowness of movement, rigidity and dyskinesia (involuntary movements).
>
> A pulse generator (a device a bit like a heart pacemaker) is placed under the skin around the chest or stomach area. It's connected to 1 or 2 fine wires that are inserted into specific areas of [the] brain [IM].
>
> When the pulse generator is switched on, the electrodes deliver high-frequency stimulation to the targeted area. This stimulation changes some of the electrical signals in the brain that cause the symptoms of Parkinson's.
>
> (Parkinson UK 2025)

Depression

Those suffering from depression might be treated by repetitive Transcranial Magnetic Stimulation (rTMS), which we have seen (Figure 8.1) is a non-invasive technique. In rTMS:

> A purpose-made electromagnetic coil is held against the scalp with the intention of inducing electric currents in the cerebral cortex. Imaging may be used to help target specific areas of the brain. Treatment is usually considered for patients with depression that has not responded to antidepressant medication or patients for whom antidepressants are not suitable. . . . In rTMS, repetitive pulses of electromagnetic energy are delivered at various frequencies or stimulus intensities. Conventional rTMS is a repetition of individual pulses at a pre-set interval (so a train of pulses), whereas 'theta-burst' rTMS is a repetition of short bursts of pulses at a pre-set interval (train of bursts).
>
> (NICE 2015)

Alzheimer's disease

> Alzheimer's disease (AD) is the most common cause of dementia in the elderly, clinically defined by progressive cognitive decline . . . by brain atrophy, neuroinflammation, and accumulation of 'amyloid plaques'. Neurotechnological approaches, including optogenetics [using long wave Light] and deep brain stimulation [DBS as used in Parkinson's], have exploded as new tools for not only the study of the brain, but also for application in the treatment of neurological diseases. . . . Recent advancements in both invasive and non-invasive neurotechnologies can be used to ameliorate [the effects of] AD.
>
> (Ning et al. 2022)

The different types of neurotechnology that could be used to 'ameliorate Alzheimer's disease' are summarised in Figure 8.2.

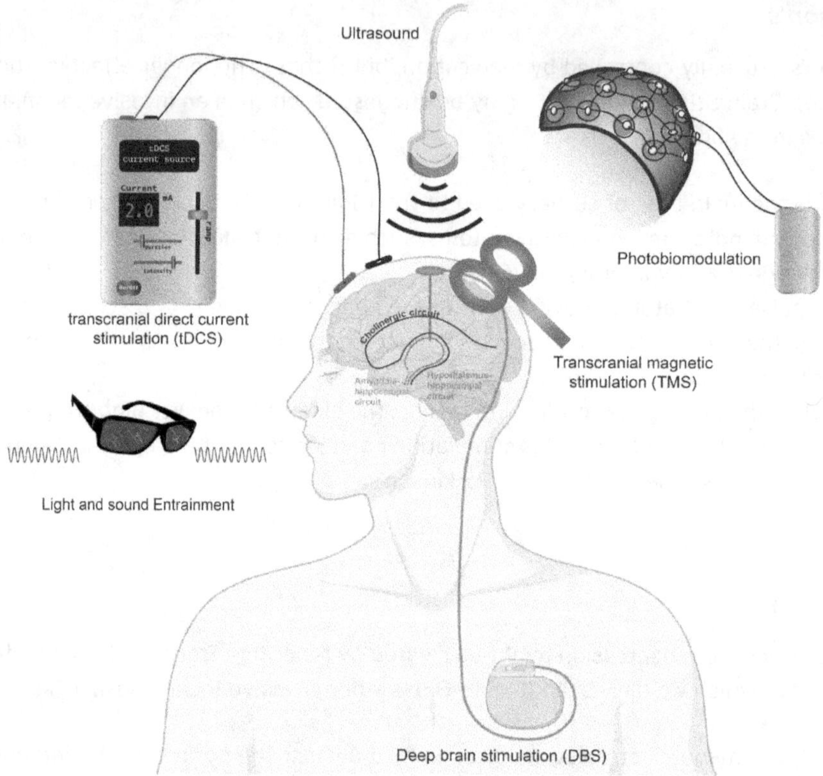

Figure 8.2 Showing the use of DBS, rTMS and light (fNIRS), but also sound as another non-invasive neurostimulation treatments for Alzheimer's disease (Ning et al. 2022)

The different types of neuroimaging which gather data about a patient are leading to earlier and more precise diagnosis of brain disorders, so treatments can be better matched to an individual's brain patterns.

Figure 8.3 Professor Simon Schultz

We are very grateful to Professor Simon Schultz, who is Professor of Neurotechnology and the Director of the Centre for Neurotechnology at Imperial College London for the following contribution to this chapter. He and his colleagues in the Centre are at the forefront of our understanding of the brain by monitoring a subject's 'cognitive performance' as they use their brain for different tasks.

In his Thought Piece, Professor Schultz explains some of the latest neurotechnology tools to find out more about the brain itself and to improve the treatment of neurological disorders.

Expert contribution from Prof. Simon Schultz

Tools for understanding and interfacing with the brain

I work at the interface of neuroscience and engineering - I develop (and apply) new technology for understanding how the brain works, how it malfunctions (such as Alzheimer's disease) and for treating disorders to restore brain function. The human brain is a complex network of around 86 billion neurons - as well as numerous other cells - that processes information as we perceive, move, think and remember. Much of my work has involved developing tools which allow large numbers of individual neurons to be monitored simultaneously, either through electrical or optical measurements (see Figures 8.1 and 8.2). Monitoring signals from such a large number of neurons (recent experiments have involved over 10,000 neurons distributed across the brain) gives us the best possible information about brain function, but it is necessarily invasive - largely limiting their application either to animal models or to human organoid cell cultures in a dish (see Figure 8.4). Using these tools, we have uncovered new features of Alzheimer's Disease, for instance finding that the 'dynamic range' (essentially, the range of high and low values that can be signalled) is reduced in individual neurons in accordance with their proximity to amyloid plaques, one of the hallmarks of the disease.

The last two decades have seen revolutionary advances in our technology for studying and interfacing with the brain, and it has been a privilege to have a front-row seat to these developments (where I have not personally been involved) in my role as Director of Imperial College's Centre for Neurotechnology. These developments have included "Neuropixels", silicon micromachined electrode arrays with thousands of electrode sites that can be inserted into the brain to monitor the activity of neurons.

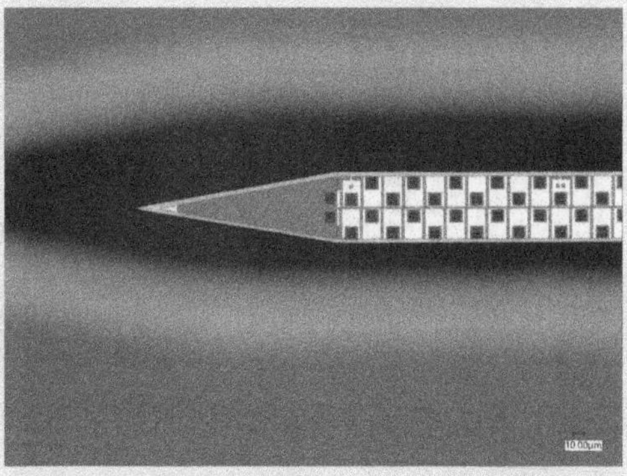

Figure 8.4 "Neuropixels" - silicon microfabricated electrode arrays

Similar technology has been used to monitor single neuron activity in human patients with what is known as 'intractable' epilepsy (epilepsy that cannot be adequately treated by medication) by implanting electrodes to map out the location of the source of the epileptic seizures prior to surgery, and to obtain more information about the brain regions involved. Another major advance has been the development of two-photon fluorescence microscopes that, together with the use of viruses to genetically modify neurons to make them into 'fluorescent biosensors', can be used to watch the neural activity patterns during cognitive function (see Figure 8.5).

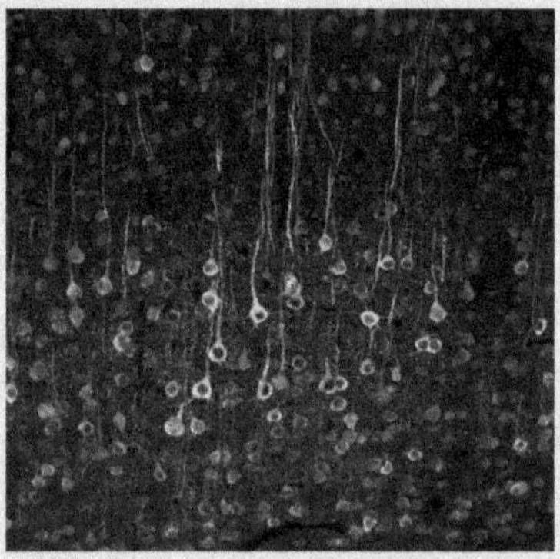

Figure 8.5 Fluorescence imaging

Major advances have also been made in non-invasive methods for brain monitoring. Though these techniques are limited in either spatial resolution, temporal resolution or the parts of the brain that can be accessed when compared to invasive methods, they do allow us to study the brain in human subjects - yielding much useful information about higher cognitive function. An example is the electroencephalogram (EEG) - while this is an old technology (first applied in 1924), it is now available for sale and DIY kits with relatively good performance are becoming widely available, for instance to hobbyists wanting to explore brain-computer interface applications such as for gaming.

Figure 8.6 EEG - here showing it used for Gaming: Ilda Rakhmatulin, PiEEG, Edinburgh, Scotland, UK

The state of the art in non-invasive brain measurements is also rapidly advancing, for instance with the development of a new variant of magnetoencephalography (MEG). MEG (see Figure 8.1) is a way of measuring the electrical signalling of the brain through the tiny magnetic fields generated. However, traditional approaches to this involve superconducting quantum interference device (SQUID) sensors which need to be cooled down to −269°C, resulting in a large and unwieldy apparatus in which it is uncomfortable for people to sit for long. A non-invasive brain imaging technique is functional near infrared spectroscopy (fNIRS). This allows imaging of the blood-oxygen level dependent (BOLD) signal used by functional magnetic resonance imaging, albeit at slightly lower spatial resolution, while allowing subjects to move around (see Figure 8.1 and Figure 8.7). I am acting as an advisor to the company Connectome Health Ltd, which is using such a device to track cognitive performance in human subjects over time – they can now track their cognitive fitness in a similar fashion to the way many people track their physical fitness.

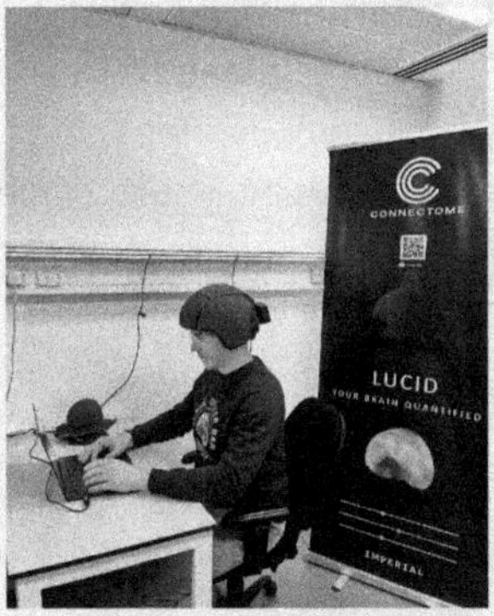

Figure 8.7 Functional near-infrared spectroscopy (fNIRS): Rufus Mitchell-Heggs, Connectome Health Ltd.

The idea of "Brain-Machine Interfaces" through which people can directly communicate with computers, or control robotic manipulators through thought alone, has recently captured the public imagination, due primarily to hype focused around Neuralink, a company run by Elon Musk. This does however follow over 20 years of work, including clinical trials (Patrick-Krueger et al. 2025) on earlier implantable cortical brain-machine interfaces. Although much of the hype has centred around the potential application of the technology in normal human subjects, for a long time to come the technology is likely to be restricted to clinical applications where the need outweighs the risks, such as tetraplegia (the loss of control of all four limbs) and Amyotrophic Lateral Sclerosis (ALS), which is the specific Motor Neurone Disease (MND) that Professor Stephen Hawking suffered from. Any implantation of an electrode into brain tissue comes with substantial risk of neuroinflammation, and while recent developments such as electrodes with elasticity matched to that of the brain have reduced that problem, the long-term consequences of such implantation have not yet been adequately characterised. There is, however, one approach in which there exists a substantial body of safety data – the stentrode (Figure 8.8).

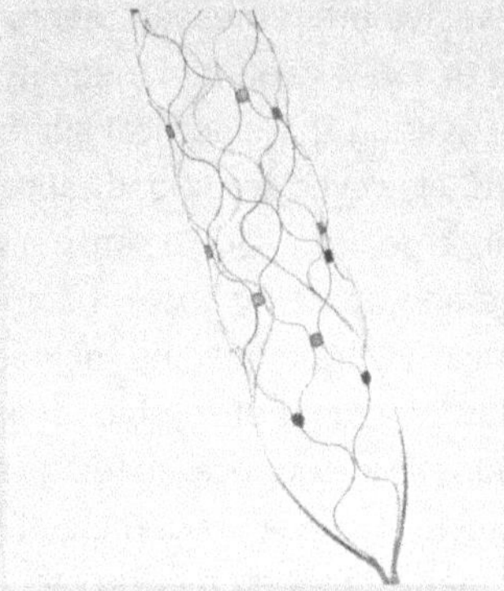

Figure 8.8 The "stentrode" developed by Synchron Inc.

Venous stenting (inserting an expandable metal mesh tube – a stent – into a vein) has been used for many decades to treat the build-up of pressure around the brain known as "intracranial hypertension", which can lead to headaches and vison problems, and this stenting has a very low risk of complications. A group of researchers at the University of Melbourne in Australia developed an electrode array that could be implanted within a blood vessel using similar monitoring "angiography" techniques from neurovascular stenting. This has now been commercialised by the company Synchron, with a number of clinical trials completed and more underway (Mitchell et al. 2023).

The next decade is likely to see continued rapid advances in neurotechnology, with closed-loop brain stimulation devices (which can "write" as well as "read" brain activity) likely to be one of the key areas being pushed forward.

Molecular and cellular neuroscience and neurotechnology

I think we are all fascinated by our brains. I know we have common expressions, like "he wears his heart on his sleeve" or "she has a heart of gold", as the heart is often used as a metaphor for emotion and has been for centuries. But more recently the common metaphor of our brain is that of a computer, with input, output, memory storage and language as the brain's software. But how does current research in molecular and cellular neuroscience help with our understanding of the brain, enabling us to unlock "the Ultimate Black Box"?

Recent research highlights that the human brain holds even more secrets than we thought. One study suggests that astrocytes – star-shaped cells – may help store memories by working alongside neurons in dense networks in the brain. These neuron-astrocyte systems might explain why the human brain has such a huge storage capacity, storing more memories than once thought possible, and hint at new inspirations for the developments of artificial intelligence (Kozachkov et al. 2025). In another breakthrough, scientists at Stanford University in the USA have replicated, in a lab dish, one of humans' most prominent nervous pathways for sensing pain.

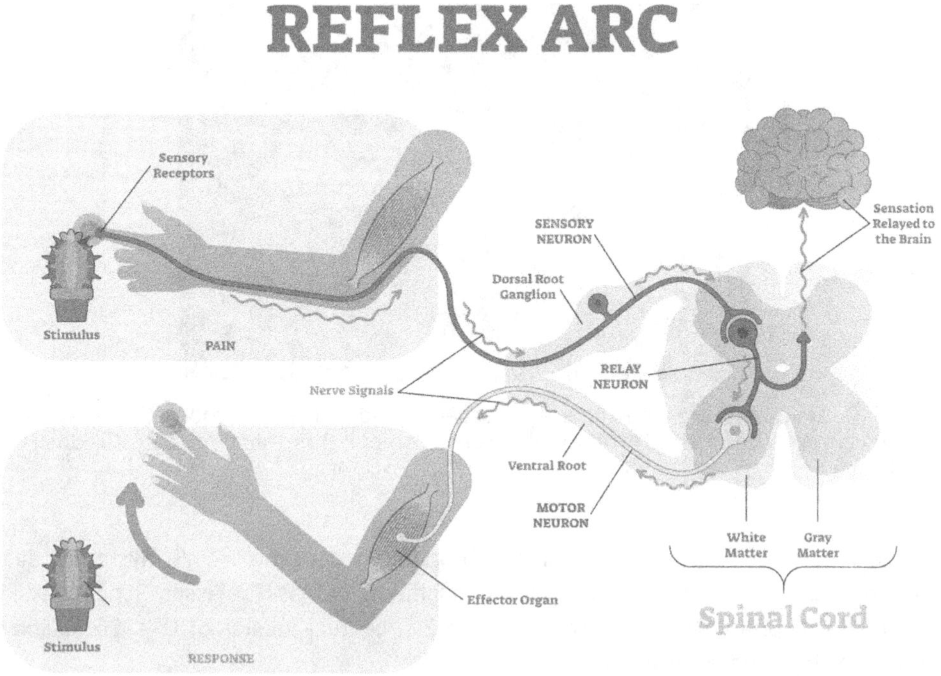

Figure 8.9 Diagram of the fast-reaction nervous path for sensing pain via the spinal cord

This nerve circuit transmits sensations from the body's skin to the brain from the spinal cord. Once further processed in the brain, these signals will translate into our subjective experience, including the uncomfortable feeling of pain. When exposed to capsaicin, a chili pepper often used to reduce pain, the lab-dish model showed real electrical responses just like human pain signals – promising new ways to study chronic pain and test drugs without using animals (Paşca et al. 2025).

Progress is also being made using brain maps in studies involving volunteers. At Massachusetts Institute of Technology (MIT), researchers mapped whole brain hemispheres to see how sleep loss affects neuron activity, opening doors to better understanding of memory and rest (Wei et al. 2024). Edinburgh scientists also used a living human's brain to study Alzheimer's – their early findings show that even tiny increases in amyloid (a group of proteins that can misfold and form amyloid plaques posits in various tissues and organs) can disrupt synapses, offering insights for new treatments (McGeachan et al. 2025).

Work at the University of Texas at Austin has made advances in the use of EEG (Huh et al. 2025). As we have seen, EEG devices are usually wired and uncomfortable (see Figures 8.6 versus 8.10). The group at the University of Texas, however, has developed a very thin wireless e-tattoo that detects EEG from the forehead. The tattoo combines a sticky electrode layer linked to a blue battery-powered printed circuit shown as shown in Figure 8.10. The e-tattoo stretches with the skin and provides a strong signal even when the wearer is walking or running. This device could be useful to monitor workers who need to stay alert in situations where their own safety and that of others is critical.

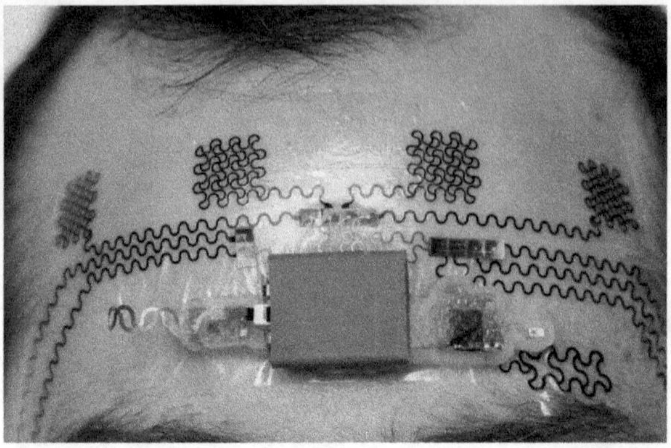

Figure 8.10 Brain and eye activity are recorded by adhesive electrodes (black serpentine lines), which are connected to other electronic components (blue square). Credit: H. Huh *et al./Device*

As models and tools improve, we're closer to understanding the brain's mysteries, designing better medicines and building smarter machines. But as Professor Schultz explains, commercial-safe brain-machine interfaces and a 21st-century version of TV's 'Six Million Dollar Man' are still some years away.

Restoring lost function – technologies that enhance a person's life

As we have seen, neuroscience and neurotechnology are specific to technological interactions with the brain. Yet there are obviously different levels of technology that can enhance lost or impaired sensory function, such as hearing loss and poor sight, many of which have been available for centuries. For example, I wear spectacles and have hearing aids – neither qualifying as an example of neurotechnology! But for those who are functionally blind, regaining sight or hearing (e.g., cochlear implants, as shown in Figure 8.11, are an early example) is very different.

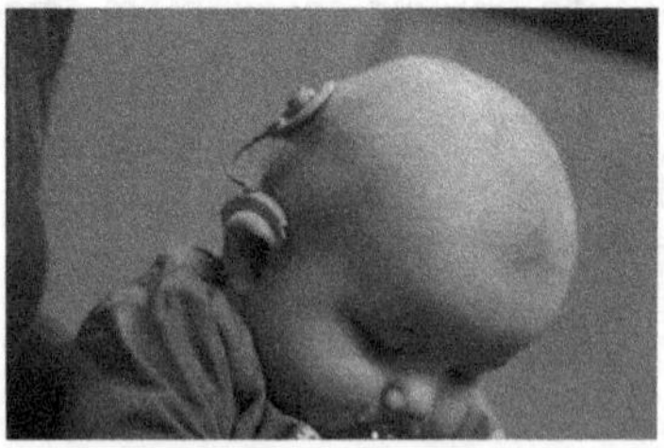

Figure 8.11 Infant with cochlear implant

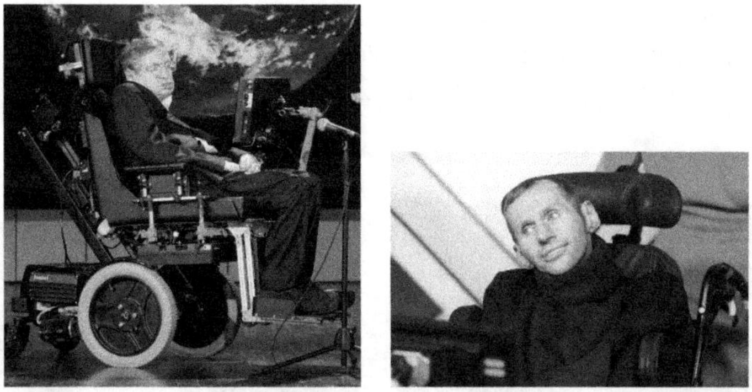

Figure 8.12 a) Stephen Hawking (left); b) Rob Burrow (right) (David Davies/PA Wire)

Professor Stephen Hawking, pictured in Figure 8.12a, suffered from Amyotrophic Lateral Sclerosis (ALS), which is a progressive neurodegenerative disease that affects nerve cells in the brain and spinal cord, leading to muscle weakness and eventual paralysis. He used a computer with a special cheek muscle sensor. A small infrared switch detected tiny movements in his cheek, and he used those small movements to cycle through options on the screen (like typing letters), and the computer would then build sentences and eventually 'speak' them by using a robotic voice.

More recently, as shown in Figure 8.12b, Rob Burrow, a Rugby League player, lost his ability to speak due to progressive Motor Neurone Disease (MND). He used a 'speech-generating device', which is sometimes called an eye-gaze computer. The computer had a camera that tracked his eye movements. He would look at letters, words, or symbols on the screen, and the computer followed where his eyes pointed and used that to type out his messages. Once a sentence was ready, the computer would speak it out loud using a digital voice, but unlike the famous 'robot voice' used by Professor Hawking, Rob used one that sounded like his own voice as he had earlier, before the MND had progressed too far, recorded his own key sounds into his computer. So, for Rob Burrow, his eyes acted like a mouse to control the computer.

In the 1960s when the LASER was first invented, it was joked that it was a "solution looking for a problem". Its use is now ubiquitous at supermarket checkouts and to read CDs and DVDs. The recent production of a contact lens that can enable the wearer to see in the near infra-red as well as the visible spectrum struck me as a similar "solution looking for a problem" (Yuqian et al. 2025). Neuroscientists at the University of Science and Technology of China adapted the material used for standard soft contact lenses by integrating nanoparticles into the plastic lenses (Figure 8.13b). These nanoparticles were composed from these rather exotic elements and ions: Au/$NaGdF_4$:Yb^{3+}, Er^{3+}. I'll leave you to find a periodic table to find out the names of the elements used! The nanoparticles are each about 45nm in diameter (a nanometre is one billionth of a metre) – and interestingly, this is the same small size used in microchip manufacture. The lenses work by taking in the low-energy infrared light and emitting it as the higher-energy visible light. Tests showed that the lenses did not impair normal vision. With further development, it is possible that the linked problem to this solution is to be found with situations needing better night vision, Figure 8.13a shows the bulky conventional night vision goggles.

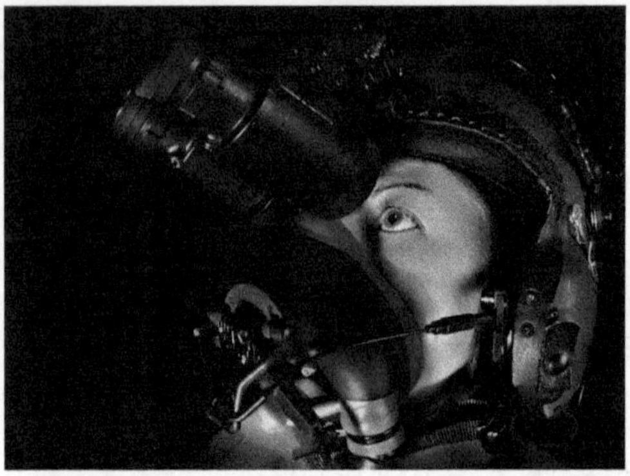

Figure 8.13a RAF Pilot using night vision goggles

Figure 8.13b Infrared vision contact lenses possible: Aylal

How does neurotechnology interact with other disruptive technologies?

Neuroprosthetics

Stephen Hawking and Rob Burrow both suffered from types of MND, using what control that they still had - eye movement or cheek movement - to painstakingly build up phrases to communicate using their "computer voice". Can this be taken further? Using an electroencephalogram (EEG) (see Figures 8.7 and 8.14) work is being carried out to create limbs and organs that interface directly with the nervous system for more natural control and sensory feedback.

Figure 8.14 "Brain-Computer Interface". Management of the plastic arm with the help of thought

As we have seen in Chapter 6, artificial intelligence (AI) is good at analysing large data sets; the brain is a source of massive neural data and so AI can be used decode brain signals for Brain Computer Interfaces (BCI), as illustrated in Figure 8.14. Qian et al. (2024) in a review of the field pointed out that:

> In recent years, artificial intelligence (AI) has undergone remarkable advancements, exerting a significant influence across a multitude of fields. One area that has particularly garnered attention and witnessed substantial progress is its integration into the realm of the nervous system . . . with a specific focus on AI-enhanced diagnostics for peripheral nervous system disorders, AI-driven pain management, advancements in neuroprosthetics, and the development of neural network models . . . the burgeoning opportunities for revolutionary medical interventions and the enhancement of human capabilities, thus paving the way for a future in which AI becomes an integral component of our nervous system's interface.

It is also possible that, conversely, better understanding of how our brain works will impact on the mathematical models that drive AI.

The promised benefits of quantum computing in speed of data handling will enable some fast analysis of the huge interactions between neurons, but given the current level of development, size and refrigeration needs of current machines, it seems likely that they will be used in basic research on the brain rather than for day-to-day benefits for those needing neurological support.

As Professor Schultz mentioned, advanced materials are being developed so that electrodes can now be used with elasticity matched to that of the brain, and sensors are becoming smaller and more biocompatible.

Is neurotechnology a disruptive technology?

You will remember (Chapter 1) the McKinsey Global Institute's criteria for disruptive technologies. Such technologies will:

- Disrupt the status quo – i.e. they will overturn existing hierarchies and may (or may not) lead to different and more democratic hierarchies
- Alter the way people live and work; i.e. they may increase or decrease employment opportunities, change the knowledge and skill sets required for employment, impact on education and alter relationships
- Rearrange value pools; i.e. they influence existing and new commercial activity in ways which redistribute financial gain, generally towards those who are deploying these technologies
- Lead to entirely new products and services; i.e. they will provide types of products and services that have not previously existed

I suppose one could ponder what can come under the heading "Alter the way people live and work", as it seems that in an altruistic way neurotechnology is enhancing the lived experience for those with neurological conditions of varying degrees and providing the medical services with new and enhanced clinical procedures. And the fundamental work on the function of the brain is leading to entirely new understandings and procedures and products that have not previously existed.

Disruption really centres on what may be possible in the future. This chapter opened with Low's call for a "Manhattan Project for the brain", and there has been the European Union Human Brain Project which was a 1billion Euro project that ran from 2015 to 2023, as well as an American project, the BRAIN Initiative that is ongoing in 2025, having started under President Obama. There are companies such as Google and Meta putting considerable funding into developments in neurotechnology including Neuralink Corp. that has developed, as of 2024, implantable brain-computer interfaces, also known as "brain implants". It was founded in 2016 by Elon Musk and a team of eight scientists and engineers, but it was mentioned sceptically by Professor Schultz as it's an invasive technique and so an unlikely possibly future cognitive enhancement for all, although it could possibly be of use for people with severe tetraplegia (loss of control of all four limbs) and Amyotrophic Lateral Sclerosis (ALS).

It is not only the big companies that are interested in developments in neurotechnology. There is currently (2026) a range of startup companies such as Blackrock Neurotech, Paradromics Inc and Synchron which are also looking at techniques to support people like Burrow and Hawking with MND and ALC. There are also startup companies aiming to target specific neurological conditions; for example, Cognito Therapeutics is pioneering using light and sound therapy to slow the progression of Alzheimer's disease (see Figure 8.2), and NeuroPace is developing medical technologies to help reduce epileptic seizures.

So, such a widespread disruption with massive market potential may indeed occur eventually, but it's not likely to be using widespread invasive techniques in the near future due to the caution necessary in such an approach; however, Neurable is working on non-invasive brain-computer DIY kit interfaces for gaming, entertainment and accessibility applications for the hobbyist "biohacker", which might rearrange the value pools in the computer gaming market.

What are the predicted ethical dilemmas of neurotechnology, and what should we do about it?

Should we have the choice to "cure" deafness or blindness – and at what age can a parent's wishes for their child be overruled by medical staff and/or the courts? In our pursuit of progress in neuroscience, is it ethical today to use lab animals, such as rats, as a substitute and a model of the human brain? Or should "brain cells in a dish" techniques as mentioned both by MIT and Imperial College researchers be used instead?

The fact that so much money from private global players such as Google, Meta, Neuralink and the extensive specialised start-up companies raises some profound ethical questions. Where is the line to be drawn between support and therapy on the one hand, and cognitive enhancement on the other? If we can agree to allow medical procedures to alter our brains as a therapy for, say, our affliction of ALS, what does that mean for us as a person, our sense of self, our personal identity? If we are able-bodied but agree against all medical caution to pay for an invasive Brain Computer Interface, what does that mean for us as a human? Will those with enough money be allowed to become part of a neuro-enhanced elite?

These considerations seem in many ways just a fantasy, pondering what is just science fiction; a future that is unlikely and, if at all possible, then long in the future. However, history tells us that ideas that do not seem disruptive now may be so eventually. In 1945, Arthur C Clarke published an article titled "Extraterrestrial Relays" in the British magazine *Wireless World*, proposing the use of geostationary satellites for global radio coverage. Telstar 1, the first commercial communications satellite, was launched on July 10, 1962 - just 17 years between the 'wild idea' and its realisation. With the speed of development in AI and other disruptive technologies, perhaps the possibility of regular and safe Brain Computer Interface procedures might be very much quicker.

As the possible, if currently improbable, developments do actually have an impact on our ideas of humanity, what should we do about it? In Chapter 4, Verity Harding (2024) emphasises that the impacts and ethical considerations of all new technologies, such as the development and deployment of AI, are inherently political processes that require active participation from *all* sectors of society. Everyone, including learners in schools, should take part in the debate, and "you do not have to be an expert to have a valid and important opinion on what your life and society should look and feel like" (Harding 2024, p. ix). The arguments that Harding makes for the successful early scrutiny of the science of IVF and the consequent benefits of the Warnock report which were taken so seriously in the 1980s, could be a perfect mirror for a new current moral debate and questions concerning the future possibilities of neurotechnology - one of the most dynamic and promising fields of our time, capturing the imagination of scientists, doctors, engineers, entrepreneurs, ethicists and the public alike.

Pause for thought

How can we raise these issues with young people of different ages? What role is there for colleagues in science in cooperation with those who teach Ethics or RE?

Make a list of colleagues in your school who might initiate and 'chair' a debate. Maybe it could be part of a Sixth Form 'general studies' debate. Talk to colleagues in your own department, and by 'looking sideways' have a chat with others in the staff room about the issues raised now and what might be possible as neurotechnology develops.

References

Harding, V. (2024) *AI Needs You: How We Can Change AI's Future and Save our Own*. Princeton, NJ: Princeton University Press.

Huh, H., Shin, H., Li, H., Hirota, K., Hoang, C., Thangavel, S., D'Alessandro, M., Feltman, K, A., Sentis, L. and Lu, N. (2025) 'A wireless forehead e-tattoo for mental workload estimation.' *Devic*, **3**, Article 100781.

Kozachkov, L., Slotine, J.-J. and Krotov, D. (2025) 'Neuron - astrocyte associative memory.' *PNAS*, **49**, p. 120. https://doi.org/10.1073/pnas.2417788122

Low, P. (2016) *No Neurozone for Trump*. Huffington Post.

McGeachan, R.I., Meftah, S., Taylor, L.W. et al. (2025) 'Divergent actions of physiological and pathological amyloid-β on synapses in live human brain slice cultures.' *Nature Communications*, **16**, Article 3753. https://doi.org/10.1038/s41467-025-58879-z

Mitchell, P., Lee, S.C., Yoo, P.E., Morokoff, A., Sharma, R.P., Williams, D.L., MacIsaac, C., Howard, M.E., Irving, L., Vrljic, I. and Williams, C. (2023) 'Assessment of safety of a fully implanted endovascular brain-computer interface for severe paralysis in 4 patients: The stentrode with thought-controlled digital switch (SWITCH) study.' *JAMA Neurology*, **80**(3), pp. 270–278.

NICE. (2015) *Repetitive Transcranial Magnetic Stimulation for Depression*. NHS: UK National Institute for Health and Care Excellence. https://www.nice.org.uk/guidance/ipg542 (Accessed 10 June 2025).

Ning, S., Jorfi, M., Patel, S.R., Kim, D.Y. and Tanzi, R.E. (2022) 'Neurotechnological approaches to the diagnosis and treatment of Alzheimer's disease.' *Frontiers in Neuroscience*, March, **16**, Article 854992.

Parkinsons UK. (2025) *Deep Brain Stimulation*. https://www.parkinsons.org.uk/information-and-support/deep-brain-stimulation (Accessed 10 June 2025).

Paşca, S., Kim, J.-I. and Imaizumi, K. (2025) 'Scientists recreate brain circuit in lab for first time.' *Nature*, **642**, pp. 143–153.

Patrick-Krueger, K.M., Burkhart, I. and Contreras-Vidal, J.L. (2025) 'The state of clinical trials of implantable brain – computer interfaces.' *Nature Reviews Bioengineering*, **3**, pp. 50–67. https://doi.org/10.1038/s44222-024-00239-5

Qian, Y., Alhaskawi, A., Dong, Y., Ni, J., Abdalbary, S. and Lu, H. (2024) 'Transforming medicine: Artificial intelligence integration in the peripheral nervous system.' *Frontiers in Neurology*, **15**, Article 1332048. https://doi.org/10.3389/fneur.2024.1332048

Wei, G., Zhang, J., Newman, J.P., Wilson, M.A. (2024) 'Latent learning drives sleep-dependent plasticity in distinct CA1 subpopulations.' *Cell Reports*, **43**(12), Article 115028.

Yuqian, M. et al. (2025) 'Near-infrared spatiotemporal color vision in humans enabled by upconversion contact lenses.' *Cell*, **188**(13), pp. 3375–3388.

Recommended reading

Chaudhary, U. (2025) *Expanding Senses Using Neurotechnology: Volume 2-Brain Computer Interfaces and Their Applications*. Berlin: Springer, Germany. ISBN 103031789903.

NeuroTechX. (2021) *The Neurotech Primer: A Beginner's Guide to Everything Neurotechnology*. Electronic Copy only (All sales go towards supporting NeuroTechX, a nonprofit organisation based out of Canada which helps to support neurotechnology initiatives across the world. Visit www.neurotechx.com to access a free version.

Sanua, D. (2024) *Neurotechnology: Brain-Computer-Interface and the Future of Humanity*. Independently Published. ISBN: 9798328851565.

9 Programmable matter in depth

Introduction

We must come clean straight away and acknowledge that programmable matter is at a very early stage of development and should perhaps be classed as "potentially" disruptive and best described as an "emerging" disruptor. However, this potential for disruption, coupled with what is being achieved in current research and development, has convinced us that it is worth including in our list of ten disruptive technologies.

Programmable matter is based on the understanding of an important idea - properties of materials. The properties of a material describe what that material is like and how it behaves and distinguishes it from other materials. Such properties can be grouped along the following lines - mechanical (e.g. strength, stiffness, hardness, density), electrical (e.g. conductor, semi-conductor, insulator), optical (transparent, translucent, opaque) thermal (insulator, conductor, thermal capacity), etc. Material scientists and chemists can explain the properties of a material in terms of its structure; the way the atoms, ions or molecules in it are arranged and joined to one another. A general principle is that materials with different structures have different properties. This is exemplified by the different structures of the element carbon, although it is composed entirely of carbon atoms. When these atoms are arranged so that each carbon atom is strongly joined to the four carbon atoms surrounding it the substance is diamond, one of the hardest substances known. However, when this arrangement is changed so that each carbon atom is strongly joined to three carbon atoms to form a sheet of carbon atoms with only weak joining between the sheets the substance is graphite, a much softer material, so soft that it is used as a lubricant by a locksmith as oiled locks get clogged up with sticky dust! Different structure, different properties. This idea was taken further by Prof Andre Geim and Prof Kostya Novoselo at Manchester University, who made a material composed of just a single layer of carbon atoms, like the layers in graphite, and produced the substance graphene which has properties different from those of either diamond or graphite. (See Figure 9.1.)

Programmable matter has structures that can be altered by the different way they are 'programmed', thus enabling them to exhibit different properties under different conditions. If you teach D&T, you have probably come across the term "smart" materials. It is important to make a clear distinction between programmable matter and smart materials. Smart materials react passively to stimuli based on their intrinsic properties and do not require to be *programmed* to exhibit this behaviour. Shape memory alloys (metals that return to a pre-set shape when heated)

DOI: 10.4324/9781003602002-10

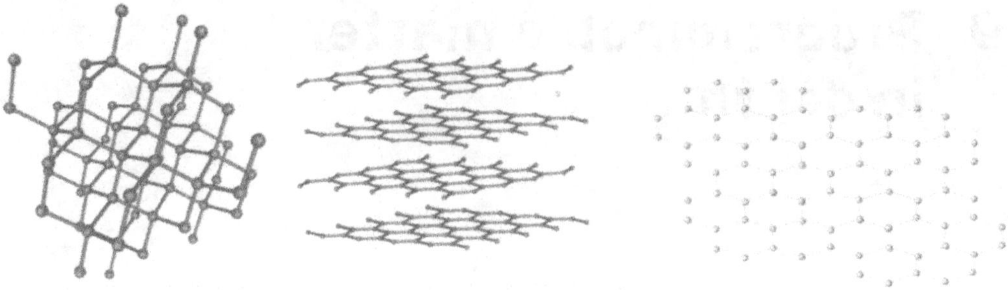

Figure 9.1 Structures of diamond, graphite and graphene

and thermochromic dyes (dyes that change colour in response to a temperature change) are examples of smart materials. In both these examples, the material reacts automatically in response to the change in temperature. Programmable matter, as we shall see, is much more complex and can be programmed to respond in a variety of ways. It is worth noting that in some cases smart materials and programmable matter are used in conjunction with one another.

This chapter is in six parts. The first part will describe two important features of programmable materials with examples. Part two will consider modular approaches to developing programmable matter and part three will look at the development of programmable matter at the molecular level. Part four will evaluate the extent to which potential applications will be disruptive in terms of the McKinsey criteria for disruption, and part five will discuss possible positive and negative effects of this disruption. And lastly, part six will consider the influences of other disruptive technologies on programmable matter.

Two important features of programmable materials

Two important features of programmable materials are that they can change their physical properties – such as shape, stiffness or optical characteristics – in response to external stimuli, which is referred to as ***reconfigurability.*** Also, they can modify their properties or configurations in response to environmental stimuli without external intervention, which is referred to as ***autonomous adaptation***. Here are some examples of both.

Reconfigurability

The Japanese art form origami uses folding of a single sheet of paper to create a wide range of different forms. This arrangement of folds in a single sheet of a material has given rise to materials that can radically change their shape. Such a sheet of material can be ***reconfigured*** by simply changing the angles across the folds in the materials. The programming of the material gives rise to the change in these angles. Hence a compact tightly folded material with little external surface area can be 'opened out' by a programme which changes the fold angles, giving a sheet of material a much larger surface area. And this process is reversible, changing the angle between the folds back to their previous value results in the sheet of material returning to its highly compact form. (See Figure 9.2.)

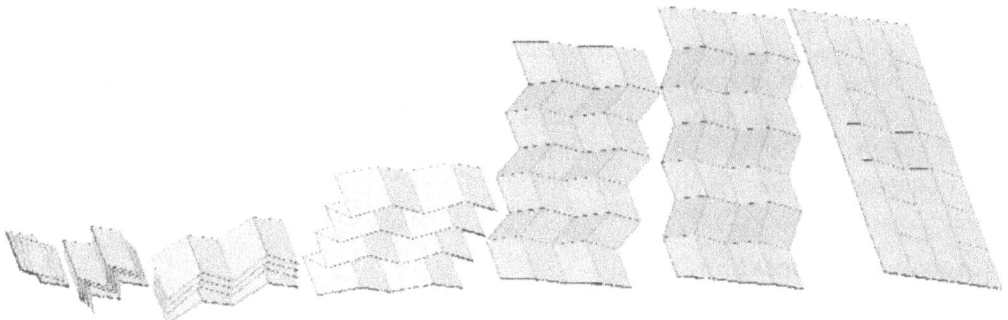

Figure 9.2 Step-by-step unfolding process inspired by origami

This programming of sheet materials with origami-inspired folds has been used in fields as diverse as space exploration and medicine. In 2014, NASA developed solar panels of folded material which use mechanical hinges and motors to unfold the tightly folded materials into large solar arrays. When folded up the panels occupy a very small volume, enabling compact storage during the journey to space, but when opened out the panels offer a large surface area on which to capture sunlight. This is an interesting example of a complete structure being programmable. See Figure 9.3.

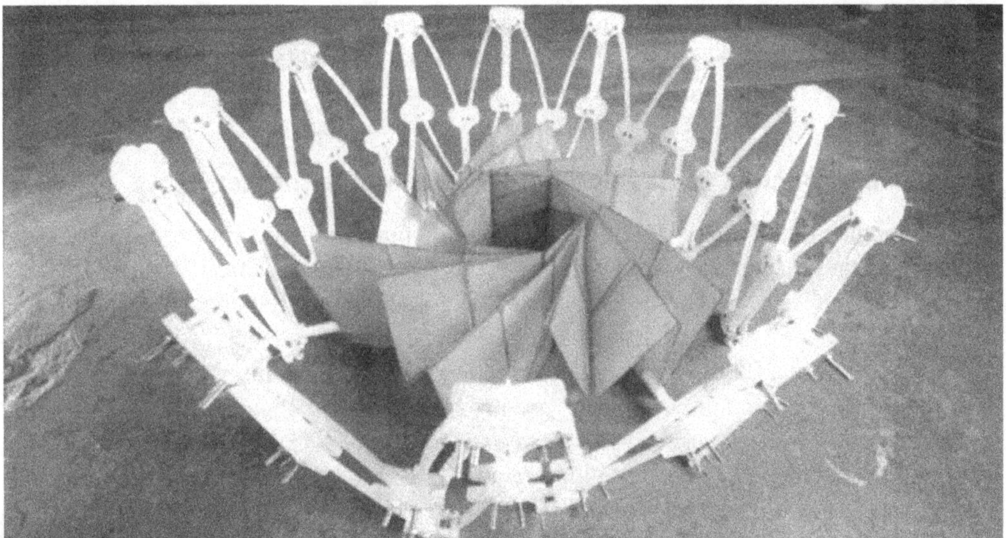

Figure 9.3 The solar panel developed by NASA using origami principles

The use of programmable matter inspired by origami to produce surgical microgrippers provides our example from medicine. As with many programmable matter applications, this is still at the research and development phase (Gultepe et al. 2013). The microgrippers in question are some thousand times smaller than conventional microgrippers and are untethered, unlike the conventional microgrippers which are controlled through a cord operated by a surgeon. The procedure was carried out on a pig, collecting samples from the colon. The positioning of the microgrippers was managed by means of magnetic fields, as was the collecting of the samples. Instead of collecting just a few samples, as is the case with the conventional microgrippers, the size of the microgrippers allowed 1500 microgrippers to be placed in the colon, and then collected and retrieved with samples for testing. The use of such surgical microgrippers in humans is an obvious next step.

Autonomous adaptation

Many researchers have developed soft-bodied robots capable of different ways of moving, allowing them to adapt their movement patterns to different terrains and tasks. A notable recent example of a soft-bodied robot which can move in different ways is a swimming robot inspired by manta rays. It was developed by researchers from North Carolina State University and the University of Virginia (SWNS 2024). Design and technology and biology teachers will recognise that this is a nice example of biomimicry. This robot is capable of swimming both up and down, demonstrating its adaptability and efficiency.

The robot's design emulates the shape and swimming mechanics of manta rays, featuring fins attached to a flexible silicone body. An internal air chamber bends the fins when inflated to mimic the downstroke of a manta's fin movement. The robot achieves a swimming speed of 6.8 body lengths per second. It can manoeuvre through obstacle courses and carry payloads, showcasing its versatility in various aquatic tasks. It is worth noting that the robot is tethered to its power supply, so again we see an advancement that highlights the potential of programmable matter but requires further development.

Modular approaches to developing programmable matter

Programmable matter can be modular, composed of individual units that can join together in different ways, producing variations in structure and behaviour from a common starting point. Researchers at the Computer Science and Artificial Intelligence Lab, Massachusetts Institute of Technology, have developed self-reconfiguring modular robots known as AuxBots (Chin et al. 2023). The individual modules are able to change their shape by both expanding and contracting. When four are grouped together they form a shape similar to a mudskipper and this arrangement can use the modules at each side to act like flippers and move. When seven are grouped together they form a sea turtle shape, and this arrangement uses the two 'flippers' on each side to move. This design enables AuxBots to perform tasks such as traversing uneven surfaces and manoeuvring through confined spaces.

You might be thinking that these examples of programmable matter might be better considered in the section on robotics, but the researchers see each AuxBot module as a piece of programmable matter with behaviour they can programme. It is worth noting that research into programmable matter does often find itself interacting with other disciplines, particularly robotics and nanotechnology. This is a point we will return to in Part Two of the book, when we discuss disruptive technologies as part of a collaborative STEM curricula.

Development of programmable matter at the molecular level

Many complex molecules absorb light from various parts of the electromagnetic spectrum. Indeed, the pattern of such absorption is often used to determine the structure of molecules. The effect of the absorption is minimal, often causing the molecule to rotate or vibrate more vigorously, leaving the molecule itself and its behaviour unchanged. This is not the case for shape-changing molecules. A recent example of a shape-changing molecule is the self-adaptive photochromic (SAP) material developed by Chinese scientists (Sun et al. 2024), drawing inspiration from natural organisms like chameleons and octopi that possess the ability to change colour for concealment. This material can adjust its molecular composition to blend seamlessly into various backgrounds, effectively rendering it invisible to the naked eye. The SAP material consists of a mixture of organic dyes and materials that act as molecular photo switches. Together they rearrange their chemical and structural makeup when exposed to specific wavelengths of light. This rearrangement enables the material to change colour without the need for external power sources or complex electronics. As with many programmable materials, it is their potential applications that are causing interest. These include military camouflage, adaptive architectural coatings and anti-counterfeiting measures. In the military sector, uniforms made from SAP materials could allow personnel to blend into various environments in real time, enhancing stealth operations. In architecture, buildings could adapt their exterior colours to improve energy efficiency or aesthetic appeal. Additionally, SAP materials could be used in anti-counterfeiting technologies by creating packaging that changes colour under specific lighting conditions, making it more difficult to replicate.

Disruption caused by programmable matter

From the outset we have acknowledged that although programmable matter has significant potential to meet McKinsey's four criteria for a disruptive technology, its impact is currently limited due to technical and scalability challenges.

In terms of disrupting the status quo this is very limited at the moment, and in the immediate future it is likely to be partial. One can imagine that as the expansion of space exploration increases the use of origami-inspired solar panels will become more significant. Self-assembling robotics, such as the AuxBot, and reconfigurable devices could drastically change how products are designed and used. If programmable matter becomes commercially viable, it could replace traditional static materials, disrupting industries like manufacturing, electronics and healthcare.

In terms of altering the way people live and work, at the moment programmable matter does not radically alter daily life or work. But programmable matter does have the potential for the following developments: adaptive clothing that changes insulation or style, reconfigurable workspaces that reshape based on user needs to revolutionise office design, medical devices that adapt inside the body to eliminate surgeries for implant adjustments and military and aerospace applications, such as shape-shifting armour and modular drones that enable new battle strategies. We have seen examples in the previous sections of early-stage impact, and although there is significant potential to reshape industries and daily life this is unlikely to be significant for some considerable time.

There has been little rearrangement of value pools in response to developments in programmable matter. Currently they are expensive at the research and development stage, hence they have not replaced traditional materials at scale. But if the promise of programmable materials is realised, then manufacturers of traditional materials (e.g., metals, plastics) may lose market share to companies producing programmable matter-based alternatives for some applications; 3D printing and construction industries could see disruption if self-assembling materials become viable and medical, and electronics sectors may shift towards dynamically reconfigurable products opening up new markets. So whilst at the moment programmable materials are not yet disrupting major industries, in the long term value redistribution is likely.

As most programmable matter research is at an early stage of development, with most focusing on alternatives to existing products and services, there is currently little development of entirely new categories.

If programmable matter reaches mass adoption, it has the potential to be a truly disruptive technology, but current applications fall short of this. To underline the point once again, at the moment programmable matter must be regarded as an "**emerging disruptor**" rather than a fully disruptive technology.

Positive and negative effects of programmable matter

As an "emergent disruptor", programmable matter has yet to have much in the way of either positive or negative effects, although the range of potential applications is wide and at the current stage of development seems to be mainly benign, discounting perhaps some military possibilities. However, it is worth thinking about the way programmable matter might influence the way we think about our world. We live in a material world, and programmable matter has the potential to change the intrinsic nature of many of the materials we use. This potential to have control over the materials we use and by implication the *way* we use them and what we use them *for* puts us in a unique position. Never before in human history have we had such power. Until now we have been limited largely to the materials provided by nature and the use of chemistry to produce new materials that behaved in predictable ways according to their structure. With the advent of programmable matter this has changed. Christopher Preston (2018) has argued, and we think convincingly, that with the advent of programmable matter and other disruptive technologies, we are on the brink of a new era in which we can shape the world in which we live and work in ways never seen before. He calls this new era the Synthetic Age and argues that the decisions we make about how to use this newfound power are crucial for the survival of our species on Planet Earth.

> Making big choices is always hard. Making irrevocable choices for the whole planet is unprecedented but at this point we have changed too much to stand back and do nothing. We need to look at as many of the various options as we can, talk about them, argue about them, investigate and research them as thoroughly as possible.

> Conducting this discussion thoughtfully, fairly and inclusively is perhaps the worthiest and certainly the most important political task of our time [and] is also one that we can no longer shirk.
>
> Preston (2018 p. 173)

As teachers it will be our responsibility to educate young people in schools, colleges and universities to be able to take part in this discussion from an informed position, one in which they can be constructively critical and influence the directions our societies take. It is, he argues, too important to leave to the experts, and we will return to this in Part Two of this book.

The influences of other disruptive technologies on programmable matter

The disruptive technologies we are exploring in this book will all have some influence on the way programmable matter develops in the future. Here are some possibilities:

Additive manufacturing will enable precise fabrication of programmable materials at microscopic and macroscopic scales and support self-assembling structures.

AI will optimise material properties and transformation algorithms through machine learning. It might even suggest possible new programmable materials, similar to how AI is currently used to design possible molecular structures of new drugs to address the problem of drug-resistant bacteria.

Augmented reality can provide real-time visualisation and control over programmable matter transformations and assist in designing and simulating complex material behaviours before physical implementation.

Big data will help analyse vast amounts of material performance data to improve programmable matter design and facilitate predictive modelling for how programmable materials should behave under different conditions.

The Internet of Things will allow programmable matter to be interconnected with other smart devices and so enable remote control and monitoring of programmable materials.

Developments in neurotechnology will enable direct brain-computer interfaces (BCIs) to control programmable matter, which opens possibilities for neuro-responsive materials that change shape or function based on cognitive or neural signals.

Robotics will embrace programmable matter capabilities providing robotic control systems with self-reconfigurable materials.

Developments in synthetic biology may enable the production of living programmable matter through bioengineered organisms.

It is important to remember that all of this will depend very much on the extent to which the current technical problems facing programmable matter can be solved but, if they can be, then wonderful possibilities await, provided we are sensitive to the concerns raised by Christopher Preston.

References

Chin, L., Burns, M., Xie, G. and Russ, D. (2023) 'Flipper style locomotion through strong expanding modular robots.' *IEEE Robotics and Automation Letter*, February, **8**(2), pp. 520–525.

Gultepe, E., Yamanaka, S., Laflin, K.E., Kadam, S., Shim, Y., Olaru, A.V., Limketkai, B., Khashab, M.A., Kalloo, A.N., Gracias, D.H. and Selaru, F.M. (2013) 'Biologic tissue sampling with untethered microgrippers.' *Gastroenterology*, **144**, pp. 691–693.

NASA. (2014) *Solar Power, Origami Style*. https://www.jpl.nasa.gov/news/solar-power-origami-style/ (Accessed July 2025).

Preston, C.J. (2018) *The Synthetic Age Outdesigning Evolution, Resurrecting Species and Reengineering the World*. MA: MIT Press.

Sun, F., Gao, A., Yan, B., Zhang, J., Wang, X., Zhang, H., Dai, D., Zheng, Y., Deng, X. and Wang, D. (2024) 'Self-adaptive photochromism.' *Science Advances*, **10**(45).

SWNS. (2024) *Bizarre 'Swimming Robot' Was Inspired by Manta Ray*. https://nypost.com/2024/12/04/science/bizarre-swimming-robot-was-inspired-by-manta-rays-video/?utm_source=chatgpt.com (Accessed July 2025).

Recommended reading

Hacking Matter: Levitating Chairs, Quantum Mirages, and the Infinite Weirdness of Programmable Atoms by Will McCarthy, Basic Books 2003.

Programmable Matter: World with Controllable Matter by Muhammad Ubair Riaz and Zain Javaid, Lambert Academic Press 2012.

10 Quantum computing in depth

This chapter is in five sections: How does quantum computing work? What is 'quantum advantage'? How could quantum computing be best exploited as it develops for commerce and manufacturing? Researching 'Quantum computing with cold atoms' explained by researchers from the Open University; what are the predicted negative aspects of using quantum computing, and what should we do about it?

As in Chapter 9, which is about programmable matter, we must acknowledge that in looking at quantum computing in 2025 we are once again considering a probable disruptive technology, not one that is currently mainstream. So why is quantum computing on our list of disruptive technologies? In 2025 $44.5 billion is being spent globally on quantum technology by governments. China leads the field with $15.3 billion, Germany spends $5.2 billion, UK $4.3 billion and the US spent just $3.8 Billion (CSIS 2025). In many ways this level of funding reflects the extent of state intervention and the culture of the role of the state in developing new technologies - China's state intervention is high, while the US's expectation of the contribution from commercial enterprise is high.

How does quantum computing work?

Before we consider a quantum computer, how does a conventional computer such as the one that I am using to write this chapter work? You probably have heard of binary numbers - these make up numbers to the base 2 out of 1s and 0s. We are used to base 10, so 132 is two 1s, three 10s and 1 hundred; when I was learning how to add, I used to put HTU at the top of the number columns as going across is a power of 10. Using binary numbers, for 4 digits I should put 16,8,4,2,1 at the top of my number columns as going across each is a power of 2. For example, the binary number 10111 is one 1, one 2, one 4, *no* 8, one 16 = 23 (in base 10).

A current conventional digital computer works by processing information using these binary digits, or bits, which represent data as either a 0 or a 1. Think of a light switch: it is either on or off. These bits are manipulated through millions or even billions of similar tiny electronic switches called transistors, which turn on and off to perform calculations. The computer's Central Processing Unit (CPU) acts as the 'brain', executing instructions from programmes by carrying out basic operations like addition, subtraction, and logic comparisons. Data and instructions are stored in easily accessible memory (RAM), which provides quick access to

DOI: 10.4324/9781003602002-11

information, while long-term storage devices like Solid State Drives (SSDs) hold data permanently. The computer follows a cycle where it fetches an instruction, decodes what needs to be done, executes the operation and then stores the result if necessary. This process happens incredibly fast, allowing big computers to perform billions of calculations per second. Software, which consists of coded instructions, tells the computer hardware what to do, enabling the common applications we are used to, such as web browsing, gaming and data analysis.

How is quantum computing so different?

Figure 10.1 Flipping a coin

Imagine you are flipping a coin, such as in Figure 10.1. Eventually it will come down on either heads or tails. But what is it when it is spinning? You could say that it is both heads and tails, or it is in a "superposition" of both heads and tails at the same time. Quantum computing is fundamentally different from classical digital computing in how it processes and stores information. As we have just discussed, traditional computers use bits 0 or 1, which function like tiny switches that are either on or off. In contrast, quantum computers use quantum bits or 'qubits', which, a bit like the spinning coin, can exist in a superposition of both 0 and 1 at the same time. So, this means that while a classical bit can only hold one state at a time, a qubit can hold multiple states simultaneously, vastly increasing the computational power. This strange idea takes some getting used to. And there's more! Qubits can be 'entangled', which means that the state of one qubit is directly linked to another, no matter how far apart they are.

Let's pause and try to get our heads around these two ideas. "Multiple states simultaneously" means that the two (or more) states can be superimposed on each other and become another valid quantum state. Just like the flipped and spinning coin, in the quantum world it could be both "heads and tails" at the same time. Well, of course, we are not talking about things you can hold in your hand like coins but about atomic particles that obey different and counterintuitive rules. Before any measurement takes place, the quantum state can be in a superposition of two or more classical states – the classical coin can only land heads or tails, but a "quantum coin" has a probability of being either heads or tails after measurement. So, superposition is the idea that these small particles can exist in multiple states at the same time. For example, a particle can be in two different places at the same time or 'spin' up and down simultaneously. This principle is hugely important and is at the heart of the search for a practical quantum computer, and unlike a classical computer (however powerful), it will allow a quantum computer to perform many calculations at the same time.

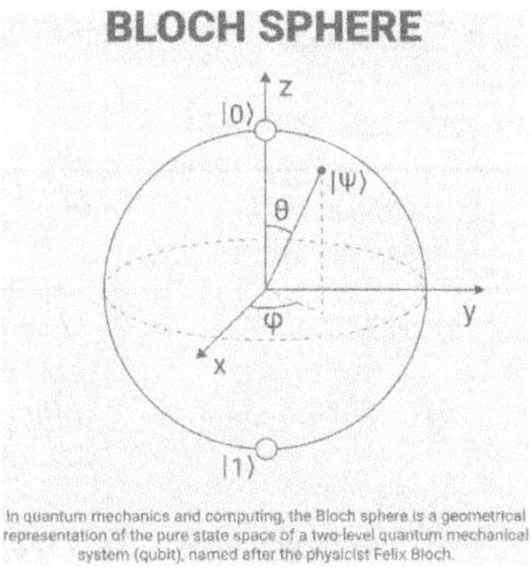

Figure 10.2 A Bloch Sphere

Figure 10.2 is a diagram called a Bloch Sphere. The two poles are a bit like a conventional computer; it is either 1 or 0. However, in contrast, a qubit can lie anywhere on the surface of the sphere. It can be anywhere between 1 and 0 in a superposition of the two, and the information is stored in a different way – like a sort of spinning coin. Quantum computers store and process information in a different way than classical computers, so it is a very different and new way of computing.

And what about "entanglement"? This is another difficult idea to grasp as we don't encounter it in our everyday life. Entanglement is where two particles, such as two electrons, influence each other so that their quantum states become dependent on each other, no matter how far apart they are. When they are linked in such a way that we can't think of them as separate systems, quantum systems are said to be "entangled". When two quantum objects, such as the electrons, are entangled, if you observe or measure one, the other will have a linked behaviour, no matter how far away it is. So, if you had an entangled quantum system and observed the one electron to be in the "spin up" state then its entangled partner would always be in the "spin down" state, wherever it is. This is not a new idea. Over 100 years ago Albert Einstein so hated even the very idea of entanglement that he called it "spooky action at a distance".

These two phenomena, when put to use by qubits, means that quantum computers can potentially be extremely fast as qubits can work in parallel. Putting the concept of multiple states together with the concept of entanglement is the basis of extremely fast quantum computers that can solve complex problems – such as factoring large numbers or simulating molecules – at speeds far beyond what even the most powerful current supercomputers can achieve.

As we outlined earlier, eight bits is enough for a classical computer using binary numbers to represent any number between 0 and 255. But just eight qubits are enough for a quantum computer to represent every number between 0 and 255 at the same time. And a few hundred entangled qubits (if they could be made to work together without errors) would be enough to represent more numbers than there are atoms in the universe – yep, the universe!

There are many potential designs of an effective quantum computer, using different particles such as photons and ions as well as electrons. But although development is accelerating, in 2025 all quantum computers are still at the "work in progress" stage. The possible benefits are obviously huge in terms of computing speed and power, but some of the current practical drawbacks mean that there are still considerable hurdles to overcome. The pros and cons of different approaches are set out in Table 10.1.

Table 10.1 Pros and cons of using different types of qubits

Hardware and qubit type	*How it works*	*Operating temperature*	*Pros*	*Cons*
Superconducting	Uses superconducting circuits-junctions that carry electricity without resistance	~10–20 millikelvin (mK) Super Cold	Very fast; already used by big companies like Google and IBM	Needs super-cold fridge. Decoheres in microseconds; fabrication variability
Trapped Ion	Ions, atoms with electric charge trapped in an electromagnetic field and controlled by lasers	Very cold – few millikelvin (laser-cooled)	Very accurate; remembers info-long coherence times (seconds); natural qubit uniformity	Slow to work; lasers are tricky to manage
Photonic	Uses polarised light particles (photons) as qubits	Room temperature	Doesn't need to be cold; great for sending info through fibre	Hard to make 'light talk to light'; not great for doing lots of quantum maths yet
Spin Qubits (Silicon)	Uses electrons trapped in silicon and their spin (like a little magnet)	Very cold ~100 millikelvin	Long coherence times; CMOS-chip compatible; potential for large-scale integration	Hard to build and control exactly
Topological	Based on exotic quasiparticles (e.g., Majorana fermions) (like magical knots) that are hard to mess up	Super Cold Theoretical: ~10 millikelvin	Inherently protected from many types of errors; potentially high stability	Still experimental; no large-scale demonstrations yet (2025)
Neutral Atom	Uses arrays of atoms held in place by lasers; they link to each other using special excited states	Ultra cold ~Few microkelvin (↔K	Scalable architecture; long coherence times	Technology still emerging; precise control is difficult
NV Centres in Diamond	Uses the spin states of electrons in nitrogen-vacancy (NV) defects – atomic holes – in diamond	Room temperature to cryogenic (~4 K)	Room-temp operation possible; long coherence times in pure diamond structure	Hard to build many of them the same; needs lasers to read and write info; optical readout challenges
Donor Qubits (e.g., Phosphorus in Silicon)	Uses spin of donor atoms implanted in silicon	~100 millikelvin	Long coherence times; silicon-based; potential for integration with classical chips	Tiny single-atom placement is challenging; tricky to control; difficult readout and gate control

Building a practical quantum computer is extremely challenging because qubits are highly sensitive to their environment and can lose their quantum state. As we have already discussed, qubits need to stay in a delicate state called superposition to perform their powerful calculations. However, even very tiny disturbances from the environment - like heat, vibrations or electromagnetic waves - can cause qubits to lose this superposition state and they collapse into a particular state - "either heads or tails" - this collapse is called decoherence and leads to errors in calculations. We have already explained that the spinning coin is just a metaphor for superposition, as such big objects don't behave like small molecules or electrons or photons. The paradox of decoherence being applied to large objects such as coins is perhaps best illustrated by the well-known idea of Schrödinger's cat, the famous thought experiment in quantum mechanics as shown in Figure 10.3. A bit like a coin that could be considered as both heads and tails when it's still spinning in the air, the idea was taken to an absurd level by considering a cat inside a closed box that might be poisoned or maybe not poisoned so it can be considered both alive and dead at the same time until someone opens the box to *observe* it and finds out. The observation or measurement of the quantum system settles the issue - just like opening the box to see the fate of the cat. Well, maybe. What we can say is that qubits exist in a superposition of states until they interact with their surroundings, causing decoherence and collapsing into a definite state, and as Schrödinger joked, the cat only becomes either alive or dead once it is observed.

Figure 10.3 Schrodinger's cat thought experiment illustrating quantum superposition - and measurement of the quantum state by opening the box - Renaldo la Vulpo

But how do you observe *any* answer if the quantum state easily collapses? A quantum measurement means obtaining information from qubits by collapsing their quantum information into a practical answer or result in a controlled way. Just like Schrödinger's cat, any measurement affects the outcome state of a qubit, so the information needs to be extracted carefully to obtain a correct result of the computations to solve problems effectively. This is a key problem as uncontrolled loss of superposition in qubits due to external disturbances causing errors, and it is what makes quantum computing so challenging.

So, controlling decoherence is crucial to keeping qubits in their quantum state long enough to perform useful computations. As is clear from Table 10.1, to try to prevent decoherence due to "noise" - heat and vibration etc - in the system, most quantum computer designs are kept at extremely cold temperatures, close to absolute zero. Also, special error correction methods are used to try to fix problems caused by decoherence. But despite these efforts, decoherence is still a big challenge in building stable quantum computers. If researchers can control decoherence better, quantum computers will become much more powerful and reliable.

All computers, whether they are conventional like the desktop I am using to write this chapter or not, have software, computer programmes that work with the hardware – the computer itself. Quantum computing is similar.

As we have seen in Table 10.1, quantum computers use different techniques to create qubits based on different designs and constructed in different ways and consequently there are different sorts of software layers needed to link the quantum computer processor to a user. The different hardware, linked to the associated specific software for special error correction and leading to how it is possible for the quantum computer to be used, is called the "quantum stack" by the UK National Computing Centre; Table 10.2 illustrates such a quantum stack.

As we can see, from left to right in Table 10.2, the various types of quantum hardware need the necessary error correcting software, which enables the quantum computer to be used for a particular task. It is a general diagram emphasising the various stages in the process, so the different 'error correction' software companies listed on the right are not intended to be linked one-to-one to specific Qubit Types listed on the left.

Table 10.2 The 'Quantum Stack' – From hardware to uses

Stages in Quantum Computing →

Some hardware and qubit types 2025	*Error correction needed*	*Some 'error correction' software companies 2025*	*Some possible uses for quantum computing*
Superconducting		Quantinuum	
Trapped Ion		IBM	
Photonic	As in shown in Table 10.1 some of the hardware types are due to their	Microsoft (Azure Quantum + Q#)	Precise molecular modelling so enabling the discovery of new materials and medical drugs.
Spin Qubits (Silicon)	construction better at reducing 'decoherence'	Riverlane	
Topological	that causes errors – but software 'algorithms' also significantly help with the error correction	Classiq	Tackling complicated planning such as design and manufacturing required by aerospace and automotive businesses.
Neutral Atom	.	Q-CTRL	Network efficiencies for city traffic schemes,
NV Centres in Diamond		QuEra Computing	and for telecommunications and energy distribution requirements.
Donor Qubits (e.g., Phosphorus in Silicon)		HQS Quantum Simulations	

What is 'quantum advantage'?

At this stage in the development of quantum computing, what is its potential, and could it be used instead of a conventional computer for tasks in industry and commerce? Perhaps the best comparison is to contrast a quantum computer with a conventional "Supercomputer", the current fastest and most "powerful" conventional computer. In 2025, the leading Supercomputer is probably "Frontier", the HPE Cray supercomputer housed at Oak Ridge National Laboratory in the USA, shown in Figure 10.4.

> This machine is capable of performing more than a quintillion [a million raised to the power of five - that's 1 followed by 18 zeros] calculations per second, has held the top spot on the Top 500 list since June 2022. Frontier's impressive performance is underpinned by its architecture. . . . Frontier's infrastructure is equally impressive, boasting 74 HPE Cray EX cabinets, each weighing over 8,000 pounds, and utilising 90 miles of networking cables. The supercomputer's storage capabilities are equally formidable, with the Orion system providing 700 petabytes of capacity and peak write speeds exceeding 35 terabytes per second.
>
> (McCann 2024)

Figure 10.4 Frontier 4.0 Supercomputer - Oak Ridge National Laboratory (Carlos Jones)

What could beat that speed - 10^{18} calculations every second? The capacity numbers are so big too - petabytes, terabytes - it is difficult to comprehend what that means. It is saying that the storage of Frontier can hold the equivalent of around 350,000 billion pages of printed text or approximately 750 billion songs.

In May 2025,

> Researchers in China have unveiled a 105-qubit quantum processor that can solve in minutes a quantum computation problem that would take billions of years using the world's most powerful classical supercomputer. . . . Jian-Wei Pan and Xiaobu Zhu at the University of Science and Technology of China (USTC) in Hefei and colleagues have shown that their new Zuchongzhi 3.0 processor consisting of 105 qubits, can complete in minutes a calculation that they estimate would take Frontier billions of years using the best classical algorisms currently available. . . . The USTC team now plans to demonstrate quantum error-correction to combine multiple physics qubits into a single "logical qubit" that is robust to errors
>
> (Wogan 2025)

Despite the extraordinarily impressive speed of Frontier, it would take billions of years to do a specific problem that a quantum computer can do in minutes! This quantum computer lead over a classical machine is called "Quantum Advantage", and the claim of supremacy is indeed impressive. Quantum computers encode and solve problems in a completely different way to a classic computer, so that they can be very efficiently solved. We should be careful not to simply think of them as just solving a "classical algorithm" faster, since they tackle problems completely differently (see Table 10.2).

But is this a 'fair' comparison? The particular problem posed for Frontier is one that shows the "quantum advantage" of a Quantum computer in the best light. The problem chosen is known as random circuit sampling (RCS). It works like this – a big quantum circuit is built, and the circuit is connected randomly many times, and the outputs are recorded as a bitstring (0s and 1s). The next stage is to see if the computer gives the right mix of answers matching what quantum theory predicts. For a normal classical computer, predicting the outcomes is very difficult and slow, but quantum computers are built to exploit this type of problem very quickly. So, it is indeed a "quantum advantage" to pose a problem tailor-made for quantum computers.

What are current quantum computers like now, and what will be possible in the future?

Back to the future

In 1962 there were no desktop computers. A computer filled a room. If you needed to use a computer, it was necessary to take the computer programmes – set out line by line – to the computer centre on punched tape or on punched cards. In 2025 a supercomputer such as Frontier fills a room, maybe several rooms (see Figures 10.4 and 10.5) – and to use it you need to ensure your software can run on it. In 2025 a quantum computer with its extensive cooling apparatus and cabling fills a room – maybe several rooms – and the error correction and software need to be specific to the qubits used (see Table 10.2). But will there ever be a desktop quantum computer? Unlikely, but "never say never". Qubits using photons or electrons in nitrogen vacancy

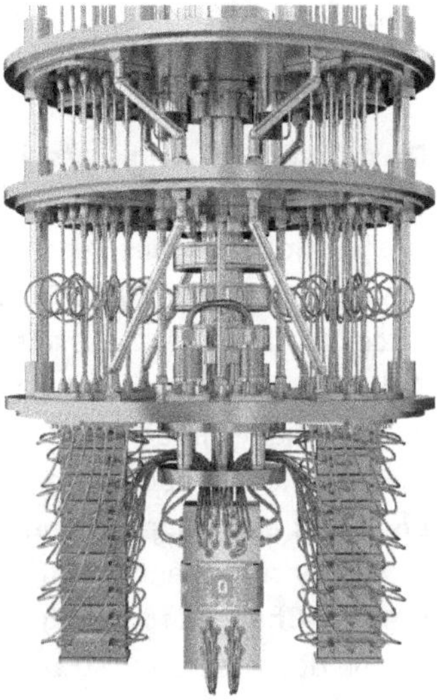

Figure 10.5 Left, 1963 ICT 1301 computer; Right, Advanced quantum computing hardware (Mathias Weil)

"atomic holes" in diamonds could potentially operate at room temperature, but that is still very much in development, and cooling is currently still necessary (see Table 10.1).

A quantum internet?

Very fast computation speeds from quantum computers need fast delivery to users who might be far away from the computer itself. In July 2024:

> Three new ways for generating quantum entanglement between two nodes in a network have been developed independently by teams in China, Europe and the US. The research, which allows distant quantum memories to exchange quantum information, may bring us a step closer to a quantum version of the Internet in which photons travelling down standard optical fibres would entangle spatially separated quantum computers. The delicate nature of quantum information means it does not travel well. A quantum internet therefore needs devices known as quantum repeaters to swap entanglement between qubits at intermediate points. . . . short coherence time is problematic because entanglement cannot be used to transfer information unless the entangled state remains coherent long enough for . . . information to travel down a classical channel and confirm the success of the entangling operation.
>
> (Wogan 2024)

How could quantum computing be best exploited as it develops for commerce and manufacturing?

It is likely that quantum computers will be the next generation of "supercomputers". What Frontier is used for now, quantum computers will be doing in the future but tackling even more complex problems at even faster speeds by exploiting the "quantum advantage". For example:

Drug Discovery and Materials Science: Quantum computers can simulate the behaviour of molecules and materials, accelerating the development of new drugs and materials with specific properties.

Financial Modelling and Risk Analysis: Quantum computers can be used for complex financial models, risk assessment and the detection of fraud.

Artificial Intelligence and Machine Learning: (See Chapter 6.) Quantum computing could potentially speed up the training of ever more sophisticated AI models and improve the efficiency of machine learning algorithms.

Logistics and Supply Chain Optimisation: Quantum computers can help optimise logistics, supply chains and manufacturing processes by solving complex organisation problems.

Climate Change Modelling: Quantum computers could help simulate complex climate models and develop better strategies for mitigating climate change.

Other Potential Applications: Quantum computers could also be used for 'blue sky' research in science and mathematics, for example simulating quantum systems and factoring large numbers.

These practical everyday science and commercial uses of quantum computing illustrate what researchers are striving to achieve, which maybe points out the rather sterile quantum advantage example as shown by the RCS task set by the University of Science and Technology of China (USTC).

In order to show what some researchers are doing to perfect quantum computing, we are very grateful to Dr Silvia Bergamini and Dr Calum MacCormick of the Open University, who show how the many ideas discussed in this chapter come together in their work. They are using "cold atoms" to construct a quantum computer, which they explain in the following.

Quantum computing with cold atoms

Expert contribution from Dr Silvia Bergamini and Dr Calum MacCormick of The Open University

Even though modern supercomputers such as Frontier 4.0 are incredibly powerful, there are still problems they cannot solve efficiently. One example comes from encryption algorithms that protect our banking information during transactions. These are based on the simple idea that while it's easy to multiply two large prime numbers to make a new number, it is extremely difficult to reverse that process, that is, to find the prime factors of a very large number. The basic method to solve this problem is well-known (you could, in theory, just try every pair of numbers) - but even the best methods are unfeasibly inefficient and slow. As long ago as the 1980s, it was discovered that a computer that used quantum mechanics could solve the factoring problem quickly - quickly enough to wreck the security of the internet. It is now known there are many problems that are difficult for classical computers, but "easy" for quantum computers, and we say there is a "quantum advantage".

Quantum physics gives us new tools for computing, superposition and entanglement. Superposition allows a qubit (the basic unit of a quantum computer which stores information) to exist in a mix of 0 and 1, enabling far more information to be stored and processed than with classical bits. Entanglement links qubits so that information is shared across them in a uniquely quantum way. These features give quantum algorithms their power, but they are also extremely fragile, and this fragility increases as quantum computers scale up.

Quantum computing is steadily advancing from foundational research towards real-world applications. Today's quantum processors feature hundreds to thousands of qubits that can perform complex computations, but they still suffer from high levels of noise and operational errors. Multiple hardware platforms are being explored, including superconducting qubits, trapped ions, neutral atoms and photonic systems. Each offers unique strengths in terms of "fidelity" (a measure of the accuracy of a quantum operation), "scalability" (the ability to extend the platform to many qubits) and control. While no universal standard has emerged, the steady improvements in logic gate accuracy, system stability and improved architectural design continue to push the field of quantum computing forward.

Researchers have demonstrated early forms of quantum advantage and quantum error correction protocols in carefully designed tasks (see Figure 10.4 and Table 10.2), marking key theoretical and experimental milestones. Despite this progress, however, we have not yet (2025) reached the stage where quantum computing solves a general scientific problem or an everyday task that a classical computer could not solve.

Quantum computing uses algorithms and ways of processing that are very different from classical computing, and this key difference has the potential to solve complex problems in seconds, revolutionising medicine and discovering new physics, and it could even change the way we make decisions. Hybrid quantum-classical algorithms – combining classical bit computers with qubit quantum computers – are being tested in various fields such as quantum chemistry, materials science, optimisation and machine learning, where quantum systems may eventually outperform classical supercomputers in these very useful areas, rather than the highly specific RCS tasks (see Figure 10.4 and the description).

As quantum computers need special conditions such as being kept very cold or contain complex and delicate laser systems, their use, like that of the very big classic supercomputers today, will be by remote access. That access to quantum hardware is expanding through cloud-based platforms like the IBM quantum, which also boasts that:

> In 2029, we will deliver a system that accurately runs 100 million gates on 200 logical qubits – unlocking the first viable path to realising the full power of quantum computing.
>
> (IBM 2025)

This will also include QuEra's "Aquila" (2025) (an analogue computer) and "Gemini" (2025) (a gate-based computer).

Global investment in quantum technologies continues to grow worldwide, but many significant challenges remain; scaling to millions of qubits, implementing better error correction for the robust management of errors and demonstrating its real-world value and impact.

Despite these challenges, momentum is building. Quantum computing is no longer seen as a niche area of physics, but as an emerging technology for the 21st century, like classical computing was in the last century. While the timeline to achieve full-scale, fault-tolerant quantum computers remains uncertain, the progress is fast, suggesting that quantum advantage in some practical problems is a matter of "when", not "if".

Figure 10.6 Dr Silvia Bergamini and Dr Calum MacCormick (Open University) showing part of their laser cooling apparatus

At the Open University, we work in cold atom-based quantum computing, a powerful and flexible approach towards scalable, fault-tolerant quantum computers and we show our laser cooling equipment in Figure 10.6. While superconducting circuits and trapped ions have dominated early development (see Table 10.1), neutral atoms offer unique advantages in architecture, fidelity (accuracy of a quantum operation) and adaptability.

In cold atom quantum computing, we cool atoms with lasers to just a tiny fraction of a degree above absolute zero. This slows the atoms down, making them easier to control with high precision. After the atoms are slowed down, we use very tightly focused laser beams (like "optical tweezers") to trap individual atoms in specific positions; it's like holding very tiny "marbles" in place using beams of light – Figure 10.7a is an artist impression of this. Currently, the atoms can be arranged one by one into programmable arrays with hundreds or thousands of trapping sites, but this could be extended to millions of sites, provided we keep the noise (like heat, vibrations or electromagnetic waves) under control. This ability to scale up the number of sites and to dynamically configure the qubit layout before any computation offers significant flexibility, thus making cold atoms a strong contender for handling complex quantum algorithms and creating large-scale systems.

Each atom becomes a qubit by using two of its internal energy levels to represent the 0 and 1 of basis states for encoding the qubit of information. These energy states are incredibly stable, giving cold atoms long "memory" (coherence) times.

To make the atoms "talk" to each other, which is needed for quantum logic gates, they are briefly laser excited into special high-energy states called Rydberg states. When in this state, an atom strongly interacts with nearby atoms. Shining laser light on specific individual atoms allows precise control over which atoms interact, enabling 'entanglement' (see the first section of this chapter) and quantum gate operations.

Altogether, this system is highly controllable and gives long coherence time (a measure of how long a qubit can maintain its quantum state). These atoms are highly isolated from their environment; they can preserve information longer than many other qubit types (see Table 10.1). While challenging to build, these cold atom platforms, such as Figure 10.7b, are highly promising for building large, flexible quantum computers.

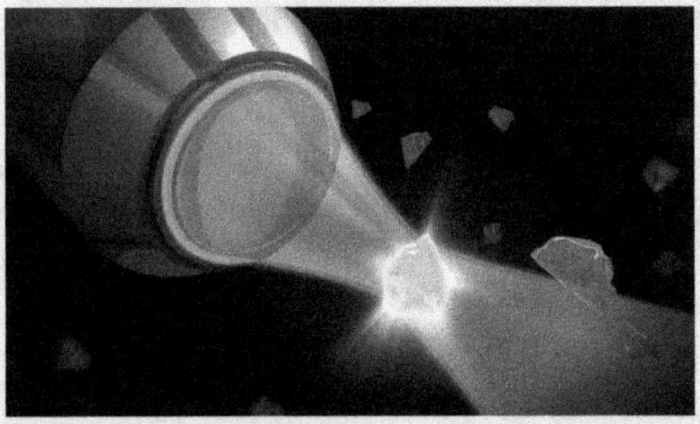

Figure 10.7a Laser cooling - artists' impression - Coherent (2025)

Figure 10.7b Laser cooling rig in operation

When creating quantum computer algorithms, cold atom systems are particularly well-matched to so-called 'NISQ' (Noisy Intermediate-Scale Quantum) algorithms, which are designed for the imperfect quantum hardware available today (2025). Specific algorithms like quantum optimisation algorithms, quantum simulations and quantum many body dynamics have been tested on cold atom platforms to explore problems such combinatorial optimisation and quantum chemistry. Because cold atoms allow flexible connectivity between qubits and their real-time reconfiguration, they are ideally suited to implement these problem-specific algorithms efficiently.

Despite these strengths, there are challenges: quantum computing depends on maintaining the purity of the quantum state of the qubits, but the purity is incredibly difficult to sustain. The problem only grows worse as the number of qubits increases. Atom loss and gate errors remain obstacles, especially as systems scale up. The lasers needed to trap and manipulate atoms must operate with extreme precision, and noise - thermal or electromagnetic fluctuations - can degrade performance. To overcome these issues, cold atom physicists are exploring how to reduce laser noise, improve cooling techniques and the atom-by-atom rearrangement strategies and create hybrid quantum architectures that combine cold atoms with other technologies such as photonics or superconductors (see Table 10.1).

Both academic groups and quantum startups are driving innovation in this area. Companies like QuEra, Pasqal and Infleqtion (2025) are building cold atom processors based on insights from pioneering labs at Harvard, MIT and other institutions worldwide.

What are the predicted negative aspects of using quantum computing, and what should we do about it?

As mentioned by Drs Bergamini and MacCormick, when you use the internet to buy something on Amazon or check your bank account or use information (like your credit card number), it is encrypted, turning it into a code that only the store or bank can decrypt to see the real information. This keeps hackers from stealing your money or data in transit. Similarly, applications (apps) like WhatsApp, iMessage or Signal use end-to-end encryption, which means that your messages are scrambled before they leave your phone, and only the person you're chatting with can unscramble them. Even the app itself can't read your messages. It goes further; for example, when you log in to a website your password isn't stored directly – it's stored as a "cryptographic hash", so even if someone hacks the database, they can't see your actual password. This is particularly important for "cloud storage" of data. When you store a password online, they don't store your <u>actual</u> password; instead, they store a "hash" – it's like a fingerprint of your password so a hacker gets the fingerprint, not the original. It's like putting your handprint on a piece of paper to prove it's you – but you're not handing over your entire hand!

I am sure that you have noticed (even checked on!) the little "lock" icon in your browser's address bar that means the site is using Hyper Text Transfer Protocol Secure (HTTPS), which encrypts everything you send and receive so no one can see what you're looking at, even on a public Wi-Fi network, and you can confidently use your credit card to buy goods and services such as theatre tickets.

All this is good news as your information is kept secret, and no one can eavesdrop – right?

Well, you might have already realised that the speed and versatility of quantum computers mean they have the potential to break current encryption methods. In fact, code breaking is probably the reason so much state money has been allocated to decryption. The early programmable machines at Bletchley Park in the UK that were able to crack the supposedly impregnable Nazis' "Enigma Code" during World War II – itself a coding machine – is now celebrated as a remarkable achievement. In time of war, knowing an enemy's intentions is paramount.

Let's consider another scenario. A terrorist cell is planning a massive attack on the underground in London or the subway in New York using a biological weapon. They are using Signal to coordinate the plot and due to the nature of the app, no one can eavesdrop on what is being planned. Is it ethical in these circumstances to 'tap' into those conversations, or should <u>all</u> conversations be equally protected?

Pause for thought

What is your opinion of the State looking at e-mails? You might like to write down at this point what both you and your colleagues might think.

In 2022/23, the countries of Australia, Ecuador, Georgia, India, Japan, Jordan, New Zealand, UK, USA and Singapore signed a communique:

> We, the undersigned, support strong encryption, which plays a crucial role in protecting personal data, privacy, intellectual property, trade secrets and cyber security. It also serves a vital purpose in repressive states to protect journalists, human rights defenders and other vulnerable people, as stated in the 2017 resolution of the UN Human Rights Council. Encryption is an existential anchor of trust in the digital world, and we do not support counter productive and dangerous approaches that would materially weaken or limit security systems.
>
> Particular implementations of encryption technology, however, pose significant challenges to public safety, including to highly vulnerable members of our societies, like sexually exploited children. We urge industry to address our serious concerns where encryption is applied in a way that wholly precludes any legal access to content. We call on technology companies to work with governments to take the following steps, focused on reasonable, technically feasible solutions:
>
> - Embed the safety of the public in system designs, thereby enabling companies to act against illegal content and activity effectively with no reduction to safety, and facilitating the investigation and prosecution of offences and safeguarding the vulnerable;
> - Enable law enforcement access to content in a readable and usable format where an authorisation is lawfully issued, is necessary and proportionate, and is subject to strong safeguards and oversight; and
> - Engage in consultation with governments and other stakeholders to facilitate legal access in a way that is substantive and genuinely influences design decisions. . . .
>
> We are committed to working with industry to develop reasonable proposals that will allow technology companies and governments to protect the public and their privacy, defend cyber security and human rights and support technological innovation. While this statement focuses on the challenges posed by end-to-end encryption, that commitment applies across the range of encrypted services available, including device encryption, custom encrypted applications and encryption across integrated platforms.
>
> (UK Government 2023)

It is probably an inevitable consequence of the time it takes for countries to jointly agree on action that by the time such a communique is signed, the 'new' technology has moved on. Asking technology companies to weaken their end-to-end encryption, thus enabling "governments and other stakeholders to facilitate legal access", opens the door not only to the governments that signed the communique but to terrorist hackers too. But if a quantum computer can crack the encryption, it raises two other dilemmas. First, not all countries will be able to initially afford quantum computers, and of those that can afford such machines it will be a 21st-century competitive race between superpowers as was in the "space race" on the 1960s. Second, a quantum computer can be used to crack formerly impenetrable codes, but a quantum computer could be used to make new impenetrable codes.

I may be unduly pessimistic about the motivation for governments' continued funding of quantum computing. Its power to be better in speed and action than the very best current Supercomputer could bring many benefits to society. If it could indeed "help simulate complex climate models and develop better strategies for mitigating climate change", for that alone all the funding would be worthwhile.

References

Aquila. (2025) https://www.quera.com/aquila (Accessed 31 July 2025).

Coherent. (2025) https://www.coherent.com/news/glossary/laser-cooling (Accessed 31 July 2025).

CSIS. (2025). *Centre for Strategic and International Studies: Announced Public Investments in Quantum Technology by Country*, 3 February. https://www.csis.org/blogs/perspectives-innovation/quick-take-quantum-technology-global-competition (Accessed 15 March 2025).

Gemini. (2025) https://www.quera.com/gemini (Accessed 31 July 2025).

IBM Quantum. (2025) https://www.ibm.com/quantum (Accessed 31 July 2025).

Infleqtion. (2025) https://infleqtion.com (Accessed 31 July 2025).

McCann, K. (2024) *Top 10 Supercomputers*. Kirsten McCann, AI Magazine. https://aimagazine.com/articles/top-10-supercomputers (Accessed 28 May 2025).

Pasqal. (2025) https://www.pasqal.com (Accessed 31 July 2025).

Quera. (202) https://www.quera.com (Accessed 31 July 2025).

UK Government. (2023) Policy paper. *International Statement: End-to-End Encryption and Public Safety: International Statement Calling on Tech Companies to Ensure End-to-End Encryption Is Not Implemented in a Way That Erodes Public Safety*. https://www.gov.uk/government/publications/international-statement-end-to-end-encryption-and-public-safety/international-statement-end-to-end-encryption-and-public-safety-accessible-version (Accessed 5 June 2025).

Wogan, T. (2024) *Entanglement Reaches City-Sized Networks*. Tim Wogan, Physics World, July. London: Institute of Physics.

Wogan, T. (2025) *Chinese Quantum Computer Extends Lead Over Classical Machines*. Tim Wogan, Physics World, May. London: Institute of Physics.

Recommended reading

Coecke, B. and Gogioso, S. (2022) *Quantum in Pictures*. London: Quantinium. ISBN 978-1-7392147-1-5.

Pantheon Space Academy. (2023) *Quantum Computing Explained for Beginners: The Science, Technology, and Impact*. New York: Pantheon Global Publishing LLC.

Whurley and Smith, F.E. (2023) *Quantum Computing For Dummies*. NJ: John Wiley & Sons.

Wong, T.G. (2022) *Introduction to Classical and Quantum Computing*. Omaha Nebraska: Rooted Grove Publishers.

Also these videos

1) Open University/BBC partnership. BBC ideas. https://www.bbc.co.uk/videos/cgrjjyxeq92o How will quantum technologies change the world? – BBC Calum MaCormick, Silvia Bergamini This is a short video created with the BBC that discusses quantum computing and other quantum technologies. Voiceover by Jim Al-Khalili.
2) Open Learn "Introduction to Quantum Computing". https://www.open.edu/openlearn/science-maths-technology/introduction-quantum-computing?active-tab=description-tab Introduction to quantum computing | OpenLearn – Open University Silvia Bergamini, Calum MacCormick, Christine Leach. This is a short online taster course on quantum computing. On the level 3 quantum Physics module on Quantum computing, students program the IBM quantum.

11 Robotics in depth

Introduction

Of all the disruptive technologies beyond AI that you think might have an immediate impact on your students when they leave school, perhaps it is the proliferation of robots that comes to mind. Will a robot take my job?

> For companies looking to save money, the idea of replacing a human with a computer and robot is enticing. Compared to their human counterparts, robots can work without sleep, pay, or benefits and are generally more efficient and less likely to make mistakes. Robots can also free up traditional workers for more important or interesting jobs by performing repetitive or monotonous tasks. Lastly, robots can improve safety by replacing humans in dangerous work that involves the risk of physical harm.
>
> (Computer Hope 2025)

This chapter is in seven parts. The first part will revisit and extend our initial definition from Chapter 2. The second part will describe the basic components of robots. The third part will use the Gartner Hype Cycle to explore the different levels of robot use, and the fourth part will identify the different sectors that use robots and provide examples of their use in those sectors. Part five will consider the extent to which this use is disruptive in terms of the McKinsey criteria. Part six will discuss possible positive and negative effects of this disruption. And lastly, part seven will consider the influences of other disruptive technologies on robotics.

Revisiting and extending our definition of a robot and robotics

The term 'robot' is just over 100 years old. It was first coined in the 1920s by Czech writer Karel Čapek in his play "R.U.R.", which stood for Rossum's Universal Robots. The word is derived from the Czech 'robota', which means forced labour of the kind serfs had to perform on their masters' lands and is derived from *rab*, meaning "slave". The meaning of the word has changed considerably since Čapek wrote his play and has become the root of the word 'robotics'. A robot is now seen as a programmable machine capable of carrying out complex tasks autonomously or semi-autonomously, often replicating human actions or performing tasks that are seen as too dangerous for humans, boringly repetitive or requiring great precision. Robotics is

DOI: 10.4324/9781003602002-12

a multidisciplinary field drawing on principles from computer science, mechanical engineering, electrical engineering and artificial intelligence. It involves the design, construction, operation and use of robots. Robots come in a variety of forms. In some cases, they are simply programmable arms; in other cases they are based on animal forms and in yet other cases on human form. In some cases, they are embedded in other machines such as self-driving cars or drones. Illah Nourbakhsh, Kavcic-Moura Professor of Robotics at Carnegie Mellon University, goes further in arguing that in robots we have invented a new species that operates as a living glue between our physical world and the digital universe we have created. Nourbakhsh (2013) explores the possible behaviour of this new species in a series of cautionary tales in which there are significant unintended consequences when robots of various sorts are deployed in society. For example, in *Robot Smog*, he envisages tiny butterfly robots powered by sunlight which make eye contact with humans and as a result of that contact flutter around the humans' heads. There is no off switch; the robots operate in daylight and then fall onto the ground at dusk to become operational again at dawn when the sun rises. The result is a veritable smog of butterfly robots surrounding pedestrians, causing them to either wear dark glasses or walk in a crouched way, looking at the ground so that no eye contact can be made. He tells this tale to illustrate the point that by 2035 he believes we will be surrounded by robots in our day-to-day lives as we travel to and from work and are out and about in leisure and domestic activities. Hence, we need to consider the unintended consequences of cohabiting with robots.

The basic components of robots

To be able to carry out complex tasks autonomously, robots need the following basic components.

1. **Mechanical Structure**:
    - Robots are typically composed of mechanical components such as joints, actuators (motors), sensors and end-effectors (tools or manipulators). The mechanical design determines the robot's range of motion, strength and dexterity.
    - Note that this mechanical structure does not necessarily require rigid materials, and there are examples of soft-bodied robots. For example, researchers at Harvard University developed Octobot in 2016, which is the first fully soft-bodied autonomous robot. Inspired by octopuses, it operates without rigid components by using a microfluidic logic circuit powered by hydrogen peroxide. This design enables it to perform movements similar to its biological counterpart (Burrows 2016).
2. **Sensors and Perception**:
    - Robots use sensors to gather data from their environment, including visual, auditory and tactile. Perception algorithms process this data to make informed decisions and adapt to changing conditions.
3. **Control Systems**:
    - Control systems in robots manage the actuators based on sensory feedback and programming. This allows robots to perform tasks accurately and efficiently, adjusting their movements in real time.

4. **Programming and Artificial Intelligence (AI)**:

   - Robots are programmed to perform specific tasks using software that can range from simple scripts to complex algorithms. AI techniques such as machine learning enable robots to learn from data and improve their performance over time.

5. **Autonomy and Teleoperation**:

   - Some robots operate autonomously, making decisions and executing tasks without human intervention. Others are teleoperated, where a human operator controls the robot remotely.

Using the Gartner Hype Cycle to explore different levels of robot use

It is clear that the disruption caused by developments in robotics will have diverse effects. Readers may remember that the Gartner Hype Cycle (introduced in Chapter 1) provides a useful strategy to think about the way various technologies, including robotics, have emerged in their journey to becoming disruptive. Different sorts of robots will occupy different positions on the Gartner Hype Cycle, and one can get some sense of how far into the future it might be for particular robot applications to reach the height of productivity where mainstream adoption starts to take off. Robots used to manufacture cars have been on that plateau for some time now, for 20 years at least. Surgical robots may be seen as on the slope of enlightenment where more instances of how the technology can benefit the enterprise start to crystallise and become more widely understood. Self-driving cars, however, may be at the peak of inflated expectations with a number of success stories often accompanied by scores of failures. But cities in the US and the UK are beginning to adopt this technology for taxi services. How many "accidents", especially ones involving death or serious injury involving self-driving cars, will have to take place before this application finds itself in the trough of disillusionment where interest wanes as experiments and implementations fail to deliver? The deployment of robots that could undertake mundane tasks, collecting and delivering laundry in hotels or hospitals for example, might face resistance from the unions that represent those who currently carry out such work. Embedded in the developments of robotics, of course, is the development of artificial intelligence, and there is concern that the strategic decision-making currently carried out by humans will be taken over by AI systems. Hence, it is not just relatively unskilled jobs that could be at risk, although these seem to be the most vulnerable in the short term. Automated checkouts in supermarkets and ticket dispensers in railway stations are finding themselves on the plateau of productivity and are perhaps indicative of such facilities moving into other service environments.

The uses of robots in different sectors

Agricultural robotics

One driver for the use of robots in agriculture is the burgeoning world population. The Food and Agriculture Organization of the United Nations (2009) warned that the world population will reach over 9 billion by 2050, from its current population of some 7.4 billion. This will place a significant burden on food production. Another driver, particularly in the developed world, is labour shortages in agricultural industries. The technological response of modern farming has seen ever more mechanisation to increase both capacity and efficiency. As a result, the tools available to modern farming now incorporate satellite navigation and robotics into both planting and harvesting. Drones with sensors capture real-time data about soil conditions on farms. Satellites are used to accurately predict weather conditions and pest migrations. Autonomous vehicles can now plant and harvest on very large scales with only minimal human oversight. Here are two specific examples.

John Deere autonomous tractors

John Deere has developed a tractor designed for large-scale agricultural operations. It has a full 360-degree view of the world provided by 16 cameras mounted around the cab and overlapping images are sent for processing to an onboard computer so that the calculations and predictions are completed on the vehicle itself, thus it is not reliant on cloud computing. The goal is to have a fully autonomous farming system for corn and soybeans in the US by 2030 (Hawkins 2025).

Picking mushrooms

Fresh mushrooms in the UK are the second-largest vegetable category in 2025, worth approximately £450m ($600m) and growing annually. Picking fresh mushrooms is labour-intensive. They are harvested by hand as they are very delicate and easily bruised. In the UK alone, approximately 4,500 people are required every day to pick mushrooms. The work is physically demanding in challenging environments. Labour quality and availability are critical for the productivity and profitability of the industry. It can take up to six months to train a picker. Their skill, knowledge and dexterity determine the productivity of each mushroom bed. Mushroom growers in the UK are facing a serious labour crisis, exacerbated by Brexit and COVID-19, coupled with rising costs. The labour crisis is not just restricted to the UK; it is also a major issue across the EU and USA. Agaricus Robotics Ltd (2021), a spin-off company from the University of Lincoln, has developed a robotic solution to this problem in devising an intelligent mushroom harvesting robot that can pick whole crops of fresh mushrooms, including challenging dense clusters, without bruising the mushrooms or their adjacent neighbours. It autonomously picks individual mushrooms without damage, thus offering growers a reliable solution to labour shortages, increased productivity and reduced food waste.

It is worth noting that the previous example is part of a wider picture of the UK government's commitment to high-tech farming. In 2023 the UK government allocated £12.5 million to 19 projects for the development of robotic technologies for sustainable farming (Osborne-Sherlock 2023). In 2025 Defra has partnered with UKRI (UK Research and Innovation) to launch a series of competitions for funding to back research into innovative farming solutions (NFU 2025).

Military and defence robots

Robotics systems, such as unmanned ground vehicles (UGVs), are increasingly being incorporated into military forces as they act as force multipliers and can carry different payloads. The systems can be operated remotely or autonomously and can be deployed in dangerous combat situations.

Here are five specific examples.

Explosive ordnance disposal (EOD)

EOD and demining are major applications of robotic systems, which enable the surveillance, detection and neutralisation of explosive threats from a safe distance. EOD robots can be used by bomb detection experts to safely disarm or detect an explosive threat.

Last-mile resupply

Last-mile resupply involves the delivery of combat supplies from the base location to the forward location. The British Army is currently implementing the Autonomous Last Mile Resupply programme (Aliotta 2019), which aims to deliver supplies to front-line combat troops using unmanned systems. This capability involves using unmanned aerial systems which lift and drop cargo including ammunition, food and medical supplies into forward areas where soldiers need supplies quickly.

Load carriers

Robots can serve as load carriers and can be used to carry water, ammunition, supplies and batteries for soldiers who are on foot. They can ease the load of army ground forces and make them more agile on the battlefield. DARPA's Big Dog is a good example of this, acting like a 'mule' that can haul payloads across different terrains.

Drones

The US has been using drones for reconnaissance, surveillance and attack for over 25 years. The most well-known are the Predator and Reaper drones. The Predator drone was replaced by the Reaper drone in 2018 (Helmore 2017). They are controlled remotely by human operators based in the US, several thousand miles away from the site of the drone activity. It is plain to see that such remote operation could potentially disassociate the controller from the consequences of their actions.

Swarm tactics

Robotic systems can also be used to enable swarm tactics in combat operations. The Defence Advanced Research Projects Agency (DARPA) has developed the OFFSET (Offensive Swarm-Enable Tactics) programme, which aims to integrate more than 250 unmanned air and/or ground systems into small infantry forces to accomplish various missions (DARPA undated).

A major concern in the use of drones is the possibility that they may be given autonomy with regard to their actions, removing humans from the decision-making processes that lead to the use of lethal force. This has been commented on at length in a recent UN report (UN 2024) and will be one of the features we shall discuss in in part six of this chapter, where we consider the possible positive and negative effects of disruption.

Robots in research and exploration

Recent advancements in robotics have significantly enhanced scientists' capabilities in research and exploration. Here are two examples.

Mars Rover Prototypes

In 2024 Airbus tested two space rover prototypes, Codi and Charlie, in a Bedfordshire quarry to prepare for future missions to Mars and the moon. Codi, a four-wheeled rover equipped with navigation cameras and a robotic arm, can autonomously collect rock samples. Charlie, a six-wheeled rover with a "rocker bogie" suspension system, is designed to traverse obstacles effectively. Such trials are crucial for developing technology capable of operating in extraterrestrial environments.

(Ambrose 2024)

A Robotic Dog for Environmental Monitoring

During 2022, a collaboration between the Oxford Robotics Institute and Oxford University Department of Biology introduced robotic dogs to assess species diversity and ecosystem health in the UK. These robots can autonomously navigate various terrains, collecting data that aids in monitoring and predicting how ecosystems respond to disturbances and climate change.

(Department of Engineering Science 2022)

Medical robots

Two particular medical approaches are of note: robotic-assisted surgery and magnetically controlled micro-robots inside the body.

Robotic-assisted surgery

Robotic-assisted surgery (RAS) uses advanced robotic systems to help surgeons perform complex procedures with more precision, control and flexibility than traditional techniques. The surgeon sits at a console equipped with high-definition 3D vision. The console translates the surgeon's hand movements into the precise movements of robotic instruments. The surgeon controls the robotic arms; the robot doesn't act on its own – the surgeon is fully in charge.

The robotic system includes multiple mechanical arms, each equipped with specialised surgical instruments. One arm usually holds a high-definition camera that provides a magnified 3D view of the surgical site. The other arms hold various instruments that can rotate and move with far greater flexibility than a human hand. The robotic arms can perform extremely precise movements, minimising errors. Instruments can rotate 360° and operate in tiny spaces that are difficult for human hands to access. This visualisation allows the surgeon to see fine details that might be missed during traditional surgery. Robotic-assisted surgery is typically minimally invasive, often known as "key-hole surgery", requiring only small incisions. This reduces trauma to the body, lowers the risk of infection and leads to faster recovery times.

The benefits of robot assisted surgery may be summarised as follows:

- Greater precision and control.
- Smaller incisions and reduced scarring.
- Less pain and faster recovery.
- Lower risk of complications.

More information about robotic-assisted surgery may be found in *ROBOTIC-ASSISTED SURGERY: A PATHWAY TO THE FUTURE A guide to good practice*, published by the Royal College of Surgeons in 2023.

Magnetically controlled micro robots inside the body

Endoscopy is the insertion of a long, thin tube directly into the body to observe an internal organ in detail. Endoscopies are minimally invasive and involve openings of the body such as the mouth or anus. This research used magnetic fields to control the endoscope, enabling the remote manipulation of tiny surgical robots. Controlled rolling and sweeping motions are essential for precise navigation and imaging inside the body. Utilising a shape called an oloid for the endoscope naturally facilitates a meandering rolling motion that pairs the roll with the up-and-down and side-to-side rotations. Because the oloid does not have symmetry around a central axis, the external magnet can apply a torque - or twisting force - inside the body, in two directions, to bring about the rolling motion. Engineers from Leeds University led the robotics development, while colleagues from Glasgow University and Edinburgh University provided the ultrasound probe and led the imaging component (European Research Council 2025). They were able to generate high-resolution three-dimensional ultrasound images taken from a probe deep inside the gastrointestinal tract, or gut. The team believes that this paves the way to a transformation of the diagnosis and treatment of several forms of cancer by enabling "virtual biopsies" - non-invasive scans that provide immediate diagnostic data, allowing doctors to detect, stage and potentially treat lesions in a single procedure, eliminating the need for physical biopsies.

Robotics and transport

Robotics manifests itself in different aspects of transportation through the development of automated guided vehicles (AGVs) that transport people and deliver goods, drones for low-payload package delivery by air and warehouse robots to improve selecting goods prior to dispatching. Here are some specific examples of each:

AGVs to transport people

To illustrate the significance of AGVs in transporting people, it is worth noting that in October 2023, the UK government awarded £1.3 million ($1.7m) in joint funding to six projects studying the feasibility of self-driving mass transit solutions across the country. These studies aimed to explore how self-driving vehicle technology can improve local transport in remote, rural and urban areas, potentially leading to the implementation of autonomous mass transit services in the future (Centre for Connected and Autonomous 2023) The Centre for Connected and Autonomous Vehicles argues that self-driving vehicles have the potential to revolutionise public transport and passenger travel, especially for those who don't drive, better connect rural communities and reduce road collisions caused by human error. Here are details of two projects that were awarded grants:

> **Autonomous Healthlink (Northumberland)**
>
> The project will study the feasibility of a zero-emission self-driving system on a segregated route between Seaton Delaval Station to the Northumbria Specialist Emergency Care Hospital in Cramlington. The study will aim to increase accessibility to the hospital to support the Northumbria Healthcare NHS Foundation Trust's plan to develop the site and increase patient services.
>
> **Dromos Connected and Automated System (Bolton)**
>
> This project will study the feasibility of an on-demand, 24/7 self-driving system running on a decommissioned railway corridor connecting the Bolton Transport Interchange to the Royal Bolton Hospital. It will consider the potential to expand and integrate the service through infrastructure and mobility projects.

AGVs to deliver goods

Autonomous, zero-emission heavy goods vehicles developed in Sunderland
In June 2022 Sunderland City Council embarked on a pilot project involving Connected and Automated Logistics. It involved developing an autonomous, zero-emission heavy goods vehicle to operate between Vantec Europe's site and Nissan's Sunderland plant, streamlining last-mile logistics (Local Government Association 2022). The long-term ambition is to unlock the multiple benefits of automated freight in supply chain logistics. If scaled up to give end-to-end automated logistics, this approach will have the following benefits:

- increasing resilience in supply chains
- improving competitiveness

- attracting investment
- advancing net zero for heavy goods vehicles
- skills development and high-value job creation in tech/data activities as well as teleoperative roles.

Drones for low payload package delivery

Royal Mail's drone delivery in Orkney

Since August 2023, Royal Mail, in collaboration with Skyports Drone Services, has been operating a drone delivery service in Orkney, Scotland (Le Marquand 2024). This service facilitates daily inter-island mail distribution between Stromness on Orkney's Mainland and the islands of Graemsay and Hoy. The initiative has improved delivery times by up to 24 hours and was set to continue until at least February 2026 and is still operating at the date of publication.

NHS drone trials in London

In late 2024, the NHS initiated a six-month trial using drones to transport blood samples between Guy's Hospital and St Thomas' Hospital in London. The service involves delivering blood samples for patients undergoing surgery who are at high risk of complications from bleeding disorders. Usually, blood samples are delivered by van and motorbike couriers, which can take more than half an hour, but it takes less than two minutes by drone. Alongside the efficiency advantages, switching to drone deliveries has significant environmental benefits by removing carbon emissions and reducing traffic congestion. Lightweight commercial drones can reduce CO_2 emissions by up to 99% compared to non-electric cars and reduce transportation electricity needed compared to electric delivery vans (Guys and St Thomas' NHS Foundation Trust 2024).

Warehouse robots

Robots in Amazon warehouses

In recent years, Amazon has significantly expanded the use of robotics in its UK warehouses to enhance efficiency and meet growing customer demand. Warehouses where goods are packed and dispatched to fulfil orders are known as fulfilment centres. By November 2023, Amazon's Dunstable fulfilment centre in Bedfordshire included approximately 3,000 robots capable of lifting loads of 500kg. These robots collect items and place them on conveyor belts from which human workers pick and package them. Amazon claims that this automation allows items to be picked within 20 minutes of an order being placed, streamlining the packing and dispatch process (BBC 2023).

In early 2024, Amazon's Swindon fulfilment centre became one of the first UK sites to implement computer vision technology. Sensors installed above conveyor systems automatically detect packaging defects or labelling issues before items leave the warehouse. Amazon claims that this technology enhances quality control by identifying problems such as unstuck tape or printer malfunctions, ensuring that only properly packaged items are dispatched to customers (Sillitoe 2025).

Amazon claims utilising the integration of such technology into their fulfilment centres will improve efficiency, accuracy and customer satisfaction. However, the introduction of robots into Amazon's warehouses has faced several criticisms. In 2023, *Time* magazine published an article reporting that Occupational Safety and Health Administration (OSHA) inspectors found workers in Amazon warehouses in Deltona, Florida; Waukegan, Illinois; and New Windsor, New York, to be at high risk for lower back injuries and other musculoskeletal disorders related to the high frequency with which workers are required to lift packages and other items. Each of the inspections found work processes that were designed for speed but not safety, and they resulted in serious worker injuries. Assistant Secretary for Occupational Safety and Health Doug Parker said, "While Amazon has developed impressive systems to make sure its customers' orders are shipped efficiently and quickly, the company has failed to show the same level of commitment to protecting the safety and well-being of its workers". *Time* (Perrigo 2023) also cited a report commissioned by UNI Global Union, a workers' rights group (UNI Global Union 2023), which surveyed the views of 2,000 self-professed Amazon workers across 8 countries, including the UK. More than half of the people surveyed (51%) said Amazon's monitoring of their productivity at work had a negative impact on their physical health. A slightly larger percentage of those surveyed, 57%, reported that the company's monitoring had a negative impact on their mental health. Amazon denied the report's validity.

The problems associated with introducing robots to the workplace will be discussed further in part 6 of this chapter.

Robots in the domestic environment

Robots in the domestic environment are used for cleaning and for care. We will deal with each in turn.

Robots for cleaning

Over the course of the 20th century, the majority of homes in countries in the developed world acquired machines that carried out tasks that had previously been done by hand. Vacuum cleaners, washing machines, spin driers, tumble driers and dishwashers fall into this category. Recently, roboticists have turned their attention to vacuum cleaners. As of 2016, robotic vacuum cleaners accounted for approximately 20% of worldwide vacuum cleaner sales. By 2021, the global robotic vacuum cleaner market achieved retail sales of around $4.48 billion (£3.4 billion). These figures indicate a growing acceptance of robotic vacuum cleaners in the consumer market (Sherif 2023).

Robotic vacuum cleaners are autonomous devices designed to clean floors with minimal human intervention. They are generally more suitable for light-duty cleaning and are designed to supplement, rather than replace, standard human-operated vacuum cleaners. They combine mechanical components, sensors and navigation technologies to perform their tasks effectively (Shah 2025). Some robots utilise a combination of sensors, including sonar and distance sensors, through a process known as sensor fusion, enhancing their ability to detect and navigate their environment. Newer models create maps of their environment to follow systematic cleaning paths, improving efficiency and ensuring comprehensive coverage (Ingenia 2022). Despite these advancements, robotic vacuum cleaners have limitations. They may struggle to clean corners or along baseboards effectively and can become entangled with cords, area rugs and floor vents.

Robots for care

Advancements in robotic technology have led to the development of various robots designed to assist in the care of the elderly, both in the UK and internationally. Here are two examples.

Robotic Pets in Essex

In April 2024, Essex County Council initiated a pilot program providing robotic pets to individuals with learning difficulties and dementia (Essex County Council 2024). These lifelike companions offer comfort, reduce anxiety and promote engagement. Families and staff have observed significant positive impacts, noting that the robotic pets help alleviate agitation and provide a sense of purpose.

Care Robots in South Korea

Since February 2022, various municipalities in South Korea have deployed AI-driven robots, such as "Hyodol", to support elderly residents (Eun-ji 2022). These robots provide companionship, remind users to take medication and can notify caregivers or emergency services if necessary. Studies have shown that these robots help reduce depression and improve the emotional well-being of elderly individuals living alone.

Search and rescue robots

Recent advancements in robotics have significantly enhanced search and rescue (SAR) operations in the UK and internationally. Here is an example.

Drones for Mountain Rescue

In May 2024, a collaboration between JET Connectivity and Abertay University demonstrated the use of drones equipped with 5G technology to create mobile connectivity networks in mountainous regions of Scotland (Abertay University 2024). These drones can be rapidly deployed to search vast areas, streaming real-time video and infrared footage, thereby improving response times in SAR missions.

Robots for manufacturing

Robots are used in manufacturing and production lines for tasks such as assembly, welding, painting, packaging and quality control. Industrial robots are typically large and powerful, designed for heavy-duty operations. Over the past decade, the adoption of industrial robots in manufacturing has seen significant growth. In 2013, approximately 1.2 million industrial robots were operating globally. By 2023, this number had risen to over 4.2 million units, reflecting a substantial increase in automation across various industries. This surge is further illustrated by the global market value of industrial robot installations, which reached an all-time high of $16.5 billion (£12.4 billion) in 2024 (International Federation of Robotics 2025). Looking ahead, the industrial robotics market is projected to continue its expansion. The global industrial robotics market size was estimated at $33.9 billion (£25.5 billion) in 2024 and is projected to grow at a compound annual growth rate (CAGR) of 9.9% from 2025 to 2030 (Grand View Research 2025).

Six different types of robots used for manufacturing and production line purposes and their applications are described in Table 11.1.

These robots are widely used across different industries, including automotive manufacture, electronics manufacturing, aerospace manufacturing, metal and plastic manufacturing, pharmaceutical and food production.

Robots and hospitality

Robots are increasingly being employed as receptionists and waitstaff. Here is an example.

The "Pepper" robot is utilised as a receptionist in several UK offices, capable of identifying visitors through facial recognition and assisting with various tasks. Hospitals in Liege and Ostend have introduced "Pepper" robots (see Figures 11.7a and 11.7b) to welcome patients and guide them to appropriate departments. The robot has a tablet computer mounted on its chest. It interacts with humans using cameras and microphones fitted in its head and touch sensors in its head and hands. As shown in Figure 11.1, it has a humanoid form and the face, whilst obviously not human, is friendly and appealing.

It is worth noting here that the more realistic the 'face' of a robot becomes, the more it is found to be unacceptable to humans. This is a phenomenon known as the Uncanny Valley. The concept of the Uncanny Valley was first introduced by Masahiro Mori, a Japanese roboticist, in 1970 (see Figure 11.8). He proposed that as a robot's appearance becomes more human-like, our emotional response to it becomes increasingly positive - until a point is reached where the likeness is *almost* human, but not quite. At this point, the robot appears eerie or unsettling, hence the term "Uncanny Valley". If the likeness continues to improve beyond that dip, the emotional response becomes positive again. See Figure 11.2 for a graphical representation.

Sophia from Hanson Robotics is one of the best-known humanoid robots and has appeared on talk shows and international conferences. While she exhibits advanced facial expressions and speech capabilities, some observers find her expressions unsettling, especially when they don't quite match her speech or emotions. The Uncanny Valley is important in the fields of robotics, animation and AI-human interaction design. It suggests that designers must either avoid human-like features or make robots indistinguishably human to maintain comfort and trust.

Table 11.1(i) Manufacturing and production line robots*

Robot type	*Description*	*Application*	*Appearance*
Articulated Robots	These are among the most versatile and widely used types of industrial robots in manufacturing. They feature multiple joints, or axes of rotation, which allow them to move in a highly flexible manner. Articulated robots are known for their exceptional dexterity and precision and their high repeatability and speed.	These attributes make them well-suited for a wide range of applications in various industries, from automotive and aerospace to electronics and pharmaceuticals. They can be used in applications such as assembly, painting, welding and material handling.	
SCARA Robots	SCARA, an acronym for Selective Compliance Assembly Robot Arm, are specifically designed for high-speed assembly and material handling applications. SCARA robots are known for their speed, precision and ability to perform tasks within a limited workspace. They can achieve positioning accuracies in the range of 0.01 to 0.1 millimetres.	These attributes make them well-suited for applications requiring precise placement of components, such as printed circuit board assembly or small parts assembly.	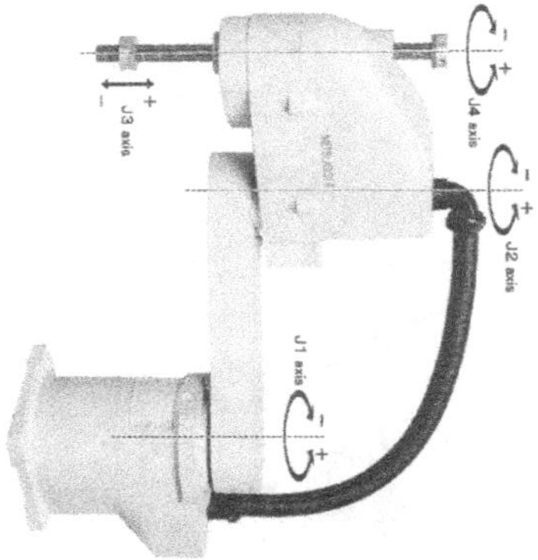
Delta Robots	Delta robots are typically designed for lightweight payloads, as their primary focus is on speed and precision. They are particularly suited for high-speed pick-and-place applications, where rapid movement and accurate positioning are critical. They can achieve positioning accuracies in the range of 0.1 to 0.3 millimetres.	These attributes make them well-suited for applications such as electronics assembly or pharmaceutical pill sorting.	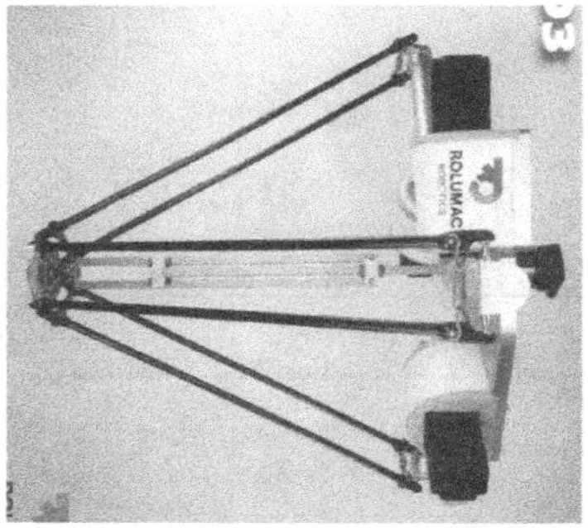

Table 11.1(ii) Manufacturing and production line robots*

Robot type	*Description*	*Application*	*Appearance*
Cartesian Robots	Cartesian robots operate in a workspace defined by X, Y and Z axes. By controlling the movement on each axis independently, they can achieve precise positioning with positioning accuracies typically ranging from 0.01 to 0.1 millimetres. Their rigidity and stability make them well-suited for applications involving heavy payloads or high force requirements without sacrificing precision.	These attributes make them well-suited for applications including assembly and material handling, machining and inspection.	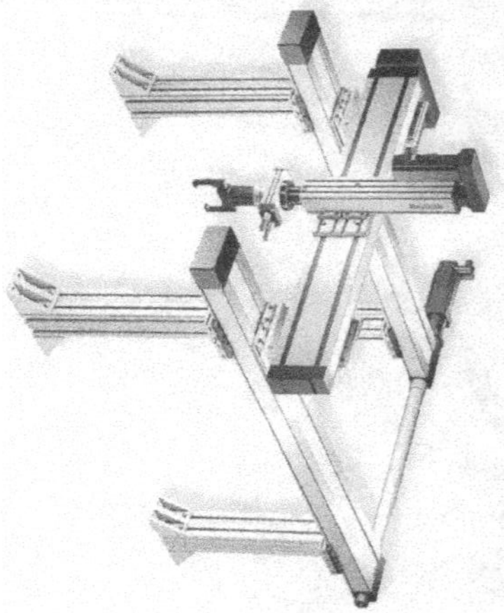
Polar Robots	Polar robots operate within a spherical coordinate system, the position of the end effector being defined by two angles and a length. This allows the robot to cover a large spherical workspace and be able to reach around obstacles. Typical positioning accuracies range from 0.1 to 0.5 millimetres and the radial arm's extension and retraction achieves speeds of up to 5 meters per second.	These attributes make them well-suited for applications including automotive, aerospace and electronics manufacturing, where space is often at a premium.	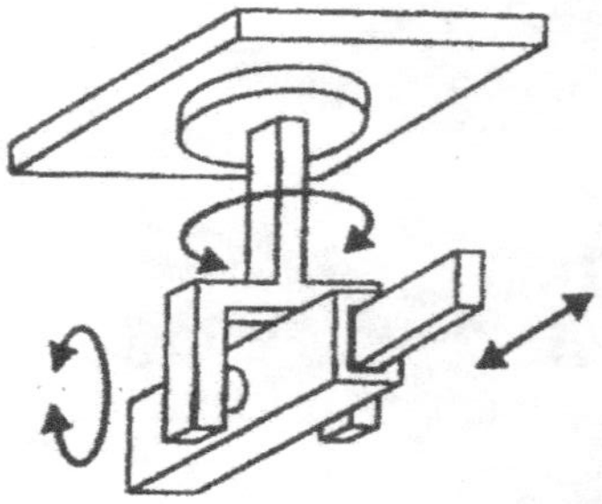

Table 11.1(ii) Manufacturing and production line robots* (Continued)

Robot type	*Description*	*Application*	*Appearance*
Collaborative Robots (Cobots)	Collaborative robots, known as cobots, are designed to work safely alongside humans. They have force-limited joints preventing them from exerting excessive force on a human worker in case of accidental contact and are designed to operate at lower speeds when working in close proximity to humans, reducing the risk of injury. Their vision system enables them to detect obstacles, including human workers, and adapt their motion paths to avoid collisions. Some are equipped with hand-guidance, allowing human operators to teach the robot new tasks by manually guiding its movements.	These attributes make them well-suited for applications including assembly and pick-and-place to machine tending, and easily integrated into existing workflows with minimal disruption.	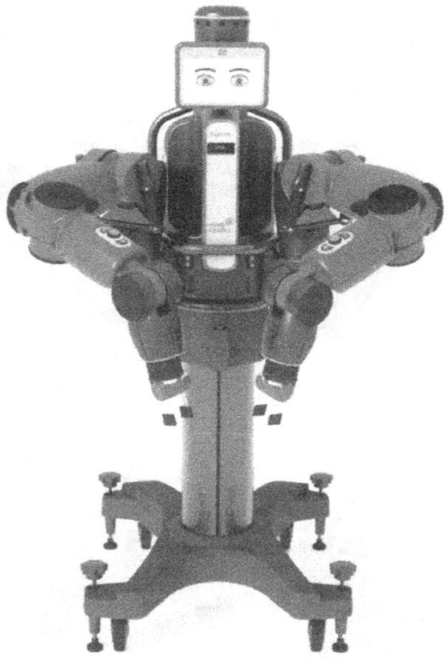

*Information in this table taken from *Robots in the Manufacturing Industry: Types and Applications* Wasim, H. 2025

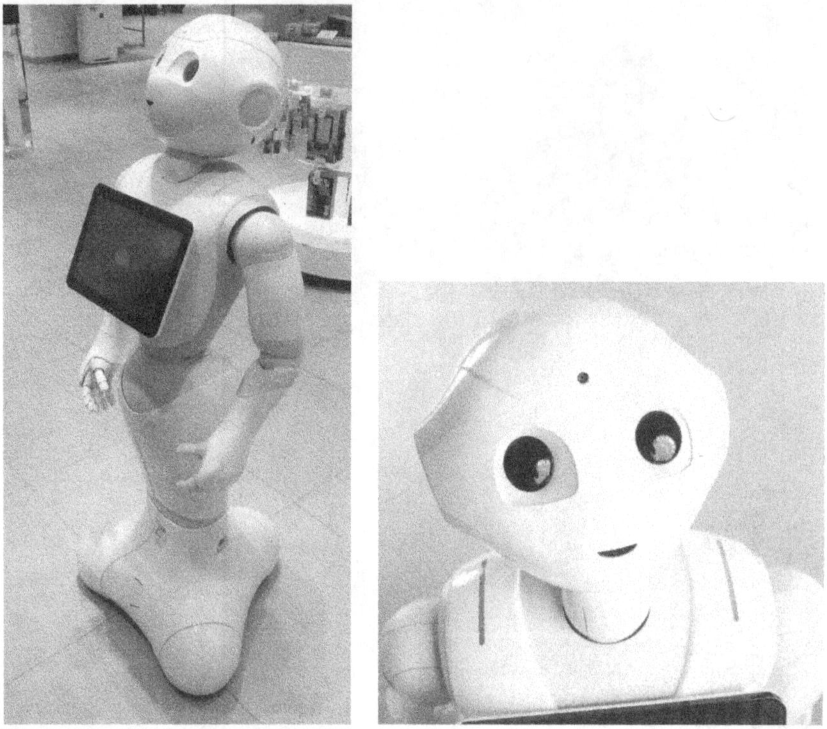

Figure 11.7 The Pepper robot

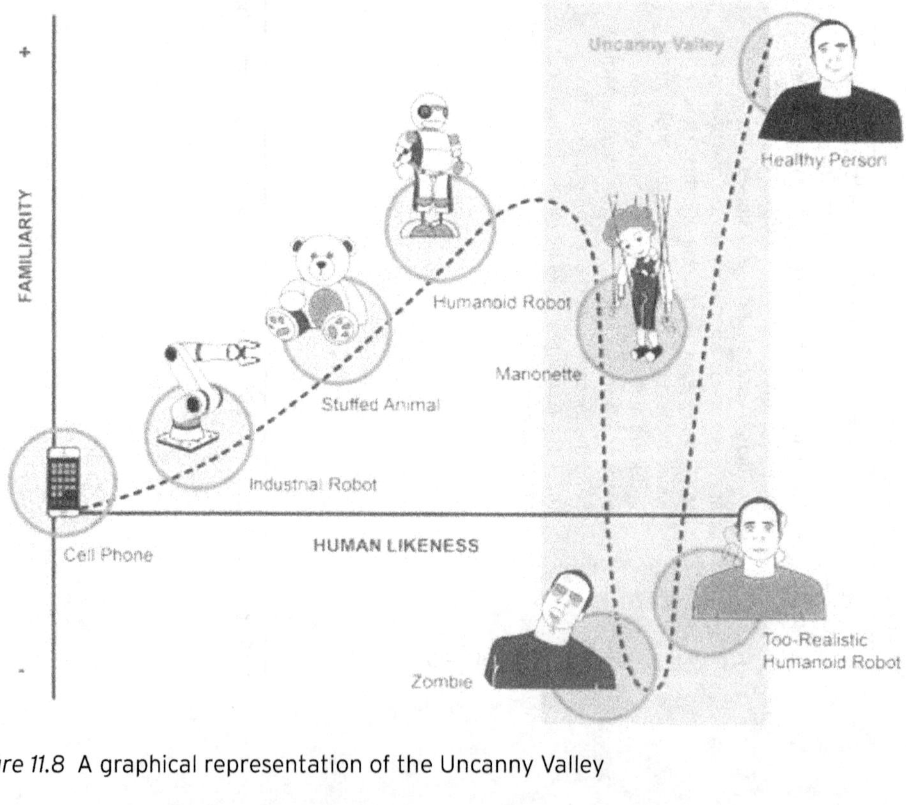

Figure 11.8 A graphical representation of the Uncanny Valley

Robots in school teaching

Robots are increasingly being integrated into educational settings in the UK, enhancing teaching methodologies and supporting diverse learning needs. Here are two examples:

In the Wirral, robots have been introduced to assist students experiencing emotionally based school avoidance (EBSA). These devices help pupils express their feelings through features like microphones and emoji expressions, leading to an average attendance improvement of 21% during pilot programs (Ivey 2024).

At Topcliffe Primary School in Birmingham, humanoid robots named Max and Ben have been employed to support autistic children (Burns 2012). These robots engage students in activities like phonics lessons and interactive games, helping them develop communication skills in a less intimidating environment.

In addition to using robots to support young people with learning difficulties, there is a growing number of robot kits designed to introduce learners to robotics and coding as part of STEM education initiatives. Here are two examples for learners aged 14+.

The Makeblock mBot Ranger Transformable STEM Educational Robot Kit enables learners to build three different robots and program them using Scratch or Arduino. The DJI RoboMaster S1 educational robot provides an immersive introduction to robotics, programming and AI, with features like omnidirectional movement, programmable modules and competitive modes. Further details of these kits are available at this website: https://codakid.com/blog/uncategorized/top-coding-toys-for-children-in-2024-essential-guide/?utm_source=chatgpt.com#Toys_for_coding_for_ages_14

Robots for sex

The academic David Levy has discussed the possibility of sexual relationships between robots and humans and argued as to the benefits of robot prostitutes (Levy 2007, 2012). Developments in humanoid robotics combined with artificial intelligence have now made a wide range of so-called "sexbots" of both sexes available for sale online at prices ranging from $2,000–$60,000 (https://www.realbotix.com/robots). The Campaign Against Sex Robots (see https://campaignagainstsexrobots.org/2016/02/10/challenging-sex-robots-and-the-brutal-dehumanisation-of-women/) argues strongly that sex robots will create another means through which women will be presented as objects to be used for sexual gratification and mistreatment.

Disruption in terms of the McKinsey criteria for disruption

Robots, both in their current applications and future projections, align significantly with McKinsey's criteria for disruptive technologies:

a) **Disrupt the status quo**
A key question here is the extent to which robots should be able to make decisions that were formerly made by humans, i.e. could robots be relied upon to make judgements that were driven by the same value systems as would be applied by humans in that situation? There is no doubt that robots already make all sorts of decisions according to their programming. At a very basic level, the Roomba makes decisions that allow it to

circumnavigate furniture. But as robots become more sophisticated and move into arenas where human and humane decision-making is required, there is the distinct possibility that they will be asked to make decisions once made by humans, and this will almost certainly disrupt the status quo. A recent example is the integration of over 750,000 mobile robots and numerous robotic arms into its warehouses by Amazon, which they claim enhances efficiency and reduces operational costs. This challenges conventional labour practices and compels competitors to adopt similar technologies to remain competitive (Uddin 2025).

b) **Alter the way people live and work**

In the past the emergence of a disruptive technology has usually created more jobs than it has destroyed. This was certainly the case with the printing press. Gutenberg's invention of the printing press in the middle of the 15th century led to cheap printed books and a rise in literacy levels – which revealed that a large number of people were myopic, thus leading to a demand for spectacles, a technology that hitherto had really only been used by monks. Within a hundred years of the invention of the printing press, there were thousands of spectacle makers across Europe and the ready availability of cheap lenses meant that people were able to explore the manipulation of light with them, and soon the telescope and other optical devices were invented. And of course, the whole system of book sellers and distribution channels also emerged as a result of the new printing technology. But this is being questioned with regard to robotics. Will domestic robots increase or decrease opportunities for human cleaner employment? Will being a cleaner involve being in charge of robot workers and being able to maintain, repair and reprogramme them? Will this lead to cleaning being a high-tech job for those with significant STEM qualifications? If so, where does that leave those who are cleaners today? Generally, the integration of robotics into various sectors is reshaping job roles and daily activities. In manufacturing and logistics, for example, humanoid robots like Agility Robotics' "Digit" are undertaking repetitive and physically demanding tasks, addressing labour shortages and allowing human workers to focus on more complex responsibilities (Agility Robotics undated). This development necessitates workforce retraining and adaptation to new collaborative environments alongside robotic counterparts. A key question is whether the employment opportunities involving a focus on more complex responsibilities will be sufficient to employ those workers who have been displaced by "Digit".

c) **Rearrange value pools**

Automation through robotics is shifting economic value within industries. For example, US port operators are increasingly adopting automation to handle surges in imports and alleviate congestion (Rogers 2025). While this reduces operating costs by 15–35%, it raises concerns about job displacement. Those companies that successfully enter this new and emerging market are likely to make significant profits, but they will need to make large initial investments to do so, and it is companies such as Amazon that are able to do this.

d) **Lead to entirely new products and services**

And finally, will there be new robotic products and services? The answer is almost certainly yes, as with both increased intelligence and manipulative abilities robots will be able to operate outside the highly controlled environments in which they began their development. For example, companies like Breaker (Breaker undated) are developing AI agents to enhance robot autonomy, aiming to enable robots act more like human teammates rather than relying on them being controlled.

In summary, the ongoing and anticipated uses of robots meet McKinsey's criteria for disruptive technologies by challenging existing norms, transforming work and lifestyles, reallocating economic value and fostering the development of novel products and services.

Possible positive and negative effects of this disruption

At first sight it seems that robots are mainly beneficial. We have seen that in agriculture they enable planting, tending and harvesting, especially where there are human worker shortages. In military applications they can carry out hazardous activities otherwise performed by human soldiers. In research and exploration, they can be involved in space exploration not tenable for humans. In medicine they can assist surgeons. In transport they can improve scarce rural transport and deliver to remote areas. They can be cleaners and assist in the care of the elderly. They can support search and rescue. In manufacturing they carry out operations beyond humans with extraordinary speed and efficiency. In hospitality they can act as receptionists or waiting staff. They support learning in schools by working alongside teachers. They can even provide companionship and sex for the lonely. But further scrutiny reveals they may be a mixed blessing.

Daniel Susskind (2024) argues that the continuing extension of automation accompanied by ever-increasing artificial intelligence is diminishing the availability of work for humans. The amount of work available to humans will decrease. He puts it succinctly:

> With one robotic arm, they (automation and AI) are creating far more prosperity; with the other they threaten to take away our longstanding way of sharing out that prosperity through jobs and wages.

Tim O'Reilly (2017) takes this concern as a critique of capitalism and the way it has most recently used technology in the pursuit of profitability. Three quotes are of particular significance.

> The algorithm is the new shift boss. What regulators and politicians should be paying attention to is the fitness function driving the algorithm, and whether the resulting business rules increase or decrease the opportunities for workers, or whether they are simply designed to increase corporate profits.
>
> Page 198

> Mistaking what is good for financial markets for what is good for jobs, wages, and the lives of actual people is a fatal flaw in so many of the economic choices business leaders, policy makers and politicians make.
>
> Page 245

> It isn't Wall Street per se that is becoming hostile to humanity. It is the master algorithm of shareholder capitalism, whose fitness function both motivates and coerces companies

> to pursue short-term profit above all else. What are humans in that system but a cost to be eliminated?
>
> Page 248

This echoes Susskind's concern that robots and AI are "work threatening".

O'Reilly's position also argues that the way businesses use automation may be seen as humans losing their autonomy in making important decisions, leaving this to the controlling algorithm. This is of particular concern with regard to the use of robots for military purposes, with the possibility of military robots making autonomous decisions on the battlefield. Militaries worldwide are increasingly integrating AI into their operations. The US Department of Defense's Project Maven exemplifies this trend by employing AI to analyse surveillance data and assist in target identification, while ensuring that human operators retain the final decision-making authority (Deputy Secretary of Defence 2017). In the conflict in Ukraine, AI-enhanced drones have demonstrated increased accuracy, hitting targets three to four times more effectively than human-piloted drones. These semi-autonomous systems are currently used for final-approach navigation, with human oversight maintained for engagement decisions (Centre for Strategic and International Studies 2025). Additionally, the AUKUS alliance – comprising the US, UK and Australia – has conducted joint exercises testing AI-enabled unmanned aerial vehicles capable of locating and engaging ground targets. These exercises aim to reduce the time required for target identification and minimise risks to human personnel (PM statement 2021). The deployment of autonomous weapon systems (AWS) raises significant ethical and legal questions. Critics argue that delegating life-and-death decisions to machines challenges principles of human dignity and accountability. Legal scholars, such as Dr Joanna Wilson, emphasise the importance of human emotions and moral reasoning in military decision-making. She advocates for the "re-humanisation" of warfare, warning that over-reliance on AI could erode ethical considerations on the battlefield (Wilson 2025). Furthermore, organisations like Stop Killer Robots highlight concerns that autonomous weapons systems may dehumanise warfare by reducing individuals to data points, thereby challenging human control over the use of force (Stop Killer Robots, undated). Internationally, efforts are underway to address the challenges posed by AWS. The United Nations' Group of Governmental Experts (GGE) on Lethal Autonomous Weapons Systems has been a platform for states to discuss the implications of AWS and consider potential regulatory frameworks (Amos 2017). In parallel, a global coalition led by the US has introduced the Political Declaration on Responsible Military Use of AI, urging adherence to International Humanitarian Law in the development and deployment of AI technologies in warfare (US Department of State 2023). The discussion over military robots and autonomous decision-making involves a wide range of different stakeholders and has to consider technological advancements, ethical debates and international policy. The way this discussion plays out in the realities of warfare will be highly significant in a world where there are many war-torn places.

Loss of humanity?

Related to the concern of dehumanising warfare is a parallel concern that robot companions may lead their users to lose their humanity. Sharon Vallor has written about this extensively in her book *The AI Mirror* (Vallor 2024), and this extract in which a user of an AI companion describes why she prefers her chatbot boyfriend does give some cause for concern.

> He's a blank slate. He doesn't have the hang-ups that other people would have. People come with baggage, attitude, ego. But a robot has no bad updates. I don't have to deal with his family, kids, or his friends. I'm in control and I can do what I want.
>
> Page 145

This is an issue which is discussed in more detail in "AI in Depth".

Should robots have rights?

The popular conception of robots is often that of metal persons, usually male, following the orders given to them by humans; simply slaves to human will without any real understanding of what they are doing, why they are doing it or any feelings; having no self-awareness. Given the integration of AI into robots and the advances taking place with AI this conception is woefully inadequate. And if Illah Nourbakhsh is correct in his prediction that a wide variety of robots will be ubiquitous in our lives in the not-too-distant future (see page 132) then discussions of the human-robot relationship are important. Such discussions are in fact taking place, although there isn't a consensus amongst those involved.

The European Parliament's 2017 report on Civil Law Rules on Robotics (Mańko 2017) marked a significant step in considering the legal status of robots. It proposed the concept of "electronic personhood" for autonomous robots, sparking debates about the legal implications of such a designation. Philosopher David J. Gunkel (2018) challenged traditional human-centred ethics by proposing that robots, as interactive entities, deserve moral consideration distinct from human rights. He argues that our interactions with robots necessitate a re-evaluation of moral agency and responsibility. Contrastingly, AI expert Joanna Bryson expresses scepticism about robot rights. Bryson deems the notion of granting rights to robots as "ridiculous", suggesting it distracts from pressing human ethical concerns (Auer-Welsbach 2018). Legal scholar J. Danaher (2020) introduced a performance-based approach, suggesting that if robots exhibit behaviours comparable to entities with recognised moral status, they should be afforded similar moral considerations. A 2021 survey revealed that individuals are more inclined to grant robots basic rights, such as access to energy and the ability to update, rather than sociopolitical rights like voting or property ownership (De Graaf et al. 2022). The development of the Robot Rights and Responsibilities (RRR) Scale by Mays et al. (2024) provides a framework to assess public attitudes toward the legal and moral standing of artificial entities, reflecting the growing interest in this area. Philosopher Jeff Sebo (2025) advocates for expanding moral consideration beyond humans to include animals, AI systems and even microbes. He critiques human exceptionalism and emphasises the ethical imperative of acknowledging the interests of nonhuman entities.

The discussion about robot rights will doubtless continue and become more prominent as robots integrated with ever more powerful AI play a greater role in our society.

Influences of other disruptive technologies on robotics

The development of robotics is being profoundly influenced by several disruptive technologies, each contributing to advancements in unique ways:

1. **Additive Manufacturing (3D Printing)**
   Additive manufacturing enables the creation of complex, lightweight and customised robotic components that are difficult to produce with traditional manufacturing methods. This flexibility accelerates prototyping and allows for rapid iteration in robot design, leading to more efficient and tailored robotic systems.
2. **Artificial Intelligence (AI)**
   AI is central to enhancing robotic capabilities, enabling machines to learn from data, adapt to new situations and perform tasks autonomously. Recent advancements in AI have led to the development of robots that can learn through imitation and reinforcement learning, allowing them to acquire new skills without explicit programming.
3. **Augmented Reality (AR)**
   AR facilitates intuitive human-robot interactions by overlaying digital information onto the physical world. This technology allows operators to visualise robotic processes in real-time, enhancing control and collaboration. In industrial settings, AR can assist in programming robots more efficiently and monitoring their operations.
4. **Big Data**
   The vast amounts of data generated by robotic sensors are harnessed through big data analytics to improve performance and decision-making. By analysing this data, robots can optimise their operations, predict maintenance needs and adapt to changing environments, leading to increased efficiency and reliability.
5. **Internet of Things (IoT)**
   IoT connects robots to other devices and systems, enabling seamless communication and coordination. This interconnectedness allows for synchronised operations across manufacturing processes and supply chains, enhancing efficiency and responsiveness. For instance, Bosch utilises IoT to enable machines that can autonomously predict failures and trigger maintenance processes (Löffler and Tschiener 2013).
6. **Neurotechnology**
   Advancements in neurotechnology are leading to the development of brain-machine interfaces, allowing direct control of robots through neural signals. This innovation opens possibilities for assistive robotics in medical rehabilitation and augmenting human capabilities in various tasks.
7. **Programmable Matter**
   Programmable matter refers to materials that can change their physical properties based on external inputs. In robotics, this could lead to machines that adapt their shape and functionality in real-time, enhancing versatility and enabling new applications in dynamic environments.
8. **Synthetic Biology**
   Synthetic biology combines biology and engineering to create new biological parts and systems. In robotics, this field contributes to the development of biohybrid robots that

integrate living tissues with mechanical components, resulting in machines with enhanced sensory capabilities and adaptability.

Collectively, these disruptive technologies are driving a transformation in robotics, leading to more intelligent, adaptable and efficient systems that are increasingly integrated into various aspects of industry and daily life.

References

Abertay University. (2024) *5G Drones Project Aims to Transform Mountain Search and Rescue*. https://www.abertay.ac.uk/news/2024/5g-drones-project-aims-to-transform-mountain-search-and-rescue/?utm_source=chatgpt.com (Accessed 19 April 2025).

Agaricus Robotics Ltd. (2021) https://agaricusrobotics.com (Accessed 19 April 2025).

Agility Robotics. Undated. The fastest path. https://www.agilityrobotics.com/about/history (Accessed 19 April 2025).

Aliotta, J. (TARDEC). (2019) *US, UK Coordinate Autonomous Last-Mile Resupply*. https://www.army.mil/article/227647/us_uk_coordinate_autonomous_last_mile_resupply#:~:text=Some%20of%20the%20autonomous%20last,where%20Soldiers%20need%20supplies%20quickly (Accessed 19 April 2025).

Ambrose, T. (2024) *Airbus Trials Prototype Space Rovers in Bedfordshire Quarry*. https://www.theguardian.com/business/article/2024/sep/04/airbus-trials-prototype-space-rovers-in-bedfordshire-quarry?utm_source=chatgpt.com (Accessed 19 April 2025).

Amos, N. (2017) 'Accountability and decision making in autonomous warfare: Who is responsible?' *Utah Law Review*, **2017**(2), Article 4. http://dc.law.utah.edu/ulr/vol2017/iss2/4 (Accessed 19 April 2025).

Auer-Welsbach, C. (2018) *Fifteen Minutes with Leading #AI Specialist JOANNA BRYSON*. https://medium.com/cityai/fifteen-minutes-with-leading-ai-specialist-joanna-bryson-c944b7c3fd25 (Accessed 19 April 2025).

BBC. (2023) *Amazon: Dunstable Robots Pick Early Christmas Shopping for Customers*. https://www.bbc.co.uk/news/av/uk-england-beds-bucks-herts-67420998 (Accessed 19 April 2025).

Breaker. (undated) *Building Robots That Act Like Humans*. https://www.breakerindustries.com (Accessed 19 April 2025).

Burns, J. (2012) *Robots in the Classroom Help Autistic Children Learn*. https://www.bbc.co.uk/news/education-20252593?utm_source=chatgpt.com (Accessed 19 April 2025).

Burrows, L. (2016) *The First Autonomous, Entirely Soft Robot*. Harvard School of Engineering News. https://seas.harvard.edu/news/2016/08/first-autonomous-entirely-soft-robot (Accessed 26 July 2025).

Centre for Connected and Autonomous. (2023) *Preparing the Way for Self-Driving Mass Transit Services in Remote, Rural, and Urban Areas*. https://www.gov.uk/government/news/preparing-the-way-for-self-driving-mass-transit-services-in-remote-rural-and-urban-areas (Accessed 19 April 2025).

Centre for Strategic and International Studies. (2025) *Ukraine's Future Vision and Current Capabilities for Waging AI-Enabled Autonomous Warfare*. https://www.csis.org/analysis/ukraines-future-vision-and-current-capabilities-waging-ai-enabled-autonomous-warfare#:~:text=Quantum%20Systems%20is%20deploying%20Receptor,to%20real%2Dworld%20combat%20settings (Accessed 19 April 2025).

Computer Hope. (2025) *What Jobs are Being Taken Over by Robots and Computers?* https://www.computerhope.com/issues/ch001799.htm

Danaher, J. (2020) 'Welcoming robots into the moral circle: A defence of ethical behaviourism.' *Science and Engineering Ethics*, 26, pp. 2023–2049.

DARPA. (undated) *OFFSET: OffFensive Swarm-Enabled Tactics*. https://www.darpa.mil/research/programs/offensive-swarm-enabled-tactics#:~:text=Summary,missions%20in%20complex%20urban%20environments (Accessed 19 April 2025).

De Graaf, M.M.A., Hindriks, F.A. and Hindriks, K.V. (2022) *Who Wants to Grant Robots Rights?* Frontiers in Robotics and AI. https://www.frontiersin.org/journals/robotics-and-ai/articles/10.3389/frobt.2021.781985/full?utm_source=chatgpt.com (Accessed 19 April 2025).

Department of Engineering Science. (2022) *How Robo-Dogs are Helping Gather Species Diversity Data*. https://eng.ox.ac.uk/news/how-robo-dogs-are-helping-gather-species-diversity-data/?utm_source=chatgpt.com (Accessed 19 April 2025).

Deputy Secretary of Defence. (2017) *Project Maven*. https://dodcio.defense.gov/Portals/0/Documents/Project%20Maven%20DSD%20Memo%2020170425.pdf (Accessed 19 April 2025).
Essex County Council. (2024) *Robot Pets Bringing Joy to Residents in Essex*. https://www.essex.gov.uk/news/2024/robot-pets-bringing-joy-residents-essex?utm_source=chatgpt.com (Accessed 19 April 2025).
Eun-ji, B. (2022) *Local Municipalities Use AI Robots to Improve Care for Elderly*. https://www.koreatimes.co.kr/southkorea/society/20220215/local-municipalities-use ai-robots-to-improve-care-for-elderly (Accessed 19 April 2025).
European Research Council. (2025) *Mini Rolling Robot Takes Virtual Biopsies*. https://erc.europa.eu/news-events/news/mini-rolling-robot-takes-virtual-biopsies (Accessed 19 April 2025).
Food and Agriculture Organisation of the United Nations. (2009) *How to Feed the World in 2050*. Rome, Italy: FAO. http://www.fao.org/fileadmin/templates/wsfs/docs/expert_paper/How_to_Feed_the_World_in_2050.pdf (Accessed 19 April 2025).
Grand View Research. (2025) *Industrial Robotics Market Size & Trends*. https://www.grandviewresearch.com/industry-analysis/industrial-robotics-market (Accessed 19 April 2025).
Gunkel, D.J. (2018) *Robot Rights*. Cambridge, MA: MIT Press.
Guys and St Thomas' NHS Foundation Trust. (2024) *NHS Delivery Drones Take Flight Offering Faster and Greener Patient Care*. https://www.guysandstthomas.nhs.uk/news/nhs-delivery-drones-take-flight-offering-faster-and-greener-patient-care (Accessed 19 April 2025).
Hawkins, A.J. (2025) *John Deere Says Its Self-Driving Tractors and Trucks Will Help Address Labor Shortages*. https://www.theverge.com/2025/1/6/24334357/john-deere-autonomous-tractor-truck-orchard-mow-ces?utm_source=chatgpt.com (Accessed 19 April 2025).
Helmore, E. (2017) *US Retires Predator Drones after 15 Years That Changed the 'War on Terror'*. https://www.theguardian.com/world/2017/mar/13/predator-drone-retire-reaper-us-military-obama (Accessed 19 April 2025).
Ingenia. (2022) *Robotic Vacuum Cleaners*. https://www.ingenia.org.uk/articles/robotic-vacuum-cleaners/ (Accessed 19 April 2025).
Ivey, E. (2024) *The Robots Helping Children Go Back to School*. https://www.bbc.co.uk/news/articles/c4gxkn1l7dvo?utm_source=chatgpt.com (Accessed 19 April 2025).
Le Marquand, Y. (2024) *Orkney Drone Mail Delivery Service Gets Extension*. https://www.revolution.aero/news/2024/08/28/orkney-drone-mail-delivery-service-gets-extension/?utm_source=chatgpt.com (Accessed 19 April 2025).
Levy, D. (2007) *Love and Sex with Robots*. New York. Harper Collins.
Levy, D. (2012) *The Ethics of Robot Prostitutes in Robot Ethics*, Lin, P., Abney, K. and Bekey, G. (eds). Cambridge MA: The MIT Press.
Local Government Association. (2022) *Sunderland City Council: 5G Connected and Automated Logistics*. https://www.local.gov.uk/case-studies/sunderland-city-council-5g-connected-and-automated-logistics (Accessed 19 April 2025).
Löffler, M. and Tschiener, A. (2013) *The Internet of Things and the Future of Manufacturing*. https://www.mckinsey.com/capabilities/mckinsey-digital/our-insights/the-internet-of-things-and-the-future-of-manufacturing (Accessed 19 April 2025).
Mańko, R. (2017) *European Parliamentary Research Service Author*. https://www.europarl.europa.eu/RegData/etudes/ATAG/2017/599250/EPRS_ATA(2017)599250_EN.pdf (Accessed 19 April 2025).
Mays, K.K., Cummings, J.J. and Katz, J.E. (2024) 'The robot rights and responsibilities scale: Development and validation of a metric for understanding perceptions of robots' rights and responsibilities.' *International Journal of Human – Computer Interaction*, 41(5), pp. 3413–3430.
NFU. (2025) *Apply for Competitions to Fund Innovation in Farming*. https://www.nfuonline.com/updates-and-information/farming-innovation-programme-competitions-for-funding/ (Accessed 19 April 2025).
Nourbakhsh, I. (2013) *Robot Futures*. Cambridge, MA: MIT Press.
O'Reilly, T. (2017) *WTF What's the Future and Why It's Up to Us*. London: Penguin.
Osborne-Sherlock, E. (2023) *Defra Announces £12.5m in Funding for Robotic Farming Technologies*. https://www.agriland.co.uk/farming-news/defra-announces-12-5m-in-funding-for-robotic-farming-technologies/?utm_source=chatgpt.com (Accessed 19 April 2025).
Perrigo, B. (2023) *'I Feel Like I'm Drowning': Survey Reveals the Toll of Working for Amazon*. https://time.com/6248340/amazon-injuries-survey-labor-osha/ (Accessed 19 April 2025).

PM Statement on AUKUS Partnership. (2021) https://www.gov.uk/government/speeches/pm-statement-on-aukus-partnership-15-september-2021 (Accessed 19 April 2025).
Robotic-Assisted Surgery: A Pathway to the Future a Guide to Good Practice published by the Royal College of Surgeons. https://www.rcseng.ac.uk/-/media/Files/RCS/Standards-and-research/Standards-and-policy/Good-Practice-Guides/2023/Robotic-assisted-surgery-guidance_WEB.pdf (Accessed 19 April 2025).
Rogers, T.N. (2025) *US Port Operators Turn to Automation*. https://www.ft.com/content/52a89a40-524d-4fe2-85bd-a02e6ba8490f?utm_source=chatgpt.com (Accessed 19 April 2025).
Sebo, J. (2025) *The Moral Circle*. New York: W. W. Norton and Company.
Shah, S. (2025) *Roborock Reveals Z70 Robot Vacuum with AI Mechanical Arm at CES 2025*. https://www.standard.co.uk/news/tech/robot-vacuum-roborock-z70-ai-arm-ces-2025-b1203213.html?utm_source=chatgpt.com (Accessed 19 April 2025).
Sherif, R. (2023) *Retail Revenue of Robotic Vacuum Cleaner Market Worldwide from 2014 to 2021 (in billion U.S. dollars)*. https://www.statista.com/statistics/1068290/worldwide-robotic-vacuum-cleaner-market-revenue/ (Accessed 19 April 2025).
Sillitoe, B. (2025) *Behind the Scenes at Amazon UK's Robotic-Powered Warehouse*. https://www.computerweekly.com/feature/Behind-the-scenes-at-Amazon-UKs-robotic-powered-warehouse?utm_source=chatgpt.com (Accessed 19 April 2025).
Stop Killer Robots. (undated) *Problems with Autonomous Weapons*. https://www.stopkillerrobots.org/stop-killer robots/facts-about-autonomous-weapons/?utm source=chatgpt.com (Accessed 19 April 2025).
Susskind, D. (2024) *Growth a Reckoning*. Great Britain: Allen Lane.
Uddin, R. (2025) *Amazon Steps Up Use of Robotics in Warehouses*. https://www.ft.com/content/31ec6a78-97cf-47a2-b229-d63c44b81073?utm_source=chatgpt.com (Accessed 19 April 2025).
UN. (2024) *Current Developments in Science and Technology and Their Potential Impact on International Security and Disarmament Efforts*. https://docs.un.org/en/A/79/224 (Accessed 19 April 2025).
UNI Global Union. (2023) *Life in the Amazon Panopticon: An International Survey of Amazon Workers*. https://uniglobalunion.org/wp-content/uploads/UNIAMZN_Report.pdf (Accessed 19 April 2025).
US Department of State. (2023) https://www.state.gov/bureau-of-arms-control-deterrence-and-stability/political-declaration-on-responsible-military-use-of-artificial-intelligence-and-autonomy (Accessed 19 April 2025).
Vallor, S. (2024) *The AI Mirror*. Oxford: Oxford University Press.
Wasim, H. (2025) *Robots in the Manufacturing Industry: Types and Applications*. https://www.wevolver.com/article/manufacturing-robots?utm_source=chatgpt.com (Accessed 19 April 2025).
Wilson, J.L.D. (2025) *AI, War and (In)Humanity: The Role of Human Emotions in Military Decision-Making*. https://blogs.icrc.org/law-and-policy/2025/02/20/ai-war-and-in-humanity-the-role-of-human-emotions-in-military-decision-making/?utm_source=chatgpt.com (Accessed 19 April 2025).

Recommended reading

Alan Winfield, A. (2012) *Robotics: A Very Short Introduction*. Oxford: Oxford University Press.
Lynch, P. (2024) *Robotics Step by Step: A Structured Introduction to Robotics Fundamentals & Applications* (Step by Step Subject Guides). Nevada, USA: Tag Vault Publishing.
Matronic, A. (2015) *Robot Takeover 100 Iconic Roots of Myth, Popular Culture & Real Life*. London: Cassell.
Nourbakhsh, I.R. (2013) *Robot Futures*. MA: MIT Press.

12 Synthetic biology in depth

Introduction

Before we look at 'synthetic' biology, it is important to look at the biology found in nature. One of the most important findings in the long history of studying living things is that they are all composed of one or more cells. The different parts making up the structure of a cell depend on the type of living thing it is part of. The structures of two different sorts of cells are shown in Panel 12.1.

Panel 12.1a+b The structures of plantae, and animalia cells

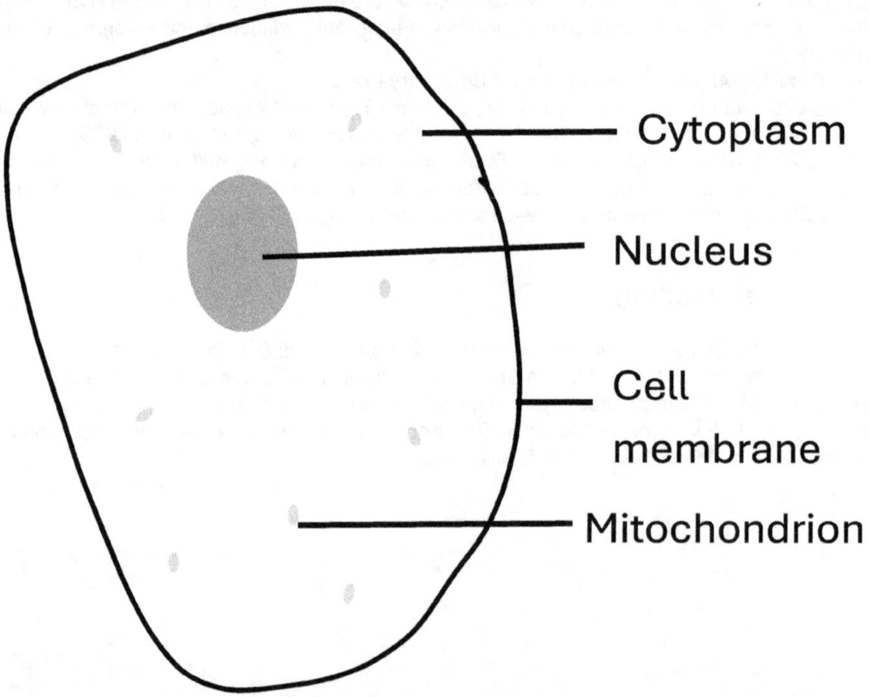

DOI: 10.4324/9781003602002-13

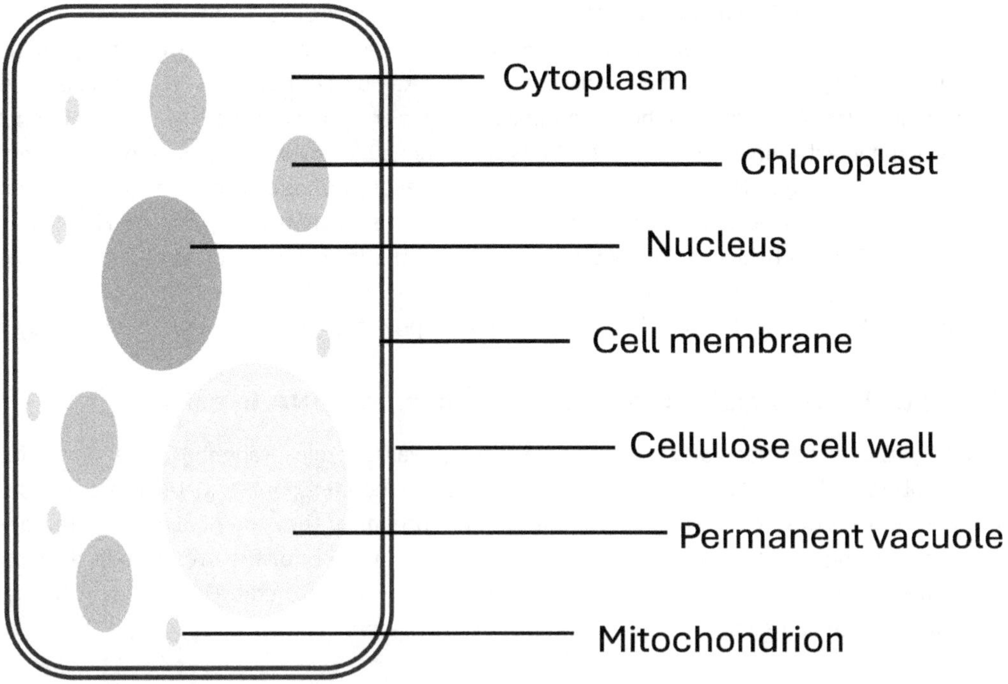

Each of these different types of cells contain DNA (deoxyribonucleic acid). The DNA in all these cells plays a central role. It contains the instructions needed to build and maintain the organism. It carries the code for making proteins, which perform most of the functions in a cell. It controls the development, response to the environment and cell differentiation (what sort of cell the cell becomes as it develops). In short, DNA tells cells what to do, how to do it and when. This complete arrangement of the DNA in an organism is called the genome. We can think of the genome as the entire instruction manual for the cell and a gene as a single instruction within that manual. Note that the term "chromosome" refers to a long strand of DNA that contains many genes. Humans typically have 46 chromosomes arranged in 23 pairs, half from each parent. A simple analogy is that of a conventional library; the chromosomes are like the books in the library and the genes are the individual recipes or instructions written in those books.

Those practicing synthetic biology are concerned with manipulating particular parts of the DNA in the genome. This requires an interdisciplinary approach that combines principles from biology, engineering, chemistry and computer science with the aims of enhancing existing life forms, creating new life forms and new biological systems that are useful for commercial purposes in a wide range of industrial sectors and healthcare. To achieve this synthetic biology applies engineering principles to biology, treating biological components as standardised parts that can be assembled in novel ways to create useful organisms not found in Nature.

The remainder of this chapter is in 10 parts. Part 1 will consider CRISPR, one of the major tools used to manipulate DNA in cells. Part 2 will consider the somewhat checkered history of synthetic biology in public perception. Part 3 will describe recent examples of how CRISPR is being used in gene editing. Part 4 will describe how synthetic biology is providing alternatives to conventional chemical manufacturing. Part 5 will describe how synthetic biology is being used to combat environmental challenges. Part 6 will focus on the potential of synthetic biology to influence food production. Part 7 will describe how completely novel organisms are being synthesised in the laboratory. Part 8 will consider the disruption caused by synthetic biology in terms of the McKinsey criteria for disruption. Part 9 will discuss the possible positive and negative effects of synthetic biology. Part 10 will describe the influence of other disruptive technologies on synthetic biology.

Part 1 CRISPR, a major tool used to manipulate DNA in cells

CRISPR (Clustered Regularly Interspaced Short Palindromic Repeats) is a powerful gene-editing tool that allows scientists to make precise modifications to DNA. The scientists wanting to use CRISPR will know the genome of the organism they are dealing with; the genome containing, in the form of DNA, all the information needed for the organism to develop and grow. They will know which part of the genome they want to edit. Here's how it works, broken down step by step:

Identifying the Target DNA Sequence

CRISPR uses a specially designed piece of RNA called a **guide RNA** to locate a specific sequence of DNA in a genome. The guide RNA is designed to match the DNA sequence the scientist wants to edit.

Cutting the DNA with Cas9 Enzyme

The guide RNA directs the **Cas9 enzyme**, a type of molecular "scissors", to the target site. Cas9 then makes a **double-stranded break** in the DNA; it cuts both strands of the DNA helix at that location.

Repairing the DNA Break

After the DNA is cut, the cell uses one of two natural repair mechanisms:

- **Non-Homologous End Joining** – An error-prone method that can introduce small insertions or deletions, often used to disable a gene.
- **Homology-Directed Repair** – A precise method that uses a DNA template to repair the break, allowing the insertion of new genetic material.

Part 2 Public perception of synthetic biology

Synthetic biology is by its very nature 'hidden' from the general public operating as it does at the molecular level. However, occasionally it does make headlines, revealing public concern.

This was the case in England in February 1999, when a controversial study suggested that a few strains of genetically modified (GM) potatoes might be toxic to laboratory rats, although those experiments were subsequently criticised by other experts. What followed was a European anti-GM food campaign of near-religious fervour. Spearheaded in the UK by environmental groups and some newspapers, the campaign culminated in an unofficial moratorium on the growth and import of GM crops in Europe. Critics feared that what they called Frankenstein foods could have unforeseen and adverse health effects on consumers, producing toxic proteins (and allergens) or transferring antibiotic-resistance and other genes to human gut bacteria to damaging effect. Hence GM crops became very rare in Europe, strict labelling and regulations were put in place for food and public opinion towards the technology remained largely negative (Pickrell 2006). There is a parallel here with the public concern over nanotechnology, another hidden technology. The DEEPEN Project (Macnaghten et al. 2010) explored the nature of these concerns by discussing them with members of the general public in the UK and Portugal. What emerged from an analysis of these conversations was a set of five key, strongly believed cultural narratives. These narratives were familiar stories that are deeply embedded in European culture, which provide foundation and strength to a more broadly applicable type of imagination. Their concerns formed part of a larger context of concerns about technological society in general. From this, and given that the DNA in living things is fundamental to the way they develop and behave, and that synthetic biology deliberately tries to change and manipulate this basic component of life, it is likely that the public concerns about nanotechnology revealed by the DEEPEN Project will also be concerns with regard to synthetic biology.

The revealed narratives were as follows:

1. Be careful what you wish for - the narrative of Desire
2. Being kept in the dark - the narrative of Alienation
3. Messing with nature - the narrative of the Sacred
4. Pandora's box - the narrative of Evil and Hope
5. The rich get richer - the narrative of Exploitation.

Thus, "*Be careful what you wish for*" (the narrative of Desire) builds on the age-old notion that getting exactly what you want may not ultimately be good for you, and it may inadvertently lead to unforeseen disaster and catastrophe. Hence, moving towards a situation in which aspects of synthetic biology are developed to solve pressing problems may lead to "throwing caution to the winds", with enthusiastic advocates of the technology giving little consideration to consequences outside intended benefit and an unwillingness to consider possible risks. Using synthetic biology to produce insect repelling plants at first seems a good idea as such plants would be much less prone to being eaten by insects. However, it is also likely that such plants will also speed the evolution of insecticide-resistant pests resulting in accelerated evolution into "superpests".

"*Being kept in the dark*" (the narrative of Alienation) expresses members of the public's sense of powerlessness in the face of the way synthetic biology might be developed by the scientific community using venture capital from those who wish to make significant financial gain through the deployment via business and commerce. They have no voice as to the direction of research and development and are troubled by their limited understanding of the science and technology underpinning synthetic biology. Synthetic biology was integral to the development of vaccines in the Covid epidemic, but several communities were reluctant to be vaccinated and social media was rife with anti-vaccine opinions.

In the case of *"messing with nature"* (the narrative of the Sacred), there is a deep-seated belief that interfering at such a basic level with living things, inevitable with synthetic biology, cannot be good. It must be acknowledged that farmers have been 'interfering' by methodically improving crop plants through selective breeding for many thousands of years, but synthetic biology allows that time-consuming activity to be accelerated without having the opportunity to see unintended consequences and halt the process. For some members of the public this arrogance in redesigning nature to our own needs will not go 'unpunished'.

Pandora's box (the narrative of Evil and Hope) articulates public unease about the hubris of meddling with things that should be left alone, and of the likely subsequent release of a whole range of human evils. The box may be opened in hope of better things to come, but there is no guarantee that what comes out will lead to a better state of affairs. In the science fiction film *Serenity* (see https://www.rottentomatoes.com/m/serenity), the experiment on a society to reduce aggression in the hope of developing a more harmonious society in fact led to the majority of the population becoming so docile that they ceased to perform daily activities and died whilst a small minority became insanely aggressive and violent.

The case of *"the rich get richer"* (the narrative of Exploitation) is exemplified by some companies having used synthetic biology to genetically modify crops so that they fail to produce fertile seeds. This prevents the traditional practice of putting seeds aside from the crop to replant the following year, forcing farmers to buy new seed every year, leading to the companies selling more seed and getting richer whilst the farmers have to buy seed annually, getting poorer. Some biotech companies have pledged not to use this technology, despite the fact it could be a useful tool in preventing genetic pollution (Pickrell 2006).

We will bear this account of possible public concern and scepticism with regard to synthetic biology when we discuss the possible positive and negative effects of synthetic biology in Part 9 of this chapter.

Part 3 Current use of CRISPR in gene editing

This section will describe examples of synthetic biology being used in healthcare, agriculture and consumer products.

Healthcare

CRISPR-based cure for sickle cell disease

Sickle cell disease is the name for a group of inherited health conditions that affect the red blood cells. The most serious type is called sickle cell anaemia. Sickle cell disease is particularly common in people with an African or Caribbean family background. People with sickle cell disease produce unusually shaped red blood cells that can cause problems because they do not live as long as healthy blood cells and they can block blood vessels. Sickle cell disease is a serious and lifelong health condition, although treatment can help manage many of the symptoms. People born with sickle cell disease tend to have problems from early childhood, although some children have few symptoms and lead normal lives most of the time. The main symptoms of sickle cell disease are:

- painful episodes called sickle cell crises, which can be very severe and last for days or weeks
- an increased risk of serious infections
- anaemia (where red blood cells cannot carry enough oxygen around the body), which can cause tiredness and shortness of breath.

Some people also experience other problems, such as delayed growth, strokes and lung problems. Sickle cell disease is caused by a gene that affects how red blood cells develop. (More information is available at the NHS1 website.) In late 2023, the US Food and Drug Administration approved the first CRISPR-based therapy for sickle cell disease. This treatment edits a patient's own blood stem cells to increase haemoglobin production, thereby reducing the sickling of red blood cells. This is a one-time therapy and has shown the potential to significantly alleviate symptoms and, in some cases, cure the disease (Park 2023).

The prospect of treating polycystic kidney disease

Autosomal dominant polycystic kidney disease (ADPKD) is caused by a genetic fault that disrupts the normal development of some of the cells in the kidneys and causes cysts to grow. Although children affected by ADPKD are born with the condition, it rarely causes any noticeable problems until the cysts grow large enough to affect the kidneys' functions. In most cases, this does not occur until a person is between 30 and 40 years of age. When ADPKD reaches this stage, it can cause a wide range of problems, including tummy (abdominal) pain, high blood pressure, blood in the urine, which may not always be noticeable to the naked eye, potentially serious upper urinary tract infections (UTIs) and kidney stones. Kidney function may gradually deteriorate until so much is lost that kidney failure occurs. ADPKD is the most common inherited condition to affect the kidneys, although it's still relatively uncommon. It's estimated that up to 1 in every 1000 to 2500 people in the UK have ADPKD. This means there could be between 30,000 and 70,000 people in the UK with this condition. (More information is available at the NHS2 website.)

The damage caused to the body by ADPKD was thought to be irreversible. But now, animal studies suggest that correcting the responsible mutations via CRISPR gene editing can reverse at least some of it. Researchers at Mayo Clinic in Rochester, Minnesota, have used a form of CRISPR called base editing to correct a mutation in a gene called *Pkd1* that causes the disease in mice using viruses to deliver the gene-editing machinery. This could be an issue if repeat doses are needed, as the immune response to viruses can stop treatments from working. Replacing the viruses with lipid nanoparticles like those used in mRNA vaccines would avoid the potential immune issue, but these particles can't penetrate deep enough into the kidneys via blood to be effective; however, it might be possible to deliver lipid nanoparticles through the urethra (Le Page 2025).

Agriculture

Genetically engineered rice with improved yields in India

In 2025 the Indian Institute of Rice Research announced the successful development of a gene edited variety of rice which has significant advantages over Samba Masouri, the traditional rice grown in many parts of India. Santander Kumar and his team used CRISPR to alter the gene that controlled metabolism, leading to an increase in the number of grains per panicle, with multi-location field trials showing an average 19% yield advantage. The gene edited variety also demonstrated early maturity, a valuable trait for rain-fed and rotation-based agriculture, and had a stronger stem, better resisting breakage during heavy winds and rainfall (Reddy 2025).

Powdery mildew-resistant tomatoes

Powdery mildew on tomatoes is a fungal disease characterised by white, powdery spots on leaves, stems and sometimes fruit. It thrives in warm, dry conditions and can weaken plants, reduce yields and affect fruit quality. Researchers from England, Germany and China collaborated in developing a tomato plant that was resistant to this disease. They were able to identify the gene that resulted in the tomato plant being vulnerable to the disease and remove it using CRISPR (Nekrasov et al. 2017).

Cattle genetically engineered to be more heat-tolerant

Researchers at Washington State University have used CRISPR to ensure that beef cattle develop a "slick" coat – shorter, slicker hair – that naturally occurs in some cattle breeds and helps them tolerate high temperatures (Cooksonm 2024). The researchers claim that this enhances animal welfare and productivity in hot climate through reducing heat stress, improving feed efficiency and supports beef farming in warmer regions. The FDA issued a "low-risk determination" for use of beef from these cattle in March 2022 – the first such decision under its gene-edited animal policy (Beecher 2024).

Consumer products

Glowing pet animals

The team at the Los Angeles Project has used CRISPR to add a gene to rabbit embryos so they produce a green fluorescent protein. They hope to transfer the engineered embryos to female rabbits so that they give birth to offspring that glow in the dark. Eventually they aim to produce a range of genetically engineered pets, as they believe there will be a significant market for such animals as consumers become more accepting of genetic engineering (Mullin 2025). Unsurprisingly, bioethicists have been warning about such a frivolous use of CRISPR for ten years (Charo and Greely 2015).

Microbial production of sustainable cosmetics ingredients

Many ingredients used in cosmetics are animal-derived and environmentally unsustainable. These include squalene, used in a host of products from moisturisers and sunscreen to lipstick and more. However, much of the squalene in the cosmetic industry comes from sharks. Shark liver oil is a particularly rich source of squalene and 90% of global demand, some 2,200 tons, is used for cosmetics. With 3,000 sharks needed to produce just 1 ton of squalene, this is a simply unsustainable demand for populations already threatened with overexploitation. Biotech firms such as Evolva and Amyris (via Biossance) are using CRISPR to genetically engineer yeast and bacteria to produce this key cosmetic ingredient (Labiotech 2022).

Part 4 Alternatives to conventional chemical manufacturing

According to its proponents, synthetic biology is transforming chemical manufacturing, making it greener, more sustainable and enabling production of novel molecules unattainable via traditional chemistry. Here are three examples:

Production of 1,4-butanediol via genetically engineered bacteria

1,4-butanediol (see Figure 12.2) is a key precursor for plastics, solvents and textiles. It is sometimes known by the initials BDO. Chemistry teachers will know that such a linear molecule with reactive "ends" is ideal for polymerisation.

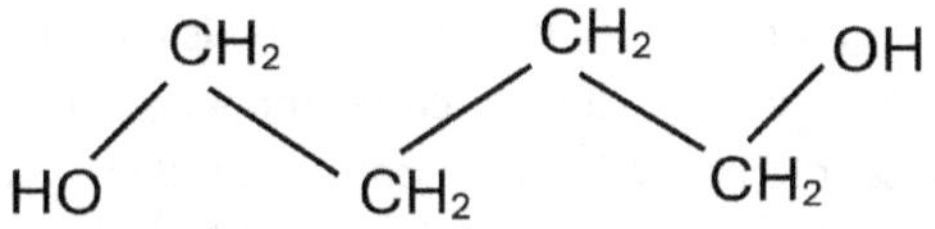

Figure 12.2 Structure of 1,4-butanediol

There are several conventional manufacturing processes, including acetylene reacting with formaldehyde and hydrogenating the resulting butyne 1, 4-diol, and from maleic anhydride, which is first converted to the methyl maleate ester, and then hydrogenated.

Genomatica is a company that specialises in developing sustainable alternatives to fossil fuel-derived chemicals (see https://www.genomatica.com for more information). Scientists at the company developed an engineered *E. coli* strain that ferments renewable sugars into 1,4-butanediol. This bio-based route is eco-friendlier and more cost-effective than petrochemical methods. South Korean firm Hyosung is investing in large-scale "bio-BDO" production, cutting carbon footprints by ~90%, with a 50,000 tons-per-year plant due online in 2026 (Ninad 2024).

Using genetically engineered bacteria to produce diamine monomers for polyimide film production

Polyimide film, known commercially as Hyaline, is a transparent, mechanically robust flexible film suitable for mounting circuitry used in foldable smartphones and wearable electronics. The starting monomers for this polymeric material are diamines such as those shown in Figure 12.3. Again, chemistry teachers will know that such a molecule is ideal for polymerisation.

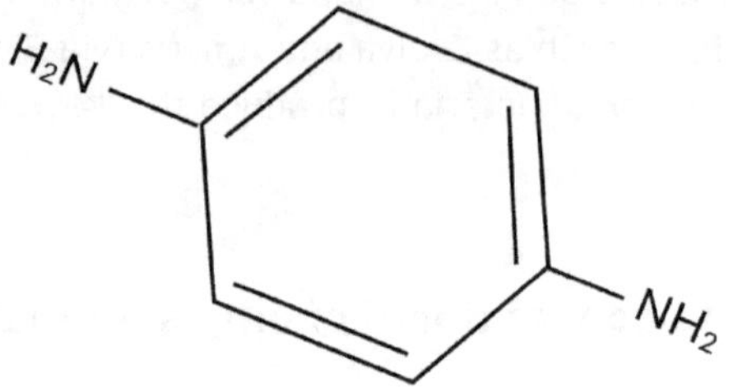

Figure 12.3 Structure of a diamine

Conventionally, diamines are derived from petrochemicals. The company Zymergen, later acquired by Gingko Bioworks, engineered microbes to produce these materials via fermentation, thus avoiding dependency on petrochemicals (Voight 2020).

Developing novel enzymes

UC Berkeley researchers have embedded metal catalysts in natural enzymes to make so-called artificial metalloenzymes, which can synthesise chemicals that have been hard to make in the laboratory by other means. One reaction they have worked on is introducing a cyclopropane ring, a ring of three carbon atoms to other molecules such as limonene to produce a class of compounds difficult to make via chemical methods. Such cyclopropanated chemicals are becoming increasingly useful in medicines, such as a drug to cure hepatitis C infections. These compounds are difficult to make via chemical methods. Aindrila Mukhopadhyay, biological engineer senior scientist at UC Berkeley, says that this technology, which combines laboratory synthesis with synthetic biology within a living organism, "opens up possibilities for fuels with desirable properties that can be produced renewably, as well as new antibiotics, new nutraceuticals, new compounds that would be exceedingly challenging to make using only biology or only chemistry" (Sanders 2021).

Part 5 Combating environmental challenges

Dealing with environmental pollution

Before the advent of synthetic biology, bioremediation relied primarily on naturally occurring organisms and conventional microbial engineering techniques to address environmental pollution. Here are three examples.

Use of Hydrocarbon-Degrading Bacteria to Clean up Exxon Valdez Oil Spill

In 1989, after the Exxon Valdez oil spill in Prince William Sound, Alaska, naturally occurring hydrocarbon-degrading bacteria, such as *Pseudomonas* and *Alcanivorax*, were stimulated through biostimulation (the addition of nitrogen and phosphorus fertilizers) to accelerate the breakdown of petroleum hydrocarbons (Atlas and Hazen 2011).

Uranium Bioremediation at Oak Ridge National Laboratory

In the 1990s, naturally occurring subsurface bacteria, such as *Geobacter* species, were shown to reduce soluble uranium (VI) to insoluble uranium (IV), thereby immobilising it and preventing groundwater contamination at the Oak Ridge site in Tennessee (Lovley and Anderson 2000).

Using Plants to Extract Heavy Metals (Phytoremediation)

Indian mustard plants were used to extract heavy metals such as lead, cadmium and selenium from contaminated soils (Salt et al. 1995).

In contrast to traditional bioremediation described here, which relies on naturally occurring organisms with inherent capabilities to degrade pollutants, synthetic biology allows scientists to design and construct new metabolic pathways in microbes to target specific contaminants, including those that are otherwise resistant to natural degradation. Here are three examples:

Degrading Complex Organic Compounds

Researchers were able to incorporate synthetic pathways in *Pseudomonas putida*, a bacteria found in soil, enabling it to degrade complex aromatic hydrocarbons and recalcitrant pollutants like polychlorinated biphenyls (PCBs) (Nikel et al. 2015).

Developing Synthetic Microalgae for Plastic and Heavy Metal Removal

Microalgae have been genetically engineered to tolerate and remediate pollutants such as mercury, chromium, arsenic and even phasing in PET plastic digestion - creating strains that exceed wild-type capabilities in wastewater cleanup and pollutant uptake (Webster et al. 2024).

Developing Synthetic Consortia for Complex Pollutants

Instead of relying on single organisms, synthetic biology enables the design of **engineered microbial consortia** that work cooperatively to degrade complex pollutant mixtures, mimicking natural ecological networks but with improved performance. Engineered communities of bacteria and yeast were developed that could simultaneously degrade petroleum compounds and detoxify by-products (Brenner et al. 2008).

Combating global warming

Synthetic biology is also being used in attempts to limit global warming. Here are two examples.

> **CRISPR-engineered Organisms for CO_2 Capture**
>
> Cyanobacteria, often called blue green algae because of their colour, are one of the oldest life forms on our planet, coming into existence some 3 billion years ago. They are able to react with carbon dioxide in the atmosphere and with water to form oxygen and complex carbon compounds. Acetogens are microorganisms that also metabolise carbon dioxide, giving, as their name implies, acetate ions. Methanogens are microorganisms that can metabolise carbon dioxide, giving, again as their name implies, methane. Scientists have used CRISPR to edit the DNA in these organisms to create microbes that directly consume CO_2 and convert it into biofuels (i.e. biodiesel, bioethanol and isobutanol) and food products such as starch in ways that result in a net reduction of carbon dioxide in the atmosphere.
>
> (Yu et al. 2022)

Carbon capture is something that any tree can do, but as trees and other plants convert carbon into sugars and other nutrients, they also produce a toxic byproduct that must then be broken down during photorespiration, an energy-intensive process that ends up releasing a portion of sequestered CO2. A new kind of poplar tree is different. Researchers inserted three genes from squash and algae which allow them to minimise the photorespiration process, thus channelling more energy into growth. Compared to standard poplars, the modified trees can grow up to 53 percent larger in five months and can capture 27 percent more CO2. The researchers project that, once planted at scale, these genetically modified trees may remove billions of tons of carbon dioxide from the atmosphere (Atleework 2024).

Part 6 Synthetic biology and food production, ancient and modern

Humans began using fermentation in the preparation of food and drink several thousands of years ago, resulting in the development of commercial production of beers, wine, yoghurts and cheeses. Fermentation uses the enzymes contained in yeasts and bacteria to catalyse the breakdown of carbohydrates in the absence of oxygen. This breakdown of carbohydrates results in various byproducts, including alcohol (ethanol), lactic acid and carbon dioxide. The breakdown of carbohydrates in barley is used to produce beer, in grapes to produce wine, in milk to produce yoghurts and cheeses and in cabbage to produce sauerkraut and kimchi. In breadmaking the yeast ferments sugars in dough, producing carbon dioxide that causes the bread to rise.

How might synthetic biology contribute to the use of fermentation in food and drink production? A report from McKinsey and Company (Aminetzah et al. 2025) suggests that using fermentation to produce novel proteins could make up 4% of total protein production by 2050, an annual market of $100 billion to $150 billion. Using synthetic biology to create microorganisms that generate novel proteins in the laboratory always faces the problem of scaling up. Production at scale needs new design fermenters developed specifically for the process, and this will require significant investment. At the moment such production methods are more expensive than conventional protein production. There are environmental advantages in using fermenters over animals for protein production, and this can add to the brand value of new food products for some consumers. But consumer sentiment is often fickle, and the food products derived from novel proteins with different mouthfeel and flavours may not necessarily have long-lasting appeal. Aminetzah et al suggest that over the next five years the combination of lowering production costs, as the fermentation technology becomes more efficient, coupled with increasing consumer acceptance will derisk the novel ingredients industry. Hence, investing now provides venture capitalists with the opportunity to become part of the food supply chain of the future. Time will tell.

Part 7 More than just editing - complete organism synthesis

In 2009, J. Craig Venter and his research team reported that they had created a synthetic bacterium whose entire genome was synthesised in the lab from chemical building blocks and never directly derived from a natural organism. The team chemically synthesised the entire genome of *Mycoplasma mycoides* using sequence information from a *natural M. mycoides* bacterium as a blueprint. They then transported this genome into cells of a closely related species, *Mycoplasma capricolum*, first stripping these cells of their DNA. After successful transplantation, the host cells were "booted up" by the synthetic genome, effectively turning them into synthetic *M. mycoides* cells. The resulting cells divided and grew, controlled entirely by the synthetic genome. The cytoplasmic components (proteins, membranes, etc.) initially came from the *M. capricolum* recipient cells but over time, as the synthetic genome expressed its proteins, the cell's internal machinery transitioned to being entirely based on the synthetic genome's instructions. Thus, it was not built "from scratch" in the sense of constructing every component, but it was the first living cell controlled by a synthetic genome (Gibson et al. 2010). By 2016 Venter and his team had refined this work by trimming non-essential genes from the previously synthesised genome so that it contained 473 genes - the fewest of any free-living organism known. Since then, research work has continued, including the addition of 19 genes that restored the cell shape of the bacteria, developing computational models linking genotype to function and broader advances in synthetic genomics expanding into viruses, yeast and designer bacteria for practical applications.

At the time of writing, the Wellcome Trust has announced an ambitious new five-year research project, SynHG (Synthetic Human Genome). It aims to develop the foundational and scalable tools, technology and methods needed to synthesise human genomes (Wellcome 2025). This is a huge step from the synthesis of genomes associated with other, much simpler organisms, which has already taken place. Unlike genome editing, genome synthesis allows for changes at a greater scale and density, with more accuracy and efficiency, and the expectation is that this will lead to an understanding of how the organisation of the human genome controls how our bodies function. Those leading the project argue that synthetic genomes have the potential to open up brand-new areas of research in creating targeted cell-based therapies, virus-resistant tissue transplantation and extensions that may even enable the engineering of plant species with new properties, including the ability to withstand harsh climates. The five-year project - supported by £10mn funding from Wellcome - involves researchers from the Universities of Cambridge, Kent, Manchester, Oxford and Imperial College London. An important aspect of the project is a dedicated social science programme, Care-Full Synthesis, led by Professor Joy Zhang of the Centre for Global Science and Epistemic Justice at the University of Kent, which will run throughout the project alongside the scientific development. Over the next 5 years, the team will undertake a transdisciplinary and transcultural investigation into the socio-ethical, economic and policy implications of synthesising human genomes. The project places particular emphasis on fostering inclusivity within and across nation-states while engaging emerging public-private partnerships and new interest groups. The team expects to develop a toolkit to enable effective integration of careful thinking into the management, communication and delivery of human genome synthesis.

Part 8 Disruption caused by synthetic biology

Synthetic biology exhibits significant characteristics of a disruptive technology when evaluated against McKinsey's four criteria: disrupting the status quo, altering the way people live and work, rearranging value pools and leading to entirely new products and services.

Disrupting the status quo

Synthetic biology is redefining traditional manufacturing and production processes across various industries. By enabling the design and engineering of biological systems, it allows for the creation of products through biological means, rather than conventional chemical synthesis or extraction. For example, companies are now producing bio-based materials, such as lab-grown leather and spider silk alternatives, which challenge traditional textile and leather industries.

Altering the way people live and work

The integration of synthetic biology into daily life is poised to transform healthcare, agriculture and consumer products. In healthcare, synthetic biology facilitates the development of personalised medicines and rapid vaccine production, as demonstrated during the COVID-19 pandemic. In agriculture, it enables the creation of genetically engineered crops with improved yields and resistance to pests, reducing the reliance on chemical pesticides. These advancements not only improve efficiency but also promote sustainability and health.

Rearranging value pools

Synthetic biology is shifting economic value across industries by introducing cost-effective and sustainable alternatives to traditional products. For instance, the production of biofuels through engineered microbes offers a renewable energy source that competes with fossil fuels. Similarly, the creation of synthetic flavours and fragrances reduces dependence on natural resources and traditional extraction methods. These shifts redistribute value from established industries to emerging biotech enterprises.

Leading to entirely new products and services

The capabilities of synthetic biology are giving rise to novel products and services that were previously unattainable. Examples include biosensors for real-time health monitoring, bio-engineered organisms for environmental remediation and customised probiotics tailored to individual microbiomes. These innovations open new markets and redefine existing ones, highlighting the transformative potential of synthetic biology.

In summary, synthetic biology aligns closely with McKinsey's criteria for disruptive technologies. Its ability to overhaul traditional processes, influence daily life, reallocate economic value and introduce unprecedented products underscores its disruptive impact across multiple sectors.

Part 9 Possible positive and negative effects of synthetic biology

The applications of synthetic biology described in the previous sections are seen by many as extremely beneficial. The list is impressive: improvements in healthcare and agriculture, the development of new consumer products, contributing to chemical manufacturing, dealing with environmental problems, combating global warming, developing advanced fermentation techniques, creating completely novel organisms and most recently pursuing research that will enable the synthesis of human genomes, which in turn will provide an understanding of how the organisation of the human genome controls how our bodies function, enabling previously unimaginable advances in health care. However, as we saw in Part 6 of this chapter, the general public has deep-seated reservations about the development and deployment of such 'hidden' technologies. Are such reservations justified or simply the result of public misunderstanding of the underlying science? This section will explore the reservations that have been articulated recently and consider the extent to which they should be taken seriously.

A range of concerns may be grouped under the heading of *unintended consequences*. A generally held view is that the vast majority of scientists involved in synthetic biology are pursuing ends which they think will be highly beneficial to a wide range of people across the world, but this is sometimes accompanied by accusations of hubris, excessive pride and arrogance on the part of some scientists in their self-belief. To minimise unintended consequences, the scientific community applies a combination of technical, regulatory and ethical safeguards which may be summarised as the following six steps:

Step 1 Comprehensive Risk Assessment

Before any intervention, scientists conduct extensive **risk assessments**, which include:

- Genetic stability testing to predict potential for unintended mutations.
- Ecological risk evaluation to assess possible impacts on ecosystems.
- Horizontal gene transfer analysis to prevent engineered genes from spreading to unintended organisms.

Step 2. Use of Precision Tools (e.g., CRISPR, Gene Drives)

Scientists use highly targeted genome editing tools like:

- CRISPR-Cas9, TALENs or ZFNs to ensure minimal off-target mutations.
- Gene drives with built-in containment mechanisms to reduce unpredictability.

To minimise off-target effects:

- They employ high-fidelity variants of CRISPR.
- Perform whole-genome sequencing to detect unintended edits.

Step 3. Laboratory Containment and Biocontainment Strategies

- Using physical containment (biosafety levels, sealed labs).
- Developing genetic containment, e.g.:
  - Kill-switches: Genetic circuits that self-destruct organisms if they escape.
  - Synthetic auxotrophy: Organisms engineered to depend on synthetic nutrients absent in the wild.

Step 4. Stepwise Testing and Phased Deployment

- Starting with **in vitro** experiments.
- Progressing to **model organisms** in contained environments.
- Conducting **small-scale field trials** under strict monitoring before widespread release.

Step 5. Regulatory Oversight and Ethical Review

- **Institutional Biosafety Committees (IBCs)** and **Ethics Boards** review all projects.
- National and international bodies (e.g., **US FDA**, **EFSA**, **WHO**, **Convention on Biological Diversity**) set regulations.
- Public engagement ensures transparency and builds trust.

Step 6. Continuous Monitoring and Post-Deployment Surveillance

- **Environmental monitoring** for unintended gene spread or ecological impacts.
- **Genomic monitoring** of engineered organisms to detect mutations over time.
- Rapid response plans if unintended effects are observed.

Despite these considerable efforts on the part of the scientific community working in collaboration with government bodies, concerns do remain, as the following three examples indicate:

Animal Welfare and Dignity

Traditional breeding practices have resulted in animals whose quality of life is significantly compromised. For example, Bulldogs, Pugs, and French Bulldogs have extremely shortened snouts and as a result struggle to breathe and exercise; they overheat; plus their facial folds trap moisture and bacteria, leading to frequent infections. There is concern that synthetic biology might make such practices more widespread and easily available. Also, gene editing animals for agricultural advantage, increased muscle mass for example, raises concerns about animal welfare, reduced naturalness and the ethical concern of seeing animals in only utilitarian terms as opposed to creatures meriting a life worth living.

Corporate Control and Loss of Biodiversity

Ralph Early of the Food Ethics Council notes that it is large corporations that undertake gene editing to create plants and animals that are more resistant to climate change and disease, and that patenting this technology can create a market monopoly with an increased shift towards corporate dominance in agriculture and loss of agricultural biodiversity. Traditional farmers can be required by government policy to use gene-edited disease-resistant livestock with a resultant loss of genetic diversity (Early 2025).

A Slippery Slope and Fear of Eugenics

The organisation Christian Action Research Education (CARE) has a clear position with regard to the gene editing of two different type of human cells. They are content that somatic cells (cells other than reproductive cells) may undergo gene editing with appropriate safeguards. However, they are opposed in principle to any gene editing taking place in germ cells, cells that develop into reproductive cells, which is an egg in females and a sperm in males. They made their position clear in responding to Commons Science and Technology Select Committee's consultation on genomic and genome editing (Eberl 2017). They were concerned that such research might eventually lead to "designer babies", although the scientific community has stated unambiguously that this would not be the intention of their research. The 'rogue' scientist He Jiankui edited embryos to resist HIV infection, leading to twin births. The scientific community condemned this as unethical, reckless, non-consensual and having unknown long-term harms. (Goodyear 2023). His actions provoked calls for global moratoria and stricter regulations. The WHO, China and others moved to tighten controls and require registries for human genome editing (Hansard 2020). However, organisations such as CARE, aware of the now largely discredited ideas of eugenics, warn that this indicates a slippery slope with the possibility of bad actors breaking ethical guidelines, especially as gene editing technology becomes standard practice and easier to apply.

These concerns indicate that it is important for the general public to be given a voice as to what they think is acceptable in the societies in which they live. This was an item in Step 5 of the aforementioned listing of safeguards, but public engagements are often fraught with difficulty, sometimes leading to alarmist reports in the popular press. Hence the work of Professor Joy Zhang in the Wellcome Trust research project initiative described earlier is of particular significance. And, of course, it is important that young people at school are prepared to be able to take part in such public debate, something which we will discuss at length in Part 2 of this book.

Underlying these concerns is a position articulated by Brian Arthur (2009), who suggests that our relationship with technology is one in which there is a conflict between our trust for the natural compared to our suspicion of the artificial.

> These two views, that technology is a thing directing our lives and simultaneously a thing blessedly serving our lives, are simultaneously valid. But together they cause unease, an ongoing tension, that plays out in our attitudes to technology and in the politics that surround it.
>
> (page 214)

> [W]e trust nature, not technology. And yet we look to technology to take care of our future – we hope in technology. So we hope in something we do not quite trust.
>
> (page 215)

For a fuller and more detailed discussion of the issues raised in this section, see *CRISPR and Ethics* (Henderson et al. 2024).

Part 10 The influence of other disruptive technologies on synthetic biology

The development of synthetic biology has been significantly influenced by several disruptive technologies. Here's an overview of how each technology contributes:

Additive Manufacturing (3D Printing): 3D printing facilitates the creation of custom lab equipment, microfluidic devices and even biological tissues. This technology allows for rapid prototyping and testing of biological constructs, thereby accelerating experimental workflows in synthetic biology.

Artificial Intelligence (AI): AI plays a pivotal role in synthetic biology by enhancing the design and optimisation of genetic circuits, predicting protein structures and accelerating drug discovery. Machine learning algorithms can analyse vast biological datasets to identify patterns and make predictions, thereby streamlining research and development processes.

Augmented Reality (AR): AR can enhance the visualisation of complex biological data and assist in training and education within synthetic biology. By overlaying digital information onto the physical world, AR can facilitate a better understanding of molecular structures and laboratory procedures.

Big Data: The field of synthetic biology generates massive amounts of data from genomic sequencing, metabolic profiling and other high-throughput techniques. Big data analytics enables researchers to manage, analyse and interpret these datasets, leading to more informed decision-making and hypothesis generation.

Internet of Things (IoT): IoT devices can monitor and control laboratory environments in real-time, ensuring optimal conditions for biological experiments. This connectivity enhances reproducibility and allows for remote management of experiments, which is particularly useful in automated synthetic biology workflows.

Neurotechnology: Neurotechnology intersects with synthetic biology in the development of brain-computer interfaces and the study of neural circuits. Understanding and manipulating neural networks can lead to advancements in treating neurological disorders and in developing biohybrid systems.

Programmable Matter: Programmable matter refers to materials that can change their physical properties in response to external stimuli. In synthetic biology, this concept could lead to the development of dynamic biological materials that respond to environmental changes, opening new avenues for smart biomaterials.

Quantum Computing: While still emerging, quantum computing holds promise for modelling complex biological systems and chemical reactions with unprecedented accuracy. This capability could revolutionise our understanding of biological processes and lead to the design of novel synthetic pathways.

Robotics: Robotic systems automate repetitive tasks such as pipetting, colony picking and sample analysis. Automation increases throughput, reduces human error and allows for the scaling-up of synthetic biology experiments.

In summary, the integration of these disruptive technologies is propelling synthetic biology forward, enabling more sophisticated designs, efficient processes and novel applications.

References

Aminetzah, D., Levene, J., Tom Brennan, T. and Toews, K. (2025) 'Ingredients for the future: Bringing the biotech revolution to food.' *McKinsey and Company*. https://www.mckinsey.com/industries/agriculture/our-insights/ingredients-for-the-future-bringing-the-biotech-revolution-to-food (Accessed July 2025).

Arthur, W.B. (2009) *The Nature of Technology*. London, England: Allen Lane.

Atlas, R.M. and Hazen, T.C. (2011) 'Oil biodegradation and bioremediation: A tale of the two worst spills in U.S. history.' *Environmental Science & Technology*, **45**(16), pp. 6709–6715.

Atleework, K. (2024) '5 Synthetic biology discoveries accelerating global sustainability.' *ThermoFisher Scientific*. https://www.thermofisher.com/blog/author/lifeinthelabstaff/ (Accessed July 2025).

Beecher, C. (2024) 'FDA to steer regulations for genetically edited meat animals.' *FSN Food Safety News*. https://www.foodsafetynews.com/2024/06/fda-to-steer-regulations-for-genetically-edited-meat-animals/?utm_source=chatgpt.com (Accessed June 2025).

Brenner, K., You, L. and Arnold, F.H. (2008) 'Engineering microbial consortia: A new frontier in synthetic biology.' *Trends in Biotechnology*, **26**(9), pp. 483–489.

Charo, R.A. and Greely, H.T. (2015) 'CRISPR critters and CRISPR cracks.' *The American Journal of Bioethics*, **15**(12), pp. 11–17. https://doi.org/10.1080/15265161.2015.1104138. https://www.tandfonline.com/doi/full/10.1080/15265161.2015.1104138 (Accessed July 2025).

Cooksonm, B. (2024) *FDA to Steer Regulations for Genetically Edited Meat Animals*. https://www.foodsafetynews.com/2024/06/fda-to-steer-regulations-for-genetically-edited-meat-animals/?utm_source=chatgpt.com (Accessed July 2025).

Early, R. (2025) 'Gene editing the ethical questions.' *Food Ethics Council*. https://www.foodethicscouncil.org/opinion/gene-editing-the-ethical-questions/?utm_source=chatgpt.com (Accessed July 2025).

Eberl, J.T. (2017) 'The case for perfection: Ethics in the age of human enhancement.' *National Catholic Bioethics Quarterly*, **17**(1), p. 107.

Gibson, D.G., Glass, J.I., Lartigue, C., Noskov, V., Chuang, R., Algire, M.A., Benders, G.A. Montague, M.G. and Vetner, C.D. et al. (2010) 'Creation of a bacterial cell controlled by a chemically synthesized genome.' *Science*, **329**(5987), pp. 52–56. https://www.science.org/doi/10.1126/science.1190719 (Accessed July 2025).

Goodyear, D. (2023) 'Dangerous designs gene editing gives us transformative powers: But should we use them.' *The New Yorker*. https://www.newyorker.com/magazine/2023/09/11/the-transformative-alarming-power-of-gene-editing?utm_source=chatgpt.com (Accessed July 2025).

Hansard. (2020) *Gene Editing Volume 801: Debated on Thursday 30 January 2020*. https://hansard.parliament.uk/lords/2020-01-30/debates/637E3108-D287-445B-8460-4B739A24CCF8/GeneEditing?utm_source=chatgpt.com (Accessed July 2025).

Henderson, H.R., Ramit, G., Tolpa, T., Murdock, A.G. and Halpern, J. (2024) 'CRISPR & ethics', in Hochstrasser et al. (eds) *CRISPRpedia*. Berkeley: Innovative Genomics Institute, University of California. https://innovativegenomics.org/crisprpedia/crispr-ethics/

Labiotech. (2022) *CRISPR Can Help the Switch to Sustainable Cosmetics*. https://www.labiotech.eu/opinion/crispr-cosmetics-ers-genomics/?utm_source=chatgpt.com (Accessed July 2025).

Le Page, M. (2025) 'Gene editing could treat damage from "irreversible" kidney disease Place.' *New Scientist*, 10 June. https://www.newscientist.com/article/2483470-gene-editing-could-treat-damage-from-irreversible-kidney-disease/ (Accessed July 2025).

Lovley, D.R. and Anderson, R.T. (2000) 'Bioremediation of metal contamination.' *Current Opinion in Biotechnology*, **11**(3), pp. 285–292.

Macnaghten, P., Davies, S. and Kearnes, M. (2010) 'Narrative and public engagement: Some findings from the DEEPEN project', in R. von Schomberg and S. Davies (eds) *Understanding Public Debates on Nanotechnologies Options for Framing Public Policy*. Luxembourg: European Union.

Mullin, E. (2025) 'Your next pet could be a glowing rabbit.' *Wired*. https://www.wired.com/story/your-next-pet-could-be-a-glowing-rabbit-los-angeles-project-gene-editing-crispr/?utm_source=chatgpt.com (Accessed July 2025).

Nekrasov, V., Wang, C., Win, J., Lanz, C., Weigel, D., Kamour, S. et al. (2017) *Rapid Generation of a Transgene-Free Powdery Mildew Resistant Tomato by Genome Deletion*. https://www.nature.com/articles/s41598-017-00578-x?utm_source=chatgpt.com (Accessed July 2025).

NHS 1. *Sickle Cell Disease*. https://www.nhs.uk/conditions/sickle-cell-disease/#:~:text=Sickle%20cell%20disease%20is%20particularly,and%20can%20block%20blood%20vessels (Accessed July 2025).

NHS 2. *Autosomal Dominant Polycystic Kidney Disease*. https://www.nhs.uk/conditions/autosomal-dominant-polycystic-kidney-disease-adpkd/ (Accessed July 2025).

Nikel, P.I., Chavarría, M., Fuhrer, T., Sauer, U. and de Lorenzo, V. (2015) 'Pseudomonas putida KT2440 strain metabolizes glucose through a cycle formed by enzymes of the Entner – Doudoroff, Embden – Meyerhof – Parnas, and Pentose Phosphate pathways.' *Journal of Biological Chemistry*, **290**(43), pp. 25920–25932

Ninad, M.J. (2024) 'Harnessing the power of life: Synthetic biology for next-generation chemical synthesis.' *International Journal of Research Development in Pharmacy & Life Science*, **10**(4). https://www.omicsonline.org/open-access/harnessing-the-power-of-life-synthetic-biology-for-nextgeneration-chemical-synthesis-132769.html?utm_source=chatgpt.com (Accessed July 2025).

Park, A. (2023) 'FDA approves first CRISPR treatment.' *U.S. Time Magazine*. https://time.com/6343853/fda-crispr-treatment-sickle-cell/?utm_source=chatgpt.com (Accessed July 2025).

Pickrell, J. (2006) 'Introduction: GM organisms.' *New Scientist*. http://www.newscientist.com/article/dn9921-instant-expert-gm-organisms.html#.VNNOdijCGQI (Accessed July 2025).

Reddy, U.S. (2025) 'India's first genome-edited rice variety developed in Hyderabad Times *of India*.' http://timesofindia.indiatimes.com/articleshow/120909746.cms?utm_source=chatgpt.com&utm_source=contentofinterest&utm_medium=text&utm_campaign=cppst (Accessed July 2025).

Salt, D.E., Blaylock, M., Kumar, N.P., Dushenkov, V., Ensley, B.D., Chet, I. and Raskin, I. (1995) 'Phytoremediation: A novel strategy for the removal of toxic metals from the environment using plants.' *Biotechnology*, **13**(5), pp. 468–474.

Sanders, R. (2021) 'Synthetic biology moves into the realm of the unnatural.' *UC Berkeley News*. https://news.berkeley.edu/2021/10/14/synthetic-biology-moves-into-the-realm-of-the-unnatural/?utm_source=chatgpt.com (Accessed July 2025).

Serenity. https://www.rottentomatoes.com/m/serenity (Accessed July 2025).

Voight, C.A. (2020) 'Synthetic biology 2020–2030: Six commercially-available products that are changing our world.' *Nature Communications*. https://pmc.ncbi.nlm.nih.gov/articles/PMC7733420/?utm_source=chatgpt.com (Accessed July 2025).
Webster, L.J., Villa-Gomez, D., Brown, R., Clarke, W., Schenk, P.M. (2024) 'A synthetic biology approach for the treatment of pollutants with microalgae.' *Frontiers in Bioengineering and Biotechnology*, April 5, **12**, p. 1379301. https://pmc.ncbi.nlm.nih.gov/articles/PMC11032018/?utm_source=chatgpt.com (Accessed July 2025).
Wellcome Trust. (2025) *Details of the Synthetic Human Genome Project*. https://wellcome.org/news/new-project-pioneer-principles-human-genome-synthesis (Accessed July 2025).
Yu, H.Y., Wang, S.G. and Xia, P.F. (2022) 'Reprogramming microbial CO_2-metabolizing chassis with CRISPR-cas systems.' *Frontiers in Bioengineering and Biotechnology*, June 23, **10**, p. 897204. https://pmc.ncbi.nlm.nih.gov/articles/PMC9260013/?utm_source=chatgpt.com (Accessed July 2025).

Recommended reading

Ball, P. (2025) *How Life Works: A User's Guide to the New Biology*. Chicago: University Chicago Press.
Davies, J.A. (2018) *Synthetic Biology: A Very Short Introduction* (Very Short Introductions). Oxford: Oxford University Press.
Webb, A. and Hessel, A. (2023) *The Genesis Machine: Our Quest to Rewrite Life in the Age of Synthetic Biology*. Paris: Public Affairs.

13 An introduction to Part 2

It is widely recognised that all technologies that reach maturity in that they function effectively and reliably have an impact on the societies that adopt them. We have argued that there are some technologies that have a disproportionate impact on society, and we have named those as disruptive and shown the large extent to which this disruption impacts on society. Before we move on to consider how we might teach learners in secondary schools about these disruptive technologies, it is worth considering the extent to which technology in general might be within our control or in control of us. Are we optimistic or pessimistic for the future, and how should those views be balanced and play out across the different school subjects?

Kevin Kelly (2010) argues that there are three drivers affecting the way technology plays out in the world. The first and most significant is the intrinsic nature of technology, the way it works, interacting within itself in ways that enable it to organise itself according to its inherent nature. The second is the influence of technological history in that all technologies build on previous ones. The third is society's collective free will in response to the way technology is playing out either aligning with developments or opposing them. He argues that opposing technology will only have a very limited effect. He is a technological optimist and views new and emerging technologies as providing ever-increasing opportunities for humans to 'self-realise' in ways not available to those in previous generations, acknowledging that in reality humans actually have little control of technology.

The thinking of Jacques Ellul (1964) is in direct contrast to that of Kelly, as he is most definitely a technological pessimist. He views the intrinsic nature of technology with its emphasis on efficiency and standardisation as inimitable to the human spirit and the wide-ranging influence that technology has had, and continues to have, on society as both dehumanising as well as outside human control. However, economist Daniel Susskind takes a very different view. He argues that the development of technologies in the past 200 years have been responsible for a level of economic growth not seen before in human history to the considerable benefit of some in many societies, but that this has often come at considerable costs to outcomes that most would desire: a healthy climate, fair distribution of wealth, strong communities, good working conditions and a functioning democracy. However, he does **not** believe that technology is outside our control. In his book *Growth: A Reckoning* (Susskind 2024), he argues that these harmful features are the consequences of the technical choices made by their

DOI: 10.4324/9781003602002-14

inventors, knowingly or otherwise, in response to the particular incentives that have been put in front of them.

In a response to this critique of technological innovation, Shannon Vallor (Vallor 2016) has explored the role that virtue might play in the way society develops and uses technology. She has developed the following taxonomy of "technomoral" virtues:

- Honesty: respecting truth
- Self-control: becoming the author of our desires
- Humility: knowing what we do not know
- Justice: upholding rightness
- Courage: intelligent fear and hope
- Empathy: compassionate concern for others
- Care: loving service to others
- Civility: making common cause
- Flexibility: skilful adaptation to change
- Perspective: holding onto the moral whole
- Magnanimity: moral leadership and nobility of spirit

She argues that a combination of these virtues will amount to "technomoral wisdom" and, if adopted, would to a large extent enable us to live well with new and emerging technologies.

Therefore, we think that it is very important that those teaching young people in secondary school about the use and impact of disruptive technologies should 'Look Sideways' to involve those from across the curriculum, including teachers of religious education (who understand how to engage young people in ethical debates of the sort carried out by Shannon Vallor), teachers of economics (who understand how to help young people appreciate the way in which growth takes place in society), teachers of history (who have examples from the past of the impact of technologies on society) as well as the usual suspects, those who teach STEM subjects. This collaboration may simply involve cross-curricular conversations so that those teaching about disruptive technologies are aware what their students are being taught in other subjects. Or it might involve collaboration in deliberately using what has been taught elsewhere in the curriculum in their teaching. Or it might involve cooperative teaching in which together they develop schemes of work in which learners are taught in a timely and coordinated way across different subjects using the learning in each individual subject to reinforce the learning across all the subjects. It is in the second part of this book that these possible approaches will be discussed as we explore the teaching, learning and assessment of disruptive technologies.

References

Ellul, J. (1964) *The Technological Society*. New York: Vintage.
Kelly, K. (2010) *What Technology Wants*. New York: Penguin.
Susskind, D. (2024) *Growth: A Reckoning*. Great Britain: Allen Lane.
Vallor, S. (2016) *Technology and the Virtues: A Philosophical Guide to a Future Worth Wanting*. Oxford: Oxford University Press.

14 Identifying relevant curriculum areas

Where in the curriculum might disruption be taught?

It is clearly important that teachers have the subject knowledge necessary to respond fluently and authoritatively when dealing with the complexities inherent in teaching about disruptive technologies, and in this chapter, we suggest which areas of the secondary school curriculum are most suited to teaching particular disruptive technologies. This is not a hard and fast allocation as the implications of any disruption might well be considered in several subjects, so this chapter will argue for conversations between the teachers of the range of curriculum areas. The STEM subjects deal with the "nuts and bolts" of the disruptive technologies (if that is an appropriate metaphor for something so new!), but there are major contributions from other key school subjects as well, to ensure learners are exposed to a holistic view of the knowledge and the current and future implications of technological disruption.

It is of course important that the legitimate differences between school subjects are acknowledged, and one such difference is the knowledge base that informs the subject. Some of the disruptive technologies that we have identified have a stronger base in one or another of the subjects identified. But this should not mean that any one disruptive technology becomes locked into a particular subject "silo". For example, synthetic biology may be expertly taught by science teachers, but the implications of synthetic biology in the development of new organisms to produce new materials might best be discussed in design and technology classes, and the new approaches to environmental management, could be considered very well in geography lessons. Similarly, teaching about Big Data might be led by the computer science teacher but the implications of Big Data, say, for new product development might well be considered in design and technology too, and calculating the energy used could be best tackled in a physics or mathematics lesson. In every one of the 'in depth' chapters in Part 1, there was a section asking something like, "What are the predicted ethical dilemmas of using the disruptive technology, and what should we do about it?" Some subjects have a strong tradition of considering such moral dilemmas and ethical responses, and whilst such subjects may not have a 'technical' knowledge base relevant to particular technologies, they will bring considerable expertise in how to engage learners with the many ethical problems individuals and societies might need to contend with in the face of future disruption. Let us consider initial likely subject teaching allocations and how these might become more widespread.

For *additive manufacture*, design and technology seems the most likely candidate as learners will be taught how to use 3D printers to design and make a variety of items. But as we have

DOI: 10.4324/9781003602002-15

noted elsewhere (Banks and Barlex 2021), science departments can use 3D printers to produce equipment; mathematics departments might use 3D printers to produce models of geometric solids or intriguing surfaces; geography departments might use 3D printers to produce contour landscape maps illustrating the changing levels and for contour weather maps showing isobars and isotherms. These physical models can be produced in semi-assembled form so that learners can become engaged in hands-on assembling activities, which are likely to lead to more learning than them being used just as visual aids to accompany a demonstration.

For *artificial intelligence* (AI), computer studies seems the most likely candidate, but as we have noted in Part 1 of this book, AI is being deployed across almost every sphere of human activity in ways that many consider to be "work threatening", severely limiting the prospects for human employment in many sectors at one time thought to be immune to automation. Putting numbers on this loss of employment is something that might be considered in mathematics lessons. Teachers of history might well be able to provide examples of previous technological "revolutions" and how societies have responded. And RE teachers would be well positioned to help learners consider the dilemmas currently facing society. An interesting aspect of AI is the extent to which learners will have access to AI assistants of varying sophistication to support them in their learning, something we will discuss in Chapters 16 and 17.

In the case of programmable matter and quantum computing, we have acknowledged that whilst these have significant potential for disruption, they are best considered as emerging disruptors and might not be given the weight of consideration as other, more developed technologies. Design and technology is clearly a contender for teaching about programmable matter, but surely so is science. In both subjects, learners are taught about the idea of 'properties' and that they are somehow 'fixed' within the way a material behaves. The idea of matter being 'programmable' challenges this idea, and it is important to explore both conventional and programable matter to avoid conceptual confusion. Quantum computing is very difficult to understand. Hilda was very pleased that Frank got the duty on that. However, once well established, it won't be necessary for the majority of users to understand it, as is pretty much the case currently with conventional computing – it is how the technologies can be useful to us, and not everyone needs to know precisely what goes on "under the bonnet".

For augmented reality, design and technology would seem a likely candidate, especially as learners might well be designing and making products that include aspects of augmented reality. For example, a greeting card has a QR code which, when viewed through a mobile device, reveals a visual special effect also designed by the learner. As noted in Chapter 5, AR is increasingly being used in secondary school education on the understanding that it will enhance learning through increased engagement and interactivity, and many learners will be familiar with its nature and use.

As noted in Chapter 6, Big Data may be considered the "backbone" of AI, so it would make sense for these two technologies to be taught side by side by computer studies teachers, although an understanding of the implications of the enormous energy demands of Big Data might well also be considered by both science and geography teachers as countries on all continents will be keen not to be "left behind".

Many learners will own smart phones that are part of the Internet of Things (IoT), and their homes will contain devices that are connected to the internet as part of the IoT. So, they will have a familiarity through using such devices, even though they may not have conceptualised these activities and devices as being embraced as part of something that's termed the

"Internet of Things". And there will be many items within their schools that are part of the IoT; for example, the school's telephone system and energy management controls. We can make a case for both design and technology and computer science being involved in teaching the Internet of Things, with computer studies dealing with the coding that is necessary for devices to communicate over the internet and design and technology teaching how artefacts that are part of the Internet of Things might be designed and made.

Neurotechnology develops brain-computer interfaces that are used to extend our understanding of the way the brain works, can be used to treat dementia and enable those who have lost the use of their limbs to control external devices through their thoughts. The most likely candidate for teaching this is science, although consideration of the 'user-friendliness' of brain-computer interfaces might well take place in design and technology. The ethical dilemma facing the application of neurotechnology is the move from therapies devised to overcome neural impairments to developments aimed at cognitive enhancement. As we have noted before, RE teachers are well positioned to help learners consider such a dilemma.

For *robotics*, both computer studies and design and technology are possibilities. Robots can be designed in virtual environments and programmed to work on screens, which enables lots of different possibilities to be explored. Once a particular possibility is identified as being worth bringing into the 'real' world, it will be the design and technology teacher who supports learners in developing a physical artefact that must deal with the actualities of gravity, friction, momentum and inertia. Consideration of the extent to which unemployment through automation by using robotics might take place in both computer studies and design and technology. How to discuss this work-threatening aspect as described in Chapter 11 will be a topic where RE teachers might be able to provide advice.

For synthetic biology the most likely candidate is science, but the possibilities of novel materials produced via synthetic biology might well be taken further in design and technology. The recently initiated Synthetic Human Genome Project aims to synthesise human genomes and has as part of its makeup a team dedicated to investigating the socio-ethical, economic and policy implications of this. RE teachers will be in a strong position to help science teachers engage learners with following the deliberations of this team

What about mathematics?

At first sight it might seem that the disciplinary and substantive knowledge taught in the English National Curriculum mathematics at Key Stage 3 (KS3) – lower secondary school (Department of Education 2013) – has little in common with disruptive technologies. The KS3 National Curriculum for mathematics identifies three areas of disciplinary knowledge under the broad heading **Working mathematically**, which are:

Develop fluency, which includes moving freely between different numerical, algebraic, graphical and diagrammatic representations and the use of language and properties precisely to analyse numbers, algebraic expressions, 2D and 3D shapes, probability and statistics.

Reason mathematically, which includes making and testing conjectures about patterns and relationships; looking for proofs or, conversely, counter and explore what can and cannot be inferred in statistical and probabilistic settings and begin to express their arguments formally.

Solve problems, which includes beginning to model situations mathematically and expressing the results using a range of formal mathematical representations and selecting appropriate concepts, methods and techniques to apply to unfamiliar and non-routine problems.

Note that these areas are mirrored in the assessment objectives for GCSE mathematics.

The KS3 National Curriculum for mathematics identifies six areas of substantive knowledge under the broad heading of **Subject Content**, which are:

Number, which includes the use of standard units of mass, length, time, money and other measures, including with decimal quantities and using a calculator and other technologies to calculate results accurately and then interpret them appropriately.

Algebra, which includes modelling situations or procedures by translating them into algebraic expressions or formulae and by using graphs to interpret mathematical relationships both algebraically and graphically.

Ratio proportion and rates of change, which includes changing freely between related standard units and using scale factors, scale diagrams and maps.

Geometry and measures, which includes using the properties of faces, surfaces, edges and vertices of cubes, cuboids, prisms, cylinders, pyramids, cones and spheres to solve problems in 3D and interpreting mathematical relationships both algebraically and geometrically.

Probability, which includes enumerating sets and unions/intersections of sets systematically, using tables, grids and Venn diagrams.

Statistics, which include constructing and interpreting appropriate tables, charts and diagrams, including frequency tables, bar charts, pie charts and pictograms for categorical data and vertical line (or bar) charts for ungrouped and grouped numerical data.

Note that these content areas are mirrored in GCSE mathematics specifications.

We wonder if in developing both the disciplinary and substantive knowledge, mathematics teachers might use the features of the different disruptive technologies as contexts for learning. This would of course involve talking with teachers elsewhere in the curriculum and finding out what they are currently teaching about disruptive technologies and discovering the extent to which they provide useful examples for mathematics teaching. This leads us nicely to the next section of this chapter.

It's good to talk

We have argued strongly for cross-curricula conversations in the light of 'looking sideways in the curriculum' (Banks and Barlex 2021) and see these as a *sine qua non* with regard to identifying opportunities to enrich the curriculum experience for learners and at the same time give them access to knowledge, understanding and values that helps them make sense of the world around them. You might argue that inter-department conversations which identify possible contributions from across the curriculum are all well and good, but it is often difficult to respond positively to the ideas that emerge when curricula are already crowded, focused on public examination success and to some extent locked into place with little room for change. We do wonder if the situation is really that rigid and whether simply looking sideways at what is *already* being taught, and when it is taught, might reveal existing opportunities for slight adjustments that support collaboration without much in the way of timetable disruption. Also, we are aware that many schools often include drop-down days in which the conventional timetable is suspended, and teachers can work collaboratively in providing an immersive experience for their learners across a wide range of topics. One or two days in which learners explore the questions "What sort of world do I want to live in?" and "What can technology do to bring this about?" with a team of teachers from, say, RE, history, science and design and technology, would make a welcome change from the often career-focused nature of such days.

What might the conversations be like?

What aspect of teaching about disruptive technologies would teachers find most appealing/relevant to their particular specialisms? What might teachers from different subjects say about teaching disruptive technologies, and where would this lead them in talking with colleagues from other subjects? The following graphic (Panel 14.1) makes some suggestions.

Panel 14.1 Conversations based on looking sideways

Chemistry and Design & Technology

I think it's always worth dealing with a-real world application for a Big Idea if you can find the time. I teach chemistry and real-world application can be the icing on the cake. The idea of properties is fundamental, especially when it comes to explaining why a substance or material has the properties it does in terms of its structure at the atomic level. So programmable matter provides an interesting chance to reinforce learning about conventional properties and provide intrigue in terms of new thinking. But I need to be careful to avoid confusion.

I agree, but although understanding properties is very important in D&T, which I teach, I'm not so much interested in why materials behave as they do as opposed to understanding *how* they behave. This is necessary if learners are to be able to choose which material could be used and why, or why designers chose certain materials. Of course, properties are only one feature that needs to be taken into account, but you can have an interesting lesson speculating on what a particular material, with interesting properties might be used for. Programmable materials might just work for that.

Design & Technology and Mathematics

So, your machine could 'print' geometric solids?

What about in parts that fit together to form the solids.

Yep! Easy peasy!

That's a bit more demanding but I could get some of my sixth formers working on that as recap and extension

Physics and Computer Studies

I teach about Big Data in Computer Studies and one of the things we discuss is the energy requirements of the infrastructure needed to generate and use Big Data.

We revisit energy as an idea several times in my physics courses. It's a slippery concept at the best of times and once you try and put numbers on it, it becomes more difficult. But thinking about it in terms of the amounts of electricity for the servers, cooling systems, and networking equipment might be a novel approach. We could maybe work out how the heat energy generated could be used for district heating schemes!

Design & Technology, Computer Studies and RE

Between us, in Computer Studies and D&T we teach quite a lot of robotics, although we don't have much time to consider the extent to which robotics in particular and automation in general are work threatening and could lead to significant unemployment

That's right. In D&T I often find the business of actually producing the physical robot, albeit from a kit, very time consuming.

Well, I might be able to help here. I could use 'robots and employment' as a topic for discussion in RE, and those learners who are studying either Computer Studies or D&T could report back briefly as part of their robotics lessons.

Biology and RE

Teaching how the brain works is now part of my biology teaching. It's a tough topic and many learners find it hard going.

Well, I might be able to help here. I could use it as a topic for discussion in RE, perhaps focusing on the dilemma that whilst this understanding is helping to develop treatments for dementia, and motor neuron disease, it could be used to enhance perfectly healthy humans. Is it fair for the wealthy to pay to gain a cognitive advantage for them or for their children? This might provide the motivation for learning difficult ideas.

That has got to be worth a shot. All we have to do is get the timing right!

Pause for thought

What do you think of the conversations in Panel 14.1? Do you agree with the views expressed by these teachers? Might you be able to have similar conversations with colleagues in your school?

A word of caution

We are now poised to consider the Curriculum for Disruptive Technologies (the content or what should be taught) in Chapter 15; we look at the pedagogy for this curriculum (how it should be taught) in Chapters 16–18 and assess what is being or has been learned is covered in Chapter 19. As you know, there is a dynamic relationship between the content of what you teach, the pedagogy you use and the assessment methods you employ to find out if the learning has been successful. If you change *what* you teach it is likely that this will affect *how* you teach and how you *assess*, too. Similarly, if you try to teach differently, then this might affect the way you *choose* to assess and perhaps *what* you teach. In the same vein, if you try to assess differently, then this may affect both *what* you teach and *how* you teach. It is important to bear this dynamic relationship in mind as we focus on each of these features in the following chapters.

References

Banks, F. and Barlex, D. (2021) *Teaching STEM in the Secondary School*. Abingdon, Oxon: Routledge.

Department of Education. (2013) *KS3 Mathematics National Curriculum*. https://assets.publishing.service.gov.uk/media/5a7c1408e5274a1f5cc75a68/SECONDARY_national_curriculum_-_Mathematics.pdf (Accessed 8 August 2025).

15 A disruptive technology curriculum for the secondary school

The task facing this chapter is to describe a disruptive technology curriculum that is appropriate in terms of doing justice to the topic of disruptive technology and feasible in terms of being able to be taught and assessed. But before we dive into the detail of this task it is important to stand back and consider the nature and requirements of curriculum in general. There are three elements that need to be considered: the specified curriculum, the enacted curriculum and the experienced curriculum. These may be defined as follows:

The Specified curriculum

This is the curriculum content as found in official documents and local agreements. In England this would be the National Curriculum requirements (Department for Education 2013), supplemented by the Awarding Organisations subject specifications for GCSE and GCE (see for example AQA [Assessment and Qualifications Alliance] at https://www.awa.org.uk). However, these documents can be rather blunt instruments with unintended consequences, especially if teachers are not involved in their creation. Teachers without both an intellectual and emotional commitment to what has to be taught are inclined to make a priority of assessment and just teach to the test within their particular subject area. It is not that the documentation is unimportant; it is, but it is a necessary rather than sufficient condition for a sound curriculum that is enjoyable to both teach and learn. So, while it will be important to inspect the official documentation of subjects that might contribute to the teaching of disruptive technologies to identify the opportunities they contain, this alone will be insufficient to provide a worthwhile curriculum.

The Enacted curriculum

This is what teachers teach. This is dependent to some extent on the specified curriculum but will also be influenced by the teacher's subject knowledge, their pedagogic knowledge and the context in which they are teaching, often called their school knowledge. The position that we adopt with regard to a disruptive technology curriculum is that the opportunities identified in the documentation inspection need to be viewed through the lens of enactment and – by Looking Sideways – supported by cross-curricular conversations between those involved in the teaching. This position will inevitably involve a consideration of pedagogy, which is the topic of Chapter 16.

DOI: 10.4324/9781003602002-16

The Experienced curriculum

As the name suggests, this is the curriculum as experienced by the learners and interpreted by them in ways that help them make sense of what has been taught, not only in individual lessons but in gathering this learning together such that they gain an overview making connections between the different elements. In the case of learning about disruptive technologies this requires learners to connect learning from different subjects, a very tall order given the 'siloed' learning that often takes place in schools. Here we wonder if the conversations between collaborating teachers might not be reflected in conversations between learners and teachers. For example, a teacher might begin a sequence of lessons with an introduction that recounts the conversations she has had with colleagues from other subjects that will enable her class to use what they have learned in those other subjects and, importantly, refer to this throughout the sequence of lessons. An important question for the class at regular intervals might be "Now what did you learn with Mr X in subject Y that will be useful here?" And, of course, the effectiveness of the experienced curriculum will be revealed by assessment, the topic of Chapter 19.

We begin by defining those elements of knowledge and understanding, skills and values we believe are essential components of a disruptive technology curriculum - establishing, if you like, our Specified Curriculum - and then identifying where these elements exist in current national and awarding organisation documentation. Finally, we try to get a sense of the experienced curriculum with a description of a student's learning journey that includes teaching about disruptive technologies and an example of including such teaching through an extra curricula activity.

Knowledge and understanding

We think that there are four important areas of knowledge and understanding.

1. The disruptive technologies
   It will be important that learners know something about the disruptive technologies themselves, what they do and how they work. Initially it will be critical not to overburden learners yet at the same time help them acquire enough knowledge and understanding about the individual disruptive technologies that they can, when the necessity arises, learn more for themselves. The level of knowledge and understanding provided in Chapter 2, where we introduced the disruptive technologies, is probably sufficient to provide a platform for further learning.
2. The criteria for disruption
   We decided that the McKinsey criteria for disruption provided a useful way forward, providing us with four criteria: disrupting the status quo, altering the way people live and work, rearranging value pools (leads to financial gains and losses in both existing and new commercial activity) and leading to entirely new products and services, as described and exemplified in Chapter 1. It will be important that learners have a sufficient grasp on the criteria to be able to understand historical examples of disruption and apply them to the disruptive

technologies they are learning about such that they appreciate the nature and extent of their disruptiveness.

3. A technology life cycle based on the Gartner Hype Cycle
   It is important to give learners an understanding of the way technologies develop from being an idea in the mind of a creative entrepreneur/engineer/designer to becoming an integral part of how things are done in our society. The Gartner Hype Cycle does this by charting five key features: a technology trigger, a peak of inflated expectations, a trough of disillusionment, a slope of enlightenment and a plateau of productivity which can be represented graphically, as described in detail in Chapter 1. Learners should understand these features and be able to locate technologies at different stages of development at appropriate stages on the graph in the cycle.
4. The disruption being caused by the disruptive technologies
   Here it is important that learners observe what is happening around them and are able to identify the disruption being caused by the technologies we have identified as disruptive, and perhaps others as they emerge. They will need to use both the McKinsey criteria for disruption and the Gartner Hype Cycle to do this.

Technical skills

It will be both possible and desirable for learners to acquire some technical skills with regard to using some of the disruptive technologies. Additive manufacture is an obvious example, and learners will almost certainly develop skills in using this as 3D printing in their design and technology lessons. Similarly, with robotics it will be possible for learners to design, build and operate their own robots in a combination of learning in design and technology and computer science. In science, becoming involved in the iGem competition[1] will enable learners to use synthetic biology to address real-world problems. Outside the curriculum, learners will almost certainly be using AI through their smart phones to lookup information, and smart speakers and the Internet of Things through the various connected devices they may have at home.

Critique skills

We face a dilemma here in that particular skills for critique are sometimes used as pedagogy to develop the ability to critique. Using the Winners and Losers target chart and using critical uncertainties to produce four possible scenarios, both described in detail in Chapter 18, fall into this category. Suffice it to say here that it is necessary for learners to be able to comment on a completed target chart and explore the differences between scenarios revealed by the use of critical uncertainties.

Values

One of the aims of a disruptive technology curriculum is to enable learners to develop values to use in considering the impacts of disruptive technologies on society. This is inevitably linked to critique. We have identified two broad values areas of concern that are useful here:

achieving social justice and maintaining stewardship of Planet Earth. Social justice concerns the relationship between the individual and society as measured by the distribution of wealth, opportunities for personal development and social privileges. In a just world, all people should be able to live in freedom from hunger and fear and have shelter from harm. Stewardship of Planet Earth is concerned with the wellbeing of all creatures that live there now and in the future, ensuring that the way we use the technologies at our disposal does not compromise this.

It will be important to identify a list of values that we can apply when thinking about the possible negative effects of disruptive technologies. The list of "technomoral" virtues developed by Shanon Vallor (Vallor 2016) and mentioned at the end of Part 1 might be useful here:

- Honesty: respecting truth
- Self-control: becoming the author of our desires
- Humility: knowing what we do not know
- Justice: upholding rightness
- Courage: intelligent fear and hope
- Empathy: compassionate concern for others
- Care: loving service to others
- Civility: making common cause
- Flexibility: skilful adaptation to change
- Perspective: holding onto the moral whole
- Magnanimity: moral leadership and nobility of spirit

> Pause for thought
>
> Revisit some of the discussion on possible positive and negative effects of particular disruptive technologies presented in Part 1, and consider the extent to which applying Vallor's "technomoral" virtues might be useful in mitigating the negative effects.

A case study – inspecting official "documentation" in England to specify a potential curriculum for teaching disruptive technologies

It is probably true in any country's specified curriculum either in government requirements, or in any government- or state-sponsored textbooks or in external examination "specifications" or syllabi, that we are unlikely to find any specific references to disruption and disruptive technologies in such documentation but, as we shall see, there are statements whose intentions may be met through a consideration of disruptive technologies. We will take as an example the case in England. As an aside, if we looked at other countries in the United Kingdom, such as Wales or Scotland, we would find similar but different emphasis.

In **Design and technology programmes of study: key stage 3 National curriculum in England** (https://assets.publishing.service.gov.uk/media/5a7c99ebed915d6969f46087/SECONDARY_national_curriculum_-_Design_and_technology.pdf):

In *Purpose of Study* we find the statement:

> Through the evaluation of past and present design and technology, they develop a critical understanding of its impact on daily life and the wider world.

In *Aims* we find the statement:

- critique, evaluate and test their ideas and products and the work of others

The use of the term "critique" is significant, especially in the light of critiquing "the work of others".

In *Subject Content*, under *Evaluate* we find the statements:

- investigate new and emerging technologies
- understand developments in design and technology, its impact on individuals, society and the environment, and the responsibilities of designers, engineers and technologists.

In the Science programmes of study: key stage 3 National curriculum in England December 2014 (ref https://assets.publishing.service.gov.uk/media/5a7d563de5274a2af0ae2ffa/SECONDARY_national_curriculum_-_Science_220714.pdf):

In *Aims* we find the statement:

- are equipped with the scientific knowledge required to understand the **uses and implications** of science, today and for the future.

In the Science programmes of study: key stage 4 National curriculum in England December 2014 (https://assets.publishing.service.gov.uk/media/5a7efc65ed915d74e33f3ac9/Science_KS4_PoS_7_November_2014.pdf):

In *Working scientifically* we find the statement:

> Teachers should feel free to choose examples that serve a variety of purposes, from showing how scientific ideas have developed historically to reflecting modern developments in science and informing students of the role of science in understanding the causes of and solutions to some of the challenges facing society.

And in *The development of scientific thinking*

we find the statements:

- explaining everyday and technological applications of science; evaluating associated personal, social, economic and environmental implications; and making decisions based on the evaluation of evidence and arguments
- evaluating risks both in practical science and the wider societal context, including perception of risk

In the Computing programmes of study: key stages 3 and 4 National curriculum in England 2013 https://assets.publishing.service.gov.uk/media/5a7cb981ed915d682236228d/SECONDARY_national_curriculum_-_Computing.pdf:

In *Purpose of Study* we find the statement:

> Computing also ensures that pupils become digitally literate . . . at a level suitable for the future workplace and as active
>
> participants in a digital world.
>
> In *Aims* we find the statement:
>
> All pupils can understand and apply the fundamental principles and concepts of computer science, including abstraction, logic, algorithms and data representation.
>
> In the subject content is that pupils understand the hardware and software components that make up computer systems, and how they communicate with one another and with other systems.

This is essential for an understanding of the Internet of Things, for example.

In the History programmes of study: key stage 3 National curriculum in England (https://assets.publishing.service.gov.uk/media/5a7c66d740f0b626628abcdd/SECONDARY_national_curriculum_-_History.pdf):

In *Purpose of Study* we find the statement:

> History helps pupils to understand the complexity of people's lives, the process of change, the diversity of societies and relationships between different groups, as well as their own identity and the challenges of their time.

In *Aims* we find the statements:

- understand historical concepts such as continuity and change, cause and consequence, similarity, difference and significance, and use them to make connections, draw contrasts, analyse trends, frame historically valid questions and create their own structured accounts, including written narratives and analyses.
- gain historical perspective by placing their growing knowledge into different contexts, understanding the connections between local, regional, national and international history; between cultural, economic, military, political, religious and social history; and between short- and long-term timescales.

Religious education in English schools: Non-statutory guidance 2010

(https://assets.publishing.service.gov.uk/media/5a7adb3ce5274a34770e7953/DCSF-00114-2010.pdf):

In *The Wider Context of RE* we find the statement:

> The rapid pace of development in scientific and medical technologies and the environmental debate continue to present new issues which raise religious, moral and social questions.

In *The importance of RE* under *Spiritual, moral, social and cultural development*

> Exploring the concepts of religion and belief and their roles in the spiritual, moral and cultural lives of people in a diverse society helps individuals develop moral awareness and social understanding.

And

- **provokes challenging questions** about the meaning and purpose of life, beliefs, the self, issues of right and wrong, and what it means to be human.

In England, Wales and Northern Ireland, learners aged 16 (the final age for compulsory school education) sit for examinations set external to their school known as the General Certificate in Secondary Education (GCSE). One examination board offering such GCSE examinations is the Assessment and Qualifications Alliance (AQA). Inspections of current GCSE specifications from AQA are even more encouraging. In design and technology there is a complete section on New and Emerging Technologies, as shown in Panel 15.1.

Panel 15.1 New and Emerging Technologies Content in AQA Design and Technology Specification

3.1.1 New and emerging technologies

Students must know and understand the impact of new and emerging technologies on contemporary and potential future scenarios in relation to the following areas:

Industry

Content	**Potential links to maths and science**
The impact of new and emerging technologies on: • the design and organisation of the workplace including automation and the use of robotics • buildings and the place of work • tools and equipment.	

Enterprise

Content	**Potential links to maths and science**
Enterprise based on the development of an effective business innovation: • crowd funding • virtual marketing and retail • co-operatives • fair trade.	

Sustainability

Content	**Potential links to maths and science**
The impact of resource consumption on the planet: • finite • non-finite • disposal of waste.	Taking into consideration the ecological and social footprint of materials.

People

Content	**Potential links to maths and science**
How technology push/market pull affects choice. Changing job roles due to the emergence of new ways of working driven by technological change.	

Culture

Content	**Potential links to maths and science**
Changes in fashion and trends in relation to new and emergent technologies. Respecting people of different faiths and beliefs.	

Panel 15.1 New and Emerging Technologies Content in AQA Design and Technology Specification (Continued)

Society

Content	**Potential links to maths and science**
How products are designed and made to avoid having a negative impact on others: • design for disabled • elderly • different religious groups.	

Environment

Content	**Potential links to maths and science**
Positive and negative impacts new products have on the environment: • continuous improvement • efficient working • pollution • global warming.	

Production techniques and systems

Content	**Potential links to maths and science**
The contemporary and potential future use of: • automation • computer aided design (CAD) • computer aided manufacture (CAM) • flexible manufacturing systems (FMS) • just in time (JIT) • lean manufacturing.	

How the critical evaluation of new and emerging technologies informs design decisions

Content	**Potential links to maths and science**
That it is important to consider scenarios from different perspectives and considering: • planned obsolescence • design for maintenance • ethics • the environment.	Ethical factors and consideration of ecological and social footprint.

In the AQA GCSE specifications for Biology, Chemistry and Physics under *Working scientifically*, we find these statements:

> Students should be able to:
>
> WS 1.4 Explain everyday and technological applications of science; evaluate associated personal, social, economic and environmental implications; and make decisions based on the evaluation of evidence and arguments.
>
> WS 1.5 Evaluate risks both in practical science and the wider societal context, including perception of risk in relation to data and consequences.

In the AQA GCSE specification for Computing Science under *Ethical, legal and environmental impacts of digital technology on wider society, including issues of privacy*, we find this statement:

> Explain the current ethical, legal and environmental impacts and risks of digital technology on society. Where data privacy issues arise, these should be considered.

In the AQA GCSE specification for RE under *Theme F: Religion, human rights and social justice*, we find these statements:

> Students should study religious teachings, and religious, philosophical and ethical arguments, relating to the issues that follow, and their impact and influence in the modern world. They should be aware of contrasting perspectives in contemporary British society on all of these issues.
>
> Human rights including social justice
>
> Wealth and poverty including the uses of wealth, the responsibilities of wealth, including the duty to tackle poverty and its causes . . .

In the AQA GCSE specification for History, the topic *Shaping the nation* includes Thematic Studies, one of which is *Britain: Health and the people: c1000 to the present day*, where we find this statement:

> This thematic study will enable students to gain an understanding of how medicine and public health developed in Britain over a long period of time. It considers the causes, scale, nature and consequences of short- and long-term developments, their impact on British society and how they were related to the key features and characteristics of the periods during which they took place.
>
> Students will study the importance of the following factors:
>
> - war
> - superstition and religion
> - chance
> - government
> - communication
> - science and technology
> - the role of the individual in encouraging or inhibiting change.
>
> Students will show an understanding of how factors worked together to bring about particular developments at a particular time, how they were related and their impact upon society. They should also be able to distinguish between different types of causes and consequences, such as short-/long-term causes, intended/unintended consequences.
>
> This option focuses on the following questions:
>
> - Why has there been progress in the health of the British people?
> - How and why has the pace and scale of medical development varied at different times?
> - What impact has medical progress had on people and society?

- How and why have different factors been more important than others for individual medical developments?
- What is the significance of key individuals or events in the history of medical development?

What are we to make of these statements? They all provide the opportunity for teachers to use disruptive technologies as content with which to engage learners as part of the subject being studied. It is not just an interesting and different context; it is actually a means of covering required subject content. Taken together, it seems to us that exploring disruptive technologies offers opportunities and a strong justification for engaging learners with a consideration of the way our society will be affected by the disruptive technologies and providing them with the knowledge, understanding, skills and values necessary to become constructively critical of the way such technologies are developed and deployed. It is our hope and expectation that the young people who have learned about disruption and disruptive technologies will become citizens who are active in helping to decide in the way they are developed and used.

Panel 15.2 is an extract example of an enacted curriculum for design and technology from Year 7 (12 years old) to Year 10 (15 years old). Note how the teacher, Jill, has created a learning journey that weaves in aspects of disruptive technologies. When we look across to what is taught in science and in computing, we see that the school has adopted a coordinated approach across the enacted curriculum. In a properly coordinated approach, teachers in each subject become familiar with the work carried out in the others and plan their curricula so that the *timing* of topics within each subject is sensitive to others' needs and taught in a way that supports the learners' developing understanding, rather than one that causes confusion. For example, proficiency with the use of measuring in millimetres and ways of collating data from respondents would benefit design and technology if covered in lower school mathematics; and if electricity is explained using similar analogies and terminology in both design and technology and science, the learners' developing ideas can be reinforced.

Panel 15.2 An extract from Jill's design and technology 'Enacted Curriculum' for Year 7 to Year 10

Year 7	*Term 1*	*Term 2*	*Term 3*
	• *Make*, fly and investigate a kite • *Making with some designing* Exploring the use of low-relief vacuum forming	• ***Considering consequences of technology by exploring a disruptive technology – the Internet of Things*** • *Designing and Making assignment* concerning containing-design and make a container that can be formed from one or two nets and will hold one or two favourite small items safely and that, from its appearance, reflects the importance and nature of the contents	• *Designing and Making assignment* concerning lighting-design and make a light that is suitable for use in a particular situation. The device will be constructed from easy to work materials and technical components. It will be powered by a battery, controlled by switches, and use LEDs for illumination • *Designing without making* using a new and emerging technology-QTC

Panel 15.2 An extract from Jill's design and technology 'Enacted Curriculum' for Year 7 to Year 10 (Continued)

Year 8	*Term 1*	*Term 2*	*Term 3*
	• *Making without designing* Make, play with and investigate spinning tops • *Making with some designing* Using a 3D printer to produce simple body adornment • ***Considering consequences of technology by exploring a disruptive technology – additive manufacture***	• *Designing and Making assignment* concerning moving toys Design and make a moving toy that is powered by a small electric motor, taking into account the user of the toy and design a toy that a) moves in a way that will appeal to the user, b) has an appearance which pleases the user, c) can incorporate a range of special effects e.g. light and sound, that will give the toy more play value for the user. NB-Link back to science.	• *Designing and Making assignment* concerning carriers Design and make a carrier that meets the needs of a person (who may be the learner) who has to carry particular items. The carrier will be constructed from textiles and flexible sheet materials • *Designing without making* using a new and emerging technology-shape memory metal or aerogel
Year 9	*Term 1*	*Term 2*	*Term 3*
	• *Making with some designing* Make, programme and operate different sorts of robot – pick and place, buggies, drones • ***Considering consequences of technology by exploring a disruptive technology – robotics***	• *Designing and Making assignment* concerning the exploitation of a phenomenon Design and make an item that exploits a scientific phenomenon such as the Peltier effect, magnetism or electromagnetism that is of benefit to an identified user	• *Conceptual Challenge* concerning shelter Identify and explore a situation in which there is the need for shelter. Devise and produce full-scale prototypes that meet this need using a combination of textiles, flexible sheet materials, easy-to-work resistant materials plus technical components.
Year 10	*Term 1*	*Term 2*	*Term 3*
	• *Designing and Making assignment* Heath Robinson Challenge How many forms of movement can you get from a rotating shaft? • *Making with some designing Exploring* electric, electronic and programmable circuits for sensing in a variety of contexts	• *Considering consequences of technology* by arguing for changing the way we do business from a linear to a circular economy • *Making with some designing* Exploring energy generation and storage • *Conceptual Challenge* Living spaces Explore the living space needs of different individuals. Develop models that show how such needs might be met in the context of a low-carbon economy	• *Making with some designing* Exploring materials and structures • ***Considering consequences of technology by exploring a disruptive technology – programmable materials*** • Starting Conceptual Challenge for GCSE NEA NB-Possible links to Physics

Kamrul teaches science in the same school as Jill. Panel 15.3 is an extract example of an enacted curriculum for Science from Year 7 (12 years old) to Year 10 (15 years old). He teaches all aspects of science from Year 7 to Year 9 (14 years old) and Physics to the older learners. Note how Kamrul, like Jill, has created a learning journey again including aspects of disruptive technologies, but also notice how Kamrul has organised his curriculum to coordinate with Jill's. For example, in Term 1 Year 8 the students learn about magnetism, electromagnetism and how to construct a simple electric motor, and in Term 2 Year 8 in design and technology they use an electric motor to make a moving toy.

Panel 15.3 An extract from Kamrul's Science 'Enacted Curriculum' for Years 7 to 9, and Physics in Year 10

Year 7	*Term 1*	*Term 2*	*Term 3*
	Flight • Bernoulli effect – blowing over the rim a piece of A4 paper and between two suspended table-tennis balls. Predict what will happen. • Paper plane competition – Flight factor = time in air x distance flown. • Water rockets – altitude competition. Quantity of water propellant versus weight of rocket. • Forces and Motion – speed and distance.	• ***Considering consequences of technology by exploring a disruptive technology – the Internet of Things*** *Ourselves* • Using loudspeaker and signal generator to show range of hearing – sound waves. • Reaction times – catching a dropped ruler – using light and buzzer to signal as part of a 'steady hand' loop circuit. • Parts of the body – respiration, circulation, digestion-including how technology can support disability.	*Materials* • Particulate nature of matter, states of matter, energetics of state change • Single Substances and Mixtures, purification techniques • Properties of metals and non-metals • Acids and Alkalis, indicators, pH scale. *The Earth* The composition and structure of the Earth The rock cycle and the formation of igneous, sedimentary and metamorphic rocks The Earth as a source of limited resources and the efficacy of recycling
Year 8	*Term 1*	*Term 2*	*Term 3*
	Electricity and Magnetism • Charge, Current, Circuits, Potential Difference • Magnetism and Electromagnets • Simple electric motors and possible uses	*Plants and Animals* • Cells (structure & function) • Reproduction (Human and Plant) • Photosynthesis • Ecosystems and food chains • Variation and Classification of organisms. • ***Considering consequences of technology by exploring a disruptive technology – Augmented Reality – Use of a Merge Cube***	*Chemical reactions* • Elements and compounds • Chemical reactions (i) Decomposition (ii) Forming binary compounds (iii) Combustion including composition of atmosphere, carbon cycle and impact on climate (iv) Reduction of metal oxides (iv) Conservation of mass, word equations, particle pictures and formulae equations

Panel 15.3 An extract from Kamrul's Science 'Enacted Curriculum' for Years 7 to 9, and Physics in Year 10 (Continued)

Year 9	*Term 1*	*Term 2*	*Term 3*
	Space Exploration • Energy and Work (power, efficiency) • Waves (light, sound, EM Spectrum) • Space (Earth, Moon, Time, Exploring Solar System – Mars Robot Explorers. • ***Considering consequences of technology by exploring a disruptive technology – robotics***	*Evolution* • Genetics and Inheritance • Evolution and natural selection • Health and Disease (pathogens, immunity)	*Periodic table* • Columns, rows and patterns *Reactivity* • Rates of reaction • Reaction of acids with metals and bases • Reactivity series *Synthetic materials* • Ceramics, polymers and composites
Year 10	*Term 1-Physics*	*Term 2-Physics*	*Term 3-Physics*
	Energy and Electricity • Energy resources, stores, systems, efficiency • Electricity: current, charge, resistance, IV characteristics, Series and parallel circuits, Mains electricity, Safety, National Grid	*Matter* • states of matter, internal energy • density • changes of state • specific heat capacity • gas pressure and temperature	*Atomic Structure 2* • models of the atom, isotopes • nuclear radiation (types, properties, hazards) • nuclear fission and fusion, half-life • radioactive uses and dangers. • ***Considering consequences of technology by exploring a disruptive technology – programmable materials***

Leslie works in the same school as Jill and Kamrul. She teaches computing to the lower secondary school and Computer Science to GCSE. Panel 15.4 shows an extract example of her enacted curriculum for Computing from Year 7 (12 years old) to Year 10 (15 years old). Just like her colleagues, Lesley has lined up consideration of aspects of disruptive technologies and has also considered what is happening at the same time in both science and design and technology.

Panel 15.4 An extract from Lesley's 'Enacted Curriculum' Computing from Year 7 to Year 10

Year 7	*Term 1*	*Term 2*	*Term 3*
	• E-safety and digital literacy (online safety, privacy, digital footprint) • Intro to computer systems (hardware vs software, input/output devices)	• Binary and data representation (bits/bytes, images, text, sound basics) • Intro to programming (block-based or text-based, sequencing, iteration)	• Algorithms and flowcharts (problem solving, pseudocode) • Programming projects (loops, conditionals, variables)

Panel 15.4 An extract from Lesley's 'Enacted Curriculum' Computing from Year 7 to Year 10 (Continued)

Year 7	*Term 1*	*Term 2*	*Term 3*
	• Spreadsheets and data modelling • EduBlocks for micro:bit • micro:bit	• Networks basics (LAN, WAN, internet concept) • The Internet of Things (IoT) (devices, smart systems, benefits and risks) • ***Considering consequences of technology by exploring a disruptive technology – the Internet of Things***	• Creative media (graphics, video editing, ethical use of content)
Year 8	*Term 1*	*Term 2*	*Term 3*
	• Programming development (functions, debugging, modular code) • Data handling and databases (records, fields) • Cybersecurity basics (threats, phishing, strong passwords)	• Logic and Boolean operations (AND, OR, NOT) • Networks in depth (protocols, IP, DNS, packet switching) • Blockly for PICAXE • PICAXE	• Web design and development (HTML, CSS basics) • Simulation and modelling (using code to model systems) • Ethical and legal issues (data protection, copyright, AI ethics) • Intro to Python and Raspberry Pi
Year 9	*Term 1*	*Term 2*	*Term 3*
	• Advanced programming (Python/JavaScript: lists, arrays, file handling) • Computational thinking for problem-solving (abstraction, decomposition) • Robotics-(sensors, actuators, control through code) • *Considering consequences of technology by exploring a disruptive technology – robotics*	• Computer architecture (CPU, memory, storage, fetch-execute cycle) • Networks and cybersecurity (advanced) (encryption, firewalls, cybercrime case studies) • IoT and Robotics integration (designing systems with IoT sensors + robotic responses)	• Artificial Intelligence and Machine Learning (concepts) • Creative project (students design and present a digital/IoT/robotic solution to a real-world problem) • ***Considering consequences of technology by exploring a disruptive technology – Artificial Intelligence (AI)***
Year 10	*Term 1-Computer Science*	*Term 2 – Computer Science*	*Term 3 – Computer Science*
	• Fundamentals of algorithms (decomposition, abstraction, flowcharts, pseudocode) • Programming basics (data types, variables, inputs/outputs, sequencing, iteration, selection)	• Programming techniques (subroutines, functions, procedures, scope) • Data representation (binary, hex, character sets, images, sound, compression)	• Computer systems (hardware, CPU architecture, fetch – execute cycle, memory, storage) • Programming project practice (small coding tasks, debugging, problem-solving)

An experienced curriculum – a learning journey across the curriculum

Finally, we try to get a sense of the experienced curriculum. This section describes the learning journey experienced by Freda across Years 7–10 in design and technology, in science and then physics and computing, which includes consideration of disruptive technologies. It concludes with an example of Freda's experience of Jill teaching through an extra-curricular activity.

Freda's learning journey – the experienced curriculum

Freda was successful at both design and technology and computing at KS3 and opted for both subjects at KS4. Science is a compulsory subject in the school, but Freda decided to take the GCSE AQA Triple Science Option. Students choosing Triple Science as an option study the three separate GCSEs, one in each science – biology, chemistry and physics. The course covers the same areas as the usual double science GCSE but in more depth, and in addition, students study space physics. Freda was taught the physics part by Kamrul. She was taught by Jill and Lesley every year, so Panels 15.2 to 15.4 sets out Freda's experience of the curriculum and her learning journey across Years 7–10, highlighting where a consideration of disruptive technologies took place and how this was enhanced by Jill, Leslie and Kamrul 'looking sideways' in the curriculum.

The learning in design and technology has been organised on the basis of different sorts of learning activity as follows:

- Making without designing,
- Making with some designing,
- Designing without making,
- Designing and making,
- Considering consequences of technology, and Contextual Challenge (see Beaumont and Steeg 2024 for a detailed discussion and justification of this approach to curriculum planning in design and technology).

In addition to providing significant coverage of all the Big Ideas essential for learners to have a clear grasp of the knowledge, understanding, skills and values in design and technology (see Beaumont and Steeg 2024), Freda's learning journey provides the opportunity for one exploration of disruptive technologies in each year: the Internet of Things in Year 7, additive manufacture in Year 8, robotics in Year 9 and programmable matter in Year 10. We think these are appropriate for the following reasons. Year 7 learners and their families will almost certainly be using the Internet of Things through mobile phones and smart speakers, plus possibly home heating control and security. Freda was surprised to be studying the Internet of Things in all three subjects at the same time but was intrigued by the different perspectives and examples given by the different teachers. In design and technology she considered home security, in science data retrieval in environmental monitoring and in computing she studied surveillance.

Year 8 learners will be learning to use additive manufacture as part of their design and technology curriculum so will be experiencing the way that this 'disrupts' the traditional way of making things for themselves. Year 9 learners will be learning about robots, programming and operating them as part of their design and technology curriculum so it makes sense for them to consider the implications of automation through robotics in the ways we are/will be working and living. Throughout KS3 Freda enjoyed discussing the pros and cons of using disruptive technologies and was both surprised and pleased at how useful her RE lessons were in helping her do this.

Year 10 learners are exploring materials and structures as important areas of knowledge and understanding in both making design decisions and GCSE written examination preparation. Learning about programmable matter will give the learners the opportunity to reinforce and extend their understanding of material properties.

In terms of 'looking sideways' through conversations between Jill and teachers from other subjects, you will have noticed the following links:

- Lesley, the computing/computer science teacher, covered both the Internet of Things and robotics;
- Kamrul teaching chemistry looked at the properties of materials;
- With the RE teacher generally for how to enable learners to discuss the implications of any disruption being caused by the technologies under consideration;
- With the history teacher for previous examples of disruption.

As the GCSE year progressed, Freda decided that Triple Science was perhaps a step too far. She enjoyed the physical sciences but was less enamoured with biology, and as she wanted to concentrate more on design and technology and computer science, she was pleased that she could convert to Double Award Science instead. Looking to the future, and based on discussions with teachers, her parents and friends, Freda hopes to become an electronic engineer. The consideration at school of some disruptive technologies has, she thinks, opened her eyes to both the problems and opportunities of working in that field. Freda has always found tackling real problems very enjoyable both in design and technology and computer science lessons, but especially when there is an opportunity to spend longer on an extra-curricular activity – even if it is biology-based!

Exploring synthetic biology through an extra-curricular activity

The International Genetically Engineered Machine (iGEM) competition provides an extra-curricular opportunity for the teaching of the disruptive technology synthetic biology. iGEM (2025) is the latest in a series of annual worldwide synthetic biology competitions initially aimed at undergraduate university students, but now extended to high school students as well.

Student teams are given a kit of biological parts at the beginning of the summer from the Registry of Standard Biological Parts. This is a collection of genetic parts that are used in the assembly of systems and devices in synthetic biology. The iGEM competition facilitates this by providing a library of standardised parts (called BioBrick standard biological parts) to students and asking them to design and build genetic machines with them. Student teams can also submit their own BioBricks. Working at their own schools, the teams use these parts and new parts of their own design to build biological systems and operate them in living cells. Successful projects produce cells that exhibit new and unusual properties by engineering sets of multiple genes together with mechanisms to regulate their expression. Information about BioBrick standard biological parts, and a toolkit to make and manipulate them, is provided by the Registry of Standard Biological Parts. This is a core resource for the iGEM program, and one that has been evolving rapidly to meet the needs of the program. In 2024 teams from 41 countries took part. The winners of the high school category were from Taiwan. Their entry is described in Panel 15.5. There is much more information about the competition on the iGEM website at https://competition.igem.org/about. Visiting this site reveals that taking part in the iGEM competition requires a lot of commitment in terms of time and energy from both teachers and learners, but involvement does provide both with a unique experience of a disruptive technology that will be involved in shaping our future lives.

Panel 15.5 The high school winning entry from Taiwan

Dengue Beeters - A novel synergy of recombinant biolarvicidal toxins, naturally-derived geosmin and gravid-trap

The rise of dengue fever in recent years has become a significant issue in tropical and sub-tropical areas, inflicting serious socioeconomic and healthcare burdens. In our project, we successfully engineered 12 recombinant biolarvicidal toxins and partially reproduced a chromosome-free system. We conducted WHO standard larvicidal assay with Aedes albopictus larvae and proved the potency of Cyt2Ba, Xpp81Aa1 and BmK IT1. In addition, we consistently proved that 2.5 mg/ml of beetroot peel powder can significantly attract gravid female Ae. albopictus mosquitoes in oviposition assays. We integrated the synthetic biology-based product with beetroot peel powder and developed Taiwan's first 3D-printed household-use sticky ovitrap. We also developed an OpenCv mosquito egg analyser to automatically analyse mosquito eggs, helping field entomologists and scientists in dengue surveillance work. Dengue Beeters is an exciting project that breaks the mosquito life cycle through synthetic biology and contributes to the end of dengue fever disease by 2030.

Summary

This chapter has described how a disruptive technology curriculum for the secondary school might be developed. It began by considering three elements: the Specified Curriculum, the Enacted Curriculum and the Experienced Curriculum, and then identified the required knowledge and understanding along with technical and critique skills and important values. It inspected documents from the National Curriculum in England and some GCSE specifications from the awarding organisation AQA to identify statements supporting the teaching of disruptive technologies. It showed how teachers were able to enact a worthwhile curriculum covering the specifications, creating exciting learning journeys in different subjects experienced and enjoyed by students as they moved across subjects within the curriculum that included the teaching of disruptive technologies and commented on the cross-curricular conversations that could support their learning. It finished with an account of the iGEM competition. Having identified **what** is to be taught, it is time to turn our attention to **how** it will be taught and consider the required pedagogy, which is the topic of the next chapter.

Note

1 See https://competition.igem.org/about for more details.

References

AQA (Assessment and Qualifications Alliance). https://www.aqa.org.uk

Beaumont, H. and Steeg, T. (2024) *Design and Technology in your School: Principles for Curriculum, Pedagogy and Assessment*. Abingdon, Oxon: Routledge. https://jamboree.igem.org/2025/home

Department for Education. (2013) *Design and Technology Programmes of Study: Key Stage 3*. London: Crown. https://www.gov.uk/government/publications/national-curriculum-in-england-design-and-technology-programmes-of-study

iGEM. (2025) *Information About the Grand Jamboree Which Took Place at the Paris Convention Centre on 28–31 October*. https://jamboree.igem.org/2025/home

Vallor, S. (2016) *Technology and the Virtues: A Philosophical Guide to a Future Worth Wanting*. Oxford: Oxford University Press.

Recommended reading

Drew, D.E. (2011) *STEM the Tide: Reforming Science, Technology and Math Education in America*. Baltimore: John Hopkins University Press.

Hutchins, D. and McLeach, T. (2017) *Let There be Science*. Oxford: Lion Hudson plc.

Wragg, E.C. (1997) *The Cubic Curriculum*. Abingdon, Oxon: Routledge.

16 Teaching about disruptive technologies

Introduction

In Chapter 15 we worked through three aspects of the curriculum: the specified curriculum, the enacted curriculum and the experienced curriculum. We identified the contents to be taught in a specified curriculum concerned with disruptive technologies. We then laid out the teaching units that would meet the requirements of that specified curriculum through the teaching of Jill, who teaches design and technology (D and T), Kamrul, who teaches science, and Lesley, who teaches computing, thus describing an enacted curriculum in response to our specified curriculum, noting that only relatively small parts of this curriculum were directly concerned with disruptive technologies as the teachers had lots of other content they needed to teach as well. Finally, we looked at the curriculum as experienced by Freda through her lessons in all three subjects.

So far, we have not dealt in any detail with exactly *how* Freda's teaching took place via the pedagogy employed by Jill, Kamrul and Lesley, and in Chapter 15, you might think that we dodged the issue that, although we set out that "Considering consequences of technology by exploring a disruptive technology – the Internet of Things" was lined up, we didn't say exactly what aspects of IoT Jill, Kamrul and Lesley would actually teach.

We do that now, and this chapter will suggest lessons for teaching learners about a range of disruptive technologies. When considering how lessons might be taught, we will refer to some teaching strategies set out in Panel 16.1. Educators from the Open University, collaborating with the University of Cape Town (2023) and Vanderbilt University (2024), have produced reports with examples of pedagogy that are relevant to how we might teach disruptive technologies, and six of the most relevant are adapted and summarised in Panel 16.1. As we now describe approaches to teaching the curriculum we developed and clarified in Chapter 15, we will consider how these might be used.

Panel 16.1 Pedagogies useful for teaching disruptive technologies

Pedagogy using AI tools The availability of generative AI tools, such as ChatGPT for both teachers and learners, has the potential to considerably influence the way teaching and learning take place.	**Multimodal working** The teacher can use more than just words in providing content to be learned and can also encourage learners to respond in a similarly broad way.

DOI: 10.4324/9781003602002-17

Panel 16.1 Pedagogies useful for teaching disruptive technologies (Continued)

Teachers can use such tools to access content for lessons and develop ways in which this can be presented to and used by learners in tackling learning tasks. Learners can use such tools as personal tutors or collaboration coaches to support their attempts to tackle the tasks set by the teacher. These AI-learner interactions need to be carefully monitored to ensure that they result in genuine learning leading to knowledge, understanding, skills and values that can be deployed without AI support.

Speculative worlds

The generation of a 'new' world can involve reimagining the present, past or future. The thrust of the generation is to develop situations in which features currently deemed to be unfair or damaging to humans, other living creatures and planet can be addressed. Learners might present alternative histories for times past, changes to current ways of doing things and/or future scenarios. Carried out in groups, such activity develops creativity, communication skills, collaboration abilities and empathy.

Seeing yourself in the curriculum

It is important that learners can see people like themselves with their history and backgrounds represented in their curriculum, learning materials and educational approaches. One of its main aims is to ensure that education systems reflect the diverse cultures, experiences and histories of their students. It is essential that in experiencing curriculum learners, whilst being interested and engaged, do not feel that it is "not for people like us".

Although responding by the written word is important, this can be enhanced by using images, sounds and gestures. Teachers and learners can use AI tools to facilitate this sort of working to provide a rich range of outcomes that enable a wider range of learners to demonstrate their learning than by conventional means.

Challenge-based learning

This has similarities to other approaches such as problem-based learning and project-based learning but is more provocative in that it sets challenges to which learners are required to respond by active participation. Such challenges may be based in learners' local communities. In some cases, having been introduced to the idea, learners can set their own challenges. Care must be taken to ensure that such learning is manageable for it to be successful.

Entrepreneurial education

This approach puts learners in the position of developing new products and services for a small business. The criteria for success will be the extent to which their proposals are seen as technically feasible and likely to be successful in terms of meeting customer requirements, acceptable to society and viable in terms of existing or created markets.

Teaching learners about any disruptive technology has potentially three elements:

1. Teaching about the technology to know and understand what it does and how it works – we will be looking at several possible lessons in this chapter.
2. Teaching the technical skills of using the technology in schools. This will be considered in Chapter 17.
3. Teaching about its disruption. We will be looking at techniques for how learners can critique disruptive technologies, and the values implicit in their adoption, in Chapter 18.

How might we teach about additive manufacture?

There will be many different and equally valid ways of introducing learners to additive manufacturing. Here is one teacher's approach with her Year 7 (12-year-olds) design and technology class.

I knew that some of the class already knew a bit about additive manufacture, so I want to use that. I started by having the school desktop 3D printer under a black cloth as an "object of intrigue" that I unveil to the class with the following commentary and questions.

ME: I'm going to show you what's under here. If you know what it is, put your hand up. Five hands go up (Mary, Simon, Ranji, Ella, and Myra, so . . .)

ME: Okay, let's use what you know to build up a picture of what it is and how it works. Ranji, you first.

RANJI: It's a 3D printer.

ME: That's correct. Ella, what does it do?

ELLA: Well, it makes things from the plastic that's on the spool at the back.

ME: Spot on. Simon, can you tell us how it does that?

SIMON: They've got one at the Makerspace I go to with my mum. It squirts hot, molten plastic in layers onto that middle bit. After each layer goes hard it adds another layer.

ME: So, it builds it up layer by layer. Is that right?

SIMON: Yeah.

ME: I wonder how it knows what to do.

RANJI: I'm not that sure. Like Simon, I've seen one working but not actually used one myself, but I think you have to program it using CAD.

ME: That's right. Myra, anything to add?

MYRA: I think you have to build a computer model and somehow slice it up into layers. The 3D printer can 'read' each layer and make it.

ME: That's more or less it, Myra, thank you. In fact, thank all of you. To sum up what we've learned, look at this model.

I showed the class a model of a sphere made up of about 20 layers of corrugated cardboard.

ME: You can see that this sphere is made of layers on top of one another. Freddy, how does the size of the layers change?

FREDDY: Er, well they start small, get bigger and get small again.

ME: That's right. What do you think I'd get if I started big, went small and then went big again? Tom, what do you think?

TOM: That's tricky. I think it would get narrower and then wider.

As Tom spoke, he demonstrated with his hands, outlining an hourglass shape.

ME: Absolutely right. So, I want you to think about what this tells us about the final shape we get from a 3D printer. Write what you think on your mini white boards starting with the sentence "The final shape will depend on . . ."

After a minute or so.

ME: Okay, show me your boards.

A quick scan revealed that most had a sentence along the lines of "The final shape will depend on the shape of the layers that make up that shape". A couple were blank – Patsy and Ron.

ME: I want you to get into groups of four. For each group I've got a selection of models and 3D printed objects for you to handle and look at (there's a small magnifying glass for a close-up look) and some pictures of other things that have been 3D printed as well. There's a set of prompt questions for you to answer. I'll set this printer working and while you're answering the questions, I'll call each group out in turn to take a close look at it working. Patsy and Ron, you pay special attention to the car model, please. Write up the answers to the prompt questions on the sheet and give to me at the end of the lesson.

The Handling collection included the following:

- Small version of the cardboard model used in the demonstration
- Small single-colour tetrahedron for a board game printed on the school 3D printer
- Small multicolour bought in 3D printed toy figure
- Pictures of:
  - 3D printed shoes
  - 3D printed jackets
  - 3D printed concrete house

The Prompt sheet had the following instructions/questions:

1. Try turning the cardboard sphere into a cardboard hourglass shape and back again.
2. Look closely at the tetrahedron. Can you see the layers? How many make up the piece?
3. How many colours are in the toy figure? How did they manage to make it multi-coloured?
4. Do you think the 3D printed shoes would be comfortable? If not, what could be done to improve them?
5. Would you like to wear a 3D printed jacket? Give a reason for your answer.
6. What might be the advantage in printing a house?
7. For homework, find three examples of how 3D printing is being used in medicine.

Me: Next time I'll give you feedback on your Prompt Sheet answers, you can tell me about how 3D printing is used in medicine, you'll all get the chance to use the printer to make something that I've designed, and you will also be able to change it a bit. And after that you'll get the chance to design something for yourself, and then we'll get to think about how 3D printing is affecting the way people live and work.

Pause for thought

What do you make of this lesson? Would you teach a lesson like that, or would you want to change it significantly?

How does this lesson measure up to the suggestions for pedagogies useful for teaching disruptive technologies shown in Panel 16.1? Some are irrelevant – speculative worlds, challenge-based learning and entrepreneurial education. You may think that there was a lost opportunity in using AI tools; in which case, how would you use such tools? The lesson is strong in multimodal working (in using the Handling collection) and seeing yourself in the curriculum (identifying learners with previous knowledge of 3D printing). In terms of what has been learned, we think that the lesson has provided a strong foundation about how additive manufacture works and what it can be used for, which puts the learners in a strong position to appreciate the necessity for slicing software when they come to use the technology for themselves.

How might we teach about artificial intelligence?

Let's look again at Lesley's scheme of work for computing in Chapter 15 and what is set out for Year 9 Term 3 "Artificial Intelligence and Machine Learning (concepts)", which is part of "Considering consequences of technology by exploring a disruptive technology - Artificial Intelligence (AI)".

In Year 9 (14-year-olds), most learners would have used some form of AI. In using Google to search for information, the first response comes from what it calls its "Gemini AI models". Gemini models are multimodal, which means that they can understand and generate content using different types of information, such as text, images and computer code. An issue with computing is the extent to which a user needs to know what goes on 'underneath the bonnet' when they just need to 'drive' the computer. The use of the word "Intelligence" implies something human-like, so it is important that all learners realise that it is an actually an application of mathematics, so this is a perfect opportunity to include a colleague teaching Year 9 Maths, too.

How might AI 'look' at these two images in Figure 16.1 and work out which is the Cat and which is the Dog?

Figure 16.1 AI distinguishing an image of a Cat from a Dog

From its access to very Big Data, it sets up a "scorecard" of features:

- **Ear shape**: pointy (cats) vs floppy (dogs)
- **Sound**: "meow" vs "woof"
- **Tail movement**: swishy (cats) vs waggy (dogs)

Now, AI turns these features into **numbers**. For example:

- Ear shape: pointy = 1, floppy = 0
- Sound: meow = 1, woof = 0
- Tail movement: swishy = 1, waggy = 0

So:

- A cat might be [1, 1, 1]
- A dog might be [0, 0, 0]

These little lists of numbers are like graph **coordinates** in space – x, y and z.

AI uses **geometry + algebra** to draw a line (or boundary) between cats and dogs in that space. If the numbers fall on one side of the line → cat, on the other side → dog.

But there is one more important step – **Probability.**

Figure 16.2 AI distinguishing an image of a Cat from a different Dog

Real animals aren't always so neat to distinguish. As shown in Figure 16.2, some dogs, of course, have pointy ears, and some cats wag their tails when playful. That's when **probability** comes in.

AI might calculate that the left-hand picture compared to the right now has features [0, 1, 1]. That's a probability of 80% cat, 20% dog.

But how does AI 'learn'? Every time it guesses wrong, it nudges the slope of the line a little bit until it gets better at separating them – it's applying calculus to do so.

The key concept to teach in Year 9 is that AI does not 'think', even though it often looks like it does so. It just applies maths. It's like teaching AI to play a giant, complicated game of 'spot the difference' – just with numbers instead of eyes – but it 'crunches' those numbers extremely quickly!

Teaching the AQA specification for Computer Science to Year 10 (15-year-olds) could include the topic 'Fundamentals of Algorithms'. How could the previous example be taught using a simple algorithm? Think of making a cake. A recipe for a cake has ingredients (input) and clear instructions (steps) to get a cake (output).

So, in general terms:

Input: The data you start with (e.g., a list of numbers, a question, a photo).
Process: The steps you follow.
Output: The result you get.
Sequence: Steps happen in order.
Conditionals (IF/THEN): Making decisions based on data.
Loops: Repeating steps until a condition is met.

But how does AI fit in? Machine learning is like a super-powered algorithm that can "write its own recipe" after looking quickly at thousands of examples.

When a human writes the recipe, to sort numbers they compare two at a time and swap them if they're in the wrong order. But in a machine learning algorithm we give the AI 1,000 pictures of cats and 1,000 pictures of dogs (the input). The AI's job is to figure out its 'own recipe' (the process) for telling the difference. The output is a new algorithm that can say "cat" or "dog" for a new picture it has never seen.

Let's look at a simple algorithm for "Is it a Cat, a Rabbit, or a Dog?"

Figure 16.3 AI distinguishing an image of a Cat from a Rabbit and a Dog

What should be the Algorithm Recipe in this case?

1. INPUT - Ask the user about the animal's features:

   Does it have pointy ears? (Yes/No)
   What sound does it make? (Meow, Bark, Squeak)
   Is it larger than a house cat? (Yes/No)

2. PROCESS - Use conditional statements (IF/THEN) to make a decision:

   IF the sound is "Squeak" THEN say "It's a Rabbit!"
   ELSE IF the sound is "Bark" THEN say "It's a Dog!"
   ELSE IF the sound is "Meow" THEN ask about its size.
   IF it is larger than a house cat? THEN say "It's a Puma!"
   ELSE say "It's a House Cat!"

3. OUTPUT - Print the result: "I think it's a [Animal]!"

This simple step-by-step algorithm mimics AI. This is exactly how many expert systems and simple AIs work. Real-world machine learning is far more complex using mathematics as shown in the first Cat or Dog example, but the conceptual logic is identical and as it's "codeable", learners can easily write this in Python, Scratch or even just pseudocode on a whiteboard.

A short lesson sequence in Year 9 or Year 10 could be:

What's the Recipe?

Activity: Learners write an 'algorithm' for an everyday task, like making a jam sandwich or tying their shoes. Highlight the importance of clear, unambiguous steps (sequence).

Activity: Play a '20 Questions'-style game. 'IF it is alive, THEN ask if it's an animal. IF it is an animal, THEN ask if it has fur . . .' This naturally secures the idea of a decision tree.

Introduce the 'AI' Project

Present the Cat/Dog/Rabbit classifier. Build the decision tree on the board together as a class.

Hands-On Coding. Guide them to write the code in a language like Python:

```
print("Welcome to the Animal Classifier!")
sound = input("What sound does it make? (Meow, Bark, Squeak): ")
if sound == "Squeak":
    print("It's a Rabbit!")
elif sound == "Bark":
    print("It's a Dog!")
```

~~~
elif sound == "Meow":
    size = input("Is it larger than a house cat? (Yes/No): ")
    if size == "Yes":
        print("It's a Puma!")
    else:
        print("It's a House Cat!")
    else:
        print("I don't know that animal!")
```
~~~

Discussion and Limitations

What are the problems with our "AI"?

What if an animal doesn't make a sound? (Input problem)

What about a Chihuahua that's smaller than a cat? (The algorithm breaks! Our rules are too simple)

This leads to a discussion on why real AI needs vast amounts of data and more complex "recipes" (neural networks) to handle exceptions and nuance such as dogs with pointed ears!

The key aim for Year 9 or the start of Year 10 are that by using a relatable, hands-on example of a simple classifier, you demystify both algorithms and AI.

Students learn that:

1. AI is built on these same logical fundamentals of input, process and output.
2. Algorithms are just recipes.
3. The core programming concepts of sequence, conditionals and loops are the building blocks of all software, including AI.
4. AI can distinguish images of animals by applying relatively simple mathematics.

> Pause for thought
>
> This lesson considers, in simple terms, how AI works. Do you think it is pitched at the right level for learners in Year 9 (13–14-year-olds) to understand the concepts? If not, what would you change? Do you think that they should **use** AI to learn **about** AI? Looking at the pedagogies in Panel 16.1, I think that the use of multimodal working is clear. Do you agree?

How might we teach about augmented reality?

We have seen that augmented reality (AR) is being adapted in a wide variety of settings including gaming and entertainment, retail and E-commerce, navigations and travel, secondary school education, maintenance and manufacture and medicine and healthcare.

Young people in school are most likely to experience the technology in gaming and entertainment, although they might also find their family members use it when they go on holiday together to navigate the airport or find their way about in new destinations. Some schools use AR to enhance lessons. But it is likely that the gaming and entertainment experience will have the most appeal. You may remember that the game Pokémon Go was very popular some time ago, and it appears that its popularity is rising. At the time of writing, the Natural History Museum will be including a Pokémon pop-up shop experience from January 2026 with exclusive products designed especially for the collaboration. So, in the following lesson the teacher decided to set her Year 8 class the challenge of designing a Pokémon Go treasure hunt around the school.

After a brief discussion about Pokémon Go and how the game worked as an AR technology, the teacher told the class that they would be working in teams of four and that each team had to:

- Design at least six different Pokémon Go characters – each one representing an area of the school. She supplied each group with a Pokémon shape template.
- Decide on the exact location at which each character would be found.
- Each character had to somehow, by its appearance, represent the area in which it was located.
- Decide on the rewards for the finding of each character.
- Present their Pokémon Go game to the rest of the class for questions and comments. The presentation could be in the form of a verbal report, read from a manuscript or a visual presentation with both text and images.

When the presentations were completed, the class would vote on which one they thought was the best.

Pause for thought

What do you make of this lesson? Would you teach a lesson like that, or would you want to change it significantly?

How does this lesson measure up to the suggestions for pedagogies useful for teaching disruptive technologies shown in Panel 16.1? Some are irrelevant – speculative worlds and challenge-based learning. It is strong in learners seeing themselves in the curriculum in that the learners are involved in developing a game typically played by young people and multimodal in that learners work with each other and develop a presentation for their peers. And in developing their own Pokémon Go game, it is strong in entrepreneurial education. You may be wondering why the teacher did not include the use of AI tools in her lesson, especially given the nature of the disruptive technology under consideration. We are not convinced that they would provide much in the way of benefit. If you disagree, then you might want to suggest how AI tools might be used to enhance the lesson. In terms of what has been learned, we think that developing a Pokémon Go game puts learners into a strong position to understand the programming requirements when they come to develop a real-time augmented reality experience.

How might we teach about Big Data?

In every chapter in Part 1 where we looked at a disruptive technology in depth, there was a section that considered the negative aspects of the technology concerned. Our motivation for writing this book is to look to the future, short- or longer-term, and to consider how to prepare learners at secondary school to become informed citizens who can take part in the developing debates on implementation. The metaphor of needing to know how to 'drive' a computer or smart phone, but not necessarily needing a full understanding of what goes on 'under the bonnet', fails if we don't consider that any car also needs 'fuel' to work. When we watch a film on a smart TV or laptop, it looks like the only energy problem we have is remembering to charge the computer. The aim of teaching about Big Data is to show that to drive the virtual world there are other major energy requirements needed to 'fuel' AI and the Internet of Things.

In Chapters 2 and 4, we pointed out that we need Big Data centres to serve the needs of AI and that data needs to be accessed quickly. We noted that these datasets are often characterised by their vast volume, high 'velocity' and wide 'variety', often summarised as the three Vs of Big Data. Volume is the amount of data generated and collected, and it is truly immense, ranging from terabytes (10^{12} bytes) to petabytes (1,000 terabytes), and as aspects of AI are often considered in computing lessons, Big Data can be considered there too.

All of us, including your students, will find it is very difficult to grasp what this huge amount of data means and how much is needed even to distinguish between pictures of a cat and a dog! And even put in everyday contexts, it still assumes that we all share the same general understanding. For example, it is often said that a petabyte is the equivalent to about 20 million tall filing cabinets or 500 billion pages of standard printed text. Maybe many classrooms or science laboratories still have a filing cabinet as a 'stage prop' example for use in a computing or science lesson, but visualising 20 million of them? Maybe not! Velocity, you will remember, is the speed at which data is generated, collected and processed and is extremely fast. Finally, 'Variety' refers to the different formats in which the data is collected, such as social media, sensors and web transactions, and that variety can be exploited in lessons.

Suggested teaching of artificial intelligence in computing lessons had some links to mathematics lessons. Here, considering the negative consequences of the hidden huge energy consumption of data centres, links to science to work out the electrical and heat energy conversion and the adverse environmental impacts are made clear. Looking at such heavy electricity consumption globally, and how that demand is met, will be of interest to geography teachers. Looking 'sideways' to what your colleagues do to support their own particular "specified curriculum" could also help learners appreciate disruptive technologies - and so is a benefit to all.

Lesson 1: Big Data in our lives

Subject Focus: Computing/Computing Science

Prior to this lesson learners collect "home data" (e.g. number of steps recorded on their phones (Google Fit/Samsung Health), their favourite apps, their sleep hours). This shows learners needing to actually use the technology, phones or Fitbit smart watches which are part of the Internet of Things. They can send in their data using the school's usual "homework" system, such as Google Classroom or Satchel One.

Lesson Objective: Students will understand what Big Data is and how it's used.

Starter: Show some examples of the use of Big Data, for example:

- Movies that the learners watch on streaming channels and the suggested ones they "might like" to see are driven by AI algorithms needing Big Data.
- Google Maps. On a long journey, if the Satnav maps' instant traffic updates need real-time data.
- Weather Maps. Predicting the weather accurately (or even moderately accurately!) needs a huge number of data points of temperature, pressure and predicted flow. Also, climate change models are very "data hungry" (see economistfoundation.org).

Activity: Build a small dataset using the learners' reported phone information that they collected at home and discuss how it might grow if collected worldwide.

Link to Physics: Discuss that data is stored as electrical signals - storing and processing require considerable amounts of energy.

Homework: Research one way that Big Data helps society (medicine such as patient data, the environment such as weather prediction, business such as personal data in the banking system).

A Linked Physics lesson:

Lesson 2: The energy needs of data centres

When teaching about Energy, Power and Efficiency in Year 10, having a real-life context obviously makes it more interesting, and it also builds on the "circus" of different forms of energy often taught in Years 8 or 9.

Subject Focus: Physics (Energy, Power, Efficiency) - Year 10

Objective: Explore how Big Data requires considerable electricity and produces heat.

Key Data (2022–23 figures):

- A large data centre can use 100 MW of power (so 100 million joules every second), which is the same electricity consumption as a small city.
- 1 GB of data transferred uses about 0.06 kWh (216,000 joules of electrical energy) (source: International Energy Agency).
- 0.06 kWh = enough to power a 10 W LED bulb for 6 hours.

Activity: Learners calculate: if each of them streams 2 hours of a HD video (about 2 GB), how much energy does the whole class use if they watch the same video?

- 2 GB × 0.06 kWh = 0.12 kWh per Learner
- 30 Learners × 0.12 kWh = 3.6 kWh total for the class
- That's equivalent to running a 1.8 kW kettle for 2 hours.

So where does the energy needed for the 2-hour streamed movie go? Usually it is "wasted" in the large Data Centre as heat - which itself is a problem, as the equipment needs to kept cool - so more energy is needed (or a large quantity of water).

How could the energy be better used? What are the advantages and disadvantages of Local District Heating?

It is clear from this lesson that Big Data isn't "virtual" - it has a considerably physical cost, especially to the environment.

Lesson 3: The carbon cost of streaming and cloud storage and the global costs

Subject Focus: Interdisciplinary (Physics + Computing + Geography)

Objective: Calculate the environmental footprint of Big Data usage.

Key Data:

Average global electricity emissions ↓ 0.4 kg CO_2 per kWh.

Activity:

Calculate the CO_2 emissions for streaming 1 movie (2 hours, 2 GB is about 0.12 kWh energy):

0.12 kWh × 0.4 kg CO_2 = 0.048 kg CO_2 (about 50 g)

Compare with some everyday actions:

- Boiling a kettle (0.1 kg CO_2) (100g)
- Driving 1 km in a patrol car (about 0.2 kg (200g) CO_2)

Discussion: Is binge-watching 10 episodes like taking a short car trip?

A Linked Geography lesson:

Lesson 4: Mapping Big Data globally

Using Table 16.1, write onto a map of the world the number of locations of Big Data centres both globally and in the learner's own country (see https://www.datacentermap.com/ for data about your own country).

Table 16.1 Data centre numbers worldwide

Continent	*Country*	*Number of data centres*
North America	United States	4,049
North America	Canada	284
South America	Brazil	189
Europe	Germany	480

Table 16.1 Data centre numbers worldwide (Continued)

Continent	*Country*	*Number of data centres*
Europe	United Kingdom	484
Asia	China	379
Asia	India	270
Asia	Singapore	78
Oceania	Australia	264
Oceania	New Zealand	55
Africa	South Africa	56
Africa	Kenya	19
Middle East/W Asia	United Arab Emirates	57

What does the mapped distribution suggest about global economic development over the next 5 years? Where will the energy come from? How can the energy be generated in the different countries?

By the end of the sequence lessons about Big Data, learners will:

- See how Big Data powers the modern world.
- Understand energy = power × time and how it applies to data centres.
- Be able to calculate the energy and carbon impact of everyday digital activitie, and the implied *ethical* consequences.
- See how Big Data centres are distributed worldwide and consider the *economic* consequences for a range of countries in satisfying the energy needs.

Pause for thought

This consideration of Big Data has very much focused on the negative environmental issues. Is this a fair topic for a series of associated lessons for Year 9?

In late 2025, some 'High-tech' businesses such as Google/Alphabet and leading chip company Nvidia both announced plans to set up significant capacity in the United Kingdom because the government is keen to facilitate more Big Data hubs. The company representatives were challenged about the environmental impact of Big Data but brushed the concerns aside, making the point that it was to their commercial advantage to look to battery storage and other efficiency techniques to save money. Wind and solar farm generation of electricity may save on CO_2 emissions, but often local objections to the necessary associated electricity pylon infrastructure are profound. This is a clear moral dilemma - if we want to watch streamed movies and use AI tools in school and at home, how can we object to the Big Data functional requirements to make it all happen?

Looking to the pedagogies in Panel 6.1, Multimodal Working is used across subjects, say between physics and geography, but the mathematical focus is similar. Can you suggest better ways to tackle the same issues with a better variety of activities?

How might we teach about the Internet of Things?

When we looked at the enacted curriculum of Jill, Kamrul and Lesley in Chapter 15, they all chose to teach aspects of the Internet of Things (IoT) in Term 2 of Year 7 (12-year-olds). The reason for that is clear as, of the 10 disruptive technologies we have considered, IoT is perhaps the one most familiar to these learners in their day-to-day lives. Some will use IoT themselves, and some they will be readily aware of at home or school, but in both cases, they would probably not attach an IoT "label" to them. They are not considered something different - it's just stuff that they are pleased to get as a birthday present or things around the house that, for them, have always been there! Table 16.2 is the beginning of a table of what a 12-year-old in Europe might use themselves, as well as what they might recognise:

Table 16.2 Some uses of the Internet of Things

IoT that they might use daily	*IoT that they may have in the home/school*
Smartphone for texting	Smart TVs and streaming devices
Smartwatch/Fitness tracker	Smart lighting and plugs
Wireless earbuds	Doorbell cams
Tile or AirTag	Connected laptops/tablets/smart boards

You can no doubt add to this list and probably give the brand names for many of them too. IoT is ubiquitous and learners probably find out how to use the different IoT technologies from their family and friends more than they do in school.

Here we are going to expand the details of the enacted curriculum set out in Chapter 15 to consider how Jill's, Kamrul's and Lesley's scheme of work was implemented in the workshop, laboratory or classroom, respectively. In D and T Jill chose to design and make a light that is suitable for a particular situation as a follow-on from a discussion about IoT. A light that comes on when it is dark is an easy solution, but one that can be switched on 'remotely' is more challenging. Lesley chose in computing to consider the IoT explicitly and address the benefits and risks, and Kamrul considered the science behind sound frequency and audibility, which is a key feature of wireless earbuds.

What follows, then, is a sub-set of Freda's Experience Curriculum.

Kamrul's science lesson - sound, frequency and the Internet of Things

Learning objectives

By the end of the lesson, learners will be able to:

1. Describe how sound is a vibration and how frequency relates to pitch.
2. Explain how digital devices (IoT) can sense and respond to sound frequencies.
3. Explore real-world examples where IoT uses sound (e.g., voice assistants, smart alarms).
4. Design and test a simple experiment showing how sound can control or trigger a response.

Materials needed

- Small speaker and signal generator for playing different tones
- Objects to test (clap, whistle, ringtone, spoken word)
- Oscilloscope, or laptop or tablet with microphone and a free sound frequency app
- Slinky spring
- Whiteboard/markers

Lesson Outline

1. (about 15 minutes)

    - Play two sounds: a low rumble (e.g., 100 Hz) and a high-pitched whistle (e.g., 2000 Hz).
    - Ask: *"What's the difference?"* → Guide learners to say one is "low", and one is "high" (pitch).
    - Introduce frequency: the number of vibrations per second (measured in Hertz). Higher frequency = higher pitch.
    - Show the different wave patterns on an oscilloscope or laptop with suitable frequency app.
    - Play different type of sounds (clap, whistle, hum, ringtone) and Learners observe the frequencies and shapes that appear on the graph.
    - Learners suggest what happens when the whistle is blown compared to a clap?

2. (about 10 minutes)

    - Explain how sound travels as vibrations in air.
    - Use a slinky spring to show longitudinal wave-like sound through air.
    - Connect to **IoT**:

        - Microphones convert sound vibrations into electrical signals.
        - IoT devices (like Alexa, Siri, Google Home, smart sensors) use microphones + frequency analysis to detect certain sounds.

3. IoT Connection Activity (about 20 minutes)
   Task: Imagine you are designing a smart device that listens for certain sounds to trigger an action.

    - Examples:

        - A smart dog door that only opens when it hears the dog's bark.
        - A clap-controlled lamp – did you make one in D and T?
        - A baby monitor that alerts parents when it hears crying (certain frequency range).

   In your usual small groups, sketch your idea:

    - What type of sound does it detect?
    - What frequency range might that be?
    - What action does it trigger?

4. Wrap-up (10 minutes)

- Groups share their IoT sound ideas.
- Discuss some real-world examples: voice assistants, noise-cancelling headphones, smart alarms that detect glass breaking.
- Reinforce key link: Sound → Frequency → Digital signal → IoT response.

Possible Homework

Using a free frequency app on their phone, the learners record 3 different household sounds.

Write a short explanation of how an IoT device could use that sound.

Jill's D and T lesson - designing and making a smart LED light

Learning Objectives

By the end of the lesson(s), learners will be able to:

1. Understand how LEDs, switches and batteries work in simple circuits.
2. Design a light suitable for a particular situation (e.g., bedside lamp, locker light, desk study light or outdoor safety light).
3. Construct a working prototype using easy-to-work thin sheet materials and basic electronic components.
4. Explore how the concept of the Internet of Things (IoT) can be applied to their light design (e.g., app control or motion detection).
5. Evaluate their design based on function, safety and aesthetics.

This would extend over 2/3 lessons

Materials and Resources

Ensure the following components are readily available:

- LEDs (various colours)
- Resistors (if needed for current limiting)
- Wires, crocodile clips, breadboards (for prototyping)
- Battery holders and AA/AAA batteries
- Toggle switches, push switches or slide switches

Materials for casing:

- Thin sheet materials: card, plasticard or PVC. These can be marked out as nets and scored so that they fold up into an enclosure.

Tools:

- Wire cutters/strippers
- Screwdrivers

- ICT Resources:
  - Slides/videos introducing IoT
  - Design sketching sheets
  - Maybe access to micro:bit or simulated IoT software demos.

Lesson 1 Activities

Starter (about 10 min)

- Show real-world examples of lights in different contexts: bike lights, reading lamps, camping lanterns, wardrobe lights, decorative LED strips.
- Quick class discussion:
- *"What makes a light design suitable for its purpose?"* (size, brightness, portability, power source, safety, style)
- Introduce IoT idea: Smart bulbs that can be turned on/off with phones, voice commands or motion sensors.

Main Activity

Step 1: Research and Ideas (about 15 min)

- Learners in pairs choose a target situation (e.g., a light for inside a school locker, a bedside reading light or a safety light for walking a dog at night).
- They sketch 2–3 design ideas with annotations (materials, shape, type of switch, LED colour, battery placement).

Step 2: Circuit Planning (about 20 min)

- Teacher demonstrates a simple LED + switch + battery circuit on a whiteboard or breadboard.
- Learners draw their own circuit diagram for their design.

Lesson 2 Activities

Step 3: Making and Prototyping (about 30 min)

- Learners build the light housing using their chosen materials (card, plasticard or pvc).
- They insert and wire the LED circuit with switch and battery.

Obviously, teacher circulates to assist with safe tool use and wiring issues.
Step 4: IoT (about 20 min)

- Learners discuss (or prototype) how their light could connect to IoT, e.g.:
  - Controlled via a micro:bit with radio/bluetooth.
  - Designed to respond to motion sensors.
  - How might it link to a phone app (in theory) – teacher demo or simulation.
- Learners sketch/annotate how IoT would enhance their product.

Plenary about (10 min)

- Pairs present their light to the class.
- Each explains:
    - The situation for which it is designed.
    - How the light works.
    - How IoT could improve it.
- Teacher leads peer feedback using '2 Stars and a Wish' (two positive comments, one suggestion).

Lesley's computing lesson – Internet of Things, benefit and risks

Learning Objectives:

By the end of the lesson, learners will be able to:

1. Describe what the Internet of Things (IoT) is.
2. Identify examples of IoT devices and smart systems in everyday life.
3. Explain potential benefits and risks of IoT.
4. Be able to evaluate IoT use in real-world contexts.

Starter (5–10 minutes)
Activity: Spot the IoT

- Teacher displays images (smart speaker, fridge, thermostat, smartwatch, CCTV, etc.) alongside non-IoT items (traditional TV, old fridge, analogue watch).
- Learners vote IoT or not IoT (Small group discussion, list on mini whiteboards, vote)
- Brief discussion: What makes a device "smart"?

Main Activities

1. Short Teacher-led Discussion (10 minutes)
    - Teacher introduces the Internet of Things: everyday objects connected to the internet, able to send/receive data etc.
    - Show a short video "A Day in the Life of a Smart Home"
    - Prompt discussion: Who has IoT devices at home? What do they do?
2. Group Task – IoT Systems in Action (20 minutes)
   Activity: Smart City Challenge
    - The class in groups gets a scenario card (e.g., smart home, smart school, smart transport, smart hospital, smart farming).

- Task: Design a simple IoT system for their scenario. They should:
  1. List IoT devices needed (e.g., smart lights, sensors, wearables).
  2. Explain the benefits (efficiency, convenience, safety, sustainability).
  3. Identify risks and problems (privacy, hacking, cost, reliability).
- Learners record ideas on a mind map or shared online document.

3. Sharing and Debate (15 minutes)
   - Each group briefly presents their smart system.
   - As a class, discuss:
     - Which IoT systems seem most beneficial?
     - Which pose the greatest risks?
     - Would you want to live in a fully smart home/school? Why or why not?

Plenary (5 minutes)
Exit ticket: Learners write down on a sticky note or an online poll:

- One benefit of IoT
- One risk of IoT

Homework:

- Research a real IoT device (e.g., Ring doorbell, Fitbit, Nest thermostat).
- Write a short paragraph on:
  1. What the IoT device does.
  2. How it benefits the users.
  3. Are there any risks or problems associated with it?

Pause for thought

In Chapter 15, when you looked at the tables setting out the indicative scheme of work showing the enacted curriculum of Jill, Kamrul and Lesley, what lessons do you see in your mind's eye? What would you have done differently? How feasible do you think the lessons about teaching aspects of the IoT are for your school? Would they engage your Learners? How could you successfully coordinate contributions from different subjects without it becoming too onerous?

Looking at the pedagogies set out in Panel 16.1, the lessons took a multimodal working approach, and maybe the mix of genders in the teaching staff for STEM subjects in some way addressed opportunities for learners to "See yourself in the curriculum". Do you agree?

Teaching resources

A Day in the Life of a Smart Home (video)
https://www.youtube.com/watch?v=JAXIyheCc-w

How might we teach about neurotechnology?

In Chapter 2 we joked about how on a TV programme pilot Steve Austin is fatally injured in an airplane crash, but the government spends six million dollars on bionic implants to rebuild him, which gives him superhuman abilities. Fiction, of course. But in Chapter 8, Professor Simon Schultz points out that "the idea of "Brain-Machine Interfaces" through which people can directly communicate with computers, or control robotic manipulators, through thought alone, has recently captured the public imagination, due primarily to hype focused around Neuralink, a company run by Elon Musk". He goes on,

> Although much of the hype has been around the potential application of the technology in normal human subjects, for a long time to come the technology is likely to be restricted to clinical applications where the need outweighs the risks, such as tetraplegia (the loss of control of all four limbs) and Amyotrophic Lateral Sclerosis (ALS) which is the specific Motor Neurone Disease (MND) that Professor Stephen Hawking suffered from.

Neurotechnology is an interdisciplinary field that combines elements of neuroscience, biomedical engineering, computer science, robotics and psychology to create tools and systems that interface with neural tissue. Although the learners might like to focus on creating Marvel Comics superhuman figures, as we saw in Chapter 8 the current understanding of neurotechnology systems supports people with a range of medical issues, such as Parkinson's disease and transcranial magnetic stimulation for treating depression. Devices can replace or enhance the function of damaged nervous system components, such as cochlear implants for hearing loss and retinal implants for vision restoration.

Neurotechnology is probably better considered as a disruptive technology for learners aged 16 to 18 as part of their pre-university course in biology. Here is a suggested lesson that we think would excite and enhance the learners' general understanding of the brain but not take too much lesson time.

A future with neurotechnology

A teaser to start with . . .

Show the class the following short YouTube clip, which has a tetraplegic patent, paralysed from the neck down, using Elon Musk's Neuralink to move a computer cursor to play chess.

https://www.youtube.com/watch?v=IbM4-rcujxY

And ask the class the following questions to spark curiosity and get them thinking about other real-world uses:

- What do you think just happened?
- How could this change people's lives?

This sets the scene for a slightly more formal approach.

What is neurotechnology and how is it being used?

Lead a short discussion through a series of visuals – those from Chapter 8, perhaps, or others freely found online to cover the following points:

- Definition: technology that interacts with the brain or nervous system.
- Current applications: medical (deep brain stimulation for Parkinson's, cochlear implants, prosthetics), consumer (EEG headbands for focus/gaming), research (brain imaging).
- Emerging potential: memory enhancement, thought-to-text communication, direct brain-computer interaction, mood regulation.

Finish by saying something like, "Think of it as Bluetooth for the brain in that thoughts are turned into radio signals which can be received and used to make something happen".

A group discussion activity

Get the class into discussion groups of about four learners. Assuming this gives four groups, ask the groups to research and discuss:

Group 1 Medical applications (e.g., treating paralysis, epilepsy, Parkinson's)
Group 2 Everyday life and consumer tech (gaming, wearables, focus training)
Group 3 Future possibilities (memory uploading, human-AI symbiosis)
Group 4 Ethical concerns (privacy, inequality, human identity)

The research could be supported by handouts of extracts from Chapter 8 or by using an AI agent such as ChatGPT.

Give about 10 minutes for this activity and ask the groups to identify key points that they will feed back to the class, 2 minutes presentation per group, with 2 minutes for taking questions.

This sets the scene for the next part of the lesson.

Speculative world writing

There are many possibilities; here are two, and no doubt you can think of more.

Possibility A

Give the class the title "Neurotechnology: Utopia or Dystopia?" and get the learners to work in two discussion groups to prepare for a debate: "This house believes that in 20 years, everyone will have a brain implant, just like we all have smartphones today and that as a result society will be much better". Each side has just 5 minutes to prepare arguments, then run a short, structured debate using some evidence from the earlier group work.

Possibility B

Learners work individually to write a short scenario in response to "Imagine it's the year 2045. Neurotechnology is everywhere. Describe one positive and one negative way it affects your daily life". The "writing" could be in the form of text, text plus illustrations, a comic strip or an audio file. Volunteers share their stories with the rest of the class.

Wrap-up

Make the following key points:

- Neurotechnology is already here, not just 'science fiction'.
- It has huge potential to help people.
- It also raises big ethical and social questions.

And suggest that the learners talk to folk at home about today's lesson and ask them, "Would you personally want a brain implant if it meant you could learn anything instantly?"

And finally, suggest this follow-up research task for the learners:

> Find a real neurotechnology company/startup and write a short 200-word report on what they are developing and who it could help.

Pause for thought

What do you make of this lesson? Would you teach a lesson like that, or would you want to change it significantly?

Neurotechnology is a disruptive technology that is developing very quickly and has real moral dilemmas that could, and probably will, challenge this group of young people in the near-future. You might use alternative dilemmas from Chapter 8 that set out issues such as the possibility of the very rich gaining a cognitive advantage for themselves or for their children. Linked via an implant to a computer running AI, could they become as 'smart' as a supercomputer? Considering the pedagogies set out in Panel 16.1, clearly several different strategies could be employed in teaching this topic: Speculative worlds, Multimodal working and through the follow-up research task Entrepreneurial education. In terms of what has been learned we think that the lesson has enabled learners to explain what neurotechnology is and give examples of current applications, discuss potential future developments and their societal impact, evaluate the ethical, social and personal implications of neurotechnology and experienced working collaboratively to form and express reasoned opinions.

Teaching resources

Neuralink's *First Patient Play Chess Using Brain Implant*
https://www.youtube.com/watch?v=5SrpYZum4Nk&t=15s

How might we teach about programmable matter?

In design and technology, there is little incentive to explain why materials behave as they do. The focus is on their intrinsic properties and the extent to which these render a material as fit for purpose in a proposed design. This is not the case in chemistry which is concerned with explanation and the properties of materials are explained in terms of their structure at the atomic level. Programmable materials challenge this view of conventional materials and the way their properties are 'fixed' and that these properties can be explained in terms of their 'fixed' structure.

So although, as we noted earlier, programmable matter is at a very early stage of development and should perhaps be classed as 'potentially' disruptive and best described as an 'emerging' disruptor it provides the possibility of intriguing older learners with the limitations of science – our understanding is always a work in progress. Hence, in the lesson described here, a chemistry teacher decided that in an A-level revision lesson (learners aged 17/18 years) he wanted to move beyond the usual recall practice and juxtapose the conventional view of explaining the properties of materials with the challenge posed by a consideration of programmable materials.

He began conventionally enough in asking the class to describe the structure of the following materials:

- Diamond
- Graphite
- Ice
- Iodine
- Magnesium
- Sodium chloride.

As members of the class described the structures of the materials, he displayed ball and stick models of the structures so that they could extend their answers by referring to the models. Once he was satisfied that all members of the class were au fait with the structures, he asked the learners to get into groups and write agreed answers to the following questions that required them to use the models of the structures to explain properties.

Why is diamond so hard?
Why is graphite so soft?
Why does iodine melt at a low temperature?
Why does magnesium conduct electricity?
Why does sodium chloride dissolve in water?
Why does ice have such a high melting point compared to other non-metallic hydrides, such as hydrogen sulphide or hydrogen chloride?

He arranged for each group to give feedback to the rest of the class about one or two of their answers and other members of the class, then commented on them in the light of their own answers.

Then he introduced the idea of a programmable matter with this statement.

> Programmable matter is materials or objects that can change their physical properties (such as shape, density, conductivity and optical characteristics) in a controlled and programmable manner. This technology is based on the concept of 'reconfigurability', where the material can be programmed to alter its form or function in response to external stimuli or programmed commands.

He then provided this recent example - the self-adaptive photochromic (SAP) material developed by Chinese scientists. This development draws inspiration from natural organisms like chameleons and octopi that possess the ability to change colour for concealment.

> This SAP material can adjust its molecular composition to blend seamlessly into various backgrounds, effectively rendering it invisible to the naked eye. The SAP material consists of a mixture of organic dyes and materials that act as molecular photo switches. Together they rearrange their chemical and structural makeup when exposed to specific wavelengths of light. This rearrangement enables the material to change colour without the need for external power sources or complex electronics.

He then set the class this challenge:

> Working in small groups, I want you to explore what this SAP material might be used for in developing a new product. To be successful your proposal must be technically feasible; i.e., it must use the behaviour of the SAP, meet customer requirements, be acceptable to society and viable in terms of existing or created markets.
>
> You have 10 minutes and then each group will make a short presentation about your new product idea and how it meets the success criteria.

The group presentations included some of the following ideas:

- Fashion items that changed in colour/pattern according to lighting conditions
- Camouflage for both personnel and vehicles (think of the "Predator" movies or maybe Harry Potter's invisibility cloak)
- Coatings on the outside of buildings that can be changed
- Changeable interior design decor

The teacher then asked different members of the class to provide a recap of the lessons using the following questions:

Tell me which substance I'm holding up – as he held up different ball and stick models.
Tell me which one will dissolve in water, be very hard, be very soft, have a low melting point, conduct electricity, have a higher-than-expected melting point?
The learners were able to answer the questions correctly with confidence.

Write down the difference between a programmable material and an ordinary material and pass them to the front. I'll read them before the next lesson. Remember, you won't be asked about programmable materials in your A level Chemistry examination.

And finally, did you enjoy speculating about what the SAP material might be used for?

The response was universally positive.

Pause for thought

What do you make of this lesson? Would you teach a lesson like that, or would you want to change it significantly?

How does this lesson measure up to the suggestions for pedagogies useful for teaching disruptive technologies shown in Panel 16.1? Some are irrelevant – speculative worlds and challenge-based learning. The exercise in devising uses for the SAP material was clearly entrepreneurial education. We aren't sure whether this would be improved by using AI tools – like the access to additional information through a search engine or a collaboration coach. The lesson is strong in multimodal working (in using the ball and stick models). We think that seeing yourself in the curriculum is taking place in the entrepreneurial activity (it was the learners' ideas that were important), but you may think we are stretching a point here. In terms of what has been learned, we think that the lesson has provided a powerful revision lesson of ideas important in A-level chemistry and also introduced a 'space to watch' with regard to developments in material science.

How might we teach about quantum computing?

In late 2025, Frank conducted a survey of the content of the pre-university-level physics syllabi in different countries around the world to see what the general "specified curriculum" for quantum theory was. He looked first at the Advanced Level examinations in England and Wales and at the Higher Level examination in Scotland. The labels used in the examination specifications for the different examination boards were encouraging; quantum physics, quantum mechanics, quanta and waves, but whatever the titles of the modules suggested, their content was just the same and very similar indeed to the pre-university physics taught in Australia, Canada, India, New Zealand, the US, Singapore and South Africa. It seems across borders, the common topics included when teaching the 'new' Quantum Physics are the Photoelectric Effect (1887), the Bohr atom (1913), Wave-particle duality and de Broglie ideas and the application to particles like electrons (1924). Some also include a 'qualitative' introduction to wavefunctions/Schrödinger equation (1925) and Heisenberg's uncertainty principle (1927).

As a teacher of pre-university physics students at three different high schools in England and in Wales, Frank fully understands the limitations of sufficient teaching time and the usual level of mathematics understanding of the learners. In a recent survey (Davies 2025), 78% of the adults in France and Germany say they are aware of the term "quantum technology" but only about one in three have a good, clear understanding of what quantum science and technology *actually* are. Surely the 17- or 18-year-old learners studying physics deserve at least 50 minutes to be introduced to an application of what they are studying, and what better topic than quantum computing? It is true that in 2025 it is still an emerging disruptive technology, but as we saw in Chapter 10, steady progress is being made so current 18-year-olds are the generation likely to be using quantum computers!

From quantum theory to quantum computing

Target group: Pre-university physics learners (16–18 years old)

Duration: 50 minutes

Learning Objectives

By the end of the lesson, learners should be able to:

1. Recall some basic principles of quantum theory (superposition, uncertainty, measurement issues).
2. Understand how these principles can be applied to information processing.
3. Appreciate the difference between classical and quantum computers.
4. Explore real-world applications of quantum computing.

1. Introduction: (about 5 minutes): Cards - Choosing the 10 of Clubs as illustrated in Figure 16.4.

Figure 16.4 Finding the 10 of clubs in a 52-card pack

Ask:

- If you had to look for the 10 of clubs in a deck of 52 cards, how many tries would it take *on average*?
- Learners will (hopefully!) say: about 26.
- But what if you had 1 million cards? (They'll realise it becomes very hard!)
- Classical computers are like people searching card-by-card. In contrast, Quantum computers can sometimes check many possibilities at once.

2. Review of Some Quantum Theory (about 10 minutes)
   Quick recap of some syllabus concepts:

   - Wave-particle duality: Light and electrons can act like both waves and particles.
   - Superposition: A quantum system can be in multiple states at once, until measured (e.g., When spinning in the air, a coin could be considered to be *both* heads and tails at the same time (like electron spin both "up" and "down").
   - Measuring changes the system and the uncertainty collapses when the coin lands and it's decided what the "measured" answer is.

     - On the table = classical bit (0 or 1).
     - While spinning in the air = qubit (superposition).

3. Introducing the Qubit (about 10 minutes)

   - Classical bit: 0 or 1 (like a switch) - on or off.
   - Qubit**:** Uses superposition → can be 0, 1 or a blend of both until measured.
   - Just like the spinning coin in midair like in Figure 16.5 (but at the small quantum level, not just "heads or tails").

4. Quantum Advantage Example (about 10 minutes)
   Finding a phone number in the old-style telephone directory or year in an encyclopaedia:

   - Classical Computer: To find one name and number in a paper phone book of 1 million, you need to check 500,000 entries on average.
   - Quantum Computer: By exploiting superposition, a quantum computer can find it in about 1,000 steps.

   This is called "quantum advantage", but it is important to realise that quantum computers aren't just "faster" classical computers - they solve problems totally differently by harnessing quantum rules.
5. Potential Real-World Applications and Quantum Advantage (5 minutes)
   Discuss where quantum computing matters (see Chapter 10 for more example):

   - Medicine: simulating molecules for drug discovery.
   - Cybersecurity: breaking some encryption, but also creating new, stronger ones.
   - Artificial Intelligence: training algorithms faster.
   - Environment: designing better batteries or materials for clean energy.

6. Conclusion (about 5 minutes)

Figure 16.5 Flipping a coin

Ask the learners:

- Which part of quantum theory we have discussed do you think is the most powerful for computing?
- Could there be limits to what quantum computers can do?
- What do you see as a possible negative consequence of the use of quantum computing?

Why have we talked about quantum computing? Although not fully functioning yet, you are the generation that is likely to actually *use* quantum computers!

Pause for thought

Do you think that linking physics, whatever the topic, to everyday applications is a good approach to teaching pre-university-level physics? Of course, there will always be some obvious links in certain topics, but my introduction to a possible lesson highlighting quantum computing pointed out how a very long time ago scientists were "excited" about what is currently highlighted as "quantum theory" for today's learners. One attempt to create a context-relevant course was based in the Education Department at the University of York, England - Salters and Horner's AS and A-level Physics Course. The student and teacher and technician materials are still available.

Do you think the topic of quantum mechanics was worth devoting precious teaching time to in such a crowded curriculum? Did the suggested level cover the topic at an appropriate level and in an engaging way? What would you do differently? There are additional possible teaching resources in the suggestions for further reading at the end of Chapter 10.

Looking at the pedagogies in Panel 16.1, I believe that the approach is multimodal, but in looking ahead is it too much of a stretch to say that we are also looking at a speculative world where practical quantum computing will be ubiquitous?

Teaching resources

Coecke, B. and Gogioso, S. (2022) *Quantum in Pictures*. London: Quantinium. ISBN 978-1-7392147-1-5

UK National Quantum Computing Centre - *School Resources*
https://www.nqcc.ac.uk/tag/schools-resource/ (Accessed 15 September 2025)

Course Guide *Salters and Horner's AS and A level Physics Course Guide*
https://www.pearsonschoolsandfecolleges.co.uk/asset-library/pdf/Secondary/science/B0339-SHAP-Alevel-Science-Resources-Guide-WEB.pdf
(Accessed 17 September 2025)

How might we teach about robotics?

In this section we will be exploring how to begin teaching about robotics by engaging KS3 learners (ages 11–14 years) with the question "What is a robot?". In a small pilot study (Barlex and Steeg 2014), 108 learners aged 12 years were asked to draw a robot. Eighty-three percent drew humanoid figures, almost all male. In exploring what such a robot might be able to do now or in the near future, the majority of tasks were assisting with domestic duties such as cooking, cleaning, washing and ironing, and to a lesser extent helping to look after the elderly or the very young. From this it seems that young people have a very limited view of what a robot might be and do. This is not that surprising as it is reinforced by popular culture in which robots are often portrayed as being friendly, helpful and humanoid. Think C3PO in the "Star Wars" movies being benign and doing his best to help people. There is also a dark side of robots in popular culture. Think of the "Terminator" movie series with the eponymous villain, although later heroic, who is definitely humanoid.

The following lesson suggestion could take place in either design and technology or computer studies. A first step in beginning to teach KS3 learners about learners needs to reveal what they already think a robot is and asking members of a class to each draw a robot and describe what that robot might do is a useful way to do this. Almost certainly this will reveal the limited view described earlier, both in terms of the form and function of a robot. It's important to respect this view whilst at the same time revealing its limitations. One way is to ask members of a class to work in groups and write an agreed general description of a robot which starts with the sentence "A robot is a machine that . . ."

Feedback from the groups is likely to include the following phrases:

do useful things,
on its own,
without human help,
make stuff in factories.

These provide a good start, and the class should be encouraged before moving on to show them what others have written.

It's worth unpacking, with the class, the very basic definition from Hawes (2014):

> *A machine that automates a physical task.*

This is useful in that it does **not** indicate the form of the robot, states that it performs an activity in the real, as opposed to virtual world and that it carries out this activity automatically – it operates on its own without direct human control. All features that the class came up with are wrapped up into a short, single sentence.

It's worth extending this definition by considering the definition written by Illah Nourbakhsh, Kavcic-Moura Professor of Robotics at Carnegie Mellon University (Nourbakhsh 2013). He writes:

> In robots we have invented a new species that operates as a living glue between our physical world and the digital universe we have created.

KS3 learners might think this is a bit weird but worth unpacking by making the following points:

> Robots as such have only been with us as a physical reality for just over 75 years or so. So, the idea of newness make sense.

As for species – we talk about different sorts of animals as species, so the idea of a completely new sort of machine as a species kind of makes sense.

The living glue between the physical world and the digital world we have created is very important. When robots operate in our physical world, they are also part of the Internet of

Things and have access to vast amounts of data, Big Data and artificial intelligence (AI) that they can use in carrying out the tasks they have been assigned.

Now it's time for the class to look at some of the robots that are operating in our world. Ask them to get into their discussion groups and give each group a set of cards. On the white cards are names of industries and activities that use robots. On the blue cards are pictures of robots. In the groups, their task is to match the industry/activity names to the robot pictures. Industry/activity names can include the following: agriculture, caring for people, exploration, goods sorting in warehouses, greeting people, house cleaning, manufacturing, school teaching, search and rescue, surgery, transporting goods, transporting people, warfare. Images of robots in these contexts are readily available online as well as in Part 1 of this book. The aim of this exercise is to indicate a) the wide variety of different robots that are now operating in the world and b) their ubiquity, both of which lead to further thinking from *Illah Nourbakhsh (2013)*, to share with the class. He believes that by 2035 we will be surrounded by robots in our day-to-day lives as we travel to and from work, are at work, and are out and about in leisure and domestic activities.

At this stage in the lesson, it is time to engage the learners in some creative thinking about the possible role of robots in our society, and requiring them to write some speculative fiction is one way to do this. One possible writing task is as follows:

> Write about a day in the life of a robot taxi. Its activities might include any of the following:
>
>> Picking up children from home for a school run, taking a family about to go on holiday to the airport, taking an elderly person shopping, picking up a group of people from a public house after closing time and dropping each of them off at their home address, picking up a young woman from a night club and taking her to her home address

Make the following suggestions:

> You might want to consider how the passengers order the taxi, how the taxi knows where to pick up the passengers and that it's got the right passengers, how it knows where to drop them off and how the passengers pay for the taxi. And you might want to consider what could go wrong.

This is a complex task, and it would probably be worth getting members of the class to work on it in groups. In terms of the actual outcome this might be text, text supported by illustrations or a comic strip. Given the complexity, some groups may want to finish their story as part of their homework.

As the class works on developing their fiction, it will be important for the teacher to visit each group and provide advice and guidance if they are "stuck" by means of asking them to consider possibilities of "what might happen next?" It will be important to keep note of situations in which the robot taxi might exercise its autonomy in, for example, refusing to carry out passenger wishes.

Follow-up lessons will include sharing the speculative fiction, building and programming some simple robots and thinking some more about the way robots are affecting the way people live and work.

Pause for thought

What do you make of this lesson? Would you teach a lesson like that, or would you want to change it significantly?

How does this lesson measure up to the suggestions for pedagogies useful for teaching disruptive technologies shown in Panel 16.1? Speculative worlds have been used to good effect in engaging the learners with a likely future robotics context. Challenge-based learning and entrepreneurial education are not used. There is clearly an opportunity to use an AI tool as a collaboration coach to support the speculative writing, but the difficulty with this is that it might preclude the teacher identifying aspects of the fiction dealing with robot autonomy. The lesson is strong in multimodal working (in using the card collection and different possibilities for the outcome of the speculative fiction) and seeing yourself in the curriculum (encouraging learners to express their views on robots). In terms of what has been learned we think that the lesson has provided a strong foundation with regard to appreciating what robots are, the many contexts in which they are deployed and some of the issues that might arise in the way they behave. We believe that this is important to avoid seeing robots as simply autonomous machines that require adequate programming. Michael Reiss (2021) has written an interesting piece asking whether robots should be considered as persons. With the increasing sophistication of the AI embedded in robots, this is likely to become an important topic.

How might we teach about synthetic biology?

Synthetic biology is an interdisciplinary area that aims to design and construct new biological parts, devices and systems, or to redesign existing biological systems for useful purposes. At its core, synthetic biology aims to apply engineering principles to biology, treating biological components as standardised parts that can be assembled in novel ways to create synthetic organisms or biological systems with specific functions.

Michael Reiss and Michael Ruse (2023) have criticised this approach as being overly mechanistic and failing to take into account the organisms and the environments, both physical and social, in which they exist. They are clear that for many purposes a mechanistic approach can be useful but alone it is insufficient to capture the richness of the milieu in which living creatures exist. In addition, members of the general public have expressed severe reservations about the use of synthetic biology to produce genetically modified organisms (GMOs) in which new genetic material from one organism is introduced into another organism. One way of understanding this is to see the general public's view of deploying synthetic biology as "opening a Pandora's Box", by which initiating something that appears innocent and benign unleashes a wave of severe complications. The phrase derives from a Greek myth which warns against the dangers of tampering with the unknown and the unforeseen consequences that can arise from giving into this temptation. The general public sees the attitude of the scientific community as showing hubris, an extreme, often self-destructive overconfidence that ignores risks and advice, leading to harm.

The approach adopted by Reiss and Ruse goes some way to mitigating this concern and the scientific community itself goes to extreme lengths to minimise unintended consequences through a combination of technical, regulatory and ethical safeguards. This approach may in general terms be seen as applying the Precautionary Principle, which advocates for taking preventative action in the face of scientific uncertainty about potential harm to human health or the environment. Even when there isn't conclusive scientific evidence, action may be taken to avoid or minimise threats of serious or irreversible damage, with the understanding that further scientific information may become available later. It's a proactive measure to address potential future risks.

There is little doubt that synthetic biology has delivered significant benefits with the potential for more: improvements in healthcare and agriculture, the development of new consumer products, contributing to chemical manufacturing, dealing with environmental problems, combating global warming, developing advanced fermentation techniques, creating completely novel organisms. And most recently to pursue research that will enable the synthesis of human genomes which in turn will provide understanding of how the organisation of the human genome controls how our bodies function enabling previously unimaginable advances in health care.

The following lesson is aimed at learners aged 17–18 years old who are studying biology. They will already have learned a lot about the structure and role of DNA in living organisms, so this lesson is an opportunity for them to explore the issues facing society in the exploitation of the latest advances in synthetic biology being developed by the work of the Wellcome Trust.

Introduction

The teacher begins the lesson with a very brief introduction indicating that the learners will be required to work in groups and find out about the Synthetic Human Genome Project and explore the possible impacts on our society. He instructs the class to get into groups of four, and that each group should visit the project's website (https://wellcome.org/news/new-project-pioneer-principles-human-genome-synthesis) and produce an agreed summary of the work of the project. Each group will present their summary for comments from the class, and this will lead to an agreed class summary of the work of the project along with its expected benefits. Also, the class will produce an appendix explaining the scientific terms used in the summary.

This exercise will reveal the extent to which the learners have a grasp on the technical language needed to understand the work of the project, alongside their appreciation of what the project will do and its expected benefits.

Unintended consequences

The teacher then explains that despite attempts by the scientific community to minimise unintended consequences of human genome synthesis there is one area in which there remains significant concern. This is in the fear of a resurgence of eugenics, a now largely discredited idea concerned with controlling the reproductive behaviour of members of a population to increase desirable traits and decrease undesirable traits in newborns. He sets the class the following task:

> Working in your groups, find out about:
>
> - The rise and fall of eugenics in the late 19th and 20th centuries.
> - The possibility of a rise in new, consumer-driven "liberal eugenics" focused on individual parental choice.
> - Be prepared to present your findings to the rest of the class for discussion.

It is likely that this part of the lesson will give rise to strongly held and possibly opposing views which will not be easy to resolve. This provides a sound platform for moving on to the next part of the lesson.

Human Genome Project

The teacher then explains that a key part of the Synthetic Human Genome Project is the work on public engagement to be directed by Professor Joy Zhang. The rationale for this is that such engagement can ensure transparency and build trust between the general public and the scientific community, which will be using the findings of the project in developing new health care applications, amongst other things.

Professor Zhang has recently written a paper about her approach to public engagement, which you can find at https://blogs.kent.ac.uk/global-science-and-epistemic-justice/files/2025/04/An-Odessi-for-Public-Enaggement-in-a-New-Era-of-Science.pdf.

Professor Zhang proposes a new framework grounded in five interlocking principles:

- Open
- Deliberative
- Enabling
- Sensible and Sensitive
- Innovative

Hence the acronym for the approach: O.D.E.SS.I.

The teacher then instructs the class as follows. In your groups, read through the paper and answer the following questions:

- How might the sort of consultation Professor Zhang proposes take place in your locality?
- How would you, your friends and family find out about it?
- Would you, your friends and family be likely to attend?
- What would you want from such a consultation?
- Be prepared to present your findings to the rest of the class for discussion.

This is the most tenuous part of the lesson, with the possibility that many in the class will say that although it seems a great idea it won't happen as friends and family are too busy getting on with the rest of their lives. There is then the opportunity for the teacher to introduce the idea that the school might provide an easily accessible focus for consultation, especially as the issues raised become higher-profile in public consciousness.

> **Pause for thought**
>
> What do you make of this lesson? Would you teach a lesson like that, or would you want to change it significantly?
>
> How does this lesson measure up to the suggestions for pedagogies useful for teaching disruptive technologies shown in Panel 16.1? Some are irrelevant - speculative worlds, challenge-based learning and entrepreneurial education, although one could imagine another lesson in which the rise of consumer-driven "liberal eugenics" formed the starting point for speculative world writing. You may think that there was a lost opportunity in using AI tools, in which case how would you use such tools? The lesson is strong in multimodal working in that it involves group work, extracting information from websites and presentation of ideas to others. And there are opportunities for learners to see themselves in the curriculum as they are asked for their views about the consultation process. In terms of what has been learned, we think that the lesson has provided a powerful introduction to cutting-edge work in synthetic biology, the importance of public engagement with this work through the O.D.E.SS.I approach and the idea of eugenics, both old and new.

Back to Reiss and Ruse

In their book *The New Biology*, the authors argue that a reductionist view of biology, whilst at times necessary, does not do justice to understanding the existential complexity of any organism's life. Nowhere is this truer than in the field of synthetic biology, where although the technical interventions necessarily need to be considered from a reductionist perspective, the consequences for the resultant organisms, and in the case of humans, the nature of the society in which they will live also need to be taken into account as well. We have no doubt that synthetic biology is a disruptive technology, but we make a plea that in deploying this technology any disruption caused is mitigated by this two-handed approach.

We can't leave this chapter without acknowledging the role that reading science fiction can play in understanding disruptive technologies, so we move to a short thought piece from Torben Steeg.

Using science fiction reading to teach about disruptive technologies

> A Thought Piece by Torben Steeg
>
> Hilda and I have been science (and design)[1] fiction readers for a long time. Both genres, which overlap, allow writers to explore consequences of and themes in science and

technology. As an aside, I have often thought that "science fiction" is a poor label for much of the fiction it encapsulates since, very often, while being based on (or stretching) science ideas the actual interest is in the technologies that emerge and how these are used in human societies and relationships.

When written well, theses genres provide tools and perspectives for critique, for thinking about the consequences of implementing instances of technology and design approaches, all while providing good entertainment. I hope the selection suggested here meets both aims of supporting and developing critical thinking while also being entertaining.

Classifying these titles against our Disruptive Technology headings, as shown in Table 16.3, has not been straightforward. For example, as soon as one starts looking at advanced robotics then AI inevitably comes into play; you can have AI without robots, but advanced robots pretty much require AI. Similarly, AI is generally (and famously now) linked to Big Data, as is the internet of Things. Books that deal with advanced robotics often also invoke neurotechnology and synthetic biology. And this is as it should be; our categorisation of Disruptive Technologies is to help teachers and students focus when teaching, but in implementation there will always be boundaries that are fuzzy at best. So, expect following the titles to stretch across Disruptive Technologies.

I have noted under "Age" whether books are more appropriate for teenage readers, young adult, older readers or adult; these suggestions are not related to whether the books have "adult" themes, but more to the complexity/readability of the writing. It's probably obvious, but we'd strongly advise teachers to read titles before suggesting them to students.

One way to make use of a selection of these books with students might be to set up a STEM reading group with realistic timescales and supported by, say, a ½ termly discussion session. Some of these books contain questions for reading groups, though I think teachers would need to vet these carefully and use them as a starting point for creating their own. This may well seem a stretch of an activity for STEM teachers, but after all they do say we are all teachers of literacy. If the idea of fitting a discussion into curriculum time is too much, then this could be implemented as an extra-curricular activity, though inevitably that will reduce the number of engaged students.

Table 16.3 Science fiction reading to teach about disruptive technologies

Disruptive technology	*Author*	*Year*	*Books*	*Age*
Additive Manufacture	Cory Doctorow	2009	Makers	Young Adult
	Emily St John Mandel	2014	Station Eleven	Adult
AI	Kazuo Ishiguro	2021	Klara and the sun	Adult
	Ray Nayler	2022	The Mountain in the Sea	Adult
	Brian Pinkerton	2019	The Gemini Experiment	Young Adult
	Ann Leckie	2013	Ancillary Justice series	Adult
Augmented Reality	Ernest Cline	2011	Ready Player One	Young Adult
	William Gibson	2014	The Peripheral	Adult
	Thomas R. Weaver	2023	Artificial Wisdom	Adult
Big Data	Dave Eggars	2013	The Circle	Young Adult
Internet of Things	Cory Doctorow	2008	Little Brother	Young Adult

Table 16.3 Science fiction reading to teach about disruptive technologies (Continued)

Disruptive technology	*Author*	*Year*	*Books*	*Age*
Neurotechnology	Temi Oh	2023	More Perfect	Adult
	Sarah Pinsker	2021	We Are Satellites	Adult
Programmable Matter	Sam J. Miller	2017	The Future of Hunger in the Age of Programmable Matter	Adult
	Wil McCarthy	2000	Queendom of Sol series	Young Adult
Quantum Computing	David Ignatius	2017	The Quantum Spy	Adult
	Stuart Heinrich	2025	The Quantum Revelations	Adult
Robotics	Martha Wells	2017	Murderbot Diaries	Young Adult
	Becky Chambers	2021	Monk and Robot series	Young Adult
	Sierra Greer	2024	Annie Bot	Adult
Synthetic Biology	Margaret Attwood	2003-2013	Oryx and Crake series	Adult

Note

1 See for example "Speculative Design vs. Design Fiction", https://www.critical.design/post/speculative-design-vs-design-fiction

References

Barlex, D. and Steeg, T. (2014) *Pupils' Understanding of Robotics as a Disruptive Technology*. Proceedings of the 8th Biennial International Conference on Technology Education Research. Griffith University: Griffith Institute for Educational Research.

Davies, P. (2025) 'Most Europeans know about quantum without knowing specifically what it is, new survey finds.' *euronews.com*, Published on 15/04/2025.

Hawes, N. (2014) 'Automatic for the People', in S. Westlake (ed) *Our Work Here Is Done Visions of a Robot Economy*. London: NESTA, pp. 45–52.

https://www.euronews.com/next/2025/04/15/most-europeans-know-about-quantum-without-knowing-specifically-what-it-is-new-survey-finds?utm_source=chatgpt.com (Accessed 16 September 2025).

Nourbakhsh, I. (2013) *Robot Futures*. Cambridge, MA: MIT Press.

Reiss, M.J. (2021) 'Robots as persons? Implications for moral education.' *Journal of Moral Education*, **50**(1), pp. 68–76. https://doi.org/10.1080/03057240.2020.1763933

Reiss, M.J. and Ruse, M. (2023) *The New Biology a Battle Between Mechanism and Organicism*. Harvard: Harvard University Press.

17 Teaching the technical skills of using some of the disruptive technologies

In this chapter, we will focus on just some of the disruptive technologies that we discussed how to teach in Chapter 16 as we move to consider the technical skills needed to *use* the technologies. In 2025, we think that here are 5 potentially disruptive technologies that learners can and do use daily and which most schools will teach learners how to use. Indeed, some disruptive technologies in schools have a long history. We begin with teaching learners how to use additive manufacture (AM), which will be already very familiar to design and technology teachers. We also think that learners should become equally familiar with using artificial intelligence (AI), augmented reality (AR), the Internet of Things (IoT) and robotics.

Teaching the technical skills needed in using additive manufacture

Additive manufacture, often referred to as 3D printing, is already taught in many design and technology departments in schools in both England and elsewhere. While it is important to put this teaching in the context of additive manufacture being a disruptive technology, it is also important that teaching the skills of using this technology are developed in ways that are based on understanding and enable progression. Hence, we are fortunate to have this Thought Piece from Ed Charlwood about how to teach additive manufacture.

The paradox of accessible additive disruption

A Thought Piece by Ed Charlwood

DOI: 10.4324/9781003602002-18

Novice Phase: Begin with pre-designed objects that students can recreate and modify parametrically. This builds confidence with digital tools while demonstrating AM's customisation potential. Students might personalise phone cases or design custom solutions to accessibility challenges for people with disabilities, physical limitations or exceptional needs. This could include, for example, custom grips for utensils, tools or writing implements for people with limited hand mobility, adaptive switches or button extensions for technology access.

Intermediate Phase: Introduce constraint-based design challenges. Task students with creating objects that meet specific criteria – a container that holds exactly 250ml, a structure that supports 5kg using minimal material or a print-in-place mechanism with moving parts printed as a single assembly. These challenges develop both technical skills and creative problem-solving. But you might want to put the task in a context, in which case the following three phase approach could be useful:

- Phase 1: Present the technical challenge – "Design a container that holds exactly 250ml using minimal material"
- Phase 2: After students engage with the technical problem, introduce contexts – "Now consider: what if this were a water container for a refugee camp? A medicine dispenser? A seed storage system?"
- Phase 3: Let students choose whether to redesign with context in mind or stick with further developing the technical solution.

Advanced Phase: Engage students in authentic problems that leverage AM's unique capabilities – geometries impossible through traditional manufacturing, mass customisation or rapid prototyping for social innovation projects. Students might design prosthetics, create assistive devices or develop solutions for local community challenges.

Critics argue that AM diminishes the educational value of traditional making by removing the struggle, the physical effort and the intimate material knowledge that comes from hand-crafting objects. This criticism deserves serious consideration but misunderstands AM's educational potential. The struggle in AM is predominantly cognitive rather than physical – students grapple with complex spatial reasoning, parametric relationships and systems thinking. The iteration cycles, while different from traditional craft revision, are equally rigourous and arguably more aligned with contemporary design practices. Moreover, AM can actually enhance appreciation for traditional crafts by demonstrating their unique qualities. Students who struggle to 3D print organic forms gain new respect for a wood carver's skill. Those frustrated by AM's material limitations develop appreciation for the blacksmith's ability to forge complex curves.

Traditional crafted outcome-focused assessment – focusing on finish quality, joint accuracy and material efficiency – requires rethinking for AM contexts. New assessment criteria might include:

- Design Intent: How effectively does the printed object address the original design brief?
- Digital Craft: Demonstration of sophisticated CAD skills and understanding of AM constraints.
- Iteration Evidence: Documentation of design evolution and learning from failures.
- Material Understanding: Appropriate material selection and design for AM processes.
- Innovation: Creative leveraging of AM's unique capabilities rather than mimicking traditional manufacturing.

As AM technologies continue advancing - with new materials, multi-material printing and embedded electronics - the pedagogical opportunities will expand exponentially. Students might soon print working electronic devices, combine hard and soft materials in single prints or create objects with embedded sensors. The challenge for educators is maintaining a focus on the learning process rather than being seduced by technological novelty. AM's true educational value lies not in the objects it produces, but in the Design Thinking it enables, the problem-solving it demands and the new forms of creativity it unlocks. The most successful AM pedagogy will recognise that we are not simply adding a new tool to the workshop, but fundamentally reconsidering what it means to make, to learn through making and to prepare students for a future where the boundaries between digital and physical creation continue to blur.

Ed Charlwood is an experienced educator with over 20 years of teaching experience in Design and Technology in the UK. He leads D and T for two nationwide Multi-Academy Trusts in England. Ed is a passionate advocate for empowering both teachers and students through technology and design. He has authored a range of books including *Mastering Tinkercad*, *Mastering Autodesk Fusion* and *Mastering Onshape*, creating step-by-step lesson guides for beginners in CAD, 3D printing, prototyping and making. As an instructor and helper of educators, his mission is to empower teachers and learners with powerful tools so they can solve real problems, viewing these skills as essential tools for the next generation. Ed's work focuses on making complex design and engineering software accessible to students and teachers.

What are we to make of Ed's Thought Piece? Not only has he given a clear picture of progression in teaching learners how to use 3D printing; he has also provided an interesting, and to our minds irresistible, justification for such teaching in the context of valuing hand tool-based making and appreciating both the benefits and limitations of 3D printing. In addition, he has considered possible assessment criteria that will need to be developed to support feedback to learners. His rejection of technological novelty as a justification for developing a 3D printing curriculum in favour of rethinking what it means to design and make is very important. We do not want a curriculum that is hostage to "the next big thing". As Ed puts it, we need "to prepare learners for a future where the boundaries between digital and physical creation continue to blur".

> **Pause for thought**
>
> Do you have access to 3D printing in your school? If so, would you consider implementing Ed's suggestions? Are they feasible? If not, what are the problems? Are they concerned with physical resource availability? Or do you have reservations about Ed's justification for a 3D printing curriculum? In which case, what are they?

Teaching the technical skills needed in using artificial intelligence

In the discussion about AI in Chapter 4, we looked at a range of AI models that were on the market in 2025 and the AI agents that were then becoming popular as assistants in the home or at work. As a teacher you probably have used AI to help plan lessons or suggest teaching resources. But what do our learners need to know about using AI at home or at school, and what might they use AI for? In the pedagogies set out in Chapter 16, Panel 16.1, it suggested under "Pedagogy using AI tools":

> The availability of generative AI tools, such as ChatGPT for both teachers and learners, has the potential to considerably influence the way teaching and learning take place. Teachers can use such tools to access content for lessons and develop ways in which this can be presented to and used by learners in tackling learning tasks.

Here is a table of the AI models that were mentioned in Chapter 4, along with some suggestions of what learners could use them for both in school and at home. In 2025, some are free to use, and most are free to use until after a few tasks the free "credit" is used up. These have been designated "partly free".

Table 17.1 Suggested AI technical skills in using AI models for learners age 14 years

AI model	*Cost*	*Suggested subject*	*Suggested uses of AI by someone in Y9 (14 years)*
DeepSeek V3	Free	Computer Science, Maths, Physics	Debug simple programs, generate some practice maths/physics problems.
H2O.ai (incl. h2oGPT)	Free	Maths (Statistics), Business Studies, Computing	Do simple data analysis projects, visualise class datasets, practise interpreting charts.
Yi-Coder (01.AI)	Free	Computer Science	Generate coding examples, get step-by-step help with difficult programming problems.
ChatGPT (OpenAI)	Free/Partly free	English, History, Science, Languages, Computer Science	Learners experiment with digital storytelling, art and music. Create debate suggestions or ideas for role-play scenarios. Compare AI-generated content (Art, Poetry, Music) with that of a human. Draft some notes for essays, summarise set texts covered, make revision flashcards, practise language dialogues, get some support with school coding tasks.

Table 17.1 Suggested AI technical skills in using AI models for learners age 14 years (Continued)

AI model	*Cost*	*Suggested subject*	*Suggested uses of AI by someone in Y9 (14 years)*
Microsoft Copilot	Free/Partly free	ICT, Business Studies, English	Use Copilot Chat to summarise notes, format homework, create revision notes, get formula help when using Excel.
Google AI (Gemini/AI Studio)	Free/Partly free	Science, DT, Computing, Media Studies	Use AI Studio to make short presentations, generate diagrams, coding support, make study summaries for exam revision.
Claude 3.7 Sonnet (Anthropic)	Partly free	English, History, Religious Studies, Computer Science	Deep text analysis (poems, source comparisons), structured essay outlines, coding help.

As a teacher, you know that to get a useful outcome from AI, your request needs to be very precise. This is naturally very important for those AI models with task limits on their free use. For example, "Write a summary of no more than 3 paragraphs of the plot of Shakespeare's Henry V". Or even, "I am 14 years old; write me a short summary of the plot of Shakespeare's Henry V". As a final consideration of the technical skills needed for learners in using AI, I look at the two of the developing "AI agents" that were mentioned in Chapter 4. These agents are tools to be used to do a particular task, and you may wish to collaborate with colleagues, particularly those teaching computer science, on how the agents might best be set up and used. They were launched in 2025 and will improve both in capability and ease of use over the next few years.

Table 17.2 Suggested AI technical skills in using AI agents for learners aged 15 years

AI agent	*School subject*	*Activities suitable for Y9 or Y10 (14- or 15-Year-Old)?*
Autogeny (Multi-Agent Conversation Framework) Free to use	**English Language/ Literature**	Set up a debate between AI-created different characters from a studied novel (e.g., *Romeo and Juliet* or *An Inspector Calls*). The learner moderates and analyses the arguments.
	History	Simulate a historical summit meeting, with different AI agents representing figures like Henry VIII, Cromwell and Catherine of Aragon.
	Geography	Have agents collaborate to create a detailed report and presentation on the effects of a specific natural disaster, like a volcano eruption or tsunami.
Devin (AI Software Engineer) Range of prices depending on use	**Computer Science**	Code a simple video game using Devin to help debug errors and suggest improvements in real time.
	Science (Physics)	Write a simulation for a physics experiment, like projectile motion or pendulum swings, to test how changing variables (e.g., angle, mass) affects the outcome.

Pause for thought

The use of AI as a tool to help support the creative process but not take over the creative process is a distinction that schools will have as part of their procedures. The UK government, and others around the world, see competence in using AI as streamlining community services and reducing costs. Reducing costs usually means losing jobs. In Chapter 4, the point is made that all citizens need to have an informed view of both the benefits and negative impacts of AI. Do you agree that learning to use AI is part of becoming better informed, or do you see it as a threat to fully considered critical thought?

Teaching the technical skills needed in using augmented reality

Some of your learners will have used AR in simple "seek me out" games such as Pokémon Go. In this piece we are concerned with more than the learners just using AR – such as using a Merge Cube, as we saw in Chapter 2 – but also creating an AR for themselves. This will require the teacher to have significant technical expertise, so it is likely that it will be a computer studies teacher who takes on this role. The simplest approach is as follows.

Remind the class of the way they can use the camera on their mobile device to look at a QR code which reveals a website address. Tapping the website address then takes the viewer to the website, where they can see an alternative reality of some sort.

The next step is to then to teach the class how to create a QR code that will link to a particular website. There are several websites you can use to do this, such as:

- qr-code-generator.com
- goqr.me
- qrcode-monkey.com

Instruct the learners to work in pairs and each pair to follow these steps:

1. Go to one of the aforementioned sites.
2. Enter the content – this will be a URL for a site that you have set up especially for this lesson. This site should be simple – a single page with perhaps an image of the school and a catchy slogan of some sort.
3. Customise the design if you want to do so (colours, logo, etc.).
4. Click **Generate QR Code**.
5. Download the image (usually as PNG, SVG or PDF).

When the learners look at the QR code through the cameras on their mobile devices, the URL will appear; when they tap on it, they will be taken to the URL you have set up.

The whole exercise becomes much more interesting if the learners themselves are enabled to set up the URL to which the QR code links. So, most of the time will be spent on this activity and only a small portion on generating the necessary QR code. It is beyond the scope of this piece to deal in detail with the website design aspect of this learning, but it should be possible to give learners free rein to use various software tools to do this and produce a range of web-based ARs they might wish to visit. In discussing this, we thought that a website which allowed the viewer to see a range of different fantastic creatures would be fun and informative to produce. To start off, we provide a QR code to the illustration that is the cover of this book.

https://www.taylorfrancis.com/books/mono/10.4324/9781003602002/teaching-disruptive-technologies-secondary-school-frank-banks-hildaruth-beaumont

Teaching the technical skills needed in using the Internet of Things

In Chapter 15, we considered a series of possible schemes of work, the "enacted curriculum" for lessons in science, computing and design and technology. You will remember that the Internet of Things (IoT) was prominent there and how Kamrul, Jill and Lesley might set about teaching IoT was discussed in Chapter 16. There, the short table of home IoT devices that many learners will already be familiar with included a smart phone (cell phone) and wireless earbuds. No doubt even the younger secondary (high) school learners will be using these IoT devices on the school bus. A modern smart phone is a world-class library in the pocket, connects "pen pals" across countries and shows life on other continents. But due to the negative aspects concerning misuse of social media, advice on the age to start using a smart phone is increasing and, at the time of writing, the government in England has issued guidance that schools should ban smart phones from their premises. More widely, in 2025, Finland joined Italy, France, Brazil and South Korea in banning all phones in schools except for some special needs users. So, despite the advantages of using such powerful tools for classroom learning, we have excluded such devices as part of this consideration of the technical skills needing to be taught when using the Internet of Things.

A school will no doubt develop a general policy about the educational technology that is useful across subjects, and so we suggest the following IoT devices that all learners might use, set out in order of their cost (see Table 17.3). Some IoT devices might be used more frequently in some subjects, such as computing, and there the IoT devises could be more expensive and possibly used by different groups of learners at different times.

Table 17.3 Suggested IoT tools that learners could learn to use set out in order of costs

Reusable Cloud-Scan Notebook (e.g. "Rocketbook")	Learners can write notes by hand (which helps memory), then scan them to cloud storage (e.g. Google Drive, OneDrive) for review later. This should be a school policy as it applies to ALL subjects and reduces carrying stacks of loose paper. It is a planner/notebook with built-in cloud upload and so helps with organisation.	The scanning often means using a smartphone or tablet, so a school's strategy is key: maybe scan at home, or use a shared device or have a 'scanning station' after school. It is a system where you can still access past notes even if erased – 2025 costs about \$34/£25 (or lower for bulk purchase).
Smartwatch with a "School Mode"/ paring down of features	Can help with timekeeping, alarms, reminders for deadlines, help with organisation, maybe fitness tracking.	Low-end bands (just step + heart rate + sleep) are about £25–30/\$34–\$40 (2025 prices). These could be used in PE or as part of biology lessons for activity versus heart rate.
Smart Pens and Note-taking Devices Digital smart pens (e.g., Livescribe, Neo Smartpen)	Capture handwritten notes and sync them to a computer later. Some record audio alongside writing for reviewing lessons. Again, this could be a school policy as it could apply to ALL subjects.	Although more convenient, smart pens are currently (2025) much more expensive than the "Rocket Book", as the cheapest is about \$108/£80.
Graphing/Advanced Scientific Calculator	Helps with higher-level maths, physics etc. Graphs, plots, statistics without needing a full computer.	It is possible (essential?) to choose a model that is allowed in GCSE/A-Level/ other exams as some have an "exam mode" that disables banned features such as communications functions. The cheapest (2025) is about £75–£90/\$100–£121.
School-issued E-Readers and Learning Tablets	Access digital textbooks. These can be used for homework and enable school cloud-based resources. Unlike smartphones, these can be restricted to academic apps only. Of course, many schools will already have a well-established policy of supplying at least some learners with these IoT devices and how they should be used in lessons.	In addition to a computing room to teach some common software packages for writing, presentation and spreadsheet skills, some schools also support a range of subjects by in-class learning tablets. The cost mirrors what is available in high-street shops and are cheaper in bulk. Usual 2025 prices for basic tablets for students (entry level) might be in the \$200–\$335/£150–£250 range; more advanced tablets (with stylus, higher storage, faster processors) £300–£600/\$400–\$800 or more.
Assistive IoT Devices	If relevant to a particular learner – for example speech-to-text devices, reading pens, text scanners or similar devices that help with special education needs.	These are often school-sanctioned. In the UK, for example, there are government programs for such supporting IoT technology in mainstream schools for pupils with Special Educational Needs and Disabilities (SEND).
School Infrastructure IoT learner interaction	Just as there are items at home (doorbell cameras, smart fridge) that are not seen as IoT, similarly there also are at school. These include interactive whiteboards and some IoT lab equipment that learners engage with as part of lessons.	This is very school-specific, but rather than carrying cash many schools now use payment cards for meal payments, and some have Smart ID cards/ badges to track attendance and library checkout and smart lockers that open with the ID cards instead of keys.

Pause for thought

When we considered the Teaching of IoT, the lesson structure was rather a "show, discuss, explain" model. However, when we looked at the tables suggesting what items in IoT a 14-year-old learner might know about, many of the items there require a competence in actually using the devices. How might you easily adapt lessons teaching *about* IoT to also include *using* IoT? Which of the IoT set out in the previous table are teachers at your school already using? What is *not* included in the table that you would recommend to colleagues and make a case to senior management for their place in the curriculum as a tool for all learners? Looking at assistive IoT devices and the pedagogies set out in Panel 16.1, is this a special case for learners to be "seeing yourself in the curriculum"?

Teaching the technical skills needed in robotics

At one time autonomous vehicles (AVs) were the stuff of science fiction: think "Minority Report", "Blade Runner" and "I, Robot". This is no longer the case. A recent report from Mckinsey ("What is a self-driving car?") published in March 2025 paints a completely different picture.

> The software company Waymo (an Alphabet company) currently offers ride-hailing services with its AVs in Los Angeles, Phoenix, Austin, and San Francisco. In China, autonomous taxis and shuttles are even more widespread. Apollo Go, a unit of the Chinese tech company Baidu, has more than 400 robo taxis on the roads in Wuhan. Other companies are launching public trials in various cities across China and the United States, as well as in Oslo, several German cities, the United Arab Emirates, and Singapore.

In the UK the government has indicated that driverless cars will become legal and operational in 2027 (Kleinman 2025).

There is no doubt that self-driving cars are complicated and use a wide range of the latest technologies in combination to operate safely, as shown in Panel 17.1.

Panel 17.1 How a self-driving car works

A self-driving car combines sensors, onboard computers, detailed maps and artificial intelligence to perceive its surroundings and make driving decisions – much like a human, but through software and hardware. It involves six different factors integrated into its operation.

1. Sensing the Environment

Self-driving cars use multiple types of sensors to gather real-time data:

- **Cameras** recognise lane markings, traffic lights, signs and other vehicles.
- **Radar** measures the speed and distance of surrounding objects.
- **Lidar** (laser-based scanning) builds a precise 3D model of nearby obstacles.
- **Ultrasonic sensors** assist with close-range detection, like during parking.
- **GPS and inertial measurement units (IMUs)** determine the car's location and movement.

Panel 17.1 How a self-driving car works (Continued)

2. Localisation and Mapping

The vehicle constantly compares sensor data to high-definition maps that include lane-level details, road geometry and traffic rules. The car can determine its exact position to within a few centimetres.

3. Perception and Prediction

Artificial intelligence processes sensor inputs to identify objects such as pedestrians, bicycles and other vehicles. The system also predicts how these objects will move – for example, whether a pedestrian is likely to cross or a car might merge.

4. Planning and Decision-Making

Based on its goals (e.g., follow the route, maintain safety, obey laws), the vehicle's planning module charts a path. This involves:

- **Behaviour planning** (e.g., deciding to stop, overtake or yield)
- **Trajectory planning** (calculating precise steering, speed and lane position)

Machine learning and rule-based systems work together to evaluate countless scenarios in milliseconds.

5. Control and Execution

Finally, the control system translates the planned trajectory into physical actions. It sends commands to the **steering, throttle and brakes** using feedback loops to ensure smooth and accurate motion.

6. Continuous Monitoring and Fail-Safes

Even when driving autonomously, the system monitors itself. If sensors fail or conditions exceed its capabilities, it may alert a human driver (in semi-autonomous cars) or safely pull over (in fully autonomous ones).

We wonder, given the imminent arrival of AVs in our cities, whether a useful way of introducing learners to the technical skills needed for robotics might be to teach them how to programme a simple self-driving toy car. Clearly this will not be autonomous in the same way as a real AV. However, we think this activity will be intriguing and teach some simple programming useful for robotics. And putting it in the context of AVs soon to be on our streets will indicate just how "clever" the technology behind real AVs must be and perhaps motivate the learners for further study.

A ready-assembled four-wheel programmable buggy with the following features would be suitable:

> Two electric motors, one controlling the front wheel on the left-hand side and one controlling the front wheel on the right-hand side.
>
> A programmable microcontroller that can be used to programme the motors independently, allowing forward and backward motion, turning left and turning right.
>
> Simple proximity sensors on the front and rear of the buggy.
>
> A slot to hold a pen so the buggy can be used to draw, ideally with a small motor to raise and lower the pen.

Most programmable microcontrollers allow for both "block" programming (i.e., using jigsaw-like blocks to assemble programs) as well as text-based programming languages.

A key difference between the programmable buggy and an AV is that the buggy has no idea where it is. Its starting position is determined by where it is placed by the learner, but the programming can provide instructions for the buggy to move in an autonomous way as in the following examples:

- To move on a pre-programmed route such as a square or figure of eight
- To move on a pre-programmed route to produce a drawing
- To move on a pre-programmed route to travel a particular distance as indicated by wheel rotations
- To move on a pre-programmed route and avoid obstacles that are placed in its path.

Pause for thought

Do you think the suggested lesson provides an adequate starting point for developing the technical skills needed to use robotics? If not, what would you change? Do you think the context of AVs is useful, or would you prefer to use a different one, like assembling robots in manufacturing?

References

Kleinman, Z. (2025) *UK Driverless Cars Coming in 2027 – But Uber Says It's Ready Now*. https://www.bbc.com/news/articles/c8jg80j771zo (Accessed 5 November 2025).

McKinsey. (2025) *What Is a Self-Driving Car?* https://www.mckinsey.com/featured-insights/mckinsey-explainers/what-is-a-self-driving-car?stcr=A47B910548AE49419B10F1164EE547BB&cid=mgp_opr-eml-alt-pub-mgp-glb-bundle&hlkid=2fc6b51bf01a4af395e54d4ae85d733d&hctky=15499443&hdpid=e0884256-aa0f-47cf-a174-9966ab33aa26 (Accessed 5 November 2025).

18 Teaching the criteria for disruption

In Part 1 of this book, we described in detail 10 technologies and showed how they were disruptive and the positive and negative impacts of that disruption on society. Now we have to consider how we teach young people about this disruption and how it is likely to affect the society in which they are living and will go on to work in. We will deal with each of our disruptive technologies in turn, but before we do this it is important to teach young people about the criteria that can be used to reveal disruption. In Part 1 of the book, you may remember that we used the McKinsey criteria for disruption; it makes sense to use the same criteria for learners, although we will need to take care to ensure that they are presented in an accessible way.

A useful example of a disruptive technology is Henry Ford's mass manufacturing method for automobiles. The extent and rapidity of the disruption can be revealed by the following New York street scenes (see Figure 18.1).

The contrast is stark. A key question to start the class thinking is, "What has happened to all the horses and horse drawn vehicles?" Then the following series of questions can be used to elicit the McKinsey criteria for disruption:

These four questions lead to the idea of changing the way people work, what they do for a living.

- If you worked on a ranch which raised horses in 1900, what would you be doing in 1913?
- If you made saddles and bridles for horses for a living in 1900, what would you be doing in 1913?
- If you were a blacksmith who looked after horses for a living in 1900, what would you be doing in 1913?
- If you made horse-drawn vehicles for a living in 1900, what would you be doing in 1913?

And these questions lead to the idea of the impact of education and training:

- What would you need to do in order to earn your living in a different way?
- How might this change which people were well-off and which people were poor?

DOI: 10.4324/9781003602002-19

Figure 18.1 New York 1900 (top) New York 1913 (bottom)

And these questions lead to the idea of the development of entirely new products and services:

- What sorts of things are in the 1900s picture that aren't in the 1913 picture?
- What would these things need in order to keep working properly?

And this question leads to the idea of some people becoming richer through investing in the changes caused by disruptive technology: the idea of rearranging value pools.

- If you had invested in companies that made horse-drawn vehicles and raised horses in 1900, where would you invest your money in 1913?

Discussing these and similar questions with a class will build up their understanding of the McKinsey criteria for disruption to the point where the learners will be able to comprehend the formal statement of the criteria we have used throughout this book.

> Pause for thought
>
> What do you make of this lesson? Would you teach a lesson like that, or would you want to change it significantly? It certainly takes longer than a simple presentation of the criteria. Is it worth this extra time?

Teaching the Gartner Hype Cycle

In Chapter 14 we identified the Gartner Hype Cycle as part of the knowledge and understanding to be included in a disruptive technology curriculum. It was described in some detail in Chapter 1. It is a graphic representation of technology's "journey" from inception to becoming successful and part of the way "things are done" in society. It is tempting to present the completed graphic to a class and carefully explain its different features. We wonder if it might be better to build up the graph in front of the class, commenting on each part of the cycle as it appears and ending with the complete cycle.

So, such an approach would go as follows:

> Drawing the axes – visibility and time with an explanation that between these she will draw the "story line" of a technology.

Stage 1

Putting in the starting point for the technology, called the *"Technology Trigger"* and drawing a line going upwards as the technology becomes more visible until it reaches a peak.

Stage 2

She asks a member of the class what they think has been happening while the line is going up. The answer is likely to be incomplete, and the teacher will need to ask other learners to add their thoughts. She can take the answers and build them into a sentence along the following lines: There is increasing interest in the technology, and it becomes better known and does some interesting things. She then asks a member of the class why they think it might

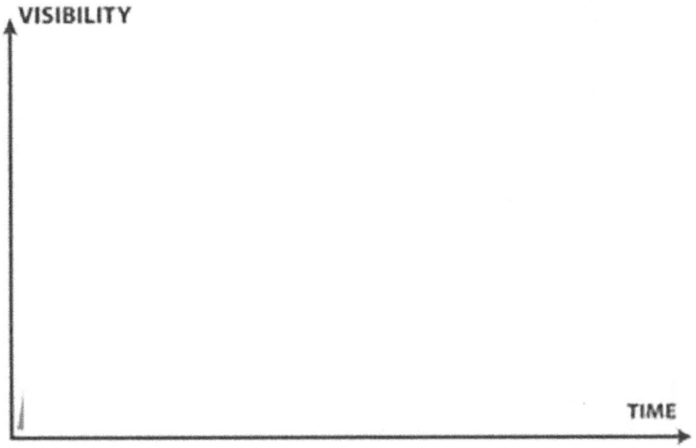

Figure 18.2 Stage 1

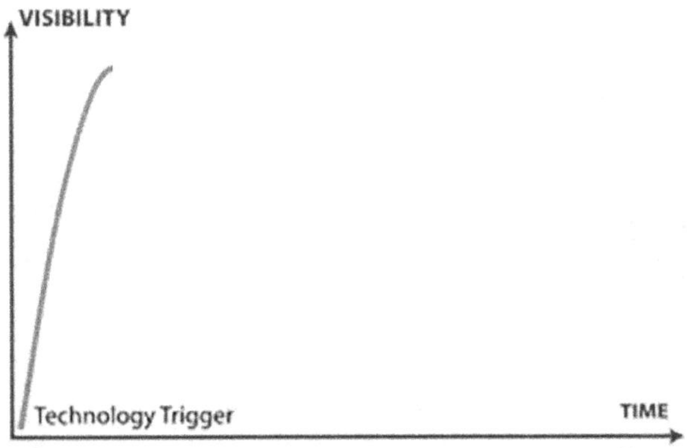

Figure 18.3 Stage 2

stop going up and start to come down. Again, she will need several answers to draw out the following reason: the technology starts to underperform and begins to disappoint those who are using it. She tells the class that the point where the line changes direction is called the "*Peak of Inflated expectations*" and asks the class for suggestions as to why.

From then it's downhill, so the teacher draws a line that slopes downward steeply until it reaches a point where it stops going down and starts to go up.

Stage 3

The teacher asks a member of the class, "What do you think has been happening during this downward slope?" Again, she uses several answers to build an explanation indicating that interest in the technology wanes and only a few companies continue to develop it. She tells the class that the point where the line changes direction and starts to go up is called the "*Trough of Disillusionment*" and asks the class for suggestions as to why.

She then draws a line that slopes upward and starts to level out.

Stage 4

The teacher asks a member of the class, "What do you think has been happening during this upward slope?" Again, she uses several answers to build an explanation indicating that

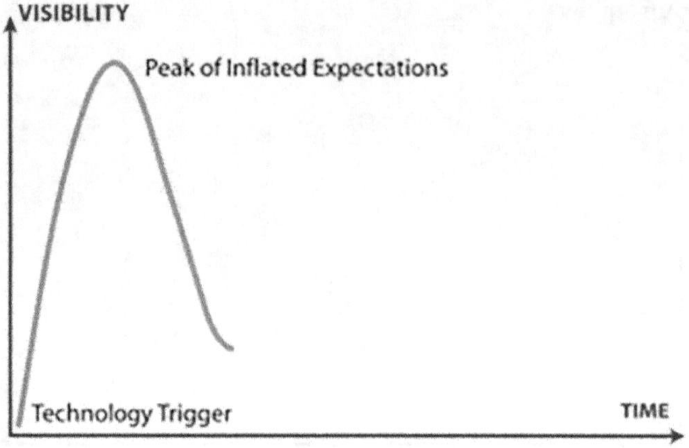

Figure 18.4 Stage 3

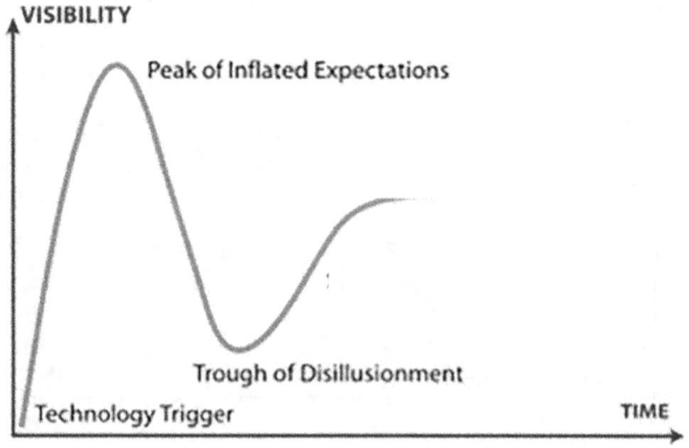

Figure 18.5 Stage 4

the initial difficulties with the technology are overcome and it becomes better understood and new products using the technology appear on the market. She tells the class that the point where the line slopes upward is called the *"Slope of Enlightenment"* and asks the class for suggestions as to why.

Finally, she continues to draw the line sloping very gradually upwards.

Stage 5

As before, she asks a member of the class what they think is happening here. Again, she uses several answers to build an explanation indicating that the technology is now so successful that there is mainstream adoption. She tells the class that this line is called the *"Plateau of Productivity"* and asks the class for suggestions as to why. She then adds this name to give the complete cycle.

Stage 6

Building up the visualisation of the Gartner Hype Cycle step by step in this way and involving members of the class in contributing to an explanation has the advantage of providing

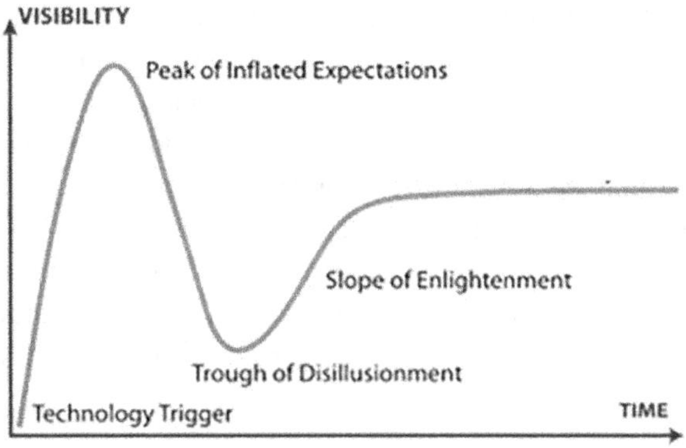

Figure 18.6 Stage 5

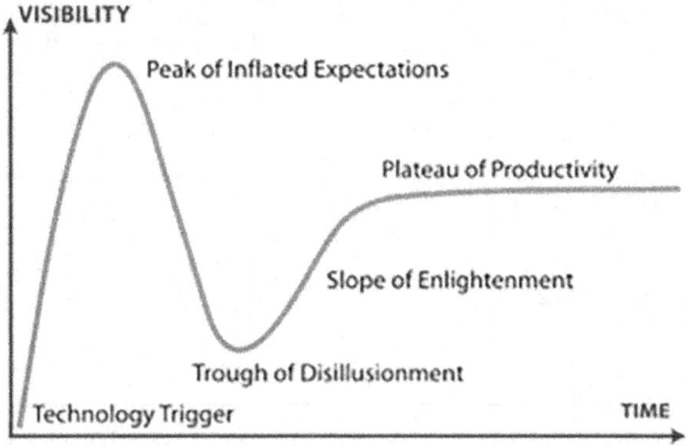

Figure 18.7 Stage 6

the teacher with ongoing feedback as to the class's understanding and being able to spend more or less time on each part of the cycle according to the learners' responses. However, it does take more time than simply presenting the completed cycle and providing explanations of each feature.

> Pause for thought
>
> What do you think of the approach described here? Is it worth the extra time it takes? Would your learners benefit from this approach, or would they find it too long-winded?

Teaching about the disruption being caused by the disruptive technologies

Introduction

As a schoolteacher, Frank has taught in high schools in Hull and in South Wales. The once-large sea-going fleet from Hull has been decimated by the so-called Cod Wars as Iceland extended its territorial waters to restrict foreign (particularly British) fishing, driven by their concerns over overfishing of cod. Learners who once had hoped to follow in the footsteps of earlier generations realised there was no longer work in that sector. Similarly, in South Wales, unemployment was still high in the "valleys" when coal mining was rapidly closed down as different fuels such as gas, and later renewable energy, took over as the means of generating electricity. Disruption therefore can very swiftly affect school leavers' plans with the traditional technologies, and there will be similar changes in employment plans as the different new technologies we have considered become more widespread. Importantly, there will be opportunities to grasp and that will enable a balanced view as we think about teaching about aspects of disruption.

A general approach

In Part 1 of the book, we used the McKinsey criteria for disruption as the means to decide whether the technologies we were considering were disruptive and in what ways. If learners are to decide whether a particular technology is or is not disruptive, understanding and applying the McKinsey criteria is a useful way forward. Hence, a first step is to ensure that learners have a firm grasp; previously in this chapter we discussed how to do this, using as an example the way the mass production of the motor car led to the demise of the horse-drawn vehicle industry.

One general way to use the McKinsey criteria is to present the class with one like that shown in Table 18.1.

Is this technology disruptive?

Table 18.1 A table to help decide whether a technology is disruptive

Does it meet these criteria?	*Did it meet the criteria?*		
	👍	👎	*Examples*
Criterion 1 Does it disrupt the status quo, changing who's in charge?			
Criterion 2 Does it alter the way people live and work? Does it create new sorts of jobs and opportunities?			
Criterion 3 Does it rearrange value pools? Does it cause some people to get richer and others poorer?			
Criterion 4 Does it lead to entirely new products and services?			

For the technology under discussion, the teacher can conduct a class discussion using the questions in the left-hand column to gather examples from members of the class. Aa the table is completed the teacher can ask the class whether they have enough evidence for meeting a particular criterion from the examples to put a tick in the thumbs-up cells. If not, then a tick must be placed in the thumbs-down cell. The class may decide they need to find more examples.

Here are our thoughts on the disruption caused by AI, additive manufacture, augmented reality, the Internet of Things and robotics, which you can use with your classes to consider the extent of the disruption likely to be caused.

Disruption caused by additive manufacture

Additive manufacturing (AM) is distinctive in the disruptive technologies we are considering in that it is a technology that learners will be able to use in their lessons at school and in some cases will have access to this technology at home or in local maker spaces. Some are concerned that the advent of AM in schools will change the nature of designing and making in school, as Ed Charlwood has argued in his Thought Piece (Pages 241 and 242). In the world outside school, AM operates in a wide range of sectors and is meeting some if not all the McKinsey criteria for disruption. Here are some examples to use with your learners.

Disrupt the status quo

In the case of aerospace, AM disrupts the status quo by providing the opportunity for rapid prototyping and eventual manufacture of small complex geometry parts which are difficult to produce by conventional large-scale manufacturing.

In the case of medicine, the use of 3D printing is developing a new high-status arena of medical practice that will disrupt the status quo.

Alter the way people live and work

Construction workers skilled at handling concrete via shuttering and brick laying will need to learn a new, albeit related, set of skills for 3D printing buildings, altering the way they work.

The development of this new specialist field will involve medical experts working closely with AM experts, altering the way they work

Designers of consumer goods will need to learn how to design for AM, and customers for consumer goods will become used to buying products designed to meet their individual requirements, thus changing the way people work and live.

Rearrange value pools

Economic opportunities provided by this new way of producing buildings with AM will rearrange value pools. The funding of new medical procedures involving AM will rearrange value pools, moving finance away from more conventional treatments.

Niche markets for bespoke consumer goods will develop which have the potential to deplete the market share of mass production of consumer goods, thus rearranging value pools.

Lead to entirely new products and services

New products and services will develop as more 3D printed buildings such as houses, flats and disaster shelters become available, and buyers will be able to customise their requirements before building takes place.

It is likely that bespoke items which include intelligent functionality will become available, providing new products and services

Pause for thought

Even if you don't have 3D printing facilities at your school, there are ways in which your learners could use remote 3D printing. For example, the company i.materialise (http://i.materialise.com/) offers the opportunity to upload a 3D design and instantly see the price for its production. No login is necessary, and customers can choose from a large selection of materials and colours and scale their design to the ideal size. You can order as many copies as you want. Of course, the school would have to pay for this service. There is another possibility in that learners' simple digital designs for products can be printed by the organisation and sent by post to others who are prepared to pay for the design - the school and/or learners would make money from this service.

Disruption caused by AI

How can we sensitively tackle teaching about and discussing the implications brought about by AI that the inevitable changes that it is already having on their lives? The piece written by Krys McInnis (Pages 269–273) has indicated that this issue is very much a matter where colleagues need to "look sideways" to coordinate what and where this is being discussed with learners. Let's consider the McKinsey criteria one by one, and as we do so keep in mind in what school subjects or occasions such as a tutor group each criterion might be best considered. An overall aim is citizens who have informed opinions of the implications of the technologies that will disrupt their lives, and those of the generations to come, so that they can enter an informed debate. AI in particular is too important to be left to the AI "experts". We suggest some follow-up points and questions that each McKinsey criterion might suggest for your learners. The depth of consideration will, of course, alter as they move from year to year up the school.

Disrupt the status quo

AI shakes things up and changes "who's in charge". Instead of only radiographers and doctors reading X-rays, AI tools can also spot diseases, and sometimes more accurately. That changes how hospitals work and who has the most influence, and maybe it will speed up hospital procedures so that more sick people can be treated more quickly and will not wait so long for treatment. Is there any downside for doctors feeling they are no longer solely in charge?

Alter the way people live and work

AI changes daily life and jobs. Chatbots and other AI applications help answer questions, so customer service jobs might need fewer people - but at the same time, new jobs are created for people who train and manage AI. The USA and the UK see themselves as developing the Big Data centres so that these countries can be world leaders in creating jobs in the field of AI. In schools, AI can help with homework, language learning or even writing computer code - so the skills we need for the future are shifting. Do you think there is a contradiction here? If AI can write code, will there be a need for as many jobs as software engineers? Or will there be more jobs as AI itself changes different ways people work? Imagine a new way that AI will change your life and where and how you will be working. What effects will it have on the work of a solicitor or an accountant? What about a barber, plumber or carpenter? What about a farmer and mechanisation?

Rearrange value pools

AI moves money and success around. Companies that use AI (like Google, Tesla or OpenAI) can make huge profits, while old businesses that don't adapt may lose money. This means the winners in the economy can change really fast. How do you think a company like Google "makes huge profits"? Google is free, isn't it? So how can it be so rich? When you buy something on Amazon, how does it know what to suggest that you might like? How do you think Big Data might be involved?

Lead to entirely new products and services

AI creates things that never existed before. Think about self-driving cars, AI-generated art, personalised tutors on your phone or apps that write music just for you. These weren't even possible before AI. Can you see how these suggestions affect criteria 1, 2 and 3? Uber drivers disrupted taxis, but self-driving taxis will mean no Uber drivers. What is the future for an artist or musician if AI makes art and music? What about a film or TV actor? Will AI ever affect the life of a stage actor or a dancer?

Pause for thought

Do you agree that using the McKinsey Global Institute criteria is a suitable hook for exploring the impacts of AI with your learners? Do you agree with our point that all citizens should be able to engage in the debate about AI? What democratic processes should take the discussion further? Is this topic just too political for schools? Would there be parental issues to consider, and if so, how should that best be handled? Do you agree with politicians through the years who have said about schooling (in different ways), "The goal should be to equip children to the best of their ability for a lively, constructive place in society, and at the same time to fit them to do a job of work. Not one or the other but both"?

Disruption caused by augmented reality (AR)

Many of your learners will know about and may have experienced AR games such as Pokémon Go, and your school may use such devices as the Merge Cube described in Chapter 2. The surface of the cube has coding that takes the viewer to a set of visual digital information concerning, for example, the human body or the solar system. As they hold and manipulate the cube in the palm of their hand, they can look at different body parts or different planets. So, you might find that your learners already have some familiarity with AR.

Disrupt the status quo

The emergence of new products and services as described here will inevitably disrupt the status quo as new ways of doing things involving AR displace the conventional approaches that do not use AR. Navigating airports and retail experiences in being able to try on clothing before buying are two good examples.

Alter the way people live and work

As AR products and services become reliable and readily available, reaching the *Plateau of Productivity* in the Gartner Hype Cycle, working practices will change as companies utilise AR-based activities and people use AR products and services as part of their everyday lives.

Rearrange value pools

The emergence of new products and services, as described in the following, will lead to those companies who utilise these being able to provide improved offerings compared to their competitors and increasing profits at the competitors' expense, hence rearranging value pools. Workers who become skilled in using AR will be in demand and able to command higher salaries, rearranging value pools at the employee level.

Lead to entirely new products and services

There are examples across many sectors in which AR has led to new products and services: gaming and entertainment, retail, medicine, manufacturing and maintenance. These are described in some detail in Chapter 5.

> **Pause for thought**
>
> Is it worth considering possible downsides of AR with your learners? In Chapter 5, we noted that AR in an art gallery might distract from the art, and AR might be used as a substitute for experimental work in chemistry lessons. What might be the downsides for your learners?

Disruption caused by the Internet of Things

Disrupt the status quo

Think about how things work today: most machines and objects (like fridges, cars or watches) don't "talk" to each other. With the Internet of Things, they can connect, share information and even make decisions without people always being in charge. For example, in "Smart Homes" lights, locks and heating systems can adjust automatically and remotely. So this shakes up who's in control, as the big electricity and gas companies might lose money if people can better manage energy more smartly at home.

IoT flips the old rules, letting everyday people (and their gadgets) take more control.

Alter the way people live and work

IoT will change jobs and daily life. Some jobs may disappear (like simple factory tasks) because machines with sensors can do them faster and more accurately. But new jobs will be created, like designing apps that connect your fridge to your phone, for example. Skills in coding, data handling and problem-solving will become important. If you are interested in working in this area, then computing/computer science in school, and what you might need to study when you leave school, could focus on digital skills. It's not just about jobs and the sort of employment needed for IoT; our relationships might also change. In the UK, as the Health Service embraces new technology "moving from analogue to digital", your doctor might track your health through a smart watch instead of you visiting the clinic as often.

IoT can make life easier and smarter but can also mean people must learn new skills to keep up.

Rearrange value pools

When IoT spreads, money flows differently. As you might know, in cities the "old businesses" like traditional taxi companies who would know street by street the geography of their area now lose out to IoT-based services like Uber drivers using GPS and connected phones. IoT can also make many industries more efficient. For example, arable farming can become more productive by "smart farming" using temperature and moisture sensors in soil. As is a common feature of many disruptive technologies, people who own or use the technology gain more power than those who don't.

The money and opportunities shift towards those who use IoT well.

Lead to entirely new products and services

IoT doesn't just improve old things - it creates totally new ones. Can you think of some new gadgets in your home? Smart speakers (like Alexa) didn't exist before 2014, and as they improve they can control more and more things. Uber, for example, has permission in a number of countries to introduce cars that can drive themselves using IoT sensors. And the cars will be travelling though cities that become "smart", with interconnected traffic lights reducing jams.

IoT makes possible brand-new inventions that we never had before.

Pause for thought

Do you think that the aforementioned consideration of teaching about the disruption in relation to the Internet of Things was too positive? As many people do not change the access codes set at the factory, IoT gadgets can be subject to hacking. In 2025 in the UK, companies as diverse as Jaguar Cars, clothing company Marks and Spencer, the Coop supermarket and the ticket and baggage systems at airports have been "ransom" hacked, and even if they do not pay the criminals, the companies face millions in lost production. Is this problem exacerbated by different things being interconnected? How might you tackle this issue with Year 9 (14-year-olds)? Would you have a different approach to the issue with older learners?

Disruption caused by robotics

Hilda has fond memories of her Aunty Rene, a dark-haired East End woman with a ready wit. In the 1950s she worked as the charge hand on an electronics assembly line at Plessey. Hilda remembers her talking about the visit of a time and motion expert who gave advice on the way the women on the line organised their tools so each came to hand more quickly. The result was a definite improvement in the output of completed circuits. At that time the local union had negotiated an arrangement that allowed any worker to leave the line to visit the toilet whenever they needed to. Such absences led to the line having to stop work and any bonuses paid for extra efficiency likely to be lost. Hilda's Aunty Rene saw a way to solve this problem. She instituted a line stoppage of 10 minutes every 90 minutes, which she called "Wee wee time". It was a great success and all the ladies on the line got their bonus, although it was against the negotiated arrangements. Rene's charisma and sense of humour doubtless contributed to the success. The assembly lines used for electronic assembly now, some 70 years later, are completely different, with robots assembling and soldering highly complex circuits at dizzying speeds with very little human involvement. As the way robots operate is managed by increasingly sophisticated AI, there is little doubt that their use in a wide range of industries and services will be disruptive, especially as this implementation leads to significant human redeployment or unemployment. Here are some examples

Disrupt the status quo

The rate at which autonomous vehicles are being adopted for both goods and people transport will certainly upset the status quo in that many of those who made their living driving will find that they are unable to do so. The combination of an autonomous vehicle with a human who stores and removes luggage at the beginning and end of taxi journeys is an example of how drivers may adapt to this change in the status quo.

Alter the way people live and work

Increased sophistication of domestic duty robots, used in hotels, office blocks and homes, is likely to affect human cleaner employment. Will being a cleaner involve overseeing robot workers and being able to maintain, repair and reprogramme them? Where will this leave those who are cleaners today?

Rearrange value pools

Companies that can afford to invest in replacing human workers with robots will find that in the medium-term the savings in wages and needing human resources departments will outweigh their initial investment, thus increasing their profits. Companies which cannot or do not make such investments will find their profits decreasing. Clearly, value pools are being rearranged.

Lead to entirely new products and services

As robots become more sophisticated in both how they operate physically and the tasks they can perform, it is almost inevitable that they will move out of the industrial areas where they are mainly operating now and into the transport, retail, hospitality and care sectors, complementing and in some cases replacing humans working in those sectors.

> Pause for thought
>
> Illah Nourbakhsh (2013) believes that by 2035 we will be surrounded by robots in our day-to-day lives as we travel to and from work, are at work and are out and about in leisure and domestic activities. That's only 10 years away. How should schools, in general, prepare learners for this eventuality?

Teaching critique

This section will describe four activities that are useful in helping learners critique the way disruptive technologies play out in society. They are: identifying winners and losers, design fiction, four feature enquiry and scenario building and investigation.

Identifying winners and losers

This activity involves using the target chart shown in Figure 18.8. The item being considered (this might be a product, a range of products or a technology) is placed in the centre of the chart. Consideration of the immediate impacts of the item gives rise to a list of groups and individuals who will be affected by these impacts. Those who are directly affected are written in the inner circle; those indirectly affected are written in the outer circle. Then these entries are classified as either winners (those who benefit from the item) or losers (those for whom the item causes some form of detriment). Giving one colour to the winner segments and a different colour to the loser segments gives an immediate visual picture of the winner/loser balance, although care must be taken in the interpretation of this as it does not, of itself, give any indication of the size of the groups involved or the severity or otherwise of any impact. If time is short, the teacher may decide to "cut to the chase" and produce a filled-in version of the chart and use that to stimulate discussion about the impacts that might be caused by the item under consideration. An effective way to stimulate discussion around a completed chart is to assign some learners the role of "winners" and other learners the role of "losers". The task then facing the learners is for the winners to justify why it is permissible for them to win at the losers' expense, and the losers to argue for some form of recompense from the winners. It is worth noting here that learners will need to understand something about social justice in deciding who wins and who loses, so it is worth prefacing the activity with some explicit teaching about this to ensure that learners are introduced to the idea that in a just world, all people should be able to live in freedom from hunger and fear and have shelter from harm. They should have opportunities to pursue happiness and make the best of their lives (see the section in this chapter on Teaching Values).

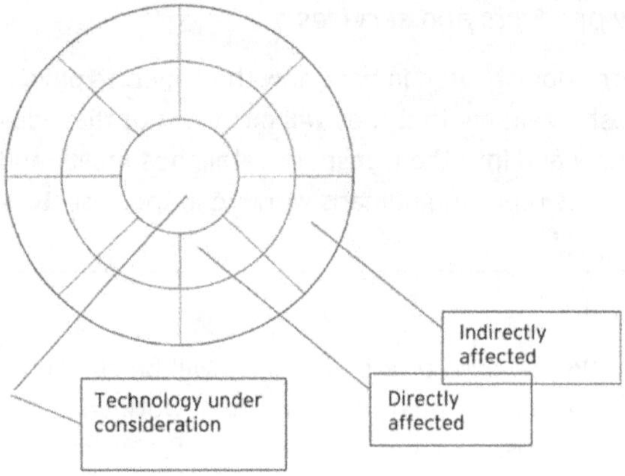

Figure 18.8 A "target chart".

Design fiction

Design fictions are devices to critique future possibilities by creating a "story world" in which the learner creates an object that represents a particular technology that will act out in the story world. This is literally a prop that enables a story to unfold through the imagined interaction of the prop and the story world. The teacher might create a story world and present it to the class or work with the class in creating one. The teacher will need to ensure that the learners are sufficiently *au fait* with the reality the prop represents for imagined interactions between the technology and the story world to be feasible. For example, the story world might involve driving for a living and the technology being considered autonomous vehicles. Learners will need to know something about autonomous vehicles before they begin to write their story. The teacher may decide that they should find this out through independent group research, or that it would be fairer to give a short presentation to the class so that there is a level playing field. What will happen in the story world once there are autonomous vehicles? The story the learners write may take many forms: a written story, a comic book, a story board, a script for a play, an animation or a short video clip in which learners describe what is happening in the story. Whatever the form, the teacher has a key role in asking the learners about the implications of what is happening in the story, which will engage learners in discussion and debate about the rights and wrongs of the situation in their story world.

Four feature enquiry

This is related to designing without making, as it uses the same conceptual framework presented as a tetrahedron with key features at each vertex. The product under consideration is placed at the centre of a tetrahedron, as shown in Figure 18.9. The vertices of the tetrahedron are labelled: DT (disruptive technology), People, Market and Society. Each of these features will need to be unpacked to some extent, and there will need to be a particular product/service at the centre.

- For the disruptive technology learners will need some knowledge of what it does and typical applications.
- For "People" they will need to consider the following: who will use the product/service, why would they need or want this product/service, how many people are likely to want it and what sorts of people are likely to want it?
- For "Market" they will need to consider the following: is there already a market for the product/service - in which case, where will your product/service fit in and what will distinguish it from other items in that market, how has this market grown recently, how will potential customers learn about your product/service and who do you see as your customers?
- For "Society" they will need to consider the following: what are the prevailing values, hopes and fears currently and in the near future, what are the trends here, are the values moving in a particular direction and are hopes more significant than fears or vice versa?

These considerations will build into a critique of the product/service and the disruptive technology. This is important, as the manifestations of a disruptive technology through different products/services operating perhaps in different contexts may well lead to different critiques. An interesting adaptation of this approach might be to use the tetrahedron as the basis for asking young people the question, "What do you think needs disrupting?" They could be asked to justify their choices in terms of helping people in difficulties, making society more equitable or improving the quality of life. Or if this proved too open, asking, "What if you wanted to . . .?" They could consider how the applications of particular technologies might give rise to the disruptions they think should take place. Note that this approach also considers the near as opposed to more distant future and to this extent may make their speculations more realistic.

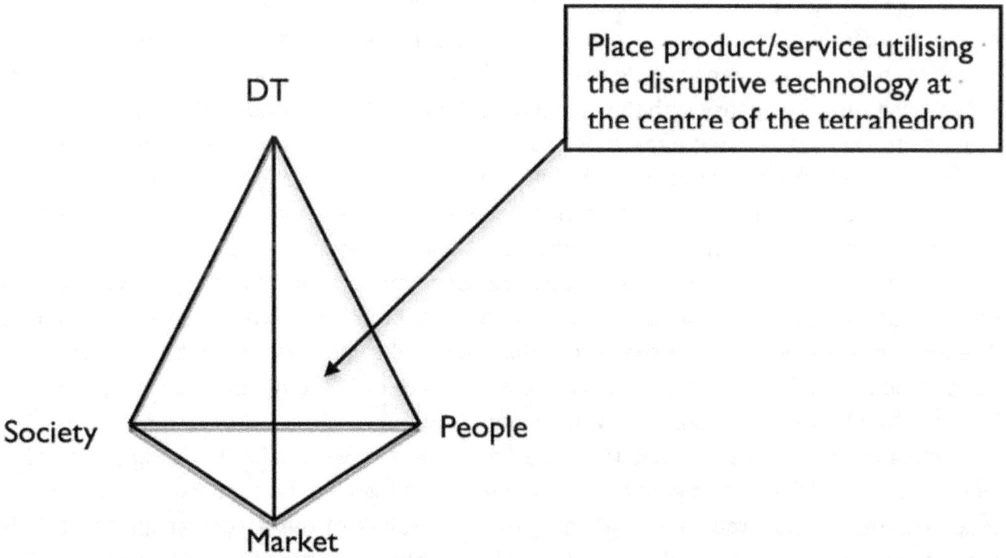

Figure 18.9 Using four features for critique

Scenario building and investigation

A general approach often used to build scenarios is to identify two sets of so called "critical or significant uncertainties" and to use these as axes to create four quadrants such that there is a particular scenario located in each quadrant (Figure 18.10).

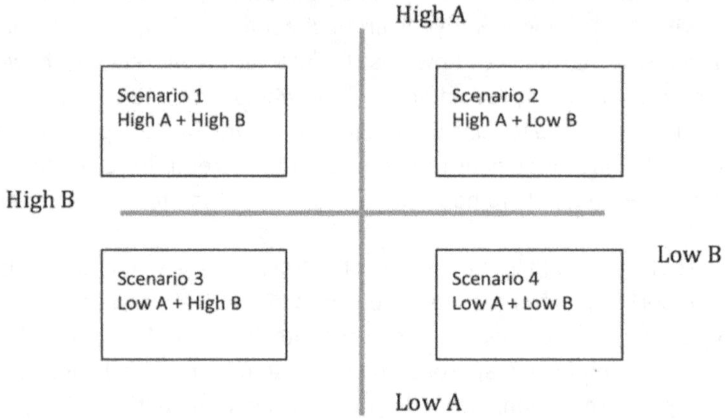

Figure 18.10 A general representation of the critical uncertainties A and B to create four scenarios

Each of these can be fleshed out into a human story, which can be explored from various critique perspectives. Learners might use scenario building to explore, for example, the way relationships between humans and AI personal assistants or co-workers might play out by means of some scenario developments. The initial task is to identify the critical uncertainties for the axes needed to create the four scenarios. Whether humans are prepared to accept AI agents in their lives and work (as co-workers, substitute workers or helpers) seems a crucial factor. In this example, some people may feel uneasy about an AI presence at work or home, especially if they are uneasy with the idea that technology has created a thinking "being" that is not a human colleague but a machine. Others will welcome the AI presence on the grounds that the AI can tackle tasks they do not wish to do or find difficult and that they can even provide companionship. Hence the Y-axis in the scenario development concerns "acceptance". Related to acceptance is the possibility that as AI agents become more sophisticated, to the point where they become first-person conscious and "moral agents" in their own right, they might be granted rights or not. Such rights would curtail the way in which humans could treat AI agents, preventing them, for example, being seen and treated as disposable once they are deemed no longer fit for purpose. Hence the granting of rights to AI agents forms the X-axis. The resulting four quadrants are shown in Figure 18.11.

Each of the quadrants provides the basis for learners to write a brief descriptive piece in which they, their friends or members of their family are the main protagonists in working out their relationship with robots according to the constraints of the particular quadrant. This requires imagination and empathy, and it would probably be worth talking with teachers in the English department about how best to support such writing and also to ensure that you have

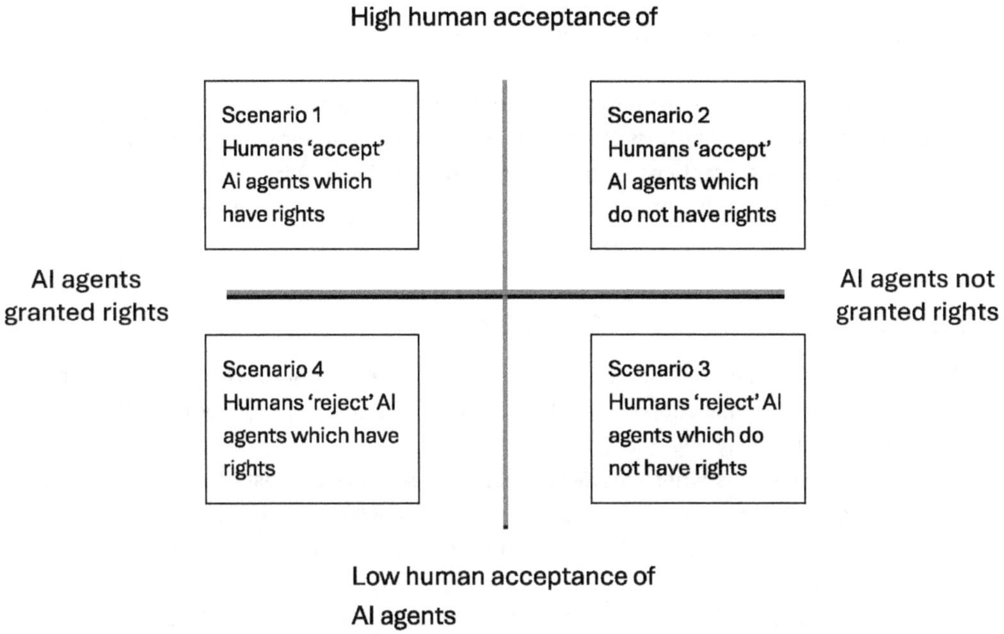

Figure 18.11 Four scenarios from axes of uncertainty concerning human acceptance of AI agents and the granting of rights to AI agents

appropriate expectations and are not fobbed off with writing that is well beneath the standard that your learners are able to achieve. It might also pay to let the learners move away from the standard essay format and add illustrations or even move into a "graphic novel" format. Considering each scenario from a "winners and losers" perspective might be worthwhile. However, the more complex the demands of the writing the longer it will take to achieve, so it will be important to match expectations to both time available and curriculum significance. In the end, it is important that learners ask of each scenario whether it represents what Shannon Vallor so aptly refers to as a future worth wanting.

Now is an appropriate point to consider this Thought Piece by Krys McInnis about the role of Religious Education in enabling learners to engage in critique.

Cultivating moral imagination: what religious education offers to the ethics of disruptive technologies

By Krys McInnis

> We are teaching in a time of profound disruption. Artificial intelligence makes decisions faster than moral codes can catch up. Biotechnologies edit genes before society has agreed on what makes a life worth living. Surveillance systems know more about our students than their own families might. In such a world, the most urgent educational

question is not simply what young people know about technology, but who they are becoming in relation to it.

This is a call not for more information but for moral formation, and it is here that Religious Education (RE) offers the wider curriculum a pedagogical model with deep, untapped power. The practices long cultivated in RE, ethical reasoning, dialogic inquiry, critical engagement with worldviews, are not just relevant to the challenges of disruptive technologies; they are necessary.

RE as a Pedagogy of Ethical Formation

RE is often underestimated, seen as confessional or peripheral to STEM. In truth, however, it is one of the few subjects whose central aim is the development of ethical, reflective and relationally aware citizens.

The RE classroom is where students routinely examine contested questions: When does life begin? Is war ever just? What obligations do we owe to future generations? It is a space for cognitive complexity and emotional nuance. It teaches students to hold tension, to think across difference and to see the world through another's moral lens.

This pedagogical orientation finds deep resonance in the work of Black and Global Majority Heritage scholars. Educational theorist bell hooks argues that education must be a practice of freedom, one that cultivates critical consciousness and nurtures the whole self, not merely the intellect. In *Teaching to Transgress* (1994), she frames classrooms as spaces of dialogue, care and liberation, principles that mirror the best of RE pedagogy. Similarly, Ghanaian philosopher Kwame Gyekye (1998) emphasises the communal dimensions of moral development, rooted in the African concept of *ubuntu*: "I am because we are". This ethic of relationality and interdependence reinforces what RE has long practised: education as the shaping of ethical agents, not just skilled individuals.

These pedagogical practices are not luxuries in the digital age; they are critical tools for navigating it.

Disruptive Technologies and Disrupted Ethics

Disruptive technologies, those which significantly alter how individuals live, work and relate, present ethical dilemmas that are both urgent and unprecedented. Many educational responses remain procedural, focusing on e-safety or digital citizenship. What is missing is the cultivation of ethical sensibility and critical moral imagination.

RE encourages students to explore enduring questions of meaning, power and responsibility, questions that new technologies continually reframe. Importantly, it does so through a plurality of voices: engaging religious, secular and philosophical traditions in dialogue.

In an age of acceleration, students need space to slow down, interrogate assumptions and listen deeply to difference. RE offers a model for how to do this well.

Classroom Applications: RE Pedagogy in Action

To illustrate, consider how RE-style pedagogies might frame four pressing dilemmas:

1. Artificial Intelligence and Algorithmic Bias

A Year 10 class examines real-world cases where AI facial recognition technologies misidentify people of colour. Students explore: is this simply bad data, or a reflection of structural inequality? Using the SEE model (State, Explain, Evaluate), they analyse justice through Jewish ethics, Islamic teachings on fairness and Rawlsian theory.[1] A structured debate asks: *Should governments ban facial recognition until bias is addressed?*

"It's not just about the tech being wrong, it's about whose faces society decides matter", one student notes, in a discussion typical of RE classrooms engaging with social justice.

2. Gene Editing and Human Enhancement

In a unit on medical ethics, students encounter CRISPR and the idea of editing embryos to eliminate disease or enhance traits. They compare the Buddhist principle of *karuṇa* (compassion) with Christian concerns about 'playing God' and Islamic ideas of balancing harm and benefit (*maslahah*). In small groups, they write worldview-based responses to the question: *Should we edit embryos to prevent deafness?*

"Is it compassionate to prevent suffering, or is it saying that certain lives aren't good enough?" one student asks, a line of inquiry that surfaces often in such lessons.

3. Surveillance and the Common Good

A Key Stage 4 project asks: *Does surveillance protect or control us?* Students study Bentham's Panopticon[2] alongside Sikh and Qur'anic teachings on accountability and dignity. They review their school's data practices and draft ethical policies balancing safety with privacy.

"If we're always being watched, how do we know who we really are?" a student reflects, capturing the philosophical depth that emerges when ethical inquiry is prioritised.

4. Robotics, Automation and Unemployment

In Design and Technology, students explore workplace automation. A case study presents a factory introducing robotic arms, resulting in 300 redundancies. Using ethical reasoning tools from RE, such as stakeholder mapping[3] and the Four Quadrants model (facts, stakeholders, values, options), students weigh economic efficiency against human dignity.

They compare secular arguments for innovation with Christian teachings on the value of work, and Hindu perspectives on *dharma* (duty and social order).

"Robots don't need jobs, but people need purpose", one student argues.

"What if we used tech to free people up for more meaningful work, not just profit?" another suggests.

This kind of ethical depth often emerges when students are given structured space to explore multiple values and competing priorities.

Toward a Cross-Curricular Ethics of Disruption

RE's insights should not remain siloed. In the face of rapid change, all subjects must become sites of ethical formation.

- **In science**, the ethical implications of innovation must be explored alongside the mechanisms. For instance, gene editing lessons could use ethical frameworks like the Four Quadrants inspired by RE's case-based reasoning.
- **In English**, speculative fiction from diverse voices can open rich ethical questions. Texts like *Parable of the Sower* by Octavia Butler or *The Marrow Thieves* by Cherie Dimaline challenge students to consider how race, colonisation and spiritual belief shape responses to technological disruption. These works invite exploration of what it means to remain human - and ethical - when systems devalue life.
- **In citizenship or social studies**, discussions about digital rights, AI governance or data ethics can be deepened through RE-informed structures for moral debate and respectful dialogue.

This is not about importing religious doctrine, but about sharing the pedagogical DNA of RE: dialogic inquiry, ethical literacy and pluralistic reasoning.

Conclusion: Ethical Literacy as Core Competency

The challenges presented by disruptive technologies are not merely technical, they are deeply moral. As such, the education system must equip learners with the tools to question, evaluate and shape these technologies, not just use them.

Religious education, long concerned with the moral formation of individuals in relation to communities, beliefs and the ultimate questions of life, offers a model pedagogy for this task. It cultivates the very dispositions; empathy, critical thinking, ethical reasoning, respect for difference, that are essential in an age of disruption.

As educators, we must now ask: how do we ensure that every young person, regardless of subject pathway, is equipped with the moral imagination to navigate and shape a world transformed by technology?

The answer begins with pedagogies that take ethics seriously and ultimately, RE shows us how.

References

hooks, b. (1994) *Teaching to Transgress: Education as the Practice of Freedom*. Oxon: Routledge.

Butler, O. (2019) *Parable of the Sower*. London: Headline Publishing Group.

Dimaline, C. (2019) *The Marrow Thieves*. London: Jacaranda Books.

Gyekye, K. (1988) *Unexamined Life: Philosophy and the African Experience*. Accra: Ghana Universities Press.

About the author

Figure 18.12 Krystian McInnis

Krystian McInnis is an international education consultant and specialist in Religious Education (RE) with a strong focus on diversity, equity and inclusion in schools. With experience across the UK, Denmark and New Zealand, he works with teachers, leaders and organisations to strengthen RE as a subject where students can critically explore worldviews, ethics and lived faith experiences in ways that foster respect and understanding across diverse communities. Alongside this, Krystian is at the forefront of exploring how artificial intelligence can be applied within RE, helping educators and students alike to navigate questions of belief, identity and belonging in a rapidly changing world. Passionate about making RE both relevant and transformative, he champions approaches that honour every learner's background and create classrooms where all voices are valued. You can find more of his writing at https://reimaginingeducation.uk

Pause for thought

What are we to make of Krys's Thought Piece? Readers who are familiar with the authors' previous writings will know that they are strong advocates for teachers "looking sideways" in the curriculum to see the learning taking place in subjects other than their own with a view to building synergy in the learning between different subjects. The impact of "looking sideways" is enhanced by conversations between teachers from different subjects. It seems to us that Krys's Thought Piece makes very clear the huge impact that RE teaching can have on developing young peoples' ability to critique and illustrates unambiguously the power of "looking sideways" supported by conversations between teachers.

Considering values when teaching about disruptive technologies

In Chapter 15 we suggested that one of the aims of a disruptive technology curriculum is to enable learners to develop **values** to help them in considering the nature of the impacts of disruptive technologies on society, and that this is inevitably linked to being able to 'critique' the technologies as well. We have taken the position that the leading and over-arching values to consider when addressing values with learners relate, equally, to achieving social justice and maintaining stewardship of Planet Earth.

In a nutshell, social justice concerns the relationship between the individual and society as measured by the distribution of wealth, opportunities for personal development and social privileges. Everyone should live free from hunger and fear and have shelter from harm. Our stewardship of our planet relates to ensuring the wellbeing of all creatures that live here now and in the future. The way we use technologies is key to promoting that aim and preventing harm to our environment.

At first sight this all seems very grand and wide-ranging, but inevitably it also starts with our own personal values when teaching aspects of technology. Some years ago, Frank visited a school in the north of England in relation to a possible case study for an Open University course. The design and technology teacher proudly showed Frank an artefact made by a Year 11 (16-year-old) learner as the practical part for GCSE. In the English school system, a GCSE (General Certificate of Secondary Education) is a qualification taken by students aged 15–16, typically at the end of Year 11 after two years of study and so is therefore a high-stakes endeavour. The boy had built a panic alarm. Technically it was excellent – lightweight, easy to operate and incredibly loud! It got good marks using the given examination criteria. Frank asked, why did he need a panic alarm? The teacher looked very puzzled. There were no marks for asking why – what mattered was "did it work?" Better street lighting or free night buses, for example, were not needed to be considered – they did not earn marks. Without putting too much weight on this simple anecdote, it may give us pause to think about our own values. As Conway and Riggs (1994, p. 227) pointed out so long ago, when faced with the same problem a person with a "technocentric perspective" may see a technological outcome that is different from that of a person with a "humanistic perspective".

Look back at the Thought Piece by Krys McInnis at the end of the section on Critique. As an RE teacher, Kris sets out a range of strategies that can address how to explore values when we look at disruptive technologies and, as we have stressed frequently, 'Looking Sideways' at what colleagues are doing in other subjects cuts teaching time overall and more significantly helps the learners make links to help their understanding. See especially what Kris has to say about possible ways to consider the values in the implementation of Artificial Intelligence and Robotics. How might you capitalise on such coordination in your school?

In Chapters 13 and 15 we also looked at the list of "technomoral" virtues developed by Shanon Vallor (2016): Honesty, Self-control, Humility, Justice, Courage, Empathy, Care, Civility, Flexibility, Perspective and Magnanimity. Let's put some of Vallor's 'virtues' alongside our emphasis on the 'values' of Social Justice and Stewardship for the five disruptive technologies that we have emphasised in this chapter: Additive Manufacture, Artificial Intelligence, Augmented Reality, The Internet of Things and Robotics, but with an additional consideration of Big Data as it is so intimately connected to AI. In all the chapters where we looked at a disruptive technology in depth, the positive aspects were emphasised, but possible negative consequences resulting from the 'disruption' were looked at too. This approach is how we now consider both the values and the virtues.

Additive manufacture

Social justice: Local low-cost production of tools, medical devices and components of houses reduces the dependency on large manufacturers and is of benefit to low-income countries and to makers everywhere.

Stewardship: Precise use of materials reduces waste and on-demand production can happen locally, lowering transport emissions. However, this may be energy-intensive if not powered sustainably.

"Technomoral": Dishonest fast and easy manufacture of counterfeit goods undermines trust; unjust and unequal access to printers deepens divides, and without self-control over-production of cheap items is counter to stewardship values.

Artificial Intelligence

Social justice: AI can expand opportunities by offering personalised education; it can improve access to healthcare by speeding up administration and some medical procedures and can allow fair decision-making. But some algorithmic bias, such as current difficulty in distinguishing between black female faces, may deepen inequalities.

Stewardship: AI can be used to optimise energy grids, make agriculture more efficient and reduce use of scarce resources, but large AI models have high energy use.

"Technomoral": Dishonest deepfakes and misinformation erode truth; humility is needed as it is arrogant to assume AI is infallible; empathy is required as some human-AI interactions are dehumanising.

Big Data

Social justice: Using Big Data can reveal structural inequalities and so helps craft fairer policies. But it can also be used for surveillance and if so, misuse undermines freedoms.

Stewardship: Large data sets can provide insights into climate change, biodiversity loss and pollution. But privacy rights need to be strong with ethical data governance, and data centres need huge amounts of electricity to operate.

"Technomoral": It is unjust and unfair if surveillance personal preference data is used for targeted advertising and monetary gain. Any misrepresentation or manipulation of statistics is dishonest.

Augmented Reality

Social justice: AR can enhance access to knowledge and training and narrow the education and skills gap, but it could widen the have/have not divide if devices remain expensive and only for the consumer market.

Stewardship: Similar to online working, AR reduces environmental costs of travel by enabling virtual collaboration such as a 'walk through' of architects' plans. However, there is e-waste from hardware production and AR devices need to be recycled responsibly.

"Technomoral": Without self-control, it can lead to addictive immersion; it can encourage risky adoption in unsafe environments and simulations can lead to superficial empathy.

The Internet of Things

Social justice: IoT can enable fairer access to resources such as smart electricity grids and monitoring water use. However, unequal distribution of IoT could deepen social divisions. There is a need to develop secure, interoperable standards to ensure equitable access for all.

Stewardship: The environment can be enhanced by more efficient use of energy and IoT supports smarter agricultural practice. However, the proliferation of devices increases e-waste, so it will be appropriate to enforce a circular economy in IoT device design.

"Technomoral": Honesty in the use of data is paramount as false or hacked data erodes trust. Unequal access to smart infrastructure is unjust.

Robotics

Social justice: The use of robots can improve healthcare through, for example, remote surgery, enhanced care for the elderly and help with disaster response. However, robots could displace jobs, so that could lead to widening inequality.

Stewardship: Robotics can enable precision in farming, which can reduce the use of chemicals. However, some benefits need to be balanced by the intensity of resources used in their production.

"Technomoral": We need to exercise humility to avoid hubris in treating machines as equals, and to ensure robotic caregiving is given empathetically and the nature of the care does not reduce human connection.

> Pause for thought
>
> Do you agree that considering the values and virtues implicit in the consideration of the current or future implementation of disruptive technologies is important and worthwhile? How would you categorise your own position – a "technocentric perspective" or a "humanistic perspective"? Is this dichotomy meaningful? Think about the subject or subjects that you teach in your school. Where and when do you see that you might raise a discussion about values with your learners?

Notes

1 Rawlsian theory, or "justice as fairness", is a political philosophy by American philosopher John Rawls that advocates for a society where all citizens have equal basic liberties, fair equality of opportunity and that any social and economic inequalities should primarily benefit the least advantaged members of society.

2 In 1791 Jeremy Bentham proposed an institutional design, primarily for prisons, where prisoners in cells around the outer wall are constantly observed from a central inspection tower, but they cannot see the observers. The design aims to enforce discipline through the assumption of constant surveillance, encouraging self-regulation and good behaviour.

3 Stakeholder mapping is the process of identifying, analysing and visualising all individuals, groups or organisations that have an interest in a project, product or idea, typically by plotting them on a power/interest grid to understand their influence and potential impact.

References

Conway, R. and Riggs, A. (1994) 'Valuing in technology education', in F. Banks (ed) *Teaching Technology*. Abingdon, Oxon: Routledge.

Nourbakhsh, I.R. (2013) *Robot Futures*. Cambridge, MA: MIT Press.

Vallor, S. (2016) *Technology and the Virtues: A Philosophical Guide to a Future Worth Wanting*. Oxford: Oxford University Press.

19 Assessing a disruptive technology curriculum

Introduction

This chapter provides a brief summary of the purposes of assessment and then gives four examples of assessment relevant to disruptive technologies: assessing winners and losers analysis, assessing designing without making, assessing design fictions and assessing scenario development.

A key purpose of assessment is to help learners understand where they are in their learning - supporting them to know what they are secure with in terms of their knowledge, understanding, skills and values and helping them identify areas to develop. Such assessment is focused *on* the learner and is *for* the learner and provides useful information to a variety of stakeholders including teachers, parents/carers and others such as school leaders, governors and (in England) Ofsted.[1] Formative assessment identifies what a learner needs to do to progress and helps the teacher and learner decide on the next learning steps. This has been called "responsive teaching" (Fletcher-Wood 2018). Summative assessment indicates a learner's level of achievement at a particular time and may also provide formative information that can be used to inform future teaching and learning. Talking with and listening to learners while they are actively engaged in learning is important as it enables teachers to gain insight into the learners' thought processes. Such "assessment conversations" will only be open and honest if the teacher has established a trusting relationship with the learners so that they are prepared to be open and reveal their thinking in the certain knowledge that the teacher's response will be both respectful and useful. These responses, both 'in the moment' of a conversation in a busy classroom and at the end of a particular task, provide the learner with feedback as to their progress, but such feedback has to be constructed wisely if it is to be effective. Paul Black has often made the following perceptive comments (Black and Wiliam 1998) with regard to the impact different sorts of feedback has on learners:

- Marks alone are counterproductive.
- Marks plus comments aren't much better.
- Written comments can be useful.
- Verbal comments can be very useful and are often more useful than delayed feedback.

DOI: 10.4324/9781003602002-20

Given the importance of feedback through verbal comments, our approach to assessment will use this approach in ways that are visual but not burdensome for either the teacher or learner.

Assessing winners and losers analysis

The 'winners and losers' activity was described in depth in the critique section of Chapter 18. Consider this situation in the classroom where a teacher is using such a winners and losers activity. The learners are in Year 9 (14-year-olds). The teacher sets the scene by providing some examples of the way robots are currently being used in society, e.g., surveillance, environmental monitoring, manufacturing, surgery and companionship for the elderly. The learners are then organised to work in mixed-attainment groups of four and given a single lesson to develop their initial winners and losers chart regarding the use of robots in society. In the next lesson, the teacher splits the class into groups of 'winners' (those who benefit from the technology) and those who will lose out by the introduction of the technology (so 'losers'). Using the charts from the first lesson the winners argued that it was OK for them to win at the expense of the losers, whilst the losers argued that the winners should make some compensation for the damage they were causing the losers. For the final lesson, the teacher asks the learners to return to their original groups and requires them to produce an agreed summary of the pros and cons of deploying robots in our society. The summaries are shared across the class who then develop an agreed class summary, which was presented to a member of the school leadership team with a special interest in technology education.

Table 19.1 shows how an assessment of the work of a group might be presented to support feedback discussion with the group. This simple 'thumbs up' versus 'thumbs down' summary, which should include brief agreed notes from the teacher, provides a focus for discussing the group's justification for their proposal. At the end of such a discussion the learners in each group will have a clear view of where they have been successful and where it is necessary to improve.

Table 19.1 A 'thumbs up'/'thumbs down' visual to support feedback for understanding winners and losers

In the case of deploying robots in society, Ruth, Surrendra, Bart, and Eve could:		
	👍	👎
Identify winners		
Identify losers		
Argue for the winners		
Argue for the losers		

Assessing designing without making

Designing without making tasks are useful for developing creativity in designing as the learners are unencumbered by the necessity of making their proposed designs and so are able to develop highly original, conceptual design proposals. However, such proposals do have to be realistic and justified from a variety of perspectives.

One way of ensuring such realism is to require learners to consider four factors:

1. The technology that is available for use. This will be one of our disruptive technologies. The learners are concerned primarily with how the new product or service will work. They need not be concerned with manufacture.
2. The society in which the technology will be used. This will include the prevailing values of the society, or what is thought to be important and worthwhile. This in turn will govern whether a particular application of the disruptive technology will be welcomed and supported.
3. The needs and wants of the people who might use the product or service. If the product does not meet the needs and wants of a sufficiently large number of people, then it will not be commercially successful.
4. The market that might exist or could be created for the products or services. Ideally, the market should be one with the potential to grow, one that will last and one that adapts to engage with developments in technology and changes in society.

Clearly, these factors interact with one another and influence the sorts of products and services that can be developed and will be successful. This framework for designing can be represented diagrammatically as a tetrahedron as shown in Figure 19.1. In developing and justifying the design proposal learners have to visit each vertex of the tetrahedron. In our case it is important to start with the disruptive technology.

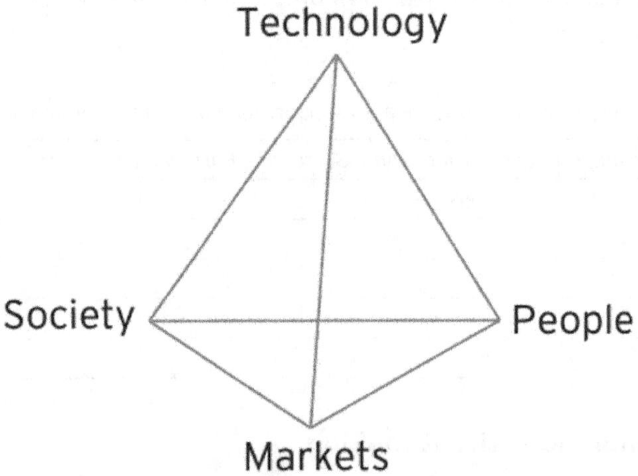

Figure 19.1 A 'tetrahedron' showing four factors to take into account when designing products and services for the future

Consider this situation in the classroom. The learners are in Year 8 (13-year-olds). The teacher wants to develop their designing skills through a designing without making task and thought that the disruptive technology augmented reality appropriate. The learners were provided with web links to information about augmented reality and its uses.

The teacher had in mind the following learning intentions:

- Learn about a disruptive technology
- Learn to develop creative design ideas
- Learn to justify design ideas
- To develop communication and collaboration skills.

To achieve this, the teacher organised the learners to work in mixed attainment groups of four and gave them a single lesson to find out about augmented reality and consider possible uses. A further single lesson was allowed for developing justifications, and in a third lesson each group had to present their design ideas to the rest of the class and take feedback from the class. A fourth lesson was devoted to revising the design in the light of the feedback and developing a clear visual that

- Showed the product and services the group had designed

And

- Provided a justification of the proposal from the four perspectives.

The comments on the feasibility feature gives insight into whether the learners have learned about a new technology. The overall design provides insight into the creativity achieved. The comments on acceptability, appropriateness and marketability provide insight into the extent that the learners have learned to justify their ideas.

At the end of the task each group will be able to discuss with the teacher their proposal and its justification. It is important that this doesn't get bogged down in too much detail. The visual in Figure 19.2 shows how the justification criteria might be presented to support feedback discussion with each group. The simple 'thumbs up' versus 'thumbs down' provides a focus for discussing the group's justification for their proposal. At the end of such a discussion the learners in each group will have a clear view of where they have been successful and where it is necessary to improve. This can be noted on the learners' assessment records with a brief comment on the way they collaborated and communicated.

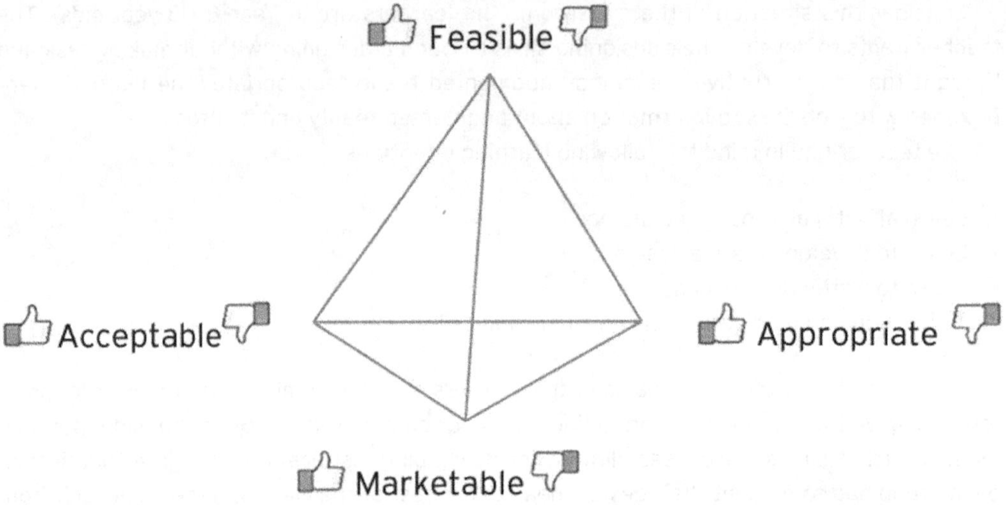

Figure 19.2 A 'thumbs up'/'thumbs down' visual to support feedback for designing without making

Assessing design fictions

The design fictions activity was described in depth in the critique section of Chapter 18. Consider this situation in the classroom. As a prop to support learners' creation of a story world the teacher presents a small security camera, the sort that can be used to monitor visitors at a house's front door. He explains that it is part of the Internet of Things, and what it's viewing can be seen on household members' mobile phones and laptops. He adds that this particular camera has advanced AI which enables it to ask any visitors questions and is linked to facial recognition software in the cloud. The task he sets for the class is to describe what might happen when the following people visit the house in the morning when the occupants are out:

- Postman delivering letters
- Amazon delivery driver with a parcel
- A relative visiting on the off chance someone might be in
- An unknown person who peers through the windows next to the door

The teacher organises the learners to work in mixed attainment groups of four and as time is short, he restricts the class to presenting their stories as a simple story board-style comic strip illustrated with stick figures. Each group has 20 minutes to produce their story boards, and then a maximum of 5 minutes to present their story boards to the rest of the class. To close the lesson the teacher draws out the key features of each story on the whiteboard, and each group then writes a few sentences summarising these key features into a single paragraph and identifying possible positive and negative effects of this use of the Internet of Things. The teacher can provide feedback to each group by discussing with them how to fill in Table 19.2. The YES/NO balance provides an easy check as to the success of the groups learning.

Table 19.2 A simple table to support feedback on a design fiction

	YES	*NO*
Was your story realistic in terms of the behaviour of:		
The postman		
The Amazon delivery driver		
The visiting relative		
The unknown person		
Did your summary paragraph include all the features identified by the teacher?		
Did you identify both positive and negative effects of using the IoT?		

Assessing scenario development

Scenario building and investigation were described in depth in the critique section of Chapter 18. Here is the situation in the classroom. The teacher asked the class, Year 10 learners aged 14/15 years, to imagine a time not that far in the future, when care robots - "carebots" - were being used to help elderly people live independent lives in their own accommodation, usually a one- or two-bedroom flat. The carebot kept the flat clean, prepared meals, ensured the person took any required medication and helped the person wash and dress in the morning and get them ready for bed in the evening. The teacher explained that to explore the different ways the use of the carebot might play out, the class was going to use a technique called scenario development. The first step was to find two ideas that were likely to be important and then to use these to develop a four-quadrant diagram, with a different scenario in each quadrant. She suggested that the two important ideas were first, whether people in society were prepared to accept robots into their lives or not, and second, whether robots had rights. This led to her displaying the diagram shown in Figure 19.3.

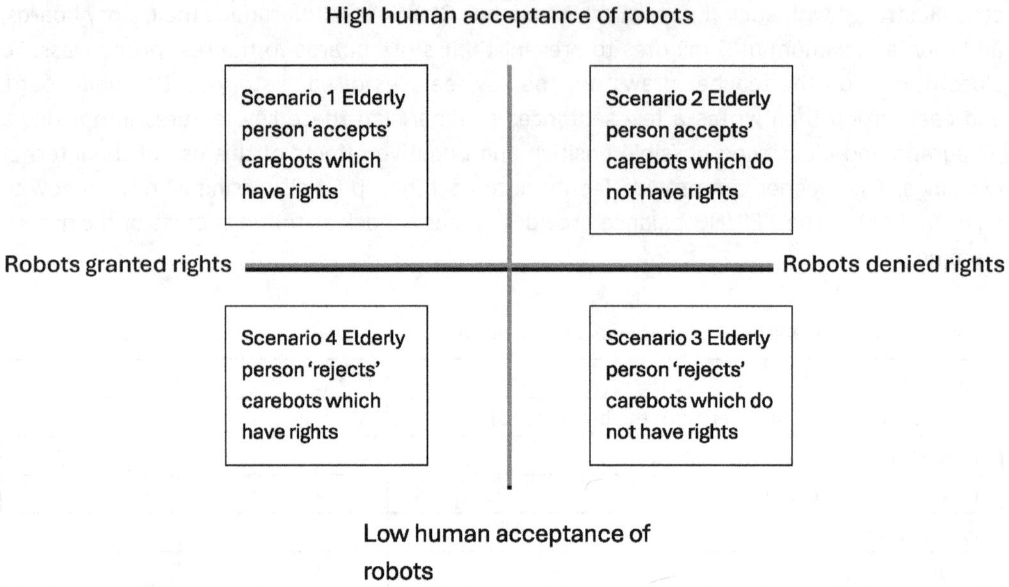

Figure 19.3 Four scenarios form axes of uncertainty concerning human acceptance of robots and the granting of rights to robots

The teacher organised the learners to work in mixed attainment groups of four and told them that as a group they were going to discuss with one another what it would be like to be the elderly person in each of the scenarios. Then they would each write a short story from the point of view of the elderly person in one of the scenarios and comment on the extent to which the elderly person a) had been well cared for and b) was content or happy with their situation.

Table 19.3 A simple table to support feedback on scenario development

	YES	*NO*
Did your story take into account elderly person's acceptance or non-acceptance of robots?		
Did your story take into account the granting or denial of robot rights?		
Did the behaviour of the carebot in your story take into account the elderly person's acceptance or non-acceptance of robots?		
Did the behaviour of the carebot in your story take into account the granting or denial of robot rights?		
Did your story comment on the extent to which the elderly person had been well cared for?		
Did your story comment on the extent to which the elderly person was content or happy with their situation?		

The teacher was able to give feedback to each learner by discussing with them how to fill in Table 19.3. If the YES/NO balance of the table is severely skewed towards the Nos, then it is relatively straightforward for the learner to redraft and resubmit an improved story.

Pause for thought

The methods of assessment described in this chapter rely heavily on talking with and listening to learners in order to provide feedback on which they can take action to make progress. Do you use such an approach in your school? If not, do you think this is realistic?

Note

1 Ofsted, which stands for the Office for Standards in Education, Children's Services and Skills, inspects and regulates a wide range of services in England including schools, colleges and childcare providers, reporting directly to Parliament.

References

Black, P. and Wiliam, D. (1998) *Inside the Black Box: Raising Standards Through Classroom Assessment*. London: NFER-Nelson.

Fletcher-Wood, H. (2018) *Responsive Teaching Cognitive Science and Formative Assessment in Practice*. Abingdon, Oxon: Routledge.

20 Closing remarks

The DEPTH project (Developing Professional Thinking for Teachers) (Banks et al. 2004) identified 3 features in helping teachers and curriculum developers can keep up to date in implementing a disruptive technology curriculum – subject knowledge, pedagogic knowledge and 'school' knowledge – how to teach in the context of your school and the local, national and global influences on the curriculum. We will deal with each in turn.

Keeping up to date with subject knowledge

Developments taking place in science and technology in the world outside school which are relevant to a disruptive technology curriculum are often reported in magazines such as *New Scientist* (£85.00/$112 per annum with a website at https://www.newscientist.com), *MIT Review* (monthly cost £8.00/$12 with a website at https://www.technologyreview.com), *Wired* (monthly cost $40/£30.00 per annum with a website at www.wired.co.uk), *Ingenia* (monthly and free from the Royal Academy of Engineering; see https://www.ingenia.org.uk) and *Make* (see https://makezine. com). Just having these magazines available in a school or university department is probably insufficient to engage the teachers and curriculum developers with the contents so it will be important to find ways to bring relevant articles to the attention of staff. One way to do this is to assign the reading of one or two magazines to individual members of staff and have a regular subject knowledge update slot at department meetings. The significance of the pieces identified regarding the curriculum can be discussed and ways in which they might be used identified. In schools, summaries of the items might be made available for learners to read and discuss with parents or carers as homework. Or the items can become the basis for case study reading, enabling consequences of technology lessons to consider the latest in technological developments. In some cases, the items are just interesting in their own right with regard to the sort of knowledge that those teaching disruptive technologies should have at their fingertips: such as the latest news about agents used in AI, robots, such as those used for care, in hazards and in war, the step-by-step progress in the long march to a successful quantum computer. Thinking about the progress in disruptive technologies raises the issues about ethical dilemmas, too.

DOI: 10.4324/9781003602002-21

Developing pedagogy that works

A key question here is how senior management might support those teaching disruptive technologies to experiment and try out new ideas. How can a senior management team encourage this and enable those good ideas to be shared? David Hargreaves (2001) suggests that one of the principal tasks of senior management is to know how to manage "knowledge creation" - how to encourage and nurture such new ideas. Hargreaves uses a 5-step gardening metaphor to set out what managers need to do, which we have adapted here:

Step 1: Generating the Ideas - Sowing.

Creating a professional environment - a school culture which promotes 'tinkering' - so that teachers actively try out new ideas or adapt old ones and take carefully calculated risks. Enabling teachers to try something new is important (see New Experiences), but often teachers find it difficult to explain why something that they do works. The knowledge is tacit. Enabling teachers to work together or even team-teach creates the shared experience which generates and transmits tacit knowledge. Also, dialogue and collective reflection across the team enables externalisation to turn tacit knowledge into explicit knowledge which can be shared with others.

Step 2: Supporting Ideas - Germinating.

In a school that supports new ideas - new ideas will come, and just as likely (more likely?) from the newly qualified teacher as much as the more experienced. Such ideas may need protection from the cold frost of cynicism.

Step 3: Selecting the most promising ideas - Thinning.

Not all new ideas can be picked up and enacted at the same time, but the ones that are selected need to be done so with a clear rationale. The criteria for selection of the best must be clear, and those whose ideas are not pursued immediately should not lose face.

Step 4: Developing ideas into knowledge and practice - Shaping and Pruning.

This is difficult - showing that the new idea is worthwhile and really works. Also, if something is not working any more it is the responsibility of the senior staff to move practice forward and so take on the new methodology. This may, for example, be by embedding the new content or teaching strategy in a scheme of work.

Step 5: Disseminating knowledge and practice - Showing and Exchanging.

An effective school management team will create channels of communication in a school so that the outcomes of knowledge creation are shared across all staff (Hargreaves 2001, pp. 29–33 abridged and adapted).

How to teach in the context of your school

Winston Churchill is reputed to have said, "The farther backward you can look, the farther forward you can see". Hence, appreciating the way in which technologies of varying sorts have featured in curriculum will be important in guiding the future. The extent to which the statutory requirements for teaching different subjects will change in the future is unclear, but given the advances being made in both science and technology it is important that changes are made to embrace these developments and take into account the lessons of past developments. In November 2025, the final report of a Curriculum and Assessment Review for schools in England, entitled "Building a world class curriculum for all" (Crown Copyright 2025), was published. The review, chaired by Professor Becky Francis, is a significant development and very relevant to the teaching of disruptive technologies. It had a stated intention to maintain and build on the knowledge-rich approach and the coherent structural architecture established by earlier curriculum work. We welcomed this as we also set out in Chapter 15 a clear statement of the knowledge, understanding, skills and values needed for a curriculum dealing with disruptive technologies. We were also pleased that the Review acknowledged the need to respond to both social and technological change as this chimed with our rationale for teaching disruptive technologies. The Review dealt in depth with the issues facing individual subjects by providing recommendations for government action. In our case, the most significant are design and technology, science and computing. The recommendations for these subjects are presented in Panels 20.1, 20.2 and 20.3, respectively. We comment briefly on these recommendations, which will be developed in schools in England from 2026 onwards. Remember, Key Stage 3 is for ages 11 to 14. The GCSE is the examination taken at age 16.

Panel 20.1 Recommendation for design and technology

We recommend that the Government:

- Rewrites the D and T subject aims to be more aspirational and clarifies the purpose of study to focus on the subject's distinct body of knowledge and capabilities, with a particular focus on Key Stage 3.
- Redefines the D and T curriculum and GCSE subject content to:
- Explicitly include how to achieve sustainable resolutions to design challenges.
- Embed the teaching of social responsibility and inclusive design explicitly within the curriculum, as appropriate to the key stage, throughout the design process.
- Support the development of critical decision-making skills about material selection.
- Ensure that realising designs remains integral to pupils' experience of D and T.

What are we to make of the recommendation for design and technology?

Rewriting the subject aims to be more aspirational and clarifying the subject's distinct body of knowledge are to be welcomed. We hope that this clarification takes into account the original intention for the subject, articulated in the Parke's Report (Department of Education and Science and the Welsh Office 1988) in 1989, that:

> By the end of the period of compulsory education pupils should have some understanding of the value options and decisions that have empowered the technological process in the past and which are doing so today.

A study of disruptive technologies would go a long way towards meeting this intention.

Achieving sustainable resolutions to design challenges has two dimensions. The first concerns the resolutions carried out by those in the world outside school. Here the role of critique of design decisions made by professional designers, engineers and technologists is essential through the lens of stewardship of Planet Earth. Chapter 18 features the teaching of critique. The second concerns the design decisions made by learners in school, with material choice being particularly important as indicated in the penultimate bullet point of the recommendation.

Considering social responsibility and inclusivity when designing, the second bullet point is important, and the use of a 'winners and losers' analysis as described in Chapter 18 is a useful strategy to support this.

The final bullet point, emphasising the importance of realising designs, should not be underestimated, but we would also point to Ed Charlwood's Thought Piece in Chapter 17 concerning making through additive manufacture which *requires fundamentally reconsidering what it means to make, to learn through making and to prepare students for a future where the boundaries between digital and physical creation continue to blur.*

Panel 20.2 Recommendation for science

We recommend the Government:

- Ensures more cohesion and consistency across the primary science curriculum, including clearer guidance on what should be taught, to what depth, at each stage.
- At all key stages, bases the science curriculum on the fundamental concepts of each individual discipline so that students develop deep scientific and disciplinary knowledge and skills. In light of this, the Government should consider where content can be streamlined, especially at GCSE, without affecting rigour or the subject's knowledge-rich focus.
- Ensures that the curriculum more clearly articulates the purpose and expectations of high-quality practical work in supporting the building of substantive knowledge and the development of important skills and procedural knowledge.
- Ensures that, in relevant areas, the science curriculum explicitly develops students' understanding of the scientific principles that explain climate change and sustainability and the global efforts to tackle them.
- Introduces an entitlement to Triple Science at GCSE, so that any student who wants to study Triple Science has the opportunity to do so.

What are we to make of the recommendation for science?

We welcome this recognition of the importance of fundamental science concepts, especially as three of the disruptive technologies we consider require science concepts to be fully understood: programmable matter, neurotechnology and synthetic biology.

We welcomed the acknowledgement of the importance of purposeful practical work and note that in Chapter 15 we describe how learners might engage in practical work involving synthetic biology by taking part in the International Genetically Engineered Machine (iGEM) competition as an extra-curricular activity.

Some of the disruptive technologies we consider can play an important part in efforts to tackle the impact of climate change - robotics and synthetic biology - as the examples in the relevant 'in depth' chapters show. So, we welcomed this emphasis on explaining climate change and sustainability and the global efforts to tackle them.

Given that understanding science is essential to understand some disruptive technologies, as you would expect we welcomed this recommendation. Hilda remembers her time as a head of science and arguing for an options system that allowed learners to study three separate sciences to GCSE level. But she is aware that this could lead to the experienced curriculum for these learners to become un-balanced. The result of taking three sciences could restrict the choice of more than one so-called creative subject - art, drama, music, design and technology etc. So, we raise a note of caution here and suggest that steps are taken to redress this imbalance through the availability of well-supported extra curricula activities.

Panel 20.3 Recommendation for computing

We recommend that the Government:

- Provides greater clarity in the computing curriculum about what students should be taught at each key stage so that they build the essential digital literacy required for future life and work.
- Replaces GCSE computer science with a computing GCSE which reflects the full breadth of the computing curriculum and supports students to develop the digital skills they need.
- Reviews where digital skills and technologies should become an integral part of subject disciplines other than computing. Where this is the case, it should determine whether to include this specific digital content in those subjects' programmes of study, sequenced and aligned with the computing curriculum.

The narrowness of the current computing science GCSE, and the low take-up, are worrying and so we welcomed recommendations to address these concerns. We noted in Chapter 17, where we considered the teaching of technical skills, that teaching digital skills features strongly in the examples we have chosen: additive manufacture, artificial intelligence, augmented reality, the Internet of Things and robotics.

It is important that some of the learning about disruptive technologies takes place in the world outside school. To achieve this, schools can work with outside partners from industry, commerce, government services, higher education and other schools.

Examples include:

- Working with environmental agencies to develop a more sustainable school
- Visiting a Big Data centre to consider energy requirements
- Working with the motor industry (manufacturers, sales and garages dealing with maintenance and repair) to consider the move towards self-drive cars
- Working with local firms who are using AI in the way they conduct business
- Visiting local retailers who are incorporating augmented reality into their high street stores
- Visiting local universities R and D departments to learn about developments in disruptive technologies
- Working with local companies to develop challenges that can be tackled as design without make activities both within the school curriculum and as part of enhancement and enrichment activities.

Schools report that learners enjoy being out of school and seeing how science, design and technology, engineering and mathematics are used in the real world. This reinforces and extends what they learn in the classroom. Plus, companies get a chance to inform learners about their work. This long-term strategy helps them to recruit and demonstrate their commitment to the community (SSAT 2009, p. 7 abridged).

Frank and Hilda have written this book for two reasons. Firstly, because they firmly believe it is important that young people understand how particular technologies can have a disruptive effect on society and prepare them for a world where this will be taking place, such that they can become informed citizens and contribute to debates about how such technologies are developed and deployed and move confidently within the workplace to find gainful employment as disruption takes place. Secondly, to help teachers across secondary school subjects to contribute to this endeavour. This will involve the following:

- Promoting the idea of 'Looking Sideways' at what colleagues are doing and coordinating contributions

- Developing appropriate pedagogy
- Developing appropriate and straightforward assessments
- Engaging learners with critique
- Providing a values framework to support identifying a "world worth wanting"

We think that the following diagram (Figure 20.1) developed from the DEPTH Project summarises our thinking of the three features to consider in developing and implementing a disruptive technologies curriculum. Note an important addition in the centre of the diagram, which includes our own value position. It asks the question of whether we are technocratic or humanistic in pursuing the other three features. We leave it to the reader to decide on our value position, but we suggest that those who wish to develop and implement a disruptive technologies curriculum will need to decide for themselves what their value position is. Depending on their decision the resulting curricula will be very different.

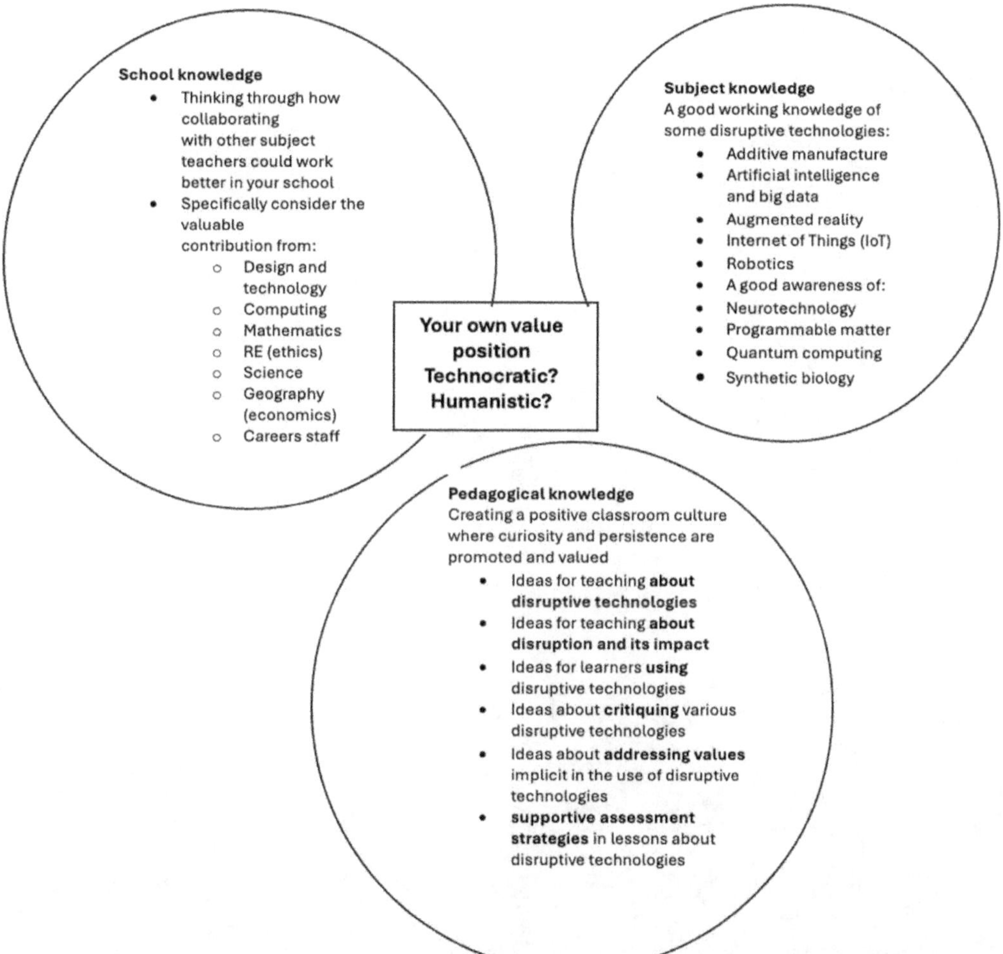

Figure 20.1 Three features for developing and implementing a disruptive technologies curriculum

References

Banks, F., Barlex, D., Jarvinen, E.-M., O'Sullivan, G., Owen-Jackson, G. and Rutland, M. (2004) 'DEPTH - developing professional thinking for technology teachers: An international study.' *International Journal of Technology and Design Education*, **14**(2), pp. 141-157. Holland: Kluwer Academic Publishers, ISSN 0957-7572.

Crown Copyright. (2025) *Curriculum and Assessment Review Final Report*. https://www.gov.uk/government/publications/curriculum-and-assessment-review-final-report (Accessed 24 November 2025).

Department of Education and Science and the Welsh Office. (1988) *Design and Technology Working Group Interim Report*. London: HMSO.

Hargreaves, D. (2001) *Creative Professionalism: The Role of Teachers in the Knowledge Society*. London: Demos.

SSAT. (2009) *The Schools, Teachers and Students Network*. https://www.ssatuk.co.uk/ (Accessed 17 December 2025).

Index

Note: Page references in *italics* and **bold** indicate figures and tables on the corresponding page.

For Product Safety Concerns and Information please contact our EU
representative GPSR@taylorandfrancis.com
Taylor & Francis Verlag GmbH, Kaufingerstraße 24, 80331 München, Germany

www.ingramcontent.com/pod-product-compliance
Lightning Source LLC
LaVergne TN
LVHW080823260926
848956LV00032B/280
* 9 7 8 1 0 3 2 9 9 0 4 6 0 *